Théophile Delcassé

Théophile Delcassé

THE CAREER OF
Théophile Delcassé

By
CHARLES W. PORTER

University of Pennsylvania Press

London: Humphrey Milford: Oxford University Press

PHILADELPHIA

1936

To
Hugh Lansing Cooke

CONTENTS

INTRODUCTION

TWELVE years after the Treaty of Versailles, the scapegoat theory of the origin of the war which maintained that one man, Kaiser William II, and one nation, Germany, were solely responsible, has been largely thrown into the discard, and a number of sober-minded historians are arguing that the blame can be more reasonably laid at the door of the European Powers as a whole. They reason that, at bottom, the catastrophe of 1914-18 was the joint product of a number of underlying causes, some as old as the dotage of Charlemagne, some quite recent, but all fitting roughly into five or six general categories such as the press, militarism, nationalism, and imperialism; the irresponsibility of diplomats to their own parliaments or peoples; and, finally, a system of secret alliances, made by these same diplomats, which divided Europe into two rival camps.

Those who adopt this broad-minded view of the origin of the war should not lose sight of the fact that these economic forces and political conditions were, in part at least, human products, and that they were directed, operated, and even at times exploited by human beings. Chief among these was Théophile Delcassé.

Delcassé was intimately connected with all six of the baneful forces just enumerated, and anyone who seriously studies the war from any one of the above angles must take him into account. He devoted twelve years of his life to ultra-patriotic journalism, and his influence in the French press, though we have no accurate way to gauge it, must have been enormous. As Colonial Minister, as Foreign Minister, he was an ardent expansionist, and furthered French economic imperialism in both Africa and the Orient. As for nationalism, he was the incarnation of that French spirit which had been outraged by the seizure of Alsace-Lorraine in 1870 and wounded to the heart by the subsequent slump in French national prestige. As Minister of Marine, as Ambassador to Russia, as an agitator for the three-years' military service law, he figures no less prominently in the "race for preparedness," or the category of militarism. As for the irresponsibility of diplomats to parliaments or people, Delcassé for seven years was allowed to run French Foreign Affairs practically to suit himself. He became olympian in his majesty, and no one, not even prime ministers, dared to pry into his secrets of state. As for the final category, Delcassé was the center or pivot of that diplomatic evolution between 1898 and 1912 which, carried out by a series of agreements of a diplomatic, military, and naval character, ended in opposing a Triple Entente to the Triple Alliance. Thus, from whatever angle one approaches the subject, Delcassé made large contributions to that fatal division of Europe into two grasping, antagonistic, and mutually suspicious armed camps out of which grew the war.

The present study aims to trace the political and diplomatic career of this remarkable man, a career replete with human interest even for the general reader. He was born in obscurity, yet came to dine in the company of kings and princes. No piece of fiction is stranger or more dramatic than his fall from the heights of power in 1905; nothing in literature is more heroic than the manner in which he chose personal disgrace rather than weaken the France of 1905 by another scandal; nothing is more admirable than the fortitude with which he successfully guarded this secret for eighteen years out of pure patriotism. Equally creditable is the way in which he raised himself to power again in the face of repeated discouragements. He was, perhaps, more dangerous to Germany from 1905 to 1914 than he had been when Minister of Foreign Affairs. Finally, there is the account of his second resignation from the government post he loved, and the pathetic story of a great man "not beaten but forgotten," a ghost, mourning the loss of his son, the gallant Captain Delcassé, and cherishing in the dimness of his apartment in the Boulevard de

Clichy a black box of papers that carried the story of his two dismissals from office.

Is it necessary to say that such a man has been variously described? His friends claim him to be one of the purest and sincerest of French patriots, and there is no doubt that their judgment is correct. They have dubbed him the Vergennes or the Richelieu of the Third Republic, and in truth there are many striking similarities between Delcassé and these prototypes. Another has called him the John Hay of France because of his efforts on behalf of peace. His enemies, however, consider that he was a monomaniac or an ogre. Kaiser William II and Prince Bülow, both inspired by the laudable motive of exculpating themselves, have daubed Delcassé very liberally with charges of war guilt; but the man who emerges from the pages of this book will be, I hope, neither a saint nor an ogre, for Delcassé was above all very human. If his system led directly to the World War, it also led to the victory of his country in that war, and therein, as in the case of Bismarck, lies his greatness.

The biographer of Delcassé does not have an easy task. Secrecy was the very breath of his diplomatic life; he flatly refused to write his memoirs, and it is said that one of his last acts was to destroy a great many personal papers. Nor need we hope for much from the archives of the Quai d'Orsay, because Delcassé's closest friend has stated that Delcassé left the emptiest files of any French foreign minister. The famed German documents, *Die Grosse Politik,* do not have the value that one would expect, because Delcassé kept the Germans completely in the dark as to what he was doing. The Russians have, unfortunately, published all too little of what must have been at one time in the St. Petersburg archives. There are, nevertheless, a number of reliable sources for the origin and evolution of Delcassé's policies. These are, in order of their importance: Théophile Delcassé, *Alerte! Où allons nous?* Paris, 1882; the early newspaper articles of Delcassé on foreign and colonial affairs; his speeches in the Chamber of Deputies and the Senate—rare but succinct; isolated letters of Delcassé published in books, newspapers, and periodicals; the official documents of the British, Belgian, German, French, and Russian foreign offices in so far as they have been published at this time, and the archives of the American State Department, now open to 1906; a great deal of memoir material left by the numerous friends of Delcassé, especially André Mévil. This last gentleman knew all the thoughts and secrets of the great Foreign Minister in both the good and bad hours, and Delcassé showed him that mysterious box of documents now said to be destroyed. His articles can be found scattered through the *Echo de Paris* as well as in certain periodicals, and together with his book *De la Paix de Francfort à la Conférance d'Algésiras* (Paris, 1909) constitute a sort of official biography of Delcassé. Another laudatory account by Georges Reynald was published in 1915 in *Pages d'Histoire*. Both see the origin of the war through Delcassé's eyes, and must be used with care.

Throughout the preparation of this work, the writer has aimed at complete independence. Yet it was thought advisable to refer to the family and to some of the friends of Delcassé for information not otherwise obtainable. M. Camille Barrère, French Ambassador and member of the Institute, especially must be thanked both for his interest and for his encouragement, and for an interview in which he threw much light upon the life and times and methods of Delcassé. The writer also wishes to acknowledge his debt to that equally celebrated diplomat, the late M. Jules Cambon, who rendered a similar service. Madame la Générale Noguès, Delcassé's daughter, contributed some invaluable details concerning the family and early life of her father, for which the author is deeply grateful. It is only fair to acknowledge here, however, that these kindly disposed persons are not to be held in any way responsible for the point of view or conclusions of this book, which are indeed unknown to them.

Similarly, the biographer wishes to express his gratitude to former Governor John Garland Pollard of Virginia, the American State Department, Mr. Theodore Marriner, American Chargé d'Affaires *ad interim* at Paris, Dr. Horatio S. Krans of the American University Union, and the staffs of the Library of Congress and of the Bibliothèque Nationale. The Institute of International Education is also to be thanked for a year of study in France which aided materially in the understanding of French character and French ideals. Here again it should be stated that while their courtesies and assistance have been invaluable in the course of this work, the persons or institutions named above are responsible only for whatever excellence this book may have, the viewpoint and conclusions of the study being those of the writer alone.

Among my friends, colleagues, and former professors, I particularly wish to thank the following: Dr. T. R. Schellenberg, Dr. E. F. Cruickshank, Dr. D. D. Irvine, Dr. O. J. Hale, and Professors A. P. Watts, E. P. Cheyney, and William E. Lingelbach of the University of Pennsylvania. Of these, I am most deeply indebted to Dr. William E. Lingelbach, in whose Seminar this study originated. His constant encouragement and criticism have been largely responsible for the book.

CHARLES W. PORTER

Richmond, Virginia, 1935

I

FORMATIVE YEARS
1852-1889

FRANCE, which breathed and felt with Gambetta, has not, however, died with him. . . . Today, she is conscious of her power. Without stopping to increase it, she watches with perfect equanimity of soul the maneuvers and wicked designs of her enemies. Without provoking trouble and without any feebleness, she calmly awaits the hour of immanent justice. (Delcassé, in the *Paris*, August 3, 1887.)

AMONG the foothills of the Pyrenees, there lay in the middle of the nineteenth century, on the site of the now flourishing city of Pamiers, a quaint little French town of about five or six thousand inhabitants. Tradition said that it had derived its name of Pamiers from the residence of Roger, Count of Foix, who called his castle Apamea after a Syrian city of great charm which he had visited during one of the crusades.

Here, amidst people characterized by an abundance of energy and fire, and active imaginations, Théophile Delcassé was born on March 1, 1852. His family belonged to the smaller bourgeoisie of the Department of Ariège, and enjoyed legal traditions dating from the time of the Monarchy.[1] His father filled the office of *Huissier*, one of the lower grades of the legal profession. These officers made known to the interested parties in a case the various deeds drawn up by the solicitors, and likewise served official copies of court judgments. Consequently, as would naturally be the case in a small French town of the Midi, the elder Delcassé was entitled to a modest amount of deference befitting one with a smattering of legal knowledge and entrusted with administrative powers.

[1] *Nuova Antologia*, Sept., 1916, p. 31; A. Mévil, *Echo de Paris*, Feb. 23, 1923.

At the time of Théophile Delcassé's birth, the political and social institutions of France were undergoing a profound change. The President of the Republic, Louis Napoleon, was a despot at heart, and before the end of the year the Second Republic was replaced by the autocratic Empire. In the field of economics, industry was expanding rapidly. The railway, the steamboat, and the telegraph were beginning to quicken the tempo of French life and to hasten the exchange of news and ideas as well as goods. Shrewd investors and speculators amassed tidy fortunes and found that wealth opened up to them still other opportunities in politics and society. Delcassé was therefore born on the threshold of a new era in which brains, ability, and money were more important than family name or title.

His youth, like his later career, was lonely. He had neither brothers nor sisters, and, when he was four years old, his mother died. Although the father remarried, Delcassé received most of his early training from his grandmother, who was very kind to him and whose memory he continued to cherish throughout his life.[2]

The young boy spent a great deal of time in the open fields and woodlands of his native Department where he learned to love the natural beauty of Ariège and where he developed a lifelong fondness for close contact with nature. The Pyrenees, which were plainly visible from the hill of the Castellat in Pamiers, became especially dear to him. Rich in history and legend as well as in scenic beauty, they came to have an attraction for him which he never outgrew, and which may even have become stronger as years went by.[3]

He received his early education in the local schools, and notably at the *college* of Pamiers, which was reputed in the region for the excellence of its classical training. At the age of eighteen, after having had his fill of the hard studies required at Pamiers, he decided to continue his education at

[2] Letter of Madame la Générale Noguès to the author.
[3] Letter of Mme la Générale Noguès. Ultimately Delcassé made his summer home in the Pyrenees.

Toulouse, which lay just forty miles north of his native town. In the twelfth century and in the first quarter of the thirteenth century the City of Toulouse had been the center of a gay, poetical, and courtly civilization. An atmosphere filled with memories of the golden past still hung over the place. Since the founding of the University of Toulouse in 1229, the city had been one of the principal seats of learning in the Midi. Three popes and a great sixteenth-century jurisconsult, Jacques Cujas, had gone forth from its academic halls.[4] The Faculty of Letters, which Delcassé was to attend, therefore enjoyed a rich cultural and intellectual heritage.[5]

The eighteen years which had brought Delcassé to the first flush of manhood had also wrought changes in the history of France. The autocracy established by Napoleon III in 1852 gave way about a decade later to the Liberal Empire. Nevertheless many people in France remained discontented. In 1868, republicanism found its champion in the eloquent Léon Gambetta, who denounced the Napoleonic government with magnificent and thrilling invectives. During the summer of 1870 the Empire tottered to its fall. War was declared against Prussia on July 19, 1870. Almost at once the French troops were driven back and France itself was invaded. On September 2, 1870, the French army, including Napoleon III, surrendered at Sedan. Trying as these events must have been to the soul of Delcassé, still other disasters were to follow in the next four months. After the fall of Napoleon III, a republic was proclaimed. All men between the ages of twenty and forty-one were recruited, and new armies were created. The favorite toasts were "Long live the Republic!" "Long live Gambetta!" "Death to the Prussians!" Raw recruits, however, could not successfully oppose the well-trained German armies. The new battalions met with defeat. Paris was besieged and,

[4] *Annuaire de l'Université de Toulouse,* 1928-1929 (Toulouse, 1928) pp. 19, 20.

[5] As a result of the centralizing policy of the Revolutionary and Napoleonic governments, the title "University of Toulouse" had given way to the term "University of France," the name given to the sum total of French public educational institutions. A. Lebon and P. Pelet, *France As It Is* (London, N.Y., and Paris, 1888) 143; *Annuaire de l'Université de Toulouse,* 1928-1929.

in spite of the genius of Gambetta, the capital surrendered on January 28 after all attempts to relieve the city had failed. Inasmuch as not a single foreign Power would come to the aid of France or intervene on her behalf, the French were left at the mercy of Prussia. Peace was made on May 10, 1871, at Frankfort, but only at the price of paying five billion francs to Germany and ceding to her Alsace and a part of Lorraine. It is worth while to emphasize the fact that France paid this great price largely as a result of her inadequate military preparation and because of her diplomatic isolation. Delcassé learned the lesson well. Moreover, during the terrible trials of 1870-71, his patriotism ripened.[6] The great leader of the national defense, Léon Gambetta, became and remained for life his idol and his ideal.[7] The Treaty of Frankfort, which deprived France of Alsace-Lorraine, outraged his ardent patriotism.[8] Henceforth, he brooded over the frontier question and continued to be profoundly distrustful of German intentions with regard to France.[9]

Perhaps Delcassé meditated too much over the German wrongs to France. Perhaps too often he indulged in what became his favorite pastime, walking along the quays alone, day dreaming. Considering how ingrained in Delcassé this habit became, it is not hard to imagine him passing by the imposing bacilica of St. Sernin, last resting place of the medieval counts of Toulouse, and making his way to the banks of the Garonne, or walking along the edges of the great Canal du Midi. Be that as it may, whether he dreamed too much or not, one thing is certain—he proved to be a student of but average ability. At Toulouse he studied for a purely cultural degree, the *Licence ès Lettres,* and like Pasteur, who was rated by his professors as mediocre in chemistry, he failed a number

[6] G. Leygues in *Journal Officiel de la République Française,* March 2, 1923, p. 2049; Louis Barthou, an intimate friend of Delcassé, Oct. 4, 1934, quoted in *L'Echo de Paris,* Oct. 4, 1934.

[7] Victor Bérard in *Journal Official* (hereafter to be cited as *J.O.*) March 2, 1923, p. 2050; A. Mévil, *Revue Politique et Parlementaire,* June, 1924, p. 395.

[8] "Nationalité," article by Delcassé in *Paris,* July 8, 1888.

[9] *Ibid., Paris,* July 8, 1888; R. Poincaré, *J.O.,* March 1, 1923, p. 2017.

of times. The archives of the Faculty of Letters of Toulouse record that Théophile Delcassé presented himself for the examinations for the *Licence* at the session of July 1873. He failed, and was again unsuccessful in July 1874, but was admitted to the honors of the degree in the session following, November 30, 1874.[10]

The *Licence ès Lettres* was roughly equivalent to a Master of Arts degree from one of the smaller American universities, consequently Delcassé was a reasonably well-educated man. He was well versed in the classics and in French literature, but in later life he could never be induced to speak any foreign language—a rather curious trait in a famous Minister of Foreign Affairs.[11]

After leaving the Faculty of Letters at Toulouse, Delcassé found it difficult to decide upon a career. It has been said that he thought of becoming a lawyer,[12] and that he began writing for the fiery little newspapers of the Midi.[13] For some months, he served as a tutor to the children of an official in the ministry of Foreign Affairs. Likely enough it was here that he first became seriously interested in politics and formed a taste for the study of diplomacy. He declared, at a later date, that he taught the children "how the French Monarchy had triumphantly organized resistance to the enterprises of the German Holy Roman Empire," and, reflecting on this phase of his life, he said, "How could I imagine that one day a like task would be incumbent upon me on behalf of the Republic?"[14]

In a sense, therefore, Delcassé belonged to that honorable fraternity of academic gentlemen who have left the paths of erudition for those of politics. Throughout his life he had,

---

[10] Letter by the Secretary of the Faculty of Letters, July 16, 1930, in the possession of the author.

[11] C. Dawbarn, *Makers of New France* (London, 1915) 37; Lord Newton, *Lord Lansdowne* (London, 1929) 343; Horace Porter to Hay, Nov. 22, 1899, State Dept. #567, France, vol. 118.

[12] G. P. Gooch, *Contemporary Review*, April, 1923, pp. 446-47.

[13] *Manchester Guardian*, Feb. 23, 1923.

[14] Pérès, in *J.O.*, March 2, 1923, pp. 2048-2049, quoting Delcassé's words of 1905.

in addition to their virtues, their prevailing weakness—a tendency to confuse ideas and dreams with realities.

During the latter part of 1875, Delcassé went to Paris, the Mecca of all ambitious Frenchmen. Here he applied himself to journalism, and in 1879 was engaged to write for Gambetta's journal, *La République Française*. This paper was a "missionary enterprise," founded in 1871. The initial capital for the undertaking had been mainly subscribed in Alsace-Lorraine.[15] Gambetta himself was the leading apostle of the reannexation of Alsace-Lorraine to France. He believed that until this was done no one would disarm, and that the peace of the world would always remain at the mercy of an incident.[16] "Think of it always; speak of it never," was his favorite injunction to his followers. The outstanding writers for the paper were all identified in some way with the defense of the country in 1870-71, or were high among the Republican leaders of France. Eugène Spuller, chief editor and *alter ego* of Gambetta, although without official title, had played an important rôle in the national defense; De Freycinet had served as head of the military cabinet and had helped to organize the armies which Gambetta used to oppose the invading Germans; Ranc had been a director of the *sûreté générale* and a member of the National Assembly; Antonin Proust had served as Minister of the Interior during the siege of Paris.[17]

One of the youngest of the editors in 1878-79 was M. Camille Barrère. He allotted Delcassé his daily task, corrected what Delcassé wrote, and initiated him into the policies of the paper. A close friendship sprang up between the two men and, thanks to Barrère, who was already well acquainted with Gambetta, Delcassé too became a friend of the celebrated Republican leader. Thus Delcassé came to know Gambetta during the last two years of the great patriot's life.[18]

The supreme political director of the journal was Gam-

[15] H. Stannard, *Gambetta and the Foundation of the Third Republic* (Boston, 1925) p. 122.
[16] Gambetta to Ranc, published in *Le Matin* (Paris) Dec. 29, 1915.
[17] Larousse, *Grand Dictionnaire Universel*, article "*République Française*."
[18] Interview with His Excellency, Camille Barrère, November 27, 1933.

betta. He was accustomed to leave the heated debates of the
French Chambers toward evening and to go to the offices of
the *République Française*. He exchanged greetings with
everybody; and then, having gathered together the leading
members of his staff, there would be a brief general discussion
of the day's events, after which the renowned orator would
launch into an eloquent speech on politics and foreign relations. His colleagues then wrote down his ideas and his
phrases.[19]

Surely this was a remarkable school for the future Foreign
Minister of France in the doubtful years of the Diplomatic
Revolution. Years later, after Gambetta's death, Delcassé in
his newspaper articles paid grateful tribute to the inspiring
genius of his former chief and recognized his own debt to
the oft-repeated discourses of the Dictator of Bordeaux. He
averred that he had "often had" the "invaluable honor" of
hearing Gambetta develop his opinions on the foreign policy
of France, and that he had heard him outline "a thousand"
diplomatic shifts by which France could realize the "supreme
purpose" of her diplomacy, which was to "reconstitute"
France and to "complete" France by the recovery of the lost
provinces.[20]

Tradition has it that one of Gambetta's brilliant discussions
turned so much upon internal policy that Delcassé became
apprehensive lest the true mission of France be forgotten.
Suddenly the group about Gambetta heard the voice of a new
arrival. The upstart responsible for it was Delcassé, a small,
dark-haired individual who peering from behind his eyeglasses said, "It is also necessary to think of remaking Europe
and of destroying the work of Bismarck."[21]

The incident is indicative of the audacity of Delcassé
throughout his entire life. He was the fervent disciple of the
man who had done so much to found the Republic, yet he had
the courage to call anyone to a strict account. Gambetta, who
was never so happy as when he had just discovered a new and

---

[19] Stannard, *op. cit.*, 123.　　　　[20] Delcassé in *Paris*, March 26, 1888.
[21] Fournol, *Revue Politique et Littéraire*, July 16, 1921, p. 444.

talented follower, commanded their respect in spite of his easy friendliness, and his influence upon the aims and purposes of their lives was indelible. He was the real inspiration of both Barrère and Delcassé, as their later careers attested.[22] So profound was the influence of Gambetta upon Delcassé that the latter could never speak of the former's affectionate familiarity toward him without visible emotion. He declared that all he accomplished in his career went back to the teachings of this illustrious man and to the precepts of Gambetta's more immediate companions and spiritual heirs, Freycinet and Ferry.[23]

Delcassé was captivated by the "grandeur'" of Gambetta's past. In the words of Delcassé,

This man, with his imperturbable faith in the destiny of the country, alone stood upright during the terrible hour [in 1870] when everything was sinking and when black despair, as well as the enemy, was invading France. By his ardent speech [he] had everywhere disseminated courage and strength for resistance . . . his genius improvised armies which, though unable to throw back the invader, had at least saved the honor of the country, the only thing left for France to lose.[24]

Delcassé was impressed not only by the warmth of Gambetta's patriotism but also by the "incredible resources of his quick and enlightened mind" and by the extraordinary energy which he displayed under the most trying circumstances. Finally, Delcassé saw in Gambetta, "who often troubled the sleep of the Iron Chancellor," the "hope" of France, the "regeneration" and "reparation" of France.[25]

Joseph Reinach, one of Delcassé's colleagues on the *République Française,* in a book setting forth the history and doctrines of the Gambetta Ministry of 1881-82, has left us an

[22] In this connection see Barrère in *Revue des Deux Mondes,* August 1, 1932, pp. 603-604.
[23] G. Reynald, *"La Diplomatie Française"* . . . in *Pages d'Histoire,* 1 Série h (Paris, 1915) 7-8; V. Bérard, *J.O.,* March 2, 1923, p. 2050; Mévil, *Revue Politique et Parlementaire,* June, 1924, p. 395.
[24] Delcassé, *Alerte! Où Allons Nous?* (Paris, 1882) 11 and 24-25.
[25] Delcassé, *Alerte!,* p. 11; Delcassé in *Paris,* August 3, 1887.

account of Gambetta's teachings. He tells us that Gambetta's ideal was the restoration of the old frontiers of France and of French prestige, together with the regeneration of France and her people. In short, to use Delcassé's favorite expression, Gambetta was dedicated to the *relèvement* (raising up again) of France. Colonial empire, a luxury in the days of French victory, was considered by him to be a necessity after the defeat of 1870. Expansion was essential in order to increase the strength of France economically and to restore the courage of the French by a succession of colonial victories. Thus, after April 1882, Gambetta and his circle considered that the acquisition of Tunis had already made France envied, respected, and even feared, and so had gone far toward wiping out the shame of Sedan. At the same time that he desired a colonial empire equal in size to that which the Old Régime had founded and then lost, Gambetta warned against scattered effort and wasted energy. Colonial enterprise should follow a well-conceived plan and be limited to reasonable proportions. Much emphasis should be placed upon getting French settlers to go to the colonies and develop them economically. Africa was considered the ideal place for France to specialize in her colonial work because it bordered the Mediterranean and was close to France.[26] These ideas were deeply impressed upon Delcassé, who sought to apply them when he became head of the French colonial office. Herein may also be found one of the explanations why Delcassé was particularly interested in the French penetration of Morocco.

"Dignity and firmness" were the keynotes of the foreign policy recommended by Gambetta. He favored an *entente cordiale* with England, and thought of the Franco-Russian Alliance as a convenient *"alliance de guerre"* because although France and Russia had "no interests in common," they might well have the same enemies.[27] About 1875 Gambetta wrote Ranc:

The political ambitions of Russia will be impeded by Austria, who is already assuming a hostile attitude. She is exerting every

[26] J. Reinach, *Le Ministère Gambetta, Histoire et Doctrine (14 Novembre 1881-26 Janvier 1882)*, Paris, 1884, pp. 193-196; 371-373.
[27] *Ibid.*, pp. 382-385; 393-395.

pressure upon Rumania. Do you see, as a consequence, Austria allying herself with Rumania and Turkey against Russia? What a conflict!

The Prince of Wales, Edward VII, however, foresees it. He does not share the hostility of a section of the English nation against Russia. With all his young authority he fights against measures which may be prejudicial to Russia. I see in him the making of a great statesman. . . .

I desire that our enemies should be Russia's enemies. It is clear that Bismarck wants an alliance with the Austrians. Russia must therefore be made to see that we might be her ally. . . . Since the revolution our country exerts great influence in Europe. Before long I see Russia and England at our side if we only have a proper internal policy.[28]

The big achievement of Delcassé's career was precisely this triple alignment of England, France, and Russia against Germany and Austria. Nothing shows more clearly than this letter that Delcassé was heavily indebted to the great French statesman whom he claimed as his teacher. If the end achieved by Delcassé was the one dreamed of by Gambetta, so were the means. As we shall see, Delcassé's actions at the time of the Anglo-French crisis of Fashoda and for the years immediately following are explicable only on the basis of the words of Gambetta quoted by Delcassé in the French Chamber of Deputies in 1890, the gist of which is that the English respect as allies only those who, taking account of their own interests, make themselves respected.[29]

That, however, is getting too far ahead in Delcassé's story. Let us note some of the descriptions of the cub reporter on the *République Française*. We are told that he soon became one of the most familiar figures among the reporters and leader writers in the lobbies of the Chamber of Deputies. "Le petit journaliste" used to buttonhole MM. les Députés and question them in a grave whisper. He was not only small but dark complexioned—

a dapper little figure, with large, smiling mouth; gold-rimmed spectacles over a thickish, slightly upturned nose, big, dark, in-

[28] Gambetta to Ranc, 1875, printed in London *Times*, Dec. 30, 1915, p. 7.
[29] Delcassé, *J.O., Chambre, Débats Parlementaires*, Nov. 6, 1890, p. 1896.

telligent eyes, thatch of dark hair plastered over a flat cranium; a most courteous, amiable mannikin, grave, precise in speech, ever alert for "tips"![30]

From the very outset of his journalistic work Delcassé specialized in foreign and colonial affairs. Hard work enabled him to earn the reputation of an expert in his chosen field. His style, devoid of all useless verbiage, was crisp, incisive, and convincing, and made foreign affairs intelligible to the man in the street. The importance of this phase of Delcassé's career cannot be overestimated. Not only was this Delcassé's real preparation for his life work, since it gave him an opportunity to study European diplomacy and to work out a French foreign policy, but the paper was the oracle of Republicanism in France, and brought his ideas daily before a circulation of forty thousand readers. Thus, at the very time Delcassé was formulating his later system of diplomacy, he was preparing a favorable reception for that foreign policy in the minds of tens of thousands of French people!

Advancement beyond the stage of lobby correspondent was very slow. It was not until 1885 that the *Annuaire de la Presse Française* carried his name as one of the leading political writers. By this time the staff of the paper had changed considerably. Gambetta had died at the end of 1882. Camille Barrère, with whom Delcassé had formed a friendship that lasted through life, had entered actively into the French diplomatic service in 1880. Other changes too had taken place, so that now Delcassé's colleagues were Spuller, Thomson, Marcelin Pellet, Depasse, Reinach, and F. de Pressensé. The *Annuaires* for 1887, 1888, 1889 carried him as secretary of the editorial staff—where his career on the *République Française* ended. The journal, besides bringing Delcassé close to Gambetta, had thrown him with many others who influenced his career. Eugène Spuller, for a while chief editor, continued to write for the *République Française* until his last years. Hero with Gambetta in the famous escape from

---

[30] *Manchester Guardian*, Feb. 23, 1923; and *Le Matin* (Paris), November 7, 1890.

Paris in a balloon, he was virtually Gambetta's other self, a matter of considerable importance in the life of Delcassé. Since the intensely active life led by Gambetta and his early death must necessarily have limited Delcassé's personal contacts with him, to know Gambetta's closest companion was a valuable privilege. President of the Republican Union group in the Chamber of Deputies, Spuller was wont to expound the Gambettist policy of union of all the Republicans, for which Delcassé was eloquently to plead in 1897. Joseph Reinach was to father the bill for the creation of a ministry of colonies, from which Delcassé was to profit in 1894 as one of the first men to hold that office. Gaston Thomson and De Pressensé will figure again in this biography because of their opposition to Delcassé. Lastly, it was also through the *République Française* that Delcassé, at one time or another, came in contact with Jules Ferry, Hanotaux, and Raymond Poincaré.[31]

Delcassé's early articles in the *République Française* are unsigned, as one would expect to be true of the writings of a new reporter. Luckily for us, during 1882, Delcassé grew tired of this anonymous existence, being then thirty years of age, and burst forth into print under his own name with a political pamphlet which he called *Alerte! Où Allons-Nous? (Look Out! Where Are We Going?)*. This tiny work consisted of only thirty-four pages, printed by E. Dentu at Paris, 1882, but, in the absence of other information, it is a most valuable source for the ideas of Delcassé on politics and diplomacy in so far as he had developed opinions on those subjects by 1882.

The following circumstances occasioned Delcassé's book. The staff of the *République Française,* like all good Gambettists, had been lifted to the heights of ecstasy when Gambetta became Premier of France on November 14, 1881. Almost at once they had been plunged into the depths of despair, because the *Grand Ministère* of Gambetta quickly

[31] Barrère, *Revue des Deux Mondes,* August 1, 1932, p. 603; Poincaré, *J.O.,* March 1, 1923, p. 2017.

succumbed and was succeeded by Freycinet's cabinet of January 26, 1882. Joseph Reinach industriously began a monumental history of the Gambetta ministry and its doctrines. Delcassé brought out his own fervent and lucid little brochure immediately, it being dated Passy, May 18, 1882.

Alerte! is above all a highly rhetorical attack on the Freycinet government of January 1882, from the standpoint of an uncompromising follower of Gambetta. The first twenty-three pages were concerned with internal questions. The Freycinet ministry was not sufficiently radical for M. Delcassé, who proclaimed himself for the Republic, against the Church, in favor of labor legislation, desirous of a more equitable taxation law, and in favor of a revision of the constitution in a democratic and progressive direction. Among the reforms demanded by Delcassé was the complete remaking and reorganization of the French military system and the introduction of a three-years' military service law applicable to all persons without distinction and without any exceptions on account of fortune or vocation. He was particularly alarmed by the weakness of the executive branch of the Government. A tendency toward political individualism in France necessitated a triple-headed or even quadruple-headed cabinet that found itself reduced to utter impotence when the aspirations of the various political leaders came in conflict. Citing the example of English politics, Delcassé said that reforms were needed in France to insure harmonious cabinets and to place the executive power in the hands of one great national figure who should enjoy real leadership and a large measure of personal power. This was an open question with Delcassé as late as 1905 and increased the awkwardness of his political position in that momentous year.[32] Preoccupied with national defense and foreign affairs, Delcassé, in later life, lost some of his interest in the social and democratic reforms, yet had the satisfaction of seeing them realized in the main by others. It would be difficult

[32] Barrère, *Revue des Deux Mondes*, Aug. 1, 1932, p. 612.

to say whether or not Freycinet knew directly or indirectly of Delcassé's fiery criticism of his administration. However, it was Freycinet who, as Minister of War, between 1888 and 1893, first began to modernize the French military system. During those five years, he introduced the three-years' service law demanded by Delcassé in 1882, and also improved the French army by the introduction of the general staff, a supreme council of war, and the army commands. Much remained to be done even after these reforms, and Delcassé still had his part to play as a staunch defender of the three-years' service idea and in coördinating the military system of France with that of her friends and allies.

The last eleven pages of Delcassé's brochure referred especially to the foreign policy of Freycinet, or rather, as Delcassé alleged, to Freycinet's lamentable lack of a definite policy at a time when Germany had just built up the Triple Alliance of Germany, Austria, and Italy.

Another danger, without doubt the greatest of all, is the complete lack of a foreign policy. . . . When on the ruins of the old balance of power a monstrous and formidable coalition has formed itself [the Triple Alliance], is it possible for France to continue to live in the isolation to which she has been reduced by her disasters [of 1870], without worrying about the future and without any determined purpose?[33]

It was a matter of national existence for France to "guarantee herself from provocations, attacks, and against all surprise," said Delcassé, and he indicated how France could be guaranteed:

Do you not see that on all sides of you in Europe there are [Powers with] interests identical to yours, and that the union of these with us would not only be a strong union because there seems to be no reason for conflict between these Powers, but, on the contrary, should form an indestructible fasces! . . . for lack of a hand to guide them and draw them together, these interests instead of seeking each other, disregard each other, flee from each

[33] Delcassé, *Alerte; Où allons-nous?* (Paris, 1882) 32.

other, and you remain isolated, living from day to day at the mercy of events beyond your control because the strings that govern them are not in your hands.[34]

How surprised Delcassé would have been if he had been told that he, more than any other Frenchman, was to furnish the guiding hand that was to draw together these Powers with identical interests, bind them fasces-like into a compact group, and place the strings of European diplomacy in the hands of France!

When he came to the details of French diplomacy, Delcassé devoted much space to the Egyptian question. Egypt, formerly under the dual control of France and England, had revolted under Arabi Pasha in 1882. England had insisted upon sending troops to put down the rebellion. The French Government, on the other hand, had waited for a mandate from the European Powers, and neglected to coöperate with England in the work of pacifying Egypt. The results were disastrous to French interests, since England, single-handed, obtained control over the country. Then the Powers declined to give the desired mandate, and France sank to the position of a mere holder of Egyptian bonds. Thus, at one blow, the French entente with England came to an end, and the equal rights of France in Egypt became a memory.

The orthodox Gambettist view was that the entente with England should not have been broken. Gambetta, in his last great speech in Parliament (July 18, 1882, two months after Delcassé's pamphlet was written), earnestly urged a close coöperation of France and England, and counseled his countrymen in the memorable words: *"Ne rompez jamais l'alliance anglaise"* (Never break the English Alliance).

This was precisely the point of view taken by Delcassé in his pamphlet. He severely blamed Freycinet for losing the confidence of England. In addition, he accused the Minister of sacrificing the interests of France to his peace policy, and tried to hold him responsible for the revolt in Egypt and for the intervention of the Powers in the dispute.

[34] Delcassé, *Alerte; Où allons-nous?* p. 32.

He said on page 26:

It was on the twenty-seventh of January that you were called to form the new Cabinet; and, three days afterwards, against us, against our influence, against our interests, the military revolution breaks out at Cairo; and the Powers send the collective note. . . . England, so firm, so resolute, with a common line of action under the preceding Cabinet [Gambetta's], since your advent to power shows a coldness which you cannot possibly disguise, and which crops out even in the articles of journals most favorable to you. . . .

And on page 28:

When the *status quo,* of which you were the recognized guardian, had been broken, and the [dual] control rendered impossible, was not this the moment to display the vigor which you retail with so much facility in your speeches? Abruptly, without hesitation, after a rapid entente with England, energetic action should have been taken to put everything back into its proper place and to safeguard our interests. It seemed preferable to you to patiently await the course of events, and you recognized the legitimacy of those national demands under which grotesque braggadocios hid their detestable appetites. Then, disconcerted by your attitude, and in every way assured of making its interests respected, the London Cabinet detached itself from you and the collective note appeared.

On the whole, this is rather strong language for a man of thirty to use in criticising so eminent a minister as Freycinet, age fifty-four, and twice Premier of France, but it was characteristic of Delcassé that he did not mince words, but stated his opinions with assurance and authority, if not with what we might call biblical directness. We gather, then, that Delcassé in 1882 was distinctly friendly toward England, though distressed by the sinking prestige of France in Egypt.

The first signed articles of Delcassé began to appear regularly on the front pages of the *République Française* in March 1886. A year later, the Egyptian question was still on his mind. On February 9, 1887, in a scathing article, he reviewed the English activities in Egypt since 1882.

She says she is impatient to evacuate the Valley of the Nile, but all her acts tend to render the occupation indefinite in point of time. She declares she is obliged to give Egypt a police force capable of maintaining order and security, but she does nothing to fulfill the obligation which she has imposed upon herself, and she thrusts aside all the means proposed to her even by those whose coöperation she has solicited.

It is a game. She may find it clever, but it is too much to pretend that France lends herself to it.

Delcassé's solution of this problem, from his article of February 26, 1887, was simple: "Neither French nor English but neutral. That is what Egypt ought to be, according to us, and we are working that it might be so."

An inkling of how Delcassé hoped to see the ideal of Egyptian neutrality realized is contained in his two-column article in the *République Française* for June 27, 1887. He knew that France alone was helpless, but had visions of aid from Russia:

As for the English notion that in the long run the possession of Egypt will constitute a title of ownership, that is all pure illusion. . . . Until now, France and Russia have confined themselves to protesting against the occupation of the valley of the Nile, but, as *le Nord* very justly recalled yesterday, "They have not made use of all the means at their disposal for giving their protestations a practical sanction." England will do well to reflect on that.

Russian assistance to France in the Egyptian question was a vain hope; Delcassé's writings on Franco-Italian relations do more credit to his perspicacity. He declared in the *République Française* on October 11, 1886, that nothing but the labors and tricks of Bismarck separated France and Italy, and added:

More than anyone else we have deplored the misunderstandings which have strained the relations of France and Italy in these last few years; but we have never thought that they could last, because national interests as well as race draw the two countries together and dictate that they mutually assist each other. All attempts to bring us into conflict in the Mediterranean are in vain. On the contrary, we think Italy has a place marked out for her in the Mediterranean and we shall see with pleasure Italy conquering her just share of influence. To be more precise, it is useless for anyone to attempt to excite the jealousy of our neighbor with regard to Tripoli: We categorically declare that we have no designs on this country and that if Italy ever wants to occupy it, she will not find us standing in her way.

Thus, in 1886, twelve years before he became Minister of Foreign Affairs, Delcassé not only desired a Franco-Italian understanding, but was willing to let Italy have Tripoli in order to establish the entente.[35]

The *République Française* carried many other articles by Delcassé in which he favored an entente between France and Italy, some of which serve to illustrate the saucy, ironical vein of humor that made it profitable to print his articles on the front page of a great Parisian journal. As the time approached for Italy to renew the bonds which tied her to Germany and Austria, Delcassé spread broadcast in his columns every possible line of argument calculated to induce Italy to refuse. To his own arguments, suitable quotations of the same nature from Italian journals were added to give the columns additional weight both at home and abroad. The Italian journal *L'Opinione* followed this astonishing press campaign and openly charged Delcassé with giving a lopsided picture of Italian opinion, since he practically ignored the arguments on the other side of the case. Delcassé, on February 26, 1887, took all the wind out of *L'Opinione's* sails by frankly admitting that he was a special pleader and at the same time he gave his reasons for his actions:

L'Opinione lets us know that they always read the *République Française:* we are much obliged to them for it. They complain that we read their journal only at intervals: They will be happy therefore to learn that we read it with the same care and with the same assiduity that we read the other great Italian papers. If we

[35] This offer of Tripoli was repeated by Delcassé in *Paris,* November 28, 1888.

cite them less, it is because, convinced partisans of an *entente cordiale* with Italy, we deliberately abstain from reprinting articles and engaging in disputes which appear to us to be of such a nature as to hinder that *entente*.

Not only was Delcassé in 1887 a convinced partisan of an *entente cordiale* with Italy, but he also appreciated the truth of the statement made by *L'Opinione* itself that the necessary basis for a durable understanding between France and Italy would have to be found in the balance of power in the Mediterranean. In the last-mentioned article of Delcassé, he staunchly maintained that France was the best friend of this Mediterranean balance of power.

Arguing against Italy's renewal of the Triple Alliance, Delcassé wrote on March 7, 1887, that Italy was "the dupe of Bismarck," and on March 15, his columns carried the following lines:

... from the Court of Vienna Italy has received up to this time only signs of a humiliating indifference; from Bismarck only sarcasm and menaces. . . .

... Italy has no claim to press against France; why then should she ally herself to our enemies?

. . . .

If the pact of 1882 is renewed, Austria will without doubt show a little more condescension toward the Quirinal; Bismarck will perhaps put a bridle on his satirical humor and will coquet less publicly with the Vatican. In reality the basis of the Alliance will not change, the three powers continuing to mutually guarantee the integrity of their respective territories. For Germany and Austria, the advantage is evident, but what about Italy, who has nothing to fear from anybody and who knows it?

After Italy's renewal of the alliance for another five years, Delcassé wrote in despair (March 21, 1887) that the alliance of Italy with Germany and Austria "shocked good sense" and "thwarted the aspirations" of Italy. In conclusion, he added: "We do not ignore the fact that the pretension of the Triple Alliance is that it is essentially pacific. But if it should form alongside of itself a league against war, what friend of

peace would complain?" Yet Delcassé refused to give up hope
of bettering relations between France and Italy. On the contrary, in his editorial of April 18, 1887, he pointed out that
the economic and material interests of Italy necessitated a
rapprochement with France, an idea to which he tenaciously
clung.[36]

Early in October 1887, the news leaked out that the Sultan
of Morocco hadn't set foot in the mosque for a solid week.
When this seemingly unimportant information was served
up to Delcassé at his desk in the office of the *République
Française,* he at once became very much excited. He concluded that the Sultan was either very ill or assassinated as
a result of a harem plot. This raised the question of the
succession to the Moroccan throne, and Delcassé considered
the matter to be of such extreme importance to France that
he not only wrote an editorial on the subject for the *République Française* (Oct. 7, 1887) but two days later wrote
another one for the *Paris,* a Parisian journal which will be
described later and with which Delcassé had established a
connection by this time.

The excitement over Morocco spread to the Italians, who
were afraid that France would take advantage of this opportunity to seize Morocco. Some Italian journals even went
so far as to propose a Mediterranean League of Italy, Germany, England, and Austria to prevent France from grabbing
the dominions of the late (?) Sultan. Commenting upon this
proposal, Delcassé said, "To class Germany among the Mediterranean Powers is a strange thing to do, and denotes a
singular state of mind."[37] He argued that of all the Powers
in Europe, France ought to be most concerned by the recent
events in Morocco. France had the same general interests
in the Sherifian Empire that England and the other European Powers had. She could evoke rights dating far back
into history just as well as Spain could, but with this difference: The Spanish touched Morocco only on one point,

[36] Delcassé, in *Paris,* Jan. 27, 1888; and Feb. 8 and 10, 1889.
[37] Delcassé, *Paris,* Oct. 9, 1887.

France bordered it along the whole western frontier of her Algerian Empire. French troops in Algeria had to fight constantly to turn back brigands from the Moroccan frontier. Then, too, most of the religious sects of Morocco counted adherents in Algeria. Every religious struggle in Morocco therefore had its repercussions in Algeria. No less vital for France was the fact that Morocco bordered the strait of Gibraltar by which the Mediterranean ports of France traded with America and West Africa, and by which French ports along the Channel traded with the Levant and the East. This was also the route by which the Mediterranean and Atlantic fleets of France would have to join each other in case of war. Consequently France must never allow Tangier to fall into the hands of Powers indifferent, jealous, or hostile to her. Delcassé proposed concordant action between France and Spain to maintain the *status quo.* Thus the question of Morocco would be "essentially a Franco-Spanish problem."[38] Delcassé did not offer to share Morocco with Italy. As we have already seen, he was willing to let Italy have Tripoli.[39] Apparently he considered Tripoli to be as much of North Africa as the Italians had a right to expect.

Before taking up the subject of Delcassé's career on the *Paris,* it should be said here that his articles in the *République Française* showed a keen penetration of the general diplomacy of Europe, which at that date was dominated by the German Chancellor. The activities of Bismarck Delcassé studied carefully day by day, and likewise searched through the published correspondence of this, the greatest of European diplomats, in order to understand him better. If the later diplomacy of Delcassé was cynical and high-handed, if he played for big stakes without too much regard for the possibilities of armed conflict, it was perhaps to some extent due to the fact that he grew up in the Bismarckian school. Not that Delcassé liked or admired Bismarck, for he thought him capable of any sort of deception or act of ingratitude,

---

[38] Delcassé, *République Française,* Oct. 7, 1887; *Paris,* Oct. 9, 1887.
[39] Delcassé, *République Française,* Oct. 11, 1886; *Paris,* Nov. 28, 1888.

and repeatedly tried to convince the Italians of this fact, but the Iron Chancellor's success forced respect for his methods, however unethical those methods might seem. Delcassé considered him France's most uncompromising enemy, and for that reason was ambitious to undo his work. But on one occasion Delcassé and Bismarck were in harmony, and since the question then at issue involved the genesis of the World War, it is too important to be passed over in silence.

On the eighth of January, 1887, in an article called "The Alliances of Germany," Delcassé informed the readers of the *République Française* that Bismarck was counseling his Austrian ally to moderate or postpone her pretensions in the Balkans. The Chancellor judged that the uncompromising opposition of Austria to Russian policy in that region was dangerous. Delcassé noted that Austria did not have the same robust confidence in Germany that she had formerly had, that the policy of expansion toward the southeast, inaugurated in 1879 and commenced by the occupation of Bosnia and Herzegovina, obliged her to watch attentively any modification in the Balkan situation, but echoed the warnings of certain Austrian papers which counseled Austria to cease keeping her eyes steadfast upon the Balkans and to come to terms with Russia. Delcassé's comment was that such a resolution on the part of Austria would completely change the conditioning forces of European diplomacy. "It would have the appreciable advantage of assuring from that day the peace of Europe."

It is impossible to state what the course of events would have been if the advice of the Iron Chancellor and the French journalist had been taken, but no one can deny the clear vision and the farsightedness of Delcassé. The World War started in the Balkans, and Austro-Russian rivalry in the Balkans was one of the major causes of that great conflict.

While on the *République Française,* Delcassé had begun an even more brilliant career with another journal, the *Paris.* Toward 1880, Jules Méline took over the *République Française* and began to color it with his moderate Republicanism. In 1881, some dissatisfied elements from another Republican organ, *La France,* resigned; and, under the leadership of Charles Laurent, founded the *Paris.* The very first number of this daily announced that it was opposed to a senile diplomacy, and desired a courageous and dignified policy: "There is somewhere in Europe a right which sleeps, a policy which causes growth, opportunities which are being born: look to them." Calling upon the name of Gambetta, it demanded less particular and private interests in the Chambers, and, significantly, more nationalism—"Men are nothing, France is everything!" This organ became the mouthpiece of the Republican Union group. Delcassé, with that lifelong ability for straddling parties which was truly marvelous, kept his position on the *République Française,* and at the same time obtained a foothold in this other camp. The political ideal of the paper, that of sacrificing one's personal interest and one's own individual political fortunes for the good of the country, remained Delcassé's through life.

He began by writing leading articles on foreign and colonial affairs, which were signed, and which attracted much attention. From 1887 to 1889 he was foreign editor of the paper.[40]

Although Delcassé was still secretary of the editorial staff of the *République Française,* his signed articles in that paper became less frequent and finally, in January of 1888, ceased altogether. However, Delcassé's agitation for his policies did not suffer. His signed articles in the *Paris* carried on the campaign without interruption. The position of foreign editor, together with the *Paris* ideal of fervent nationalism, permitted him to be more outspoken in his opinions than before, and consequently his writings in the *Paris* are less restrained in their language and uniformly more radical than his earlier articles. The result was a more vigorous exposition of his ideas.

He continued to preach the mutual advantages of a rapprochement of France and Italy, declaring on September 8,

[40] E. Mermet, *Annuaire de la Presse Française,* 1888-1889.

1887, that he was "obstinately set on its realization." During the year 1888, he sought to dispel the Italian fear that France might intervene on behalf of the Pope. Since the general elections of 1887, France had not seriously thought of restoring the Pope, he said. Indeed, the Pope had complained of anti-clericalism in France. Delcassé even tried to shift Italian fears by saying that Bismarck and Francis Joseph were carefully courting the Roman Pontiff, and were really more of a menace to Italy than France. About the same time, he reminded the Italians that their close union with the Teutonic Powers was in direct conflict with their longing for the Irredenta. Moreover, he again offered Tripoli to Italy. Even the erratic and hostile acts of the new Italian Foreign Minister (Crispi) and the outbreak of a Franco-Italian tariff war failed to shake his faith. He remained a "convinced partisan of a political entente with Italy."[41]

Until 1886, the foreign policy of France had been timid, reserved, and uncertain. France was present at the great European congresses, out of pride; but in reality, because of her weakness and diplomatic isolation, she had relatively little part in the decisions taken by the great Powers. She seemed to be waiting for an immanent Justice to restore her rights. Delcassé was among those who thought that Justice did not perform such miracles single-handed, that it was necessary to solicit her, and, above all, to fix clearly upon the objects and design of French foreign policy.

When at last, in 1886 and 1887, the French Foreign Minister, Flourens, began to work actively for a Franco-Russian alliance, Delcassé supported him joyfully, and took the occasion to outline a complete foreign policy for France, which anticipated in a large measure the policy that he was to pursue himself as Foreign Minister. It must be admitted, however, that in one respect he departed sadly from his political faith. These ideas are summarized in the signed article by Delcassé which appeared on the front page of the *Paris* for Sunday, June 5, 1887.

[41] Delcassé, *Paris*, March 23, Sept. 17, Oct. 14, Nov. 28, 1888.

This veritable masterpiece begins by declaring that a democratic government is not absolutely incapable of having a continuous foreign policy, that universal suffrage and diplomacy are not radically different terms. It was only necessary that the diplomacy of a republic should not be like that of certain monarchies.

If one understands by diplomacy that science which has dynasticism for its principal interest and intrigue for its favorite means; which operates only in darkness and mystery; which results in bizarre combinations all the more arrogant because they choke nature and good sense; which couples together in monstrous alliances nations separated by race, language, customs, institutions, hatreds of the past, the claims of the present, the hopes of the future, as, for example, the alliance of Austria and Italy: for whom the people are only instruments and remain the monopoly of a caste rigorously closed: if such is the significance attached to this word, the French Republic will never have a diplomacy.

Note well this paragraph. The inconsistency of Delcassé's denunciation of secret diplomacy, which he afterwards developed into a fine art, is merely the age-old difference between being in and out of office. Like Woodrow Wilson, he was forced to give up this article of his political faith. More important is the fact that even at this early date, Delcassé appreciated the unnatural aspects of Italy's adhesion to the Triple Alliance. In the third place, the same argument he gives against the union of Austria and Italy applies to the rapprochement of Germany and France actually desired by a party in France. Here again, the nations were separated by race, language, customs, institutions, hatreds of the past, the claims of the present, and the hopes of the future. Delcassé, as a skillful protagonist of *Revanche* (revenge for 1870), knew how to get his ideas across and yet to live true to Gambetta's precept—"Think of it always; speak of it never." Delcassé then continued:

The only rule which inspires her [France] in her international relations is the defense of rights, that is, the protection of French interests. Evidently the accomplishment of these obligations can lead her to search for friendship and support on the outside. All the art of her diplomacy consists in finding the nation to whom the friendship of France appears equally advantageous and her support precious; and, when she has found it, to avoid all that might compromise an entente founded on reciprocal sympathies and common interests.

Here Delcassé has propounded the ardent defense of French interests for which he was to strive during the Fashoda crisis, and has stated the doctrine of Gambetta's letter to Ranc that a proper internal policy in France would be necessary for the Russian rapprochement.[42] His argument for the Russian alliance continued as follows:

Well, this nation exists, and it is our most inveterate enemy, Bismarck himself, who has taken care to point it out to us. It is he who, on the 26th of April, 1856, in a report to the Prince-regent of Prussia, now the Emperor of Germany, wrote this sentence which should be continually in the mind of all those who give themselves to politics: "The alliance of France and Russia is a thing so natural that it would be folly not to expect it; because, of all the powers, they are the only ones which, by reason of their geographic position and political aims, have the least elements of hostility, not having any interests which necessarily conflict."

This is still the truth today, a truth which time has fortified, which events have rendered more forceful. To all the causes of friendship between France and Russia described thirty years ago by Bismarck, there has been added one other which makes a close union of these two nations a superior law: that is, a common danger. Between them, united Germany raises herself, formidable by her military power, disquieting because of her encroaching tendencies, bruising by her arrogance the most legitimate susceptibilities, ruining the economic interests of her neighbors whose national existence she still menaces. It is against her attacks that France and Russia have to fortify themselves beforehand; it is upon her that they have to press identical claims. To the east and to the west of Europe, they act as a counterpoise to the German colossus, just as on the north and south of Asia they act as an obstacle to the invasions of China and England. Everywhere the

[42] Cf. G. Michon, *L'Alliance Franco-Russe*, p. 60.

same enemies, everywhere the same interests, everywhere the same aspirations. What is puzzling is that an entente so natural has been so long in becoming established.

Such were the arguments for the Franco-Russian Alliance employed by Delcassé in 1887. Is it necessary to analyze them? The great enemy of France was Germany; the alliance was to be directed against her for the purpose of pressing certain claims. . . .

The succeeding paragraphs praised Flourens for dissipating the misunderstandings of Russia, and for overcoming her hesitations. Then Delcassé put in a plea for a Franco-Italian entente. Flourens had indeed "not been able to prevent the Italian Government from concluding with Germany and Austria an alliance which injured the aspirations and the patriotic sentiments of Italy." But his policy toward her had been reassuring, and had "dissipated the ill will of the Quirinal and singularly seconded the party, each day more powerful on the other side of the Alps, which sees in France a natural friend of Italy." "That is not a small service either," remarked Delcassé.

The article closed by exhorting France not to deviate from the simple, clear, and determined system so auspiciously begun, and congratulated Prime Minister Rouvier for maintaining Flourens in office. Taken as a whole, it anticipates the major part of Delcassé's own program from 1898 to 1914. The only notable exception is that England figures as one of the mutual enemies of France and Russia instead of as their friend. But does this mean that Delcassé despaired of the complete Gambettist policy of a triple entente of France, England, and Russia? The primary object of the article of June 5, 1887, was to promote the Russian Alliance. Relations between Russia and England were then sorely strained because of Russia's continued advance toward India. To speak of England as the friend of France would have endangered the immediate end that Delcassé desired to obtain, and it was true that the French and English were bitter colonial rivals in almost all parts of the world.

Delcassé's columns in the *République Française* also supported the Franco-Russian Alliance, and other articles by Delcassé favoring it appeared in the *Paris* during 1887.[43] The excellence of his work was not lost on Flourens—nor his flattering praise of Flourens himself. July 16, 1887, President Jules Grévy, on Flourens' nomination, signed a decree making Delcassé a Chevalier of the Legion of Honor.[44]

The picturesque legends that gather about the great, and were not lacking in Delcassé's case, say that during this same year Delcassé had a duel "à la Grande Jatte" with a colleague of the South. An anecdote connected with this alleged affair is too humorous to be passed over in silence. It seems that in the middle of the combat the swords became badly bent. While this difficulty was being adjusted, Delcassé disappeared, to the great consternation of the seconds. He hadn't gone far, though. As a young man, he had been accustomed to exercise as a gymnast, and he had just gone off to renew his strength by working on a trapeze. Reinforced by this excellent exercise, he came back and wounded his opponent in the thigh.[45]

After receiving the cross of the Legion of Honor, Delcassé continued to labor whole-heartedly for the alliance of France and Russia. We gather that he saw in the Franco-Russian Alliance a chance to cripple Germany by obliging her to fight on two sides at once,[46] and that he considered Russia to be the natural leader of the Slavic peoples in the Balkans. Russia was extolled as the "beloved liberator" of Bulgaria and the Tsar as the "father and protector" of the Slavs.[47] Finally, we learn that Delcassé thought it unnecessary to seal

---

[43] Delcassé, *République Française*, Sept. 26, 1886; Jan. 8, June 27, 1887; *Paris*, April 21, May 15, July 29, Aug. 3 and 15, Sept. 1, 1887.

[44] *J.O.*, 1887, p. 3314.

[45] *Nuova Antologia*, vol. 185, p. 33. His Excellency, Camille Barrère feels sure that Delcassé never had a duel. "If he had, I'd have known about it because I should have been his second." However, the reader cannot see Delcassé as his contemporaries saw him without a knowledge of these anecdotes, true or false.

[46] Delcassé, *Paris*, Nov. 26, 1887.

[47] Delcassé, *Paris*, Aug. 15, 1888; Feb. 21, 1889.

the rapprochement of France and Russia by a formal alliance. Even then, he understood that a well-established entente was better than a signed treaty. The will and the desire to work together was the important thing, not the paper document:

> . . . there is between France and Russia a community of interests which renders treaties superfluous and which is one hundred times preferable to the best of treaties. The important thing is to avoid any misunderstanding which might, either in Paris or St. Petersburg, interfere with the clear perception of the solidarity of interests that unites us. This is the policy we have recommended for years with diverse fortune, but with equal perseverance. In the end, it has triumphed. Today, [article dated Nov. 21, 1888] no minister having in mind its abandonment could last twenty-four hours.[48]

Delcassé joyfully noted the signs of German anger. In his estimation, the choler of the Germans manifested the value of the new Franco-Russian rapprochement.[49]

The year 1888 found Delcassé agitating in the *Paris* for a triple entente of France, England, and Russia. Two years before, September 27, 1886, he had repeated in the *République Française* the statement of another journal that France had done all that she could possibly do in order to maintain the *entente cordiale* with England and had stopped short only when it became evident that England was imposing upon France. The French became defiant of England, and the entente then seemed an "idle fancy." After the neutralization of the Suez Canal in October of 1887, Delcassé's hopes of a restoration of the *entente cordiale* began to revive. He believed that the Egyptian question was the only important bone of contention between England and France, and hoped that before long the neutralization of the Canal would be followed by the neutralization of Egypt and perhaps English evacuation of the country.[50] By February 18, 1888,

---

[48] Delcassé, *Paris*, Nov. 21, 1888; also May 24, 1887.
[49] *Ibid.*, Nov. 21, 1888, "Colère Instructive."
[50] Delcassé, *Paris*, Oct. 25, 1887.

Delcassé considered the rapprochement of France and Russia to be an accomplished fact, and the diminutive journalist enjoyed the high satisfaction of pronouncing the diplomatic position of France to be "good," but he quickly added, "Let nothing prevent us now from making it excellent." He was of the opinion that this could be done by contracting a new friendship with England. Opponents of this idea were eagerly demonstrating the many reasons why the French should hate the English. The English had abandoned France in 1870 and had "confiscated" Egypt, they argued. All very true, and a long list of other sins committed by the English might be added, said Delcassé but "Nevertheless, it is impossible for us to hate them. . . . The past is not to be thrown as an insurmountable barrier between France and England." His point of view was that both countries must act in accord with their national interests, which drew them together, and forget the bitter memories of other days.[51]

Instead of dwelling upon the disagreeable incidents of recent years, Delcassé, who had taught history, found in the past ample argument for Anglo-French cordiality. He cited the *"fraternité anglo-française"* championed in 1791 by Mirabeau and pursued by Talleyrand during his mission to London in 1792, and said that Mirabeau and Talleyrand were right in declaring that England had every reason for drawing closer to France and that "what was true at the end of the eighteenth century" was "still more true today."[52]

The last sentence was written by Delcassé in April 1889. Progress toward contracting a friendship with England had meanwhile gone on very slowly. A part of Delcassé's article of May 21, 1888, in the *Paris* reads:

The journey of Lord Randolph Churchill to Saint Petersburg has certainly not taken place against his will; and, at the same time, the Marquis of Salisbury himself concerted with M. Flourens. There is much talk therefore of an entente between France, England, and Russia. Public opinion in the three countries is

[51] Delcassé, *Paris*, Feb. 18, 1888.
[52] Delcassé, *Paris*, April 20, 1889.

favorable to it; their respective interests command it. Why has the accord not been made?

The chief reason for failure, according to Delcassé, was the pro-German bias of Queen Victoria, whose will always prevailed. Then, too, Salisbury was prejudiced; England feared the Boulanger movement in France; and M. Flourens, poorly seconded by the French Ambassador in England, had not been able to send over the right man to persuade Salisbury.

On the eighth of June, 1888, Delcassé wrote in the *Paris* an answer to those Englishmen who were foolishly talking of a war between France and England. His love of sarcasm and his sense of humor compelled him to twit the English for believing that they had a natural right to every piece of land surrounded by water; yet, on the whole, his attitude toward the Britons was distinctly friendly.

But, after all, why should we make war on the English? To take a strip of territory from them? But we acquired our natural frontiers on the northwest centuries ago, and it is not on the Channel that we have been mutilated. To take away their colonies? But the exploitation of those we already possess will keep us employed for a long time to come. . . .

The last sentences in this quotation are the most important. Fourteen years later (August 1902), in the epoch-making negotiations with Lansdowne, which laid the basis of the Anglo-French Entente, Delcassé empowered Cambon (the French Ambassador) to use almost the identical language of this newspaper article, and, fifteen years later (July 7, 1903), Delcassé in his personal conversation with Lansdowne brought forward the same point to help win over the English statesman.[53]

Delcassé asserted many times that an Anglo-French entente was perfectly consistent with the Franco-Russian rapprochement already established. He steadfastly maintained that

[53] Gooch and Temperley, *British Documents on the Origins of the War,* 1898-1914, II, 264 and 294.

there was no real conflict between England and Russia, that
England had nothing to gain in taking an aggressive attitude,
and that an Anglo-Russian entente would be beneficial to
England.[54] Especially notable was his clear perception of
that trend of events which was making Germany rather than
France and Russia the great opponent of England, and he
developed this idea at considerable length.[55] He also saw
that time, circumstances, and national interests were all on
the side of the triple entente of France, England, and Russia
which he desired.

The Prime Minister of the Queen [Lord Salisbury] has not
been able to disembarrass himself of the prejudices and hatreds
which have it that France and Russia are the born enemies of
England. They prevent him from taking well into account the
modifications which have taken place in the respective situation
of the Powers, and from seeing clearly that England's danger now
lies elsewhere. What umbrage could England possibly take from
France? Without speaking of the vigilance which our eastern
frontier demands, is it not true that the organization of our empire beyond the seas is sufficient to employ our efforts?

The same thing is true of Russia. She does not seek any new
conquests in Asia. She contents herself with the glorious task of
civilizing the immense countries which she ought to subject to
herself. If she has advanced to the doors of India, she does so in
order to be able to repulse by a decisive blow the attacks which
official England is obstinately bent upon contriving against her
in Europe.

But the democracy which is rising, and which is fated to have
the government of England, does not share these prejudices [i.e.,
those of Salisbury and official England]. Its arrival in power will
lead to a different foreign policy. Lord Randolph Churchill
formulated it a year ago on his return from his trip to Russia.[56]

The diplomats must play their part. Time goes beyond their
little calculations and their artificial combinations. To arouse the

---

[54] Delcassé, *Paris*, March 2, April 27, 1888; March 1, 1889.
[55] Delcassé, *Paris*, Aug. 15, 1888; Jan. 17, 26, and 28, 1889.
[56] His visit was unofficial, but he discussed, and was in favor of, an Anglo-
Russian rapprochement. W. L. S. Churchill, *Lord Randolph Churchill*, II,
357-358, 365-366.

people one must convince them that their national interests are really menaced, and in regard to these interests it will be less and less easy to deceive them.[57]

Delcassé contemplated rounding out this triple entente of France, England, and Russia not only by the addition of the Slavic Powers in the Balkans, which naturally looked to Russia as father and protector, but also by the inclusion of Austria. Making use of the tactics employed to wean Italy from Germany, Delcassé, between 1887 and 1889, used his influence in the French press to detach Austria from the nation which had conquered and humiliated her at Sadowa.[58] He endeavored to arouse the national spirit by questioning the wisdom of Austria in contenting herself with being the "satellite" and "tool" of Germany, or the "first of the feudatories" of William II. He alleged that Germany dictated to Austria and interfered in her affairs.[59] He told the Austrians that they could leave the Triple Alliance without fear of isolation. The entente of Austria and Russia was easy. Austria had only to give up her policy of expansion in the Balkans, a policy that was exceedingly dangerous to herself anyhow because she already had too many Slavs within her borders. To secure the friendship of France, Austria had only to recover her independence and dignity—no rival interest or national antipathy stood between the two nations. There was even a certain common interest between them, forgetfulness of which had cost dear. Both had been defeated by Prussia, Austria in 1866 and France in 1870, and both had paid heavily for the blunder of not helping the other in its hour of need. There was consequently "nothing to prevent Austria from becoming the center of a Franco-Austro-Russian Alliance."[60] As for England, Delcassé had written in the *Paris* as early as April 27, 1888, that the entente of England and Austria was for the best interest of England and

[57] Delcassé, *Paris*, Sept. 27, 1888.
[58] Delcassé, *République Française*, Jan. 8, 1887; *Paris*, April 20, May 9, Aug. 12, Sept. 27, Oct. 7, 1888.
[59] Delcassé, *Paris*, Dec. 13, 1887; Dec. 2, 1888; June 29, 1889.
[60] Delcassé, *Paris*, Dec. 9, 1888; See Dec. 5, 1888.

the rest of Europe. Moreover, in a remarkable editorial which appeared in the *Paris,* September 27, 1888, under the title *Ce Qui Devrait Etre* (What Ought to Be), Delcassé not only declared the close coöperation of France, Russia, and England to be both possible and desirable, but urged Austria to turn her attention from the Balkans and make her peace with Russia, thereby gaining the natural allies of Russia. This would have meant a quadruple entente of France, Russia, Austria, and England, and, taken along with Delcassé's well-known desire for a rapprochement of France and Italy, would have amounted to a more complete diplomatic isolation of Germany than Delcassé later on achieved.

There is nothing particularly reprehensible in this idea of isolating Germany. It merely involved undoing the work of Bismarck and isolating Germany as Bismarck had isolated France. Delcassé thought it could be done because he fully appreciated the flimsy nature of the cords that bound Austria and Italy to Germany, and at the same time saw that they, and other Powers too, could be bound to France by stronger and surer ties based upon national interests.

The policies advocated by Delcassé were, in each case, parts of a well-organized and well-thought-out system of diplomacy. Consequently they did not vary from day to day but were pursued doggedly. However, fate stepped in to virtually wreck one of his pet schemes, the addition of Austria to his system of ententes. His Austrian hopes rested to a large degree on Rudolf of Habsburg, heir to the Austrian throne and reputed to be a friend of the idea of Austrian rapprochement with France and Russia. This Prince died early in 1889, and Delcassé wrote:

How wise it would have been for Austria to have worked to regain the position she lost in 1866! At the same time, she would have made two powerful friends of France and Russia, and their assistance to her would have been all the more certain because every bit of assistance given by them to her would have been to their own profit. They say that the Archduke Rudolf always had in mind the rank that his country once had in Germany and

that he did not despair of restoring it. . . . There is no use to
await any energetic resolution on the part of Francis Joseph. He
certainly sees the better course, but either through timidity or
discouragement he will continue to follow the worst path.[61]

The foregoing analysis of Delcassé's writings shows that,
even as a journalist, he was working for what he strove to
build up in later life—a rapprochement with Italy—a triple
entente of France, Russia, and England—and that he likewise
contemplated adding Austria to the system. Those who have
already studied Delcassé's career will want two questions
answered: What did he say about Alsace-Lorraine? What
was his attitude toward a reconciliation with Germany? Both
questions can be answered at the same time.

As for Alsace-Lorraine, in the article for *Paris*, June 5,
1887, we have already found Delcassé referring to the lost
provinces indirectly in order to live true to Gambetta's motto,
"Think of it always; speak of it never." He often did this.
Writing in the *Paris* on April 9, 1888, he spoke of Alsace-
Lorraine in the same guarded manner as the "obstacle
separating us from Germany." On September 27, 1886, in
the *République Française,* Delcassé examined the prospect
of a Franco-German alliance, only to dismiss it with the curt
remark that there was "a grave question" [Alsace-Lorraine]
which divided Germany and France, the name of which it
was quite unnecessary to mention. So far as Delcassé was
concerned, this unnamed argument was final.

Similarly, in the columns of the *Paris* for December 28,
1888, Delcassé rejected the idea of a French rapprochement
with Germany. This time he subscribed to the widespread
feeling that France had a right to expect "substantial satisfaction" from Germany, and denounced the very idea of a
rapprochement as a German trap to prevent the union of
France and Russia. He then argued for the Franco-Russian
Alliance, and said that good sense would prevent the French
people from falling into the snare Germany desired to set
for them. "Germanic perfidy" was a part of Delcassé's

[61] Delcassé, *Paris,* April 23, 1889.

working vocabulary, hence perhaps, his suspicion on this occasion.[62]

However, Delcassé by no means contented himself with speaking of Alsace-Lorraine and Germany in such restrained language:

It has been eighteen years since Alsace-Lorraine was taken away from France. Has France become less dear to her and Germany less odious? The persistence of the Alsace-Lorrainers in electing candidates of the party of protest, the desertion of their young men *en masse* at the moment of conscription, declare well enough that their feelings have not changed. And there is no indication that they are changing.

Farsighted as he is, Bismarck understands that his last conquest has not been accepted, and that the years in passing by will render it still more contestable.[63]

. . . .

It was in 1793, March 21. The population of the left bank of the Rhine, from Bingen to Spire, had enthusiastically voted their reunion with the French Republic. The Rhenish Convention nominated after this vote ratified it, and here is the message it sent to our Convention.

"By union with us you acquire that which by right belongs to you; by union with us you gain your [city of] Mayence, the only gateway by which the cannons of the enemy can penetrate into your provinces. Nature herself has desired that the Rhine should be the frontier of France: it was in the first centuries."

History sometimes repeats itself.

Delcassé[64]

As the last days of the old Emperor William I drew to a close, liberals in Germany and France were hopeful that the accession of the progressive and enlightened Ferderick III would inaugurate a new era in Franco-German relations. Profoundly skeptical on this score, Delcassé nevertheless hastened to Berlin as special correspondent for the *Paris* in the middle of March 1888, after the news of William's death had been reported.

---

[62] Delcassé, *Paris*, Nov. 9, 1888.   [63] Delcassé, *Paris*, Jan. 6, 1889.
[64] Delcassé, *Paris*, article "Nationalité," July 8, 1888.

There in Berlin, he watched the crowds before the coffin
of the old Emperor, and sensed that the German people felt
as he himself had felt when he stood before the coffin of
Gambetta. This man, William I, had incarnated for them
the greater Germany. He was the "Father of Germany," said
a humble newspaper vendor. Leaving the crowd, Delcassé
talked with a number of German progressives and was told
that the liberal intentions of Frederick III were quite sincere
but that he would have to struggle against great obstacles.
He needed strength, but was weakened by illness. He needed
time, and yet he could not possibly live longer than August.
This depressing news gave the funeral of William I the air
of a double tragedy. Absorbed in this feeling, Delcassé, on
the morrow, stood before the forged grillwork guarding the
entrance to the Royal tombs and watched the nobles file in
for the last rites. Suddenly he heard the crowd about him
shout, "Es lebe kaiser Friedrich!" "Cruel irony!" said Delcassé to himself, reflecting that in a few months Frederick
would have to join his ancestors in the tombs at Charlotten-
bourg.[65]

It is clear that the trip to Berlin confirmed Delcassé in his
pessimism with regard to Germany. He was told "ten times"
that he would not find in the capitol a single merchant,
farmer, laborer, or peasant who professed bellicose ideas;
but this was overshadowed and outweighed in his mind by
the fact that, although they were the most numerous element
in the State, they did not exercise a determining influence
upon the Government. Above them stood the military or
war party, "two million more or less," making up in activity
what they lacked in numbers. Their songs and toasts to the
accession of Crown Prince William were still ringing in
Delcassé's ears as he sat at his desk in Paris ten days later:
"When Prince William, the hope of Germany, puts on the
Imperial Crown . . . Then the enemies on the East and West
shall tremble." And Delcassé reasoned that there were only

[65] Delcassé, *Paris*, March 16 and 17, 1888.

too many causes or pretexts for conflict because matters were going from bad to worse in the Balkans.[66]

On March 21, 1888, Delcassé read the special manifesto of Frederick III to Alsace-Lorraine, a manifesto that plainly indicated Frederick's intention of preserving every bit of that territory for Germany. This confirmed Delcassé in his opinion that the lost provinces must inevitably be a "barrier" between France and Germany. He persistently refused to believe in the rumors that Germany was about to give back Alsace-Lorraine, or give back part of it, or even a morsel of it such as Metz. The notion was baseless, said Delcassé, who was in all things a realist. Germany could never restore these territories. To do so would be either a confession that she had done wrong in taking them in the first place or an admission that she was too weak to defend them. National pride in Germany would of course never permit this. Germany would not restore Alsace-Lorraine until she was forced to do so.[67]

Hence, to Delcassé's mind, a policy of rapprochement with Germany was useless because the very object sought in the rapprochement would be unattainable. But, not only was a policy of rapprochement with Germany useless, it was also positively dangerous in his opinion because drawing closer to Germany might alienate Powers otherwise friendly to France or about to throw in their lot with France.[68]

Popular rumor had it that Gambetta in his last years had favored a rapprochement of France and Germany. Delcassé indignantly refused to believe that Gambetta had ever seriously thought of such a thing.

We have many times had the invaluable honor of hearing Gambetta develop his views on the foreign policy of France. He always envisaged the country reconstituted and made complete; he cited a thousand different ways of achieving this supreme purpose: he never once spoke of an entente with Germany![69]

[66] Delcassé, *Paris*, March 28, 1888.
[67] Delcassé, *Paris*, March 6, 1888, March 21, 1888, Oct. 14, 1888.
[68] Delcassé, *Paris*, March 6, 1888, March 21, 1888.
[69] Delcassé, *Paris*, March 26, 1888.

Delcassé declared that, while France would respect the terms of the Treaty of Frankfort, it was too much to expect her to consider that this treaty was beyond revision. "They may judge our actions, but our thoughts are not beholden to anybody," was his declaration.[70]

Having already cheerfully admitted that he looked upon the charge of being a chauvinist as a compliment to himself, Delcassé gloried in the French desire for *Revanche* as "dignified" and contrasted it with the Austrian policy of alliance with Germany after the defeat of 1866, which he said was "shameful."[71]

Like a man ringing fire bells in the night, Delcassé repeatedly warned his countrymen that Germany was France's "mortal enemy," that she had "sworn the ruin" of France, and that she was preparing for a "war of extermination" against her. Not that Delcassé thought Germany would attack France first, rather he always asserted that Germany was deliberately trying to exasperate France beyond the limit of endurance in the hope that the French Government would declare war, thereby putting itself in the wrong in the eyes of other Powers.[72]

Speaking of Germany and her plans, Delcassé said on November 20, 1887, in the *Paris:*

> This situation deserves all of our attention. At any moment, our national existence may be found to be at stake. Let us, then, settle our internal problems as quickly as possible in order that we may devote all our attention to the enemy. Let us hold ourselves in readiness.

The death of Frederick III and the accession of William II was, according to Delcassé, a sensible aggravation of the situation. If the new Kaiser either read or heard of Delcassé's editorials, he must have felt far from happy, because therein he was usually described as a dangerous man. Delcassé emphasized that he was a friend of old traditions and the

[70] Delcassé, *Paris*, July 29, 1887.
[71] Delcassé, *République Française*, Aug. 29, 1886; *Paris*, Jan. 2-3, 1889.
[72] Delcassé, *Paris*, May 24, Nov. 2, 1887; July 1, 1888, and many others.

idea of Divine Right and that he praised his grandfather, William I. He preoccupied himself with everything and interested himself in everything. His care on the day of his accession to address himself to the army before speaking to the nation, the affectation with which he identified himself with the army and gloried in its past and future, aroused the gravest apprehensions in Delcassé. Some of his characteristics, however, augured well for Delcassé's system of French ententes with other Powers. Delcassé perceived that the Kaiser's high words and airs displeased many of the foreign peoples he visited, and predicted that he would one day be hostile to England and be instrumental in sharpening Anglo-German colonial rivalry.[73] Germany's loss might be France's gain.

Delcassé also wrote that it was not improbable that the Kaiser meditated "a definitive partition of Europe" between Germany and her allies.[74] Yet it was an open secret that he longed for the friendship of France. Delcassé commented on this longing in the following terms:

On what does William II build his hopes of having us for allies? He knows what barrier separates France from Germany; but did he not say recently that to maintain this barrier [Alsace-Lorraine] he would sacrifice his forty million subjects to the last man? And, moreover, his power cannot so far blind him as to imagine that he can have France for a vassal.[75]

Delcassé's note of pessimism became accentuated in the early months of 1889. He saw before Europe only the prospect of a gigantic armament race for which he always blamed Germany. This race for armaments he described as mutually ruinous and as exceedingly dangerous because sooner or later some Power would use these war supplies in order to escape from the vicious circle of more preparations. However, there was no help for it. France must "go get her woolen stocking and dig into it," he said.[76]

He warned his readers that the Balkans were like a powder

---

[73] Delcassé, *Paris*, June 16, Aug. 15, Oct. 18, 1888; April 9, 1889.
[74] Delcassé, *Paris*, Oct. 18, 1888. [75] Delcassé, *Paris*, Oct. 14, 1888.
[76] Delcassé, "La Liquidation Européenne," in *Paris*, March 19, 1889.

magazine. A single spark might explode it at any minute and involve everybody in ruin. He maintained that the peoples in the Balkans (Serbians, Rumanians, and Bulgarians) looked toward Russia as their protector but that their governments leaned on Austria and Germany. If to defend themselves, or to execute their will, the governments turned to Austria, reinforced by Germany, for aid, could Russia remain deaf to the call of her protégés? This, said Delcassé, was the delicate point in the international situation.[77] The people of Serbia would never pardon Austria for taking Bosnia and Herzegovina, which they regarded at Serbian. Radicals in Serbia believed that their King was committing a crime in being the vassal of a Power (Austria) that held so many of their brothers under the yoke. A revolution was imminent. All Europe might be drawn into the ensuing conflict.[78]

Delcassé, who saw with this unerring eye whither Europe was drifting, was ambitious for France to be ready. Even then, he was studying strategic railroads, war plans and military preparations, and calculating the speed of mobilization of France and Russia as over against the preparations of their enemies. As early as December of 1887, he had called attention to the fact that Russia had only three railroads of less than 3,000 kilometers on her Austro-German frontier, while Germany and Austria had seventeen railroad lines by which they could throw their armies into Russia. On the other hand, he pointed out the advantages of the Franco-Russian rapprochement which obliged Germany to face the prospect of fighting on two sides at once. The German plan of campaign would be to crush France by a rapid advance of German troops and then to turn back on Russia. Delcassé soberly pronounced this to be "overconfidence." In 1870, it took France six months to get herself in fighting shape and even then she was not fully prepared. It wouldn't take Russia that long now. Likewise France, instead of obligingly waiting to

[77] Delcassé, "L'Etincelle," in *Paris*, Dec. 18, 1887; "Petites Causes . . .," *Paris*, Dec. 22, 1888; "Le Point Délicat," *Paris*, Feb. 21, 1889.
[78] Delcassé, *Paris*, Dec. 22, 1888.

be attacked, might take the offensive and Germany be caught between two fires. In fact, after the Franco-Russian rapprochement, Delcassé was confident of French victory. If war came, the Germans would discover that France was not alone, and that French veins were not full of beer![79]

It was in his newspaper days, too, that the future Minister of Marine began studying the state of the French navy, the part that it would have to play in war time, and the need of reforms. The defects that Delcassé espied in the French marine were four in number. Most ministers of marine had been more concerned with realizing their personal theories than in building up a fleet ready for quick action. The navy lacked organization. There were not enough ships and submarines. Like the army, the fleet should be capable of instant mobilization. This was not the case. Delcassé admitted that building more ships and submarines would be very expensive business, but he reminded the French people that they should not forget the Italian fleet and the recent augmentation of the German fleet. He pointed out that in the next war the rôle of the navy would be of capital importance, and that France must at the same time be master of the Mediterranean and the North Sea.[80]

Delcassé's signed editorials began with a number of more or less well-defined introductory articles. In the succeeding issues of the *République Française* and the *Paris,* he sketched the foreign policy and system of national defense which we have given here. He closed with a last signed article on peace conferences and peace:

War appears to us as a necessity. It is found everywhere in nature. For a long time it has been the normal state of Europe. Animals hardly ever fight except in case of need. Men often fight over nothing, just for the pleasure of it. Today, wars are becoming more rare. That is because they are too deadly and too costly. Humanitarian considerations do not count for much in the hesitation of one rival nation to throw itself on another. But what of it? *N'est-ce pas au résultat qu'il se faut surtout attacher?*[81]

[79] Delcassé, *Paris,* Nov. 26, Dec. 18, 1887; June 24, Oct. 18, 1888.
[80] Delcassé, *Paris,* Jan. 10. 1888.   [81] Delcassé, *Paris,* May 16, 1889.

To Delcassé's mind, the prevention of war was a "seductive dream."

There are always nations more intelligent, more enterprising, more covetous, more prolific, more strong than others. Therefore, there will always be conflict among men. The duty of a government is to stave off war as long as possible at the same time that it prepares to engage actively in war when it comes.[82]

Enough has already been said to indicate the close connection between French newspapers and politics. From one to the other was a very short step. The earliest election campaign in which Delcassé figured was that of 1885. At that time, he presented himself in his native Department of Ariège as a candidate for the Chamber of Deputies. After the first balloting, he withdrew his name "in favor of one belonging to a list less favored," in order to permit the formation of a ticket by the advocates of Republican Concentration.[83] The purpose of such a party was to unite Republicans of various groups and to concentrate them against the opposition. Delcassé was too profoundly Republican not to sacrifice himself in such a cause.

The next parliamentary elections would not occur for four years. During the interim, Delcassé engaged in local politics. He at once proclaimed himself a faithful disciple of Gambetta. Those were the stirring days of the Boulanger crisis when the Republic of Gambetta seemed in danger of dissolution; but on July 15, 1888, the constituency in the Canton of Vicdessos elected Delcassé to represent them in the *Conseil Général* of the Department of Ariège.[84] The *Conseil Général*, an elective assembly with one representative for each canton in the Department, met twice a year at Foix, the capital of Ariège, and deliberated on departmental affairs. On July 28, 1889, at the general elections for the renewal of the *Conseil*, Delcassé was reëlected.

Delcassé was now thirty-seven years old, and was already married to a young woman née Mademoiselle Wallet, the

[82] Delcassé, *Paris*, May 16, 1889.   [83] Reynald, *op. cit.*, p. 8.
[84] *J.O.*, 1888, p. 3110.

widow of Massip, a wealthy deputy from Ariège. Camille Barrère had been best man at the wedding. Massip, for whom Delcassé had served as secretary, died in 1885, and Delcassé, in marrying his widow, fell heir to both his wealth and his political fortunes. The money that Mme Delcassé brought her husband not only freed him from all material cares but allowed him to pursue unhampered his natural inclination for politics. That was not all. A charming woman of medium height, Mme Delcassé presided gracefully over the social functions incumbent upon Delcassé and, in this way, too, she assisted him in his rise to political power and high office. Their home in Paris was a modest apartment at 11 Boulevard de Clichy.[85]

As we have said, Delcassé also fell heir to Massip's political fortunes. At the general elections for the Chamber of Deputies in September of 1889, the Radical-Liberals of Foix, despite the agitations of the Boulangists, selected Delcassé to succeed Massip in the representation of their city.

Delcassé, for at least twelve years, had been thinking very deeply about the position of France in the colonial field and in Europe. He saw that in each case the situation of France could be greatly improved. Under the immediate inspiration of Gambetta and his followers, from Bismarck's speeches, writings, and actions, and from his own studies of European international politics, he had developed a clear-cut program for France to follow. This program included policies relating to national defense, an equally definite colonial policy, and a remarkable system of diplomacy calculated to remake Europe in accordance with his heart's desire.

That part of the program relating to national defense called for, first, the complete reorganization of the French military system and the establishment of the three-years' service law in order to guarantee a strong and efficient army; second, a wholesale reform and reorganization of the marine and the

---

[85] Reynald, 36; Interview with Camille Barrère already cited; *Annuaire de la Presse Française . . . et du Monde Politique*, 1890, p. LXIV; London *Times*, Feb. 23, 1923, p. 11; *Qui Etes Vous.*

building of a stronger navy capable of controlling both the Mediterranean and the North Sea.

The colonial policy was that of an ardent defense of French interests in all parts of the world and especially in Egypt, where French rights were of great pecuniary value, and in Morocco where they were vital to the national safety of France. Even then, he contemplated Tripoli going to the Italians and Morocco falling under the influence of France and Spain to the exclusion of Germany and the rest of Europe.

The system of diplomacy included: first, the ardent protection of French interests in Europe as well as in the colonial field; second, the Franco-Russian Alliance for the double purpose of defending France from the German Colossus and of wringing from Germany certain claims (Alsace-Lorraine); third, the rapprochement of France and Italy, involving at once the weakening of the Triple Alliance and the strengthening of France against Germany; fourth, the rapprochement of England and France and the Triple Entente of France, England, and Russia; fifth, Russia as the father and protector of the Slavic people in the Balkans; sixth, the rapprochement of Austria and Russia (marred by the death of Rudolf); seventh, non-coöperation with Germany lest the Treaty of Frankfort be more firmly established and in order to avoid alienating Powers otherwise friendly to France or about to throw in their lot with France. The combined Delcassé program, as he must have envisaged it when he wrote *"Ce Qui Devrait Etre"* for the *Paris,* September 27, 1888, aspired to the complete diplomatic isolation of Germany through the alignment of France, Russia, England, Austria, and Italy, and would have guaranteed the security and preëminence of France in Europe. This would have been the *relèvement* of France with a vengeance! As we have said, he considered it possible to undo the work of Bismarck and to turn the tables because he fully appreciated all of the inherent weaknesses in the union of Germany, Austria-Hungary, and Italy, Powers with conflicting aims and hopes, and at the same time saw that Italy and Austria, and other Powers too, could be bound to

France by stronger and surer ties based on national interests. Delcassé had carried on a lively press campaign in favor of his policies. Even before this press campaign was finished, the foundations of the Franco-Russian alliance that he desired had been laid by the establishment of a Franco-Russian rapprochement. The French Minister of Foreign Affairs, by conferring upon Delcassé the cross of the Legion of Honor, had signalized the importance of Delcassé's journalism as a force helping to bring about that rapprochement. Delcassé had also prepared the minds of a large section of the French public for the execution of the remainder of his program. He was now, thanks to a fortunate marriage, free from the distractions of "making a living," and was a member of the Chamber of Deputies, one of those to whom the future of France had been confided.

The formulation of Delcassé's policies called for hard study, hard sense, and stern realism; advertising them in the press called for patriotism and courage; the actual execution of these policies required genius in practical politics, patience, and statesmanship of the highest order. The real greatness of Delcassé lies in this fact, that having fixed his policies clearly in his own mind, he was able to make his personal program become the national policy of France.

II

FINDING HIS PLACE
1889-1898

1. Speeches and Commissions

. . . to be ready at any moment to take the hand of our friends and natural allies: that is what our policy should be.

As you hold to this policy . . . you will create a powerful center of attraction toward which all those in Europe for whom France is a security will turn more and more. . . . (Delcassé, Nov. 6, 1890.)

M. BUVIGNIER reported on the fifteenth of November, 1889, that Delcassé had been elected by 10,836 votes against 8,086 of his aristocratic competitor in Foix, M. Alberic de Narbonne-Lara. Thereupon, Delcassé was admitted to the Chamber of Deputies.

The political atmosphere in which Delcassé was to move henceforth was much different from that of England or America. Those who called themselves Monarchists, Socialists, or Republicans did not belong to single organized parties. The Republicans, for instance, had split into two major divisions after 1870, the Opportunists under Gambetta and Jules Ferry, and the Radicals under Floquet and Clemenceau. The latter demanded far-reaching reforms at once, regardless of circumstances. But the Radicals were themselves split into groups and sub-groups, and it was to these that the French politician held allegiance. Yet even these groups were as uncertain and changeable as clouds. Against this system, which made every Frenchman virtually a party all to himself, Gambetta had raved: "What do I care for your groups and sub-groups, their names and their surnames? They don't interest either me or France."[1] He sought to conciliate them and to mold the groups into one Republican union. Never-

[1] E. Bourgeois, *Modern France*, II, 280.

theless, when he died in 1882, the "Republican Union" was just one of a large number of such groups.

If we are to understand the political faith of Delcassé, we must realize that here again he was a disciple of Gambetta. For him, likewise, group names were meaningless. He was Republican to the depths of his being, but he would not identify himself with any Republican group, though he was perfectly willing to coöperate with any one of them or all of them for the good of the Republic. He said in his political circular, "I am a faithful disciple of Gambetta, a Republican for whom the Republic is indissolubly connected with France, for whom the enemies of the Republic are perforce the enemies of the country."[2] Thus one might argue that he was an Opportunist; but Delcassé also had leanings in the other direction. He has been constantly labeled a Radical;[3] and he maintained a close connection with the very Radical *Dépêche de Toulouse,* which supported him even in some of his darkest hours.

As time went on, Delcassé came to have, potentially at least, a place in all of the Republican camps. By refusing to join any one particular body of politicians, he straddled all of them, and remained available to all. As one French writer has put it, he was isolated among the parties, but belonged to the Party-of-the-Republicans-in-Office.[4]

His spirit was large and free. He refused to think of other politicians as enemies merely because they did not share his political convictions. He saw in them first of all Frenchmen, and he wished to reconcile them to one another. He had the making of a great leader. He did not fear unpopularity. On the contrary, he disdained the plaudits of the multitude. Madame Delcassé's wealth was of importance in this connection. Her fortune gave him a position of independence with respect to both Parliament and electorate. Since office and reëlection were not vital necessities, he never compromised

[2] A. Bertrand, *La Chambre des Députés,* 1898-1902 (Paris, 1899) 39.
[3] S. Grenier, *Nos Députés,* 1902-1906 (Paris, 1903) 44; *Le Temps* (Paris), Feb. 23, 1923.
[4] Cf. Fournol, *Rev. Pol. et Lit.,* July 16, 1921, p. 446.

his principles on their account, but worked definitely and obstinately toward his goal.[5]

Opposed to no one, supported only by a few friends who admired his fervent patriotism, Delcassé worked alone, rarely acting even as vice-president of a group in opposition. What he did, he accomplished without any collective preparation or assistance.[6] He was oblivious to parties because obsessed with his schemes for reconstructing the world to the profit of France, and this political habit explains much that would otherwise be puzzling in his career.

Before Delcassé could reconstruct the world in accordance with his desires, he had to make up for certain grave handicaps. He was insignificant in his appearance, being no taller than Napoleon. Indeed, it would perhaps be accurate to say that he was half a head shorter than the average Frenchman. His voice was thin, almost too thin to be heard in the noisy Chamber of Deputies. Lacking "the gift of improvisation, he had to prepare his speeches with the utmost care and forethought, often only to see them utterly drowned in the tumult of the session."[7] Energy and tenacity, hard study and hard work, made him the powerful figure that he became.

The year 1889 in the Chamber of Deputies passed by without any notable achievement on the part of Delcassé who rapidly earned a reputation for silence. The first session did, however, yield him some valuable contacts and friendships, the most important of these being with Raymond Poincaré who has given us an account of it. Poincaré recollected that when Delcassé entered the Chamber of Deputies in 1889, they had been drawn together quickly by common friendships and by a collaboration on the *République Française*.

. . . In an epoch when the familiar thee and thou were rare in the Assemblies, we rapidly came to disembarrass ourselves of a

[5] G. Leygues, *J.O.*, March 2, 1923, p. 2049-2050; Poincaré, *J.O.*, March 1, 1923, p. 2017; Die Grosse Politik der Europäischen Kabinette, 1871-1914 (Berlin, 1922-1927) No. 4231 Eulenburg to Hohenlohe, Oct. 23, 1898, Vol. XV, p. 163.

[6] Fournol, p. 447; Pressensé in *Monthly Review*, July, 1905, p. 23.

[7] C. Seymour, *The Diplomatic Background of the War*, 1870-1914 (New Haven, 1916) 143.

too ceremonious plural. Something which Delcassé had in his nature, his Southern impetuosity, at first disconcerted my Lorraine
habits, but I was quick to perceive that this son of the Ariège
lived under the obsession of the frontier [pushed back in 1871]
and no effort on the part of my soul was necessary in order to fra-
ternize with his.[8]

Poincaré bears witness that even then Delcassé "had his
eyes obstinately fixed upon the same ideal" that he pursued
"for twenty-nine years of parliamentary life" and that he "had
only one thought: to secure France from the peril of German
hegemony and from the mortal risk of a new aggression."[9]

The same statesman also tells us that Delcassé "had such
a mastery of himself that at times superficial observers were
deceived by the part of impassivity which he had assumed."
In the management of affairs "he made silence and discre-
tion an imperative rule. He voluntarily took refuge in himself,
a sort of intellectual retreat in which he meditated his vast
projects."[10]

During the time between November 1889 and March 1890,
Delcassé was conspicuous only because of his hard labor on
a number of minor commissions. On March 24, 1890, as
reporter for the commission charged to consider the convention signed at London on December 4, 1889, by France,
England, and Belgium relative to the exchange of telegrams
between the three countries in case of partial or complete
interruption of their direct telegraphic communications, Delcassé declared the commission to be in favor of this convention.[11] His very first introduction to the practical aspects of
diplomacy had afforded him the opportunity of helping to
draw France, England, and Belgium closer together. His contribution was undeniably small but not less characteristic or
prophetic on that account. It marked a beginning.

As late as the first days of November 1890, eleven and a
half months after his admission to the Chamber of Deputies,

[8] Poincaré, *J.O.*, March 1, 1923, p. 2017.
[9] *Ibid.*, p. 2017.   [10] *Ibid.*, p. 2017.
[11] *J.O.*, *Débats, Chambre*, March 24, 1890, p. 609.

Delcassé still had not yet made his maiden speech. The day selected for this carefully prepared début was Thursday, November 6, 1890. The excuse was a debate on the budget of the Ministry of Foreign Affairs for 1891.

Delcassé began timidly enough by asking the Chamber to permit him to give some reflections on foreign policy; he promised to be discreet. Growing bolder, he announced that he had a penchant to be a Minister, that he would not bury himself in internal questions, but, while in opposition, would devote himself systematically to foreign affairs. He had only praise for the spirit and intentions of French policy, he said, but was dissatisfied with the results.

The question of converting the Egyptian debt had arisen in 1890. Delcassé said that he thought the French Government should have seized upon this as a chance to make their country the equal of England in Egypt. (A course of action made possible by France's position as a bondholder. On pretense of protecting French bondholders, the French Government could veritably plague the English Administration in Egypt.) France could not very well send troops to Egypt in 1890 as England had done in 1882, but she could have been vigorously insistent that England evacuate Egypt. "Give Egypt to herself, and France will naturally, pacifically, recover the influence which tradition and a thousand scattered favors assure to her," said Delcassé.[12]

He told the Chamber that for eight years all the English Ministers had affirmed they could not evacuate Egypt until they had accomplished their mission, which they said consisted in (1) the reëstablishment of order, (2) the restoration of Egyptian finances, (3) the organization of an armed force capable of repulsing aggression. The first, said Delcassé, had been fulfilled since England was absolute master of Egypt. Any admission by England to the contrary would be an acknowledgment of unfitness for the task she had imposed upon herself. Encouraged by signs of approbation from the Left, Delcassé went on to argue that the demand for the conversion

[12] *J.O., Débats, Chambre,* Nov. 6, 1890, p. 1895.

of the Egyptian debt was itself proof of the fulfillment of England's second aim. As for the Egyptian army, money was lacking; but France was about to supply the funds that were needed. She should therefore stipulate that as fast as the Egyptian army augmented, the English corps should be reduced.[13] The preceding French Minister had made this the *sine qua non* of his adhesion to the conversion of the debt. Why had not the present Minister, Ribot, maintained this demand?

Delcassé then bitterly attacked Ribot for a policy which had neither advanced the date of the English evacuation of Egypt for so much as one hour, nor fortified in any way French interest in that country. "The fact is that you have gratuitously made an important concession to England, who never makes gratuitous concessions herself."[14]

Delcassé maintained that it was the imprescriptible right of France to establish that her signature to the convention did not in any way imply French recognition of that which had occurred in Egypt since 1882, and that it did not indicate the abandonment in any measure whatever of the rights and traditional policy of France in the Nile valley.

The excuses given by the Ministry for "the perpetual and, unfortunately, non-reciprocal, concessions" which it had presented to England, were based on the policy of not separating the two great Western Powers that represented in the world the idea of liberty. "That would be perfect," said Delcassé, "I understand this desire, but on one condition, which is to find a like preoccupation and care in English policy." No trace of it could be found, said Delcassé. Too many proofs attested the fact that the entente between France and England in regard to Egypt had been profitable to England alone; French patriotism could not indefinitely resign itself to such a situation.

Gambetta from the first hour, said Delcassé, had marked out the proper course for France in Egypt. In his last speech at the French tribune, Gambetta had said, according to Del-

---

[13] *Ibid.*, p. 1895. [14] *Ibid.*, p. 1896.

cassé: "I am, certainly, a sincere and enlightened friend of the English, but not so much so as to sacrifice to them the interests of France. . . ." "And," said Delcassé, "Gambetta added with admirable justice, 'Be convinced that the English, good politicians as they are, esteem only those allies who take account of their interest and know how to make themselves respected.'"

"Yes, M. le Ministre," continued Delcassé, "if you had shown more firmness; if you had convinced England that you knew your strength and the value of the coöperation of France; if you had proved to her that you were fully conscious of representing—according to the magnificent expression of Gambetta—'the highest moral entity in the world,' I am convinced that the Egyptian Conversion would have marked an important step toward the evacuation of Egypt."[15]

Here we have the roots of that policy toward Great Britain which Delcassé pursued as Colonial Minister and as Foreign Minister of France, and which was to bring his country to the very brink of war with the English people in 1898. He believed that France had as much right to Egypt as England. He was convinced that if France resolutely took account of her interests, the respect of the English people would be gained, and England would act in a more reasonable manner. Likewise, this first part of Delcassé's speech foreshadows the policy that he followed after the crisis with England in 1898. It is clear from what he said that he desired the friendship of the neighbor across the Channel if she could only be made to respect French rights.

So far, Delcassé had only scratched the surface in discussing French colonial and foreign affairs. He likewise blamed Ribot for the stand he had taken with regard to the independence of Zanzibar. Two days before this speech, after English concessions to Germany and the renunciation of British claims on Madagascar in favor of France, Zanzibar had been declared a British protectorate. Delcassé complained that proper care was not being taken of French rights in Africa. He also

[15] *J.O., Débats, Chambre,* Nov. 6, 1890, p. 1896.

severely criticized the Minister of Foreign Affairs for signing a Convention on August 5, 1890, which surrendered to England the region between the Niger and Lake Chad in Africa. He was evidently disgusted with the way French foreign affairs were being conducted, because he made the following remark:

I say with a profound conviction that when the responsible chiefs of our foreign policy have ceased to take speeches for actions; when they show that they realize the power of accomplished facts as a basis for negotiations; then it will be demonstrated that it is no longer possible to swindle us out of our rights and interests.[16]

At the time of the Zanzibar negotiations, Great Britain and Germany had settled the boundaries of other great stretches of Africa. Approaching the subject of foreign affairs proper, Delcassé said that he did not undervalue the points in common between France and England, but was struck just then by the rapprochement of England and "the Empire, the Chief of which lately proclaimed himself at Königsberg 'Sovereign by the Grace of God alone.'" Delcassé feared a "colonial marriage" between Great Britain and Germany; and, consequently, "that in the solution of questions vital to France . . . England would not be on the side of the Great Western Power next to her, on the side of the nation which had made [the democratic reforms of] 1789."[17]

Waxing humorous, Delcassé implied that Germany had duped England:

It is not our business to discover if there is perfect equality between the two halves of this union. I should, however, for my part, be very much surprised if the negotiator of it, Bismarck, shares on the subject of political marriages, or at least on colonial marriages, the ideas professed by the hero of *The School for Wives*,[18] and if he accepted for his country, in this colonial marriage with England, the secondary rôle which Arnolphe reserves for the feminine half of society.[19]

[16] *Ibid.*, p. 1896. [17] *Ibid.*, pp. 1896-1897.
[18] *L'Ecole des Femmes*, by Molière, 1662.
[19] *J.O., Débats, Chambre*, Nov. 6, 1890, pp. 1896-1897.

Delcassé now came to the climax of his speech, the Franco-Russian Alliance as a safeguard against the neighbor across the Rhine.

Messieurs, you have seen Germany first of all conclude an alliance with Austria against Russia. That much is inferred from the published treaty of October 1879. You have then seen Germany ally herself with Italy, and to say against whom, the world has no need to know the terms of the contract.

The alliance of Germany with Italy was a "hard task," a "difficult enterprise," said Delcassé. There was no real interest involved except that of Germany and the ambitions of Germany.

While this strange and formidable coalition—more strange than formidable—was shaping and knitting itself together in Central Europe, at two extremes of that Continent, two great nations [France and Russia] demonstrated by their very calm but resolute attitude that they were conscious of the common peril, and that this peril, the day when it should burst upon them, would not surprise them at all.

I wish to consider, I consider sincere the representatives of the Triple Alliance who are proclaiming their love for peace amidst the heavy crash of armaments and who are underlining each of their pacific utterances with redoubled military preparations.[20]

After this bit of sarcasm, Delcassé said that he personally thought the Franco-German war scare of 1887 and the Franco-Italian crisis of 1888 would have taken on vaster proportions but for the justice of the French position, but for the skill with which her case was presented, and, to some little extent, but for the doubt which existed as to whether a flagrant violation of French rights would leave Russia impassible and motionless.

As a matter of fact, said Delcassé, the Triple Alliance was no longer considered by its authors strong enough to prevail against an entente established on such a solidarity of interest as that between France and Russia. The Central Powers were

[20] J.O., Débats, Chambre, Nov. 6, 1890, p. 1897.

opening their doors to all the world: to Sweden, to the Sultan, and to England, who had a foot on the doorsill.

Certain groups of people in France laid great stress upon the incompatibility of the political systems of France and Russia. Such differences were of no importance, declared Delcassé. "It is *national interest alone* . . . that maintains and cements alliances."[21]

Was a formal treaty necessary to seal the union of France and Russia? Delcassé answered:

I avow that I do not have any superstitions with regard to alliances. It is important to consider how alliances are made and what they represent. Do you believe that even the author of the Triple Alliance, Bismarck, has any illusions on this subject? Do you think that if there had existed between Germany and Austria the same solidarity of international interests which manifestly exists between France and Russia, Bismarck would have exhausted himself in erecting alliances, and in concluding treaties which more often than not destroy the reason for which they are concluded?

What is necessary is that two Powers which have the same international interests should preserve as long as possible an identical attitude in foreign affairs . . . avoid obscuring the conception of solidarity of interests, or of shaking the conviction that a strong France is indispensable to a powerful Russia, and that the enfeeblement of one would leave the other alone in the face of its enemies.[22]

Toward the close of this remarkable speech Delcassé broached what was perhaps the most important single idea in it. Perhaps the plan was partly inspired by the actions of the Triple Alliance which he had just described as "opening the door to all the world."

To live in peace with all the world; not to suffer the least attack upon our rights; and to be ready at any moment to take the hand of our friends and natural allies: that is what our policy should be.

As you hold to this policy . . . you will create a powerful center

[21] *Ibid.*, p. 1897, italics mine.   [22] *Ibid.*, p. 1897, italics mine.

of attraction toward which all those in Europe for whom France is a security will turn more and more. . . .

Delcassé was anxious to compete with Germany in the solicitation of new rapprochements. He wanted France to "open the door to all the world," likewise. This is virtually the same as the policy which he had advocated in his political pamphlet in 1882, and in the press from 1886 to 1889, only the policy is more definitely expressed as a broad, general principle. It is easily recognizable as the basis of that system of rapprochements and ententes which Delcassé built up between 1898 and 1905.

Delcassé closed with an admirable apostrophe to universal suffrage. Besides what has been given here, the speech had been full of those phrases likely to excite the fevers of chauvinism and imperialism. Twenty-nine times it brought applause or other signs of approval. There had been reassuring clauses for autocratic Russia to the effect that Republican France would not conspire against foreign governments, but would be loyal to all of them. As he finished speaking, lively applause broke out on the Left, and when he returned to his seat, his friends rushed up to extend their congratulations.

Those who are acquainted with the subsequent history of France and of Europe will agree that this was a most prophetic début. Delcassé had announced that he wanted to be Minister of Foreign Affairs. He had displayed an ardent zeal for French expansion in Africa, and had advocated a policy of firmness toward England—to gain her respect—which led at first to the Fashoda crisis but eventually to the *Entente Cordiale*. The virtues of the Russian Alliance, as a security from the German danger, he had expounded and defended in the Chamber of Deputies as he had formerly written of them in the French press. Ribot, the very man that Delcassé had taken to task, by negotiating a written understanding with Russia in August of 1891, was to turn the Franco-Russian rapprochement into an entente, the second great step toward the Franco-Russian Alliance of 1894, but Delcassé was himself to give this alliance active force and to transform it into a working diplomatic instrument. Delcassé's description of the alliance of Germany and Italy as "more strange than formidable," and as contributing to the interests and ambitions of Germany alone, was little short of a plea for Italy to abandon it. This, together with his newspaper articles on the same subject, indicates that Delcassé has a very strong claim to the title of father of the Franco-Italian rapprochement.

There is also Delcassé's recognition that the forms and signatures of alliances are unimportant—that the vital fact is that two Powers with identical national interests should preserve as long as possible an identical attitude in international affairs. This last constituted the real alliance. What a world of light this throws on Delcassé's actions in 1902 when he was dealing with Italy, and in 1905 when France and Germany stood, seemingly, on the verge of war! In 1902, Delcassé was positive that Italy would never go to war with France; in 1905, he was equally sure that if war came, England would be with him on the French side.

Finally, there is the enunciation of that last principle of French policy: "to be ready at any moment to take the hand of France's friends and natural allies," and to make France "a powerful center of attraction" toward which other countries might turn. It is surely not difficult to see in this last statement a plea for the Delcassé system of ententes which was so momentous in European history.

M. Ribot, Minister of Foreign Affairs, and the object of Delcassé's onslaught, was driven to defend his foreign policy, which he did cleverly enough. Ribot freely admitted that Delcassé had developed his subject with "very much talent," and agreed with Delcassé that in the future France should have cognizance of her own strength. Henceforth, Ribot had his eyes fixed upon the author of this "lively" attack. Delcassé settled back into his customary silence, but who could tell what was going on in that head of his? Ribot was worried and gradually came to the conclusion that the only safe and sure way to handle a critic of his caliber was to take him into your own camp.[23]

[23] Ribot, March 11, 1903, *J.O.*, *Chambre*, p. 1105.

On November 21, Delcassé was accordingly slated for his first really important committee, namely, that charged to examine proposals and bills relating to the marine. Freycinet was even then industriously reorganizing and reforming the military system of France along lines agreeable to Delcassé, but the navy had not yet found anyone capable of performing a similar work and Delcassé was glad to have this opportunity of serving it himself.

Delcassé's hardest labors between November 1890 and November 1891 lay with still another commission. This was the most important of all commissions because it dealt with the budget for 1892. Associated on it were such illustrious statesmen as Pelletan, Barthou, Millerand, Poincaré, Félix Faure, Charles Dupuy, and Brisson. Delcassé was assigned to work on the colonial section.

Colonial projects and foreign policy were so closely connected that Delcassé welcomed the task before him. The Under Secretary of State for the Colonies was Eugène Etienne, deputy for Oran in Algeria, where he was born, December 15, 1844. His father was an officer who had taken part in the conquest of that country. Etienne, after finishing his studies, began life in commerce, but had been closely associated with Gambetta in politics as early as 1869.[24] He likewise wrote for the *République Française*,[25] and his connection with Gambetta continued until the latter's death. Thereafter, until his own departure from this world, he regularly made a pilgrimage each year to Nice to lay a wreath on Gambetta's grave.[26] Etienne had sustained French colonial enterprises in the Chamber of Deputies since 1881, and had first served as Under Secretary of State for the Colonies in 1887. He was given the office a second time, March 14, 1889, and again on March 17, 1890.[27] By his own admission, Etienne was regarded as an "ardent Jingo."[28]

[24] Curinier, *Dict. Natle. des Cont.*, I, pp. 2 and 3.
[25] London *Times*, Jan. 25, 1909. [26] P. Deschanel, *Gambetta*, p. 329.
[27] Louis d' Haucour, *Gouvernements et Ministères de la IIIe République Française*, pp. 268-270.
[28] *National Review*, Aug., 1904, p. 924.

The colonial budget, in the first instance, would be prepared by Etienne. Delcassé would then be expected to study it. The past history of French colonial budgets had been little short of scandalous. French colonial expansion awakened lusty opposition both in the country at large and in the Chamber of Deputies. Some felt that too much interest in the Colonies would distract France from her true mission, the recovery of the "lost provinces," or would weaken her position in Europe by dispersing her efforts. Still others caviled at the expense of colonization which threatened to swallow up all the resources of the mother country. The masses were left untouched by the enthusiasm of those who wished to engage in a scramble for swamps and deserts, and if not actually hostile, they were at least indifferent to imperialism.[29] Even the most successful of French colonial enterprises, such as Tunis, had its detractors in the doctrinaires, who declaimed vigorously against all kinds of conquest.[30]

The result was that the French Government carried on a colonial policy that it did not dare to avow, but in fact tried to conceal. Insufficient funds were therefore appropriated, but rather than ask for more money and provoke dangerous debates, the authorities dissimulated each year in regard to the sacrifices that would be necessary. The local colonial budgets were not distributed to Parliament, but could be had at the *Bibliothèque Nationale*. Doubtless it was hoped that no one would go there to see them, but, with his customary industry, Delcassé did just that. He found they were written up in a manner calculated to keep parliamentarians in the dark in regard to the totality of expenses, their utility, and their effect.[31]

Delcassé worked assiduously with his friend Etienne and uncovered other crying abuses. The most notable related to the new colony of Tonkin, which had been added to the French possessions in Indo-China. Alarmed by resounding

[29] P. de Coubertin, *Evolution of France*, p. 171.
[30] Reynald, p. 9.
[31] Delcassé, *J.O., Débats, Chambre*, Nov. 30, 1891, pp. 2361-2362; Cf. J. Chailley-Bert, *Dix années de politique coloniale*, pp. 20-21.

debates and passionate polemics, public opinion was not favorable to the new colony. The Chambers did not like to be importuned, and the Administration, fearing opposition, had been led to dissimulate to Parliament, and perhaps to itself.[32] The annual subvention of the Home Government had been reduced in four years from thirty million francs to ten million; but as the needs of Tonkin had not diminished, the Administration had sought to make up the difference by means of local receipts. Unfortunately, these could not be made to increase as rapidly as the subvention had shrunk. There was nothing to do but to present the deficit as a bill to Parliament, and Parliament had paid it. The action of Parliament had cured the deficit but not its cause. Meanwhile, heavy taxation kept Tonkin in the doldrums by ruining its prosperity.

When Etienne tackled his budget for 1892, this same inevitable deficit stared him in the face. Delcassé recommended to the budget commission that they get to the root of the matter by suppressing the cause of this constantly recurring shortage. This could be done, he claimed, by detaching from the colonial budget the military expenses for Tonkin. The colony could meet its own civil expenses, and, if relieved of the military burden, would take heart and become prosperous. A nominal sum of ten thousand francs, however, could be safely charged up to its budget for military expenses, thus preserving the rights of the French Government without injuring the colony financially. The budget commission adopted this idea by a large majority, and the Government, as well as Etienne, rallied at once to the proposition.[33]

The colonial budget for 1892 came up for the consideration of the Chamber of Deputies on November 30, 1891. The budget commission made Delcassé its reporter for this section of the budget, and in this capacity Delcassé took the tribune for his second extended discourse.

Twelve months had gone by since Delcassé's last speech.

[32] Delcassé, *J.O.*, *Débats, Chambre*, Nov. 30, 1891, p. 2359.
[33] Delcassé, *J.O.*, *Débats, Chambre*, Nov. 30, 1891, p. 2361.

He was apparently a bit nervous. He repeatedly asked the Chamber to be quiet, and assured the five hundred members that he would be concise and to the point.

He decided to defend the cause of good sense and truth— to expose the situation in all of its ugly details and, at the same time that he called the attention of Parliament to Germany's determined effort in the colonial field, to appeal to it to support the French Government in a frank and clear colonial policy of its own. As a matter of fact, his description of the disorders and deceptions in the Colonial Administration caused Deroulède to exclaim aloud that the report was like the harangue of a prosecuting attorney! Delcassé severely criticised the Government for "misconceiving what was perhaps the most essential of the constitutional prerogatives of Parliament," the right to be adequately informed on the Government's policy in the Sudan and its method of executing that policy. The Budget Commission, he said, felt that the Government should justify before the eyes of the country the sacrifices for which it was asking.[34]

Tonkin, with its subvention reduced to ten thousand francs, could not bear the weight of both its military and civil expenses. No other colony, not even Tunis, said Delcassé, was expected to do so. This unreasonable policy was robbing the colony of its means of livelihood and killing its prosperity. He urged that the sensible and best policy in the long run was to detach all but ten thousand francs from her military expenses—this last sum to be retained as a matter of principle.

He likewise proposed a thoroughgoing reform of the local colonial budgets, to make them more honest and understandable. This was also his idea originally and had been adopted by the Budget Commission. He pointed out how the budgets could be made more truthful and comprehensible if prepared on a more logical basis; that is to say, not by nature of the service collectively, but by a budget for each individual colony.

The Colonial Administration was at that time joined to the

[34] *Ibid.*, pp. 2358-2359.

Department of Commerce and Industry. He suggested that it should be made into a special ministry as the extent of the French empire justified. Parliament would then have someone upon whom they could fix responsibility. He personally thought that France should adopt a definite colonial policy. Whatever opinions Frenchmen might hold on the nature of the policy, they were no longer free, in that day and time, to be without one, he said.

Delcassé then launched into his own philosophy of colonial expansion:

If it has its extra expenses, which are apparent, it also has its advantages. Without doubt France is great because of the brilliance of her ideas; but do you think that the far-off manifestation of her material power will harm her prestige? Do you think that the flag is without influence in the determination of commercial currents, and that we should enjoy four-fifths of the commerce of Algeria if Algeria were not French? Do you think that it could be pure folly which animates this expansive movement of all the Great Powers, and among them that one which is least given to sentiment and to vain pursuits, she who prides herself on determining her actions by positive reasons?

And do you think that, under these circumstances, we are able to abstain without "going under," or without at least belittling ourselves?

Why should we abstain? Because we are not colonizers! . . .

Is it not a German, Gerhardt Rohlfs, who declares that whoever has seen, as he has, the prodigious work executed by the French in Algeria can have only pity for all those who, in the presence of these marvelous works, dare to pretend that the French do not know how to colonize?

And what is to be said of Tunis . . . where we have almost attained the results obtained in Algeria?

Why, again, should we abstain? Because we have here, in Europe, a task that is more important? Ah! Messieurs, there is a reason which, if it were well founded, would efface from my spirit every other consideration. But is it true that these two tasks exclude each other?

The deputies now sat bolt upright. Would this bellicose little fellow behind eyeglasses dare to speak in full Parliament the dreadful word *Revanche*—revenge for 1870, and the recovery of Alsace-Lorraine? But Delcassé was mindful of the founder's precept, "Think of it always, speak of it never"; having directed the deputies to the very doorsill of *Revanche*, he skillfully drew them back from it: "Is it not true, on the contrary, that the achievement of our colonial work depends on the success of our European policy?" The deputies had expected the exact converse of this. Relieved of their tension, they broke into cries of *"Très bien! Très bien!"* The oratorical trick was all the more effective because one could not but turn the argument around and conclude likewise that the success of France in Europe depended upon success in the colonial field.

Continuing, Delcassé said, "You are struck by the rapidity and dexterity of the colonial enterprises of Germany in these last few years?"

This was too much; some of the deputies began to grow impatient. Nevertheless Delcassé went on with his subject: "Do not seek for the explanation other than in the preponderance which of late Germany has been credited with exercising in Europe, that is to say, it is in Europe that you will most effectively defend your colonies."

The Radicals broke into applause. Delcassé, in pointing out the direct connection between European power and colonial policy, had hit upon an absolutely sound doctrine of great importance. Not the least part of Delcassé's genius lay in this ability to envisage matters in all of their ramifications and connections.

Continuing the development of his theme, Delcassé remarked that the Franco-Russian rapprochement had once more placed France in the front rank of European Powers. The entente secured August 27, 1891, by Ribot had not yet been made public, but the French Fleet had quite significantly visited Cronstadt; and M. de Giers, Chancellor of Russia, had paid a flying visit to Paris, where the Grand Dukes Wladimir and Alexis, the closest relatives of the Czar, were already to be found vacationing.[35]

[35] *Revue des Deux Mondes*, Nov. 30, 1891, pp. 710-712.

"Recent events have magnificently revealed what our situation in Europe is," said Delcassé;

The world has just seen the affirmation of an accord, determined by reasons which Bismarck ably described as early as 1856, and which he has since employed all his genius to retard; an accord toward which the French nation, with her marvelous instinct, surer than science, and sometimes too profound for statesmen, has felt invincibly drawn; which she has imposed by force of courage, wisdom, and application to the restoration of international loyalty and of her own power; [applause from the Left and Center] and which she salutes proudly, because she well knows that it costs nothing to her dignity [*"Très bien! Très bien!"*], because she realizes that the support which she should receive from this friendly State, she renders to it in turn, just as firmly, just as sincerely, and just as efficaciously. [More applause.]

Already you see in outline the movement of attraction, which last year (in some reflections that I took the liberty of submitting to the Chamber) I indicated as the inevitable consequence of the policy that has just been consecrated: you see turning toward united France and Russia all those for whom this union is a reason for confidence and a gage of security. [*"Très bien! Très bien!"*]

Forward this movement, then, using a right which belongs to all independent Powers, and which others around you have exercised for a long time. Whatever may be the humor with which other Powers view the rebirth of the sentiment of international solidarity and the reconstitution of a moral Europe, be convinced that they will hesitate very much before troubling you in your task, or creating obstacles to the pacific development of your colonial empire, the establishment of which, despite its recognized and partly inevitable faults, will not be among the least of the titles of glory of the Third Republic.[36]

Delcassé bundled up his papers and looked about the room through his glasses. His sincerity, his emotional voice, and the air of honesty and patriotism with which he delivered his report did not fail to win over the Chamber.[37] There was repeated applause from the Left and Center. He stalked down

[36] *J.O., Débats, Chambre,* Nov. 30, 1891, p. 2363.
[37] *Le Matin,* Dec. 1, 1891, p. 2.

from the tribune and regained his bench, where a number of his colleagues extended their felicitations. His second speech had been "eloquent, brilliant, and decisive," and he had achieved a second triumph.[38] Perhaps the most important part of the oration was the last, in which he urged France to encourage that "movement of attraction" which was drawing still other nations around her. As has been said, that was the basis of Delcassé's system of ententes.

The debate lasted until the first days of December 1891. Delcassé's advice in regard to the adoption of a colonial policy was, if anything, only partially adopted; the Colonial Administration was not made a separate ministry; but the Chamber did hearken to his budget reforms; and, as he had requested, Tonkin was given a new lease on life by being relieved of the burden of its military expenses. The mind behind a policy actually in force in Tonkin, the defender of that policy in Parliament, Delcassé was from that moment a marked man with a career before him.

During the succeeding year, 1892, Delcassé continued as reporter for the colonial budget. In March he submitted and defended a report for a supplementary credit of twelve million francs for Tonkin. Delcassé claimed that the credits followed naturally from the course which the Chamber had adopted in December of the previous year. The action of the Chamber in voting to relieve Tonkin of its military burden had already made a profound impression and cheered up the spirits of the colonists, he said. They were now delivered from uncertainty. Confidence and prosperity reigned, and the future of the colony was assured. The debate was lively, but the credits passed.[39]

On November 9, 1892, Delcassé rendered a report in favor of the projected law of Joseph Reinach and his colleagues relative to the creation of a Ministry of Colonies. As reports go, this was a masterpiece.[40] It pointed out that the French

[38] *Ibid.*, p. 2; Etienne, *Annales de la Chambre*, Dec. 1, 1891, p. 618.
[39] *Annales de la Chambre, Documents Parlem.*, 1892, vol. 37, p. 379; Delcassé, *Annales, Débats*, March 22, 1892, pp. 422-425.
[40] *Annales de la Chambre, Docs.*, 1892, vol. 39, pp. 259-260.

colonies had grown to vast proportions. The foundations of a great empire had been laid in the extreme East; Madagascar was a protectorate, and then there was Tunis. France dominated one-fourth of the continent of Africa, as a diplomatic document attested. French influence in 1880 had extended over seven hundred thousand square kilometers; in 1892 it extended over three million; and the colonial population, which in 1880 had not passed the five million mark, exceeded thirty million in 1892. Delcassé argued that such profound changes necessitated new methods, new instruments, and new organization.

The report said that a recent decree had detached the Colonial Administration from the Department of Commerce and Industry and attached it to the Department of Marine. But should the colonies be left attached to the marine? Were they not a burden to the Navy Department, which, like the War Department, should be left free to prepare itself for service to the country in time of war? True, on the day after the last war, France had dreamed only of remaking her army, which at that time seemed the one defense of the country.

The reconstitution of our military forces, the modifications which have taken place in the foreign policy of certain powers, and the alliances which have been made, have very happily rectified our views on this point. It is always the army, in a day of supreme proof, which must make the decisive effort. But [think] of what assistance the navy will be, either in preparing or seconding the army's action! . . .

But to hold constantly in good condition, and constantly to improve this enormous machine; to eliminate all unnecessary cogwheels; to stop all wasted effort; to obtain, in a word, from the devotion of the sailors and the sacrifices of the country all the effect necessary, what a task! And how evident it is that this demands all the intelligence, all the care, and all the time of the Minister who has the honor of holding the responsibility.[41]

Next, Delcassé launched into a series of arguments for colonial expansion: The marine needed naval bases in different

[41] *Annales de la Chambre, Docs.*, 1892, vol. 39, pp. 259-260.

parts of the world both for supplies and as a place of refuge in war time, but there was another reason for expansion, "larger and more conformable to reality":

A great people to whom nature has given only a relatively small territory, which mistakes of policy and hazards of war have still further diminished, is compelled to make up for this inferiority by her power of expansion. The generous ideas which she disseminates about the world gain sympathy for her; the beauties of her artistic productions attract admiration; but, above all, the manifestation of her material strength in distant lands conquers esteem and respect. It is with astonishment that one has seen France raise herself with prodigious rapidity from the disasters under which it seemed that she would remain crushed; it is with envy that one sees France today planting her flag in all parts of the world and taking millions of men under her civilizing influence. One may ignore, if he wishes, the satisfaction thus procured for the national self esteem: We believe, however, that such a result is a source of rejoicing for the practical spirit of farsighted patriots.[42]

Still, said Delcassé's report, neither prestige nor raw material was the principal advantage to be gained from expansion. Because of the restrictive policies of other nations, the time might well come when each Power would be able to trade only with its own people and its own colonies. What, in that day and time, would become of the surplus products which France was already producing? In the final analysis, then, colonies should be preserved in order to insure markets for French goods.

In conclusion, Delcassé said that it was not a question of further conquests. If France took up arms, it would be only to preserve her actual domain; but organizing and exploiting the colonies constituted a great problem, and the Department of Marine was not adapted to this essentially utilitarian purpose. Either the marine or the colonies would have to be sacrificed if they remained joined together. The same logic applied to the attachment of the colonies to any other depart-

[42] *Ibid.*, pp. 259-260.

ment of government. Moreover, the well-known evils and the dodging of responsibility would continue until the colonies were made a separate ministry.

Shortly after Delcassé had submitted this report, his attention was momentarily distracted by internal affairs. The wholesale bribery and corruption of the French company which had been engaged in the construction of a Panama Canal had discredited the Government, the legislature, and the press. Once more, the Republic seemed to be sinking into an abyss. Unable to ignore the situation, the French Chamber elected a commission to pry into the Panama scandal. This was on November 22, 1892. Delcassé was one of those selected for the commission, along with Brisson, Barthou, Pelletan, Déroulède and other notables.[43] Toward the beginning of 1893, the French Cabinet went to pieces. Early in January, Ribot was called upon to reconstitute it. This was the same Ribot whom Delcassé had attacked so energetically in his maiden speech, and whom he had supported later in the negotiation of an entente with Russia. Ribot decided that the critical nature of the political situation demanded a cabinet which could work in unison with all the Republican groups, one which would follow, not the policy of a single group, but a program of Republican defense.[44] Delcassé, though not a member of one himself, then counted friends in all of the party groups,[45] and had found numerous sympathetic followers. One of the youngest and most distinguished members of the Republican majority, he was already known as a hard worker, and his reports on colonial questions had been very much remarked upon both in Parliament and in the great Parisian dailies.[46] Consequently, his arrival at power would be well received, and it was therefore natural that Ribot should desire to take him into the Government. Accordingly, when Ribot formed his Cabinet, he asked Del-

---

[43] *Annales de la Chambre*, Nov. 22, 1892, p. 498.
[44] Ribot, *J.O., Chambre*, Jan. 12, 1893, p. 15.
[45] *Le Figaro*, Jan. 14, 1893.
[46] *Ibid.*, Jan. 14, 1893; *République Française* and *Le Matin*, Nov. 10, 1892.

cassé to take charge of the French colonial empire. The proposal had been made to exclude the Under Secretary of State for the Colonies, whoever he might be, from all Cabinet deliberations except those pertaining to his own administration. Delcassé at once took a firm stand on this point. He reminded Ribot that he stood for increasing the power and prestige of the Colonial Administration by making it into a separate ministry, and that consequently he could not accept the headship of the colonies under the conditions which had been proposed. A day or two later Ribot surrendered and Delcassé took over the office with its authority undiminished.[47]

Delcassé's hope of the formation of a Ministry of Colonies did not materialize, but a decree of January 11, 1893, detached the colonies from the marine, as he requested, and joined them once more to the Department of Commerce and Industry. This left the marine free to devote all of its energy to the preparation of the national defense. The decree making Delcassé Under Secretary of State for the Colonies was signed January 17, 1893.[48] Working side by side with Delcassé in the Cabinet was his friend Poincaré.

2. Head of the French Colonies

A great people to whom nature has given only a relatively small territory, which mistakes of policy and hazards of war have still further diminished, is compelled to make up for this inferiority by her power of expansion. (Delcassé, Nov. 9, 1892.)

When Delcassé took charge of the French colonies in January of 1893, the Colonial Administration was still housed in unhygienic and cramped offices in a wing of the Ministry of Marine at Rue Royal. Delcassé had made the removal of the Administration from this place the first condition of his entrance into the Cabinet.[49] He said he would be content to be Under Secretary of State for Colonies, but that he would

---

[47] République Française, Jan. 18-19, 1893, and May 31, 1894, p. 1.
[48] J.O., Documents, 1893, p. 329.
[49] A. Duchêne, La Politique Coloniale de la France (Paris, 1928) 256.

install himself elsewhere than at the Ministry of Marine. Luckily for him, a whole wing of the Louvre, the Pavillon de Flore, was vacant at the time. It was a marvelous location. The western end of the southern extension of the Louvre, it commanded on the left a view of the garden of the Tuileries, the Champs Elysées and the Arc de Triomphe. In front, and a little to the right, were the Arc du Carrousel and the monument to Gambetta. Some weeks after taking office, Delcassé was in full possession of this Pavillon.

True, the Pavillon de Flore had never been intended for an office building, but for the residence of a prince, and the modesty of Delcassé's budget prevented him from furnishing it as he desired, but the propagandic effect of a separate building was a happy one. Viewed from the outside, the quarters of the Colonial Administration were palatial. Moreover, as one writer has said, the event was of consequence because the Under Secretariat of State for Colonies became, in the eyes of all, a distinct establishment; and, from that day, everything was ready to transform the Under Secretariat into a special ministry.[50]

The new Under Secretary was able to count on the support of numerous friends in the journalistic world. They advertised his colonial projects and promoted them. They loved to describe their former colleague as one who had great competence in colonial matters and as an active little man with dark complexion who ravenously ate up any amount of work set before him. They tell us that in those days he was thin, that even then he was very myopic, and his spectacles were always seen saddled across his nose. He wore the moustache that became so well known at a later date, and he still had a decided Southern accent. Moreover, in the early days of the "Gay Nineties," he was sufficiently fond of music and the theatre to be a marked man on that account.[51]

The year 1893 found France in the full flush of her colonial

[50] Duchêne, op. cit., p. 256.
[51] Paris, Jan. 20, 1893; May 31, 1894; République Française, Feb. 5, 1893; Dawbarn, p. 37.

activity. She possessed Annam and Tonkin in Asia; Algeria and Tunis in North Africa; Ribot had secured promises of Madagascar; and French explorers were active in the Sudan, the Upper Congo, and along the Niger, laying the foundations of a vast Empire to extend from Equatorial Africa to the provinces of Algeria.

Engaged with France in the same business of developing "the backward areas" of the world were the newly united countries of Germany and Italy, as well as England, Belgium, and Russia, to mention only the chief objects of Delcassé's concern. A great part of Africa was still unexplored and still unclaimed, and consequently Delcassé knew that much diplomacy and some combat would be necessary to protect the interests of France.

The race for territory was made more hectic by the fever of nationalism which animated everybody, and by the spread of the Industrial Revolution, which provided surplus products to sell and necessitated more raw materials and markets. Missionaries, patriots, Jingoes, concession hunters, capitalists, and manufacturers all over Europe were putting pressure on their respective legislatures and colonial ministers. These, in addition to the politicians and bona fide colonists, were the types of persons with whom Delcassé had to deal.

Colonization in the late nineteenth century was far different from colonization in the seventeenth or even the eighteenth century, so that we now speak of the old and the new imperialism. The French peasant departed in the seventeenth century for Canada with plow, seeds, and axe, and upon arrival tilled the soil himself. But in the nineteenth century in Indo-China, Madagascar, or Africa, this was not possible. The white man could not labor with his hands in such a climate, even if he had been willing to compete with native labor on its low standard of living. The modern colonist had need of capital. Instead of toiling himself, he directed native labor on a large scale, and concluded with the black, brown, or yellow men agreements of one sort or another, designed to be advantageous to both parties. One furnished the labor;

the other, the capital and instruments of labor, and brought new talents and new methods to bear upon production.[52] Such colonial adventurers desired Government concessions of land or raw products, and large measures of Government protection to spur them on with their task.

Delcassé was not long in outlining to the French Chamber of Deputies the colonial policy that he intended to follow.[53] He promised first of all to carry out the reforms he had advocated as a member of the Budget Commission. These, it will be remembered, related to financing the colonies, and keeping Parliament informed with regard to proceedings in the empire. More particularly, he desired that Tonkin be left free of the expenses of military occupation. The subject of colonial expansion he straddled. He declared that his program from a military point of view was to maintain present possessions; yet he would not say that the limits of France's colonial domain were forever fixed, for no one ought to set bounds to the genius of the French; but he promised to place the emphasis upon the organization and development of the French domain, which he said was already immense and sufficient to occupy the activities of the French people for a long time to come. The military period was at an end; the "utilitarian" period was at hand, he loved to say. The sword would be an agent of conservation, for the moment had come to let agriculture, public works, and commerce enrich and exploit what the sword had conquered. The colony of which he dreamed was one with the least possible number of troops, the least number of functionaries, and the largest possible number of planters and merchants.

Jaurès exclaimed that Delcassé was about to produce a Socialist paradise. Another deputy described the program as a "fine dream." Friendly journalists declared that the speech gave the measure of what was to be expected of Delcassé. They felt that he had the firm resolution to resolve the colonial problems before him in accordance with a gen-

[52] Cf. Chailley-Bert, *Dix Années de Politique Coloniale*, pp. 115-117.
[53] Delcassé, *Annales de la Chambre*, Feb. 4, 1893, pp. 511-514.

eral line of conduct which he was able to trace out already, although he had been in office only a few weeks. Moreover, they were confident of a successful administration because they found him wide awake and precise in his thinking and "prompt and energetic in decision."[54]

His first difficulties were with Siam. The Siamese began making incursions east of the Mekong river into territories claimed by Annam and Cambodia, then under French protection. Delcassé flatly proclaimed that this was an infringement of French rights, that the left bank of the Mekong river on the north of Indo-China was the extreme western limit of French influence in Indo-China, and that France would brook no interference therein.[55] The same evening (February 4) Delcassé ordered the Governor of Indo-China to take steps to obtain the evacuation of the country by the Siamese.[56] He himself began the construction of two gunboats.[57]

As the Siamese did not yield to the French claims, armed encounters took place in the disputed area. French gunboats were then sent to Bangkok, the capitol of Siam, to enforce French demands. Since the French Minister of Foreign Affairs, Jules Develle, skillfully obtained the neutrality of England, the result was not long in doubt. Delcassé reported to the Chamber on July 4, 1893, that all the Siamese posts from the Mekong to the sea and from Kammon to Stung-Treng had passed into the hands of either the French or the Annamites. Annam and Cambodia now knew that French protection was not a vain word.[58]

There remained the double task of collecting damages and of forcing Siam to recognize formally all of the French claims, which now amounted to a considerable enhancement of French territory and prestige at Siam's expense. Develle and Delcassé, together with their colleagues in the departments of War and Marine, coerced Siam by force of arms in an "un-

---

[54] Jaurès and Baron Reille, *Ibid.*, p. 513; *République Française*, Feb. 5, 1893, p. 1.

[55] Delcassé, *Annales de la Chambre*, Feb. 4, 1893, p. 513.

[56] *Ibid.*, July 4, 1893, p. 957.   [57] *Ibid.*, March 2, 1895, p. 826.

[58] *Ibid.*, July 4, 1893, p. 957.

declared war." French relations with England became strained because of an indiscretion on the part of the French commander at Bangkok, but Develle and Delcassé had no desire to fight England and the matter quickly blew over. The treaty of October 3, 1893, between France and Siam was not especially hard upon the smaller Power, because Develle and Delcassé had meanwhile decided that an entente with England was preferable to wringing money and new territory from the Siamese. Siam renounced her claims to the left bank of the Mekong and to the islands in the river. A neutral zone twenty-five kilometers wide was created on the right bank of the Mekong, and Chantaboum, in the heart of Siam, was left in French hands as a guarantee. French and English diplomats in Paris then reached an agreement on a limited number of points touching trade in Siam and made arrangements for a joint investigation of the geography of the country so as to be able to coöperate with each other in the future.[59]

All of this sounds very simple on paper. Actually, problems did not occur, or work themselves out, one at a time. On the contrary, everything seemed to happen at once. For instance, it was in Dahomey, a purely negro state of West Africa recently conquered by General Dodds, that Delcassé had counted on establishing what Jaurès had been pleased to call a "Socialist paradise." The day after that speech Delcassé got in touch with General Dodds. The correspondence and the events which followed are a good sample of Delcassé's activities as Colonial Administrator, and offer explanation enough of his budgetary difficulties. His first telegram to Dodds read:

I have need of knowing before the end of the discussion of the budget, which is very close, the number of the effective troops that you count on maintaining this year, and the amount of money for which you are asking. Please cable your answer to the Government.

[59] F. L. Schuman, *War and Diplomacy in the French Republic* (New York and London, 1931) pp. 99-104; W. L. Langer, *The Franco-Russian Alliance* (Harvard Press, 1929) pp. 325-333.

I have promised the Chamber to establish at Dahomey, both on the coast and in the interor, the simplest possible organization. You will please facilitate our task in holding to those expenses strictly indispensable.[60]

On February 20, General Dodds answered in the following dispatch:

It will be necessary to keep in Benin [another name for Dahomey] eight European companies, ten native companies, a battery of artillery, an auxiliary section. . . .[61]

Next day, Delcassé communicated this dispatch to the Cabinet, and on the twenty-second telegraphed the General once more:

I have communicated your dispatch to the Government; we are resolved to accord to you the troops and the credits necessary to consolidate the results acquired, and to definitely reduce Behanzin [the former king of Dahomey] . . . but are 3,000 men indispensable? It seems to us that 1,500 soldiers, 500 of them European, well armed and well commanded, and one battery would suffice to prevent any idea of a return to the offensive, all the more since 200 civil guards, distributed among our establishments on the coast, will leave all of your effective soldiers free. Our strict duty is not it impose upon the country any sacrifice which is not absolutely necessary. . . .[62]

General Dodds sent this dispatch in answer on February 28:

The troops asked for are determined by the following considerations:

So long as Behanzin neither disappears nor is displaced, it will be necessary

1. To keep at Abomey a company of whites, three native companies, and a section of artillery, in order to prevent all attempts at return on the part of the former king.

2. To connect these troops to Porto-Novo and Whydah by intermediary posts, necessitating altogether three European companies and four native companies.

[60] Delcassé, *Annales de la Chambre,* March 28, 1893, p. 1416.
[61] *Ibid.,* p. 1417.　　　　　　　　[62] *Ibid.,* p. 1417.

3. To affirm our possession of the littoral by the momentary occupation of the principal centers annexed. [Whydah and the adjacent territory were annexed to France Dec. 3, 1892, by General Dodds. The rest of Dahomey was declared a Protectorate.] This occupation should be made by four European companies, two sections of artillery, and three native companies.

The pacification of the annexed territory is today complete. I now hope to obtain the same result in that part of the Protectorate occupied by our troops. But I do not count on a definite solution of the Dahomeyan question until a month after the flood of the Ouème in October.[63]

There was nothing for Delcassé to do but grant General Dodds the three thousand men and a credit of five to six million francs. That done, it was necessary to get the Chamber of Deputies to ratify what he had given the General. Etienne and Emile Jamais aided Delcassé in the debate which took place on March 28, 1893. Finally the Chamber passed to the order of the day, leaving Dodds his soldiers and credits. Béhanzin had then suddenly become redoubtable, and constituted a grave peril to the new colony. He was not caught, however, until January 25, 1894.

North of Dahomey, in the Sudan, the activities of the British had long been disquieting to the French. The conquest of Dahomey had now made it relatively easy to forestall the English in this territory. Unhappily, there was another native chief by the name of Samory who disputed this region with France. By June of 1893 Delcassé was able to report to the Chamber of Deputies that Samory had been driven out, his power destroyed, and the French frontier pushed as far as the bend in the Niger River.[64] Delcassé considered that it was time to organize this new conquest, and in October, after long reflection, sent out a civil governor. However, it amounted to little more than a change of command, because administration as well as defense remained in the hands of French officers, and the corps of occupation was strengthened rather than diminished. The change was nevertheless important, because the French Parliament had many times

[63] Delcassé, *Annales de la Chambre*, March 28, 1893, p. 1417.
[64] Daniel, *L'Année Politique*, 1895, pp. 135-136.

manifested a desire to see an end of the purely military period, and the nomination of a civil governor betokened Delcassé's willingness to coöperate.[65]

Reading between the lines, one can suspect that Delcassé did not always find it easy to live up to this ideal of political and economic organization in place of conquest. The intrepid Captain Marchand, whom Delcassé had sent in March to reconnoiter the Ivory Coast country,[66] took up the pursuit of Samory on the environs of the Kong, and wrote Delcassé beseeching letters in December, asking for four hundred riflemen. With their aid he promised to capture Samory in a month.[67]

The other major campaign begun by Delcassé in 1893 had grandiose possibilities. It will be remembered that Delcassé believed France had as much right to Egypt as England, and that he had urged Ribot to force her to evacuate it (November 6, 1890). Ribot, however, had done nothing toward that end. England was too firmly entrenched for France ever to hope to penetrate Egypt from the north, but is was still possible to bring pressure to bear upon her from the south in territories largely unexplored. If France forestalled England in this region she might be able to provoke, at an opportune moment, a European conference for the settlement of the Egyptian question in a way more favorable to France.[68] The scheme had the added merit of giving to the French the possession of Ubanghi, an outlet on the Nile, and, if luck were with the French, might give them an African empire, extending from the Atlantic to the Red Sea. How much of this was in Delcassé's head in 1893 may never be known, but we do know, from his own admission, that in 1893 he decided to send Colonel Liotard into the upper Ubanghi "to give the French possessions of Ubanghi an outlet on the Nile."[69]

[65] Daniel, p. 136; Delcassé, *Annales de la Chambre*, March 2, 1895, p. 827.
[66] Delcassé, *Annales de la Chambre*, June 27, 1895, p. 622; *Ibid.*, p. 827.
[67] Cochery, *Annales de la Chambre*, June 27, 1895, p. 617.
[68] Vizetelly, *Republican France*, pp. 437-438. Actually desired by President Carnot, 1893, M. B. Giffen, *Fashoda*, pp. 13-14.
[69] Delcassé, *Annales de la Chambre*, Jan. 23, 1899, p. 149; *Documents Diplomatiques, Haut-Nil et du Bahr-El-Ghazal*, No. 29, p. 24; (Col.) Monteil, *La Colonne de Kong*, p. 9, and pp. 41-44.

There seemed to be every chance of success. The Sudan had been lost to Egypt for a long time, and Egypt, counseled by England, had done nothing to regain it. Indeed, she had not even spoken of it. Moreover, the two provinces of the Equator and the Bahr-el-Ghazelle had been formally abandoned.[70] This was the origin of the French expansive movement in the direction of the Nile, which culminated when Marchand nearly precipitated war between France and England by raising the French flag at Fashoda five years later.[71] How Delcassé fared in that crisis will be seen in a later chapter.

As if all these matters were not enough to occupy the attentions of the Under Secretary of State, Delcassé had been obliged to engage in other pressing matters. There was, first of all, an argument in January with Admiral Veron, who objected to having the colonies taken away from the Ministry of Marine.[72] Then the Ribot Cabinet fell from power, and Delcassé might well have lost his office had not the new Premier, Charles Dupuy, retained him at his post by decree of April 4, 1893.[73] Delcassé's spiritual brother, Raymond Poincaré, likewise remained to serve in the new Cabinet.

On May 10, Joseph Reinach's proposal to create a Ministry of Colonies was debated at length. The Premier expressed the opinion that the Government could create such a ministry by simple decree. The Senate, meanwhile, tried to attach the colonies to the Department of the Marine. Dupuy went before Parliament and declared his intention of creating a new Ministry of Colonies by executive order. Delcassé, in a "magisterial discourse" to the Senate, neglected the question of legal right in order to demand the creation of a Ministry of Colonies on the ground of necessity and in the name of the colonial policy of France. The arguments he used were, on the whole, similar to those he had employed in his earlier report on Reinach's proposition, with the added one that there could be no real colonial army until there was a Minis-

[70] Delcassé, *Annales de la Chambre*, Jan. 23, 1899, p. 149.
[71] *Ibid.*, p. 149; Liotard, interview reported in *Le Matin*, Oct. 7, 1898. See also *Le Matin*, Oct. 4 and 24, 1898.
[72] A. Daniel, *L'Année Politique*, 1893, p. 28.
[73] *J.O.*, 1893, p. 1710.

try of Colonies to furnish it with a chief.[74] Impressed by Delcassé's speech, the Senate left the matter to the Chamber of Deputies, where the fight was continued on May 15. Etienne, now Vice President of the Chamber, put all of his influence behind Delcassé, but the proposition to create a Ministry of Colonies was lost by a vote of 260 to 239. Delcassé had succeeded, though, in keeping his organization separate from the Marine.[75]

M. de Montfort, on the fourth of July, took occasion to criticise Delcassé for the manner in which he strove to balance his budgets. He asserted that Delcassé's method consisted in petty economies on shoes and provisions at the expense of French colonial soldiers. He charged that they were ill fed, ill clothed—some even without shoes. The instances cited, he alleged, were not isolated facts, but a general tendency discernible because of Delcassé's economies.[76] Decidedly the life of an Under Secretary was not a happy one!

The legislative elections also required attention in the summer months. Delcassé had not neglected his constituents. The miners of the valley of Vicdessos in Ariège had unanimously complained of the hard living conditions of those who worked in the public mines of the region. The men could work only on fixed days, and could mine only a stated amount of mineral, which had to be sold to the first muleteer who asked for it. The miner was then paid, not in cash, but in kind, at a price fixed by the local Prefect. New methods and new competition, born of the railroad and steam, caused the production of the mines to dwindle in value until the workers were on the point of starvation. During June of 1892 Delcassé had rushed through a bill reorganizing the direction and the methods of these mines, and ordering the miners to be paid in real money.[77] The local credit of Delcassé was therefore immense. He was reëlected at once on August 20,

[74] A. Daniel, L'Année Pol., 1893, pp. 201-202.
[75] L. d' Haucour, Gouvernements et Ministères de la IIIe République Française, 1870-1893, pp. 263-4.
[76] Montfort, Annales de la Chambre, July 4, 1893, pp. 957-958.
[77] Annales de la Chambre, Documents Parlem., vol. 38, tome 2, p. 271; Delcassé, Annales de la Chambre, June 23, 1892, pp. 403-4.

1893, by 14,171 votes to 100 for a Socialist named Theron.[78] This reëlection gave Delcassé another four years in the Chamber of Deputies. The Dupuy Government, however, was forced to resign in the last days of November, 1893. Delcassé was succeeded, as Under Secretary of State for the Colonies, on December 3, 1893, by Maurice Lebon. Delcassé had been in office only about ten and a half months, and was just in the middle of his colonial projects.

While Delcassé was out of office, the proposition to create a Ministry of Colonies came up once more. This time, March 20, 1894. Etienne and Reinach easily carried the measure. The first Minister of Colonies was not Maurice Lebon, but M. Boulenger, who was chosen at the dictation of the Senate.[79] Boulenger had trouble in finding a personnel. Many of Delcassé's old collaborators were dismissed because Boulenger had ideas of his own about the organization of his Ministry.[80] Among Boulenger's appointees was Bienvenu-Martin, who was named director of the personnel and of administrative and commercial affairs, a position which made him the first person in the Ministry after Boulenger himself.

The new Minister took until the beginning of May to get his house in order, only to find himself overthrown and succeeded by Delcassé upon the formation of another Dupuy Cabinet.[81] This was on May 30, 1894.

Delcassé modified the organization of the preceding Minister, and made some changes in the office force. Among the last was the substitution of Jacques Haussmann for Bienvenu-Martin, of whom more will be heard in 1905.[82]

Subject to the changes wrought by six months' time, Delcassé again took up his plans, the difference being that he was now a full-fledged Minister and, as such, strictly responsible for the success of the Colonial Administration. His tenure of the office lasted until January 14, 1895.

In Indo China, Delcassé continued the policy, begun in

[78] A. Bertrand, *La Chambre des Deputés*, 1898-1902, p. 40.
[79] Duchêne, *op. cit.*, pp. 257-258.   [80] *Ibid.*, pp. 258-259.
[81] *Ibid.*, pp. 258-259.   [82] *Ibid.*, p. 259, note 1.

1890, of making peace with the Mandarins and governing through them. Delcassé admitted that the Mandarins were little more than ex-pirates or brigands, but he was convinced that only they could maintain order in the country. The plains of Hanoi and Monkay became peopled with farmers who were pirates yesterday but who were now wedded to order and tranquillity because of their landed interests. The surveillance of the ex-pirates was managed through the Court of Hue, which lived only because of the sufferance of the French Republic and was too well aware of the fact to be disloyal. The protectorate system thus established enabled France to govern an immense territory and a huge number of people with the least possible cost, and with the smallest possible number of French officials. The other advantage lay in the relative contentment of the people under the government, as they thought, of their native chieftains, and secure in the enjoyment of their age-old customs and habits.[83]

During 1894, the prosperity of Tonkin was increased by the completion of a railroad line which became a paying concern. Delcassé also suppressed the export duty on coal by his own decree, and reduced the taxes on its extraction, which had hampered not only that industry but at the same time, the prosperity of the colony.[84]

War again broke out in Dahomey in January of 1894. This time Béhanzin was captured. It fell to Delcassé's lot to organize the colony. Even General Dodds judged that the time had come for the civil administration to take over the country. Delcassé organized it as simply as he could. His dominating idea was to group together people of the same race and to attach them to the French régime by respecting their ancient laws, mores, and institutions, and by leaving them under the immediate direction of their natural chiefs over whom France would act as a protecting power. Thus, at the head of Dahomey, reduced to its primitive limits, Delcassé placed a brother of Béhanzin who would be watched and counseled

[83] Delcassé, *Annales de la Chambre*, March 2, 1895, pp. 821-823.
[84] *Ibid.*, p. 825.

by a resident Frenchman "appropriately escorted." The ancient kingdom of Allada, formerly conquered by the princes of Dahomey, was made independent, and the government confided to a descendant of the old dynasty under the control of another "resident." The kingdom of Porto-Novo was left under France's "faithful ally," King Toffa, while other territories were formed into five circles under administrators. In all, there were just eight administrators or residents partaking in the administration of the government of Dahomey under a governor—a reasonable approximation of Delcassé's goal of "the least possible number of functionaries."[85]

The activities of Delcassé in the direction of the Nile constituted a cause of alarm to the British. Thinking to offset French movements in this direction, and by virtue of Egypt's claim to the Sudan, Great Britain leased to King Leopold of Belgium, as Sovereign of the Congo Free State, the left bank of the Nile from Lake Albert to a point north of Fashoda.[86] This was in May 1894.

The French Parliament was determined, on this occasion, to protect French interests, and unanimously voted 1,800,000 francs on the seventh of June to be used by Delcassé to reënforce the French posts in the Upper Ubanghi, and to tie them to the coast by telegraphic and river communications.[87]

Hardly had the bill passed before Delcassé organized a column to reëstablish the French position in the Upper Ubanghi, compromised by the English action. At the same time, he ordered the material for a telegraph line to connect Loango to Brazzaville, the point at which the Congo was navigable. He also ordered two gunboats and ten barges to insure communications between Brazzaville and the French posts of M'Bomou. Delcassé selected Colonel Monteil for the expedition, and placed the Upper Ubanghi under his control.

Monteil's troops and materials were debarked at Loango

[85] Delcassé, *Annales de la Chambre*, March 2, 1895, pp. 829-830; *L'Afrique Française*, April and July, 1894.   [86] Vizetelly, p. 438.

[87] Cochery, *Annales de la Chambre*, June 27, 1895, p. 617; Couchard, *Annales de la Chambre*, Feb. 28, 1895, p. 767.

in the first days of August. Meanwhile, the Congo Government had been much impressed by the action of the French Parliament and by the energetic measures of the French Minister. Diplomacy now seemed to them to be the best possible line of action and, on the fourteenth of August, a Congo-French Convention was signed which gave satisfaction to the most important French interests. All the posts created on the right bank of the M'Bomou were abandoned to France. The object of the vote of June 7 had thus been achieved.[88] Delcassé had once more been instrumental in forestalling the British.

While he was immersed in these events, distressing news reached Delcassé of the activity of Samory in the Kong country. A king without definite people or country, he now lived by conquest and pillage, bartering women and children for powder and arms, and leaving desolation wherever he went. The Kong country was well watered, rich, populous, the seat of a thriving commerce, as Delcassé said:[89] "a new Sudan more rich and more accessible"[90] than the French Sudan. Could Delcassé, after driving Samory out of the French Sudan, permit him to ravage at his ease "a colony of the future?"[91] Marchand wrote Delcassé alarming dispatches; the native chiefs of Kong implored his aid; and Captain Binger, Governor of the neighboring French colony of the Ivory Coast, also asked Delcassé to intervene.[92] Unhappily, Delcassé had no authority to engage France in such a war as would be required.

Could Delcassé have asked for credits and permission to engage in this venture? His enemies claim that he had ample time.[93] Marchand's letters had been coming in regularly since December of 1893.[94] He had written specifically in the month of January:

[88] Delcassé, *Annales de la Chambre*, March 2, 1895, p. 829.
[89] *Ibid.*, p. 828.
[90] Chautemps, *Ibid.*, March 1, 1895, p. 801.
[91] Delcassé, *Ibid.*, March 2, 1895, p. 828.
[92] *Ibid.*, p. 828.
[93] Couchard, *Annales de la Chambre*, Feb. 28, 1895, p. 767.
[94] Cochery, *Annales de la Chambre*, June 27, 1895, p. 617.

If I had four hundred riflemen I would regulate once and for all the question of Samory at Sakala and Kane, where the columns now are. But I do not have them, and the inauspicious action of the French Sudan in driving back the bands of Samory on the rich Ivory Coast is going to continue.[95]

Delcassé, however, did not decide to act until the Congo-French Convention of August 14, 1894, put a sudden end to the Upper Ubanghi expedition, and left him with a large sum of surplus money and a great many extra soldiers. The Chamber of Deputies was then on vacation. The same day, August 14, Delcassé sent Monteil a telegraphic dispatch, ordering him to divide his forces, to send one part to occupy the posts abandoned to France in the Upper Ubanghi, and to embark himself with the others for the Ivory Coast.

"As for you," read the dispatch, "accompanied by your staff and the surplus troops, you will make your dispositions for presenting yourself without delay at Grand Bassam, where you will find instructions in view of military operations to take place in the region of Kong and the hinterland of the Ivory Coast invaded by the bands of Samory."[96] Before taking this step Delcassé had obtained the approbation of the Cabinet,[97] but the idea of the expedition was Delcassé's own. It was he who proposed and ordered the formation of the Monteil column, and the responsibility for the expedition was inevitably his, as he himself acknowledged before the Chamber of Deputies in June of 1895.[98] At that later date he justified himself by saying that Kong had for some years been under French protection, and that he felt the honor and interests of France to be at stake.[99]

Having decided upon the Kong expedition, Delcassé entered into this unlucky enterprise with great zest. His plan was to drive Samory from the Sudan; to bar his route in front

[95] Document quoted by Cochery, *Annales de la Chambre*, June 27, 1895.
[96] Cochery, *loc. cit.*, p. 617.
[97] Dupuy (the Premier), *Annales de la Chambre*, June 27, 1895, p. 622.
[98] Delcassé, *Annales de la Chambre*, June 27, 1895, pp. 621-622, and March 2, 1895, p. 829.
[99] *Ibid.*, pp. 621-622.

with the Montiel column; to enclose Samory on the left by troops of the allied states of Tieba, reënforced by Sudanese troops, and on the right by a column from the Ivory Coast and the sea.[100] If Samory, caught in this trap, would renounce his vagabond habits, he was to be allowed to cut out a kingdom for himself in the region between the extreme French posts of the Sudan and states of Tieba, Kong, and Boudama; and France would help him organize it. Otherwise, France would crush him.[101] Even Delcassé's detractors recognized that the design of this campaign was "perfect,"[102] on paper.

A telegram of August 15, 1894, informed Marchand of Monteil's expedition, and said that the latter would begin to march in September.[103] Monteil's instructions were to go into Kong by the surest route, and to establish himself strongly in the region.

On September 12, Monteil debarked at Grand Bassam on the Ivory Coast. Here he was delayed by local revolts until the thirtieth of November.[104] Meanwhile the French Parliament had resumed its sessions. Delcassé still had time to get the authority of Parliament before engaging in military operations in the Kong states. He did not do so.[105] Probably there would have been a terrific amount of opposition in the Chamber to his scheme, but by keeping the Chamber in ignorance, Delcassé committed a blunder which gave his political opponents a handle that they did not fail to use at a later date.

One delay after another held up Monteil for months. His men became sick and the columns enfeebled. Samory managed to get between Kong and the sea, and instead of the Monteil column marching peacefully to Kong, as Delcassé had imagined, it was forced to fight every step of the way. There were twenty-six combats in thirty days, not counting skirmishes. Kong itself fell into the power of Samory,[106] and

[100] Delcassé, *Annales de la Chambre*, March 2, 1895, p. 829.
[101] *Ibid.*, p. 829.
[102] Cochery, *Annales de la Chambre*, June 27, 1895, p. 617.
[103] *Ibid.*, p. 617.   [104] *Ibid.*, pp. 617-618.   [105] *Ibid.*, p. 617.
[106] *Ibid.*, p. 618; Monteil, pp. 11-39; (Col.) Baratier, *Epopées Africaines*, 41-43; 109.

the Ivory Coast was thrown into turmoil and devastation.[107]
The expedition, by the end of 1894, not only used up
1,100,000 francs of the surplus from the Upper Ubanghi expedition, but also 330,000 francs besides.[108]

On January 14, 1895, Delcassé resigned his post as Colonial Minister because of the fall of the Dupuy Cabinet.
His successor in office recalled Colonel Monteil on the ground
that the expedition was a hopeless failure.[109]

Delcassé left his offices in the Pavillon de Flore without taking any documents. That was "a grave error," to use his
own expression.[110] It was not long before M. Cochery, reporter for the budget commission, as well as certain of Delcassé's political opponents, began to search among the papers
of the late Minister. They came forth elated, and marched
into Parliament with their "fists bulging with official documents!"[111]

The storm began to break on Delcassé's head in the first
days of March, 1895. Conservatives like M. de Montfort,
partisans of the colonies like MM. Couchard and Isaac and
members of the new Government all began to attack him
at once. De Montfort said there were occult and suspicious
operations in the Bank of Indo-China which hid behind the
Protectorate; Couchard and Isaac made it known that entire
territories had been conceded to particular individuals, while
merchants already installed had been expropriated, and natives menaced likewise with the loss of their properties. M.
Turrell inquired into a long-standing railroad scandal.
Jaurès deplored the passing of personal and family colonization which could no longer compete with the wealthy capitalists and their financial societies, bolstered up as they were
by concessions of immense size.[112]

The pressure was too great for Delcassé to remain silent.

---

[107] Cochery, June 27, 1895, *Annales*, p. 618.   [108] *Ibid.*, p. 616.
[109] A. Daniel, *L'Année Pol.*, 1895, p. 137.
[110] Delcassé, *Annales de la Chambre*, June 27, 1895, p. 625.
[111] Delcassé, *Ibid.*, p. 625.
[112] Jaurès, summarizing the charges, March 2, 1895, *Annales de la Chambre*,
pp. 838-839; *L'Afrique Française*, April, 1895, pp. 105-113.

He rose on March 2 to defend his colonial administration. The greater part of his speech had been written three months before, when he was still Minister of Colonies.[113] Not having had a chance to use these materials because of his fall from power, Delcassé was determined to use them now. Writing speeches was a difficult task and, besides, the earlier speech had contained much useful instruction for Parliament that he hated to see utterly lost. The figure cut by Delcassé on March 2, 1895, was therefore perhaps unique in parliamentary history. He appeared not so much like a former minister defending himself from serious charges as like a minister still in office, benignly lecturing the Chamber on the colonial mission of France and the best means of carrying out that mission. He gave a specific answer to only a few of the charges that had been made against his administration, but dealt at length with the general lines of his policy. The whole was a "brilliant discourse" which showed great "erudition." It painted the colonial situation of France in the brightest possible colors and was "optimistic in almost every line."[114] The merit of the speech lay in the fact that it outlined a complete program of colonial policy and expounded a colonial doctrine.

Delcassé resolutely defended the arrangement, which he had continued, of governing Indo-China as a protectorate. He argued that this was, at the same time, the least costly way of governing and the best because it left the inhabitants free to enjoy their time-honored customs and habits. A few more years of patience and continued effort, he said, would make Indo-China a splendid empire.

Passing to the discussion of African questions, Delcassé declared that the Sudan had once been fertile and prosperous and would become so again if centers of agriculture were created and if the population were assured of peace. Political and economic interest alike, he said, necessitated the construction of permanent modes of transport to drain this trade.

[113] *République Française*, March 3, 1895 (friendly to Delcassé).
[114] *Ibid.*, March 3, 1895; *L'Afrique Française*, May, 1895, pp. 137-145.

Touching the subject of colonial finance, Delcassé put forward the theory that the colonies should be made to bear all of their own expenses, both those of the local administration and those of sovereignty. It was the French Government's "imperious duty," though, to encourage, and even to stimulate, the initiative of private persons, and to make itself the protector of French colonists, industrialists, merchants, and farmers. He said he was opposed to the old system of past centuries by which great colonizing companies were given quasi-sovereign powers. Yet he agreed that isolated effort could hardly be successful. Intelligence should be "double headed" in the colonies; consequently he favored the association of two or a limited number of persons for enterprises which should remain exclusively commercial, agricultural, or industrial. To these gentlemen concessions should be given by the Government upon proof of the seriousness of their endeavor.

Delcassé described briefly four important concessions that he had made. The first, dated 1893, was to M. Verdier, a merchant on the Ivory Coast, who by preserving his stores there in 1870 had saved the territory for France. The second was in the Ogôoué region "behind the Gabon," and was granted to a M. Daumas, who had rendered a service similar to that of M. Verdier. The third was to certain French industrialists engaged in the cloth industry who promised to substitute French products for foreign goods then being sold in the colony. The last was to the *Societé d'études du Congo* in return for what it had spent in studying ways and means of constructing a route from Loango to Brazzaville.

Delcassé flatly denied the charges that troops had been neglected or ill clothed, except for the matter of provisioning which, he explained, had been rendered difficult by the dispersion of the soldiers over great areas. As for the Monteil expedition, Delcassé said he was ready to assume full responsibility for it.

In regard to the old colonies of the Western Hemisphere Delcassé had very little to say, but he did urge that the sugar

magnates be put on a plane of equality with those concerns
in France which received bonuses. This could be done if the
sugar manufacturers were allowed to receive their bonus in
the colony without the obligation of exporting the sugar.

After comparing the French, German, and English possessions in Africa, Delcassé justified the French in having hope
and pride in their colonial future. He went on to say that it
was necessary to have paying colonies, because, by the con-
tinual raising of tariff barriers, the Great Powers were more
and more becoming reduced to the extremity of having to
export to their own people in their own colonial empires.
So far as France was concerned, "the crop was certain if she
would but plant the seeds."

Delcassé did not seek to minimize the expense of this
colonial effort. Commenting upon it, he said:

. . . but would this [the expense] be our excuse if one day it could
be said that for some hundreds of thousands of francs we allowed
our rivals to occupy territories of which we have legitimately
dreamed ourselves? Do you think that even the present generation,
on whom the expenses of colonial policy weigh, would be pleased
by an abstention from which our rivals would profit?

No! In this country of France, above all sensible to honor, where
the humblest laborer, where the most ignorant peasant has the
liveliest feeling for the singular grandeur and superior destiny of
his country, no Government would long be tolerated if it could
invoke only monetary reasons to explain its lack of enterprise.

As for those who are especially preoccupied by our situation in
Europe—and I beg you to believe that he who is at this tribune
is far from being disinterested in this matter—as for those who
dread that France should expand abroad and radiate afar, I shall
confine myself to asking them this question:

Do you think that we should be stronger today, that our prestige would be greater, that we should enjoy more confidence and
respect, if we had continued to shut ourselves up in the policy of
abstention to which we were condemned during the ten years
which followed 1870; if we had not proven—Yes! even by our ex-
uberance—the depth and extent of our national restoration; if,
in short, the English, the Italians, the Germans, and others still,

held in Tunis, Madagascar, Indo-China, the Congo, Dahomey and on the Guinea Coast, the empire which places us after England and Russia in Asia, and which in Africa, permits us to dispute the first rank?[115]

Delcassé concluded his speech of March 2 by asking the Chamber of Deputies to support the Government in continuing its colonial policy. Subtracting two hours for the midday meal, it had taken Delcassé about four hours to deliver this speech, and when he finished it was approximately three o'clock.

A discussion so general and so academic could hardly have been expected to moderate the temper of the storm which had begun to brew about the person of Delcassé. Marcel-Habert was disgusted. Four hours of general "talk" did not enlighten him at all in regard to his specific grievance. Jaurès, the genial and scholarly socialist, found Delcassé's words in regard to the concessions "more disquieting than decisive." Neither was he satisfied on the score of the Bank of Indo-China. M. Isaac replied that Delcassé, "in withdrawing into the regions of pure principle," seemed invincible, but that institutions did not live simply by the enunciation of pure principles, however good they might be. It was the proper application of them that counted.

M. Isaac declared that in the case of the Ivory Coast mahogany concession to Verdier, there were 5,000,000 hectares (about 12,500,000 acres) in the limits of the colony as of 1893, enough forests for fifty concessions. Where 100,000 hectares of mahogany forest would have sufficed, Delcassé gave 5,000,000 to one man and his *société* for the low sum of 5,000 francs. This one organization with a capital of two million francs could not reap the just value of such a vast extent of forest. Moreover, he charged that the Verdier contract carried a secret clause remitting to Verdier fifty per cent of the export duty to the damage of his competitors, a great number of whom were French.[116] M. Isaac expressed the opinion that

---

[115] *Annales de la Chambre*, March 2, 1895, p. 837.
[116] Isaac, *Annales de la Chambre*, March 2, 1895, p. 840.

the Ogôoué concession was equally unfair. This was for a monopoly over 11,000,000 hectares of land in the Congo and carried the right of armed police.[117] At the end of the debate of March 2, a motion of Marcel-Habert for a committee of inquest to investigate irregularities in the Colonial Administration was lost by the uncomfortably close vote of 285 to 175.

The charges occasioned another lively debate in June 1895, when Delcassé's opponents came into the Chamber of Deputies with their hands full of official documents taken from his office in the Pavillon de Flore. The Ministry of Colonies had just presented a bill for 330,000 francs to liquidate the expenses of the Monteil expedition through 1894. The Budget Commission flatly refused this money on the ground that the expedition had been irregularly engaged without the consent of Parliament and badly managed.[118] In spite of Delcassé's objections, the Commission seems to have proved its case from official documents. The Chamber of Deputies adjourned indefinitely the matter of paying for the expedition by a vote of 423 to 81. Even if one granted that no modification of the credits for the Upper Ubanghi was necessary, Delcassé should not have engaged in a military expedition into Kong without the consent of Parliament. The charges of mismanagement were little short of astonishing in their character, and serve to justify a criticism of Delcassé's method which even his admirers have admitted, namely, that Delcassé endeavored to carry out his general idea of scheme with such whole-hearted fervor that he sometimes overlooked or neglected the practical means to his end. He pursued his dominating idea obstinately and feverishly but neglected the details of application.[119]

Perhaps this explains likewise the faults that were found in Delcassé's concessions. The Verdier grant particularly was exploited as a scandal. Chautemps, Delcassé's successor, annulled the concession on the advice of his committee on dis-

[117] *Ibid.*, p. 840.
[118] Cochery, reporter, *Annales de la Chambre*, June 27, 1895, pp. 616-617.
[119] Cf. *Le Temps*, Feb. 23, 1923.

putes, and on the ground of protests from the Governor of the Ivory Coast to the effect that the monopoly was driving away trade and harming the colony.[120] Echoes of the affair lasted well into 1898, when Delcassé was forced to defend himself again on this same score. At that time he said, "What I regret is not that I accorded some concessions, but that seven hundred million more hectares are still awaiting concessionaires."[121]

Meanwhile, in June of 1895, it was again proposed that a committee of inquiry be named to investigate Delcassé's colonial administration. This time the proposal failed by a large margin, having received only 96 votes, while 333 were cast against it. Outside of Parliament, less partisan critics of Delcassé, in reviewing his administration, saw in him a statesman who had bravely answered all of the direct and indirect attacks made against him, who might at times have been wrong, but who had had the singular merit of following a clear and well-conceived colonial policy.[122] No one, not even Jaurès, doubted Delcassé's "perfect loyalty or his probity."[123]

Such is the complicated story of Delcassé's brief tenure of office as head of the French colonies. The administration was marred by charges of mismangement in the details of execution; by the unwarrantable size and character of the Verdier concession, and by the fiasco of the Kong expedition, which had been undertaken without consulting the French Parliament. The expedition in the direction of the Nile was yet to cause Delcassé considerable trouble. On the other hand, thanks to him, the Colonial Administration was neatly housed in a wing of the Palace of the Louvre, the Pavillon de Flore,[124] the colonial territories of France had been rounded out and their material prosperity advanced in many

[120] Chautemps, *Annales de la Chambre*, March 1, 1895, p. 803; Cf. also *L'Année Politique*, 1898, p. 81, and *L'Afrique Française*, July, 1894, p. 98.

[121] *L'Année Politique*, 1898, p. 81.

[122] *Revue des Colonies et des Pays de Protectorat*, 1 année, No. 1, April, 1895, p. 8.

[123] *République Française*, March 4, 1895; June 29, 1895.

[124] Now in the hands of the Ministry of Finance, 1934.

ways. Finally, his fervent speeches on colonial policy and colonial doctrine had given an impetus to French colonial enterprise and colonial expansion, as the creation of a Ministry of Colonies indicated to all the world, though it must be remembered that his friends, Etienne and Reinach, also shared in this work.

Delcassé's conception of the place of colonial expansion in French politics had been that France should expand abroad, not in order to forget the defeat of 1870, but to heal her wounds and to recover her former strength.[125] The restoration of France to first importance in Europe was the real goal.[126] Once rid of the thankless task of building up the French colonial empire, Delcassé turned his attention to this other field of activity where, as Minister of Foreign Affairs, a glorious career awaited him.

3. Transition to Foreign Affairs

. . . it is in Europe that you will most effectively defend your colonies. (Delcassé, Nov. 30, 1891.)

During the latter part of the nineteenth century, the Ministry of Colonies was a logical stepping stone to the more important Ministry of Foreign Affairs. Every attempt at colonial expansion involved delicate diplomatic negotiations with one or more of the great imperialistic Powers, and the ability of a nation to expand depended to a considerable degree upon the strength of its position in Europe. Even a colonial policy directed to the peaceful development of territories already acquired might necessitate the whole-hearted coöperation of the Colonial Minister and the Foreign Minister as had been true during the crisis with Siam in 1893 when Delcassé and Develle had worked together to avoid a possible conflict with England. In fact, the connection between Colonial Minister and Foreign Minister was such a close one that, when Delcassé left office in 1895, he was no longer a stranger to the practical aspects of European diplomacy. Yet it required until June of 1898 to work himself

---

[125] Reynald, pp. 13-14.   [126] *Ibid.*, pp. 13-14.

into the post of Foreign Affairs, an interval of time which perhaps begs some pages of his biography.

Among the noteworthy speeches made by Delcassé while in opposition was that of May 29, 1897, in which he outlined his political faith. The Republicans were torn by their disagreements on the subject of an income tax. More than ever they were becoming split into two factions, one Radical, the other Moderate. The speech of May 29, 1897, was intended to conciliate both divisions of the Republicans in the hope of getting them to present a united front at the coming general elections.

The Premier of the day was that same M. Méline who had taken over the direction of the *République Française* toward 1880. There had been a disaster at a charity ball (May 4, 1897), when an ancestor of the present movie machine set fire to a flimsy structure; a fanatical priest, who acted as though he were just out of the Middle Ages, had made a funeral oration for the victims which scandalized Catholics as well as Anti-clericals in France; a debate on the subject arose in Parliament, and Méline, in a moment of exasperation, invited a discussion of the general policy of his Government.

Delcassé accepted Méline's challenge, and criticised at the same time the composition of the ministerial majority and the results of its labors. The last, he said, had produced only some deceptions and some grave subjects to preoccupy the minds of all reflective persons!

He found the Government's foreign policy deplorable, but tripped lightly on to discuss internal questions. He said a preceding cabinet, that of Bourgeois, had alienated one-half of the Republican party by leaning on the Socialists, and that the Méline Ministry, by leaning on the Right or Conservative wing, had forced the other half of the party into opposition. Estimating these props as equally dangerous, Delcassé concluded that a policy of Republican concentration was alone possible if the Republicans were to avoid presenting themselves divided at the elections, avoid alienating the country from both of their divisions and causing it to vote to enlarge the ranks of the two extreme parties. He made a motion that the Chamber declare itself "convinced that a new policy alone, founded on the union of all Republicans, is able to reassure the country and give satisfaction to the just demands of universal suffrage."[127]

The skilful tactics of Delcassé might well have caused the fall of the Méline Ministry, but for the fact that the lively applause of the Socialists put the Chamber on its guard.[128] Méline cautiously replied that his party would not sacrifice any portion of its Republican principles to the Conservatives. Delcassé's motion was lost by 274 to 239 votes.

The importance of this speech lay in the fact that it enabled Delcassé to straddle both of the Republican factions. Since he stood for the unity of the Republicans, he could at any time, on the ground of expediency, join hands with any prospective Premier who needed his support. At the same time it made him a logical member of any cabinet that claimed to desire to work with all of the Republicans. Is there any wonder that such a politician survived the downfall of four cabinets between June 1898 and June 1905 and remained in office for seven consecutive years?

Usually, however, the speeches made by Delcassé while in opposition between 1895 and June 1898 dealt with naval affairs. Such a subject, from its nature, is largely statistical and technical, but to Delcassé's credit be it said that he interspersed between the figures and technical phrases bits of humor and no little amount of sound theorizing about the functions of a French Navy. He declared its chief business was to protect the country and to secure and develop French colonies. Comparing the French Marine with that of other countries December 12, 1896, Delcassé said he thought the French qualified to handle the fleet of the Triple Alliance, but that there was no hope of equalling England's pace. The best that France could hope to do would be to build swift

---

[127] Delcassé, *J.O., Débats Parlem.*, May 29, 1897.
[128] Daniel, *L'Année Pol.*, 1897, pp. 113-114.

little ships [commerce destroyers] to attack England where she was most vulnerable.[129]

Another speech[130] on the same subject delivered by Delcassé February 1, 1898, stated very precisely his feelings in regard to England: "I am neither Anglophobe nor Anglophile, but my preferences in foreign policy are above all determined by the interests of my country."[131] And again in the same speech Delcassé said:

In the establishment of our naval program we should be pre-occupied with England. Are we not a great colonial Power, having points of contact with her in almost all parts of the world, and interests which make it necessary for us to prepare the means to assure ourselves of protection from her?

Delcassé then said it was not necessary to have a fleet as large as England's. She was weakened by the fact that her possessions were scattered: the essentials were for France to possess intruments which should be "adapted to the task that they were to fulfill, and that England should know the fact!"

I do not pretend that England should be our only concern. I do not care to play the game of anybody whatever, by embittering French opinion against her, [or] by turning aside and leading astray a national feeling to the conservation of which both the situation of France among the greatest Powers and the reparations of the future are attached.

However numerous, however important our differences with her may be, none is so considerable or so vital as to justify a war of extermination between her and us. Be sure that you are in a position to defend yourself and that you also have the resolution [to defend yourself]; no more is necessary to cause her to abstain from encroachments and provocations, but rather to incline her to seek a friendship the logical outcome of which seems to make the price worth while.[132]

---

[129] *Annales de la Chambre*, Dec. 12, 1896, pp. 1121-1122.

[130] *Annales de la Chambre*, Feb. 1, 1898, p. 430.

[131] *Annales de la Chambre*, Feb. 1, 1898, p. 430.

[132] . . . qu'on incline plutot a rechercher une amitié dont les événements, qui paraissent devoir se précipiter, se chargeront de faire ressortir tout le prix. Delcassé, *Annales de la Chambre*, Feb. 1, 1898, p. 430.

This policy toward England, expounded by Delcassé February 1, 1898, was not modified by his accession to the post of French Minister of Foreign Affairs; nor was it modified by the Fashoda crisis, which so nearly embroiled England and France in war; but rather it was the beginning of the Anglo-French Entente. Delcassé by his own admission was as firmly attached to this policy in January of 1899 as in February of 1898.[133]

The truth is that Delcassé adopted his ideas after much reflection and study, and they remained relatively fixed over long periods of time. This particular policy, based on the idea that the English respect only those allies who take account of their interests and make themselves respected, Delcassé derived from his contacts with Gambetta, as has already been pointed out.

As surely as Delcassé was ready for an Anglo-French Entente in February of 1898, just so was he eager for an Italian rapprochement.

In the spring of 1898, Delcassé visited Camille Barrère, who was now French Ambassador at Rome. Delcassé profited by this visit to the extent of a number of interviews with the Marquis Visconti-Venosta, Italian Minister of Foreign Affairs. The two men exchanged views on Franco-Italian relations. Both were agreed on the necessity of establishing a solid and durable Franco-Italian understanding, "on a basis of a mutual recognition of accomplished facts," such as the French occupation of Tunis, "and of existing obligations," such as Italy's signature to the Triple Alliance.[134] "There is plenty of room for both of our countries in the Mediterranean," said Delcassé; "That which has separated us is able to unite us."[135] The Marquis indicated his approval by nodding his head.

Back in Paris again, and reëlected to the Chamber for another four years on May 8, 1898, by 9,241 votes against 8,296

[133] *Ibid.*, Jan. 23, 1899, p. 148.
[134] Mévil, *Natl. Rev.*, July, 1908, p. 716.
[135] Reynald, p. 30.

accorded to M. Lafayette, a Radical Socialist, Delcassé held himself in readiness to take over a Cabinet post when, on June 19, 1898, President Faure began to struggle with the task of forming a Ministry which would conciliate the two divergent Republican factions. Delcassé's recent efforts at conciliation made him a logical member of any new Cabinet that might be proposed. The chief question was the portfolio which should be assigned to him. The interest which he had manifested in the Marine, of late, seemed to recommend him for the position of Minister of Marine. As a matter of fact, Delcassé had a strong desire for this portfolio.[136] The reforms in the Marine which he had advocated as early as 1888 had never been put into effect, and the Marine was very much in need of someone who would make it a really efficient instrument of national defense. The Ministry of Colonies was offered to Delcassé from the beginning of the Cabinet crisis, and in truth there was still considerable work for him to do in that field if his early colonial program was to be carried out in its entirety. A third choice was offered to him on the 27th and 28th of June, when he was requested to become Minister of Foreign Affairs in the proposed "homogeneous" Radical Cabinet of Brisson. Delcassé seemed equally well qualified for this post. His tenure of the office of Minister of Colonies had given him practical experience in dealing with problems of foreign policy, and he had been a close student of foreign affairs for more than twenty years. An amateur diplomat, he was even then working behind the scenes unofficially, as his journey to Rome attested.[137] It was for the Ministry of Foreign Affairs that Delcassé finally spoke. The decrees nominating the new Ministers appeared on the thirtieth. Brisson's name came first as Minister of the Interior and Premier; Delcassé's was second as Minister of Foreign Affairs. In this capacity, he could still look after the interest of the French colonies—perhaps be of more service to them than he could be in the Ministry of Colonies which

[136] *Le Matin*, June 25, 1898.
[137] Cf. *Grosse Politik*, XIII, 241.

carried less prestige. The reform and reorganization of the
Marine would have to be deferred, but meanwhile he could
fortify France to a much greater degree by giving her a dignified and courageous foreign policy directed toward his ideal
of acquiring new friends and allies. As he envisaged the fun-
damental problem of defense, it was not enough for France
to have a strong army and navy herself; it was necessary, in
time of war, to have the friendship and coöperation of as
many as possible of the great military and naval Powers of
the world.[138] Logically, then, of the three positions open to
him, the Ministry of Foreign Affairs seemed to offer the
greatest possibilities. He would not have to sacrifice either
the colonies or the fighting strength of France, and at the
same time he could go forward toward his goal by executing
his ambitious program in foreign affairs. The opportunity
for which he had been patiently waiting had come to him
at last.[139]

[138] Delcassé, *J.O.*, *Chambre*, March 11, 1903, p. 1108.
[139] Cf. Auguste Gérard, *Mémoires* (Paris, 1928) p. 316, where the statement
is made that Delcassé had been secretary-general of Déroulède's League of
Patriots and that he entered the Brisson Cabinet as the friend of the Radicals
and as the protégé of Paul Déroulède.

III

MINISTER OF FOREIGN AFFAIRS
1898-1905

1. *The Reversal of Hanotaux's Policy Toward Germany*

FRANCE has only one enemy, that is Germany. (Bülow, September, 1898.)

FEW events in modern history are more important than Delcassé's accession to office in June of 1898. When he entered the Quai d'Orsay, France was almost at the sword's point with England over the question of how the "backward areas" in Africa and the Orient ought to be divided. France and Italy were scowling at each other across the Alps. The Italians could not find it in their hearts to pardon France for seizing Tunis; Frenchmen could not forgive Italy for making an alliance with their German enemy. The interest taken by some Frenchmen in the temporal pretensions of the Pope was also a long-standing grievance to the Italians. Trade and financial relations reflected this political situation with the result that France and Italy were economically and morally at war. To do away with this ill feeling and to restore cordial relations seemed almost impossible.[1] The picture was made even darker by the fact that certain rival nations were profiting from this Franco-Italian discord, especially Germany, who desired to see France remain at odds with her Latin cousins, and England, whose preponderance in the Mediterranean depended upon quarrels between France and Italy. The one hopeful consideration was that France had an alliance with Russia, but Russia was remote and devoting most of her energies to Far Eastern interests. Moreover, although it had considerable value as a guarantee against German aggression, the alliance was of little use in

[1] Barrère, *Revue des Deux Mondes*, Aug. 1, 1932, p. 607.

European politics because of its limited scope and purely defensive character.

Germany appeared to be in a much more enviable position than France. Everyone knew that she was allied to Austria-Hungary and Italy. Relations with Great Britain and Russia were still intimate. Queen Victoria was a living pledge of good will, and the Kaiser exchanged friendly letters with the Czar of Russia in which they referred to each other as "Dearest Nicky" and "Dearest Willy." Moreover, Roumania had secretly joined in a Quadruple Agreement with Austria-Hungary, Italy, and Germany, and Serbian policy had for a long time been Austrophile. In short, the prestige of Bismarck had been so great that European diplomacy still gravitated around Germany. There were, however, signs of an approaching break-up in the Bismarckian system—for instance, Bismarck's Reinsurance Treaty with Russia had not been renewed in 1890—but, nevertheless, the Germans might well expect to be the arbiters of Europe. Seemingly, they had only to play England against France and Russia, a game that appeared to be easy, because England was suspicious of Russia and continually wrangling with France, anyway.

The relatively unimportant rôle that France was playing in this alignment of the Powers haunted Delcassé, who could not erase from his mind the thought of how weak France had been since 1870.[2] For more than sixteen years he had agitated for the adoption of that portion of his program which pertained to foreign affairs, believing that it was the proper means by which France could improve her position in Europe and enhance her prestige. Only one portion of his elaborate plan had been definitely adopted. This was the establishment of the Franco-Russian Alliance, a work in which Delcassé himself had played a modest part. He had pointed out the way, but his countrymen had taken only a few steps in the direction which he had indicated. Virtually the whole program was left for Delcassé himself to realize.

[2] See an exclamation made by Delcassé in the Chamber of Deputies, Nov. 3, 1896, quoted in *Œuvres de Jean Jaurès*, I, 132.

Many of his projects were incompatible with the German dream of hegemony in Europe. The Franco-Italian entente, the triple entente of France, England, and Russia, and the entente of France, Austria-Hungary, Russia, and the Slavs, still desired by Delcassé in 1898,[3] would be mortal blows to the Bismarckian system if ever realized. Germany would therefore strive by every possible means to prevent their realization, and Delcassé's success would depend to a large extent upon the skill or lack of skill of the German diplomats. Fortunately for Delcassé, German diplomacy was no longer in the hands of one great, single genius. Bismarck, who had not been an active force in diplomacy since his resignation in 1890, died at the end of July 1898, a little over a month after Delcassé became Minister of Foreign Affairs, and too soon to appreciate the ability of the tiny man who wanted to be his nemesis. Four would-be pilots were optimistically trying to steer the German ship of state through the troubled seas of European politics. First of all, there was William II, an impetuous man of genius and restless energy, whose typically Hohenzollern love for the army would have been taken as a matter of course by a Europe long used to this Hohenzollern trait if his tactless self-assertion, his dramatic and spectacular poses, and his extravagant language had not caused alarm. He was not without original ideas in matters of foreign policy. Again and again he toyed with the idea of a continental coalition to be formed by merging the Franco-Russian Alliance with the Triple Alliance, but he was impatient and could not adhere very long to a steady course. Moreover, he was doubly unfortunate in that, even when he desired the friendship of a people, he often unwittingly alienated them. Standing next to the Kaiser was the Chancellor, Prince Hohenlohe-Schillingsfurst, who was seventy-nine years old in 1898. He had only two more years to live, and, because of his feebleness, the management of foreign affairs fell to a

---

[3] *Grosse Politik*, (hereafter to be cited as *G.P.*) XIII, 241; Delcassé's history of his own policy in *J.O.*, *Chambre*, Nov. 10, 1904, p. 2381; and Jan. 24, 1908, p. 106; Reynald, p. 30.

younger and more energetic man, Bernhard von Bülow, who had become Foreign Secretary in July 1897, and who succeeded to the Chancellorship in October of 1900. Like Delcassé, Bülow was an incurable optimist, but there the resemblance comes to an end. He was three years older than Delcassé and had fought in the German Army in 1870. The path to office had been made easy for him. He was the eldest son in a distinguished German family, and had been carefully educated for the diplomatic service by his father, who had been Prussian Secretary of State for Foreign Affairs and one of Bismarck's most faithful henchmen. Bülow himself was a fluent speaker and a brilliant courtier with a gift for flattery far beyond that of most men in the "Byzantine court" of William II. As slippery as an eel, he ingratiated himself with the Kaiser, the Parliament, and the people, heedless of the fact that his flattery, his promises, and his concessions might excite hopes and desires which he himself would have to combat later. That he ever worked out a theory of politics or diplomacy is doubtful,[4] and his aims were equally obscure. He seems to have preferred to drift with the tide and to compromise, sometimes abetting the schemes of William II, sometimes fighting them, and at other times accepting the advice of the fourth would-be helmsman, Baron von Holstein.[5]

Holstein, who acted as political director of the Foreign Office, has been styled the "man of mystery" or the "Grey Eminence of the Wilhelmstrasse." There is this much to his nicknames. He loved power and intrigue but disliked the publicity and responsibility that go with power. He therefore remained shut off from the world and worked in the dark. His principal defect as an adviser came from the fact that he was abnormally suspicious. His keen eye, sharpened by a fertile but morbid imagination, espied plot, intrigue, and duplicity on every hand, perhaps even when none was intended. The influence of this man on German affairs has

[4] Cf. O. J. Hale, "Prince von Bülow: His Memoirs and His German Critics," *Journal of Modern History*, June, 1932, p. 272.

[5] *Ibid.*, pp. 261-271; J. W. Swain, *Beginning the Twentieth Century* (New York, 1933) pp. 67; 216-217; 247; 269.

doubtless been exaggerated, yet it is true that his superiors often listened to his arguments because, although he had been only a tool in the hands of Bismarck, he was the last important survivor of the most successful period of German diplomacy. But how different the new régime was! Power was divided and no one could foretell what shift in the course would be made next.

French diplomacy under Delcassé had the advantage of being more definitely conceived, more unified and more continuous in its execution. A succession of Radical Cabinets enabled him to remain at his post from June 28, 1898, until June 6, 1905, giving him seven years in which to realize his projects. He was convinced that only national interests ought to determine the diplomacy of states. Mere sentiment, differences in or similarity of institutions, political faith, and internal conditions, were of no importance in his estimation. The only vital question was the strength of a given nation and what it was willing to give in exchange for French aid.[6] This was Delcassé's first premise. His second was that, master of Indo-China and possessor of one-third of Africa, the principal problem of France was one of preserving and developing these vast holdings and of obtaining strategic frontiers for them. More particularly, the approaches to this empire would have to be secured by obtaining supremacy in Morocco and preponderance in the basin of the Mekong; elsewhere the policy of France could be conservative. This conviction that the colonial ambitions of France were virtually realized was the source of much fruitful diplomacy. Delcassé reflected on the position of England, Italy, and Spain in the Mediterranean, and on the large sections of Africa still undivided. He asked himself if it would not be possible to obtain Morocco and the basin of the Mekong by a series of territorial trades and bargains. France had so much territory already that she could afford to be generous with what was left of Africa. The scheme had one added advantage that he did not overlook.

⁶ Delcassé, Sept. 17, 1886, in *République Française*; Sept. 1, 1887, in *Paris*; *J.O., Chambre*, Nov. 6, 1890, p. 1897 and Jan. 21, 1902, p. 102.

The territorial trades and agreements could easily be made the basis of new friendships, since something was to be given away, and could also be made to create new bonds of common interests binding other Powers to France. That is to say, each trade or agreement would not only give security to the French Empire by rounding out the frontiers, but would also make a new friend or ally for France. This in turn would contribute to the realization of his policy of surrounding France with as many friends and allies as possible in order to build up a bulwark against Germany and to fortify and aggrandize the position of France in Europe. Such was the plan that Delcassé had in mind at the beginning of his ministry.[7]

The reader already knows what Powers Delcassé wished to have for his friends. We have seen him pointing out to Ribot the advantages of a *fait accompli* in diplomatic negotiations. It is reasonable to suppose that he meant to employ the device himself whenever he could. Moreover, he continually urged that the army and navy be strengthened and kept in good repair. This was partly because he still had no faith in disarmament or peace conferences and believed that war was sure to come sooner or later.[8] It was also because he knew that, in diplomacy, bargaining power comes with strength and that, at bottom, the army and navy are the last trump cards in the diplomat's hands. As he said in April of 1900, "In the final analysis, what is diplomacy if not the art of taking advantage of the might of the nation in order to protect and advance the national interests?"[9]

With the above theory of diplomacy and the above policy well fixed in his mind, Delcassé worked alone and in deep secrecy at the Quai d'Orsay. He made treaties which he communicated only to the President of France. The President signed them, placed the originals in a red portfolio with

[7] Delcassé, *J.O., Sénat*, p. 1048, Dec. 7, 1904; *J.O., Chambre*, p. 2381, Nov. 10, 1904; also Jan. 24, 1908, pp. 104 ff. (the most complete history of his policy).

[8] Delcassé, *Paris*, July 22, 1888; *J.O., Sénat*, pp. 299-300, April 3, 1900; *J.O., Chambre*, March 11, 1903, p. 1107; *J.O., Sénat*, Dec. 7, 1904, p. 1050.

[9] *J.O., Sénat*, April 3, 1900, pp. 299-300.

other secret papers and locked them up in a steel safe built into the wall of his office.[10] Delcassé kept one copy for himself and held it in ultra-secret reserve. His colleagues in the Cabinet, and even Prime Ministers, were not informed of these secrets of state because Delcassé knew that a secret disclosed in a Cabinet meeting was a secret no longer.[11] He therefore refrained from advertising his methods, his purposes, and his secret arrangements, as he had a constitutional right to do.[12] Political circumstances were especially favorable to this course of action. The nation was absorbed in its domestic quarrels, and except for one brief interval during the Fashoda Crisis, paid almost no attention to what the Minister of Foreign Affairs was doing.[13] Those members of Parliament qualified to speak on the subject of foreign affairs kept silent either through lassitude, reserve, or confidence in Delcassé's ability. The Senate, in the space of four years, did not judge it necessary to open a single serious debate on foreign affairs. Even Jaurès was strangely neglectful in calling Delcassé to account.[14] Occasionally Delcassé had to answer interpellations, but the Chamber and general public were acquiescent, and brief explanations or a few patriotic words sufficed on these rare occasions. Thus, for virtually seven consecutive years, the diplomacy of France was the personal diplomacy of Delcassé.

The strictest possible secrecy also characterized Delcassé's negotiations with other Powers. He found that the Quai d'Orsay had a full-fledged decipherment service which made a business of reading the secret correspondence of other Powers. For instance, whenever a foreign diplomat in Paris sent or received a telegram, a copy of it was sent by the bureau of telegraphs to the Quai d'Orsay where the decipherment serv-

---

[10] A. Combarieu, *Sept Ans à l'Elysée* (Paris, 1932) pp. 33-34.
[11] Barrère, *Revue des Deux Mondes*, Aug. 1, 1932, p. 612; M. Paléologue, *Revue des Deux Mondes*, June 15, 1931, pp. 786-787; Schuman, pp. 162 and 183; Lord Newton, *Lord Lansdowne* (London, 1929) pp. 287-289; 341-342.
[12] Schuman, pp. 18-19.
[13] R. Millet, *Nôtre Politique Extérieure* (Paris, 1905) p. 2.
[14] E. Drumont, in *La Libre Parole*, Jan. 23, 1906.

ice puzzled their heads over it and soon made out the message. The content of the telegram would then be made known to the French Minister of Foreign Affairs.[15] The information gained might be of the most astonishing character and, in order to avoid having his own telegrams read in the same way, Delcassé was constantly devising new ciphers or making use of special couriers. Carrying secrecy one step further, he preferred, whenever possible, to negotiate verbally. His ambassadors were encouraged to make frequent trips to Paris to consult directly with him; and, in cases necessitating extreme secrecy, he visited the foreign Power himself.

He likewise encouraged his ambassadors in the habit of sending him long personal letters. Although the main lines of his foreign policy were clearly fixed in his mind when he came to power, he needed the advice of seasoned diplomats. For seven years these letters poured in, giving him the benefit of the experience and opinions of a whole corps of the ablest diplomats in Europe. As time went on, the chief mentors upon whom he relied were Paul Cambon, Ambassador at London, Jules Cambon, Ambassador to the United States and Spain, and Camille Barrère, Ambassador at Rome. The openness of Delcassé's mind to advice of this sort readily explains how, in spite of his lack of training in the arts of diplomacy, he came to be one of the most astonishingly successful foreign ministers in Europe.[16]

There are some interesting facts connected with this personal correspondence of Delcassé. One of his letters to President Loubet arrived covered with the word *"confidentielle"* and with the signature *Delcassé* written across all of its seams lest someone attempt to pry into it.[17] The Marquis de Montebello, Ambassador at St. Petersburg, was among those writing confidential letters which the Minister prized highly, and,

---

[15] The service was flourishing as early as 1894 when Pannizardi's despatch was intercepted, *L'Année Politique*, 1900, 361-364; Paléologue, *Revue des Deux Mondes*, June 15, 1931, pp. 765-766; for similar Russian service, *Documents Diplomatiques*, 3rd S., tome 3, pp. 54-56.

[16] Interview with Jules Cambon and Barrère (1933); Combarieu, 185.

[17] Combarieu, 141.

although the aristocratic airs of the Marquis and his wife were very much frowned upon in French political circles, Delcassé defended his Ambassador stoutly, saying, "He is very much devoted to me and I make him do what I wish." Montebello's easy compliance with Delcassé's wishes, so flattering to Delcassé himself, made him stand in marked contrast to Barrère, who, as late as 1902, found it difficult to realize that his "pupil" had grown up, and who, on occasions, did not hesitate to "lecture" Delcassé and his official household.[18]

These confidential letters gave an added personal touch to French diplomacy under Delcassé. He was particularly fond of doing business in this manner because the contents of such letters need not be known to anyone except the sender and the Minister of Foreign Affairs. They did not have to be filed at the Quai d'Orsay, hence there was no danger of their contents "leaking out" to the public. For the same reason, they left no traces of his policy or actions at the Quai d'Orsay.[19] Apparently he had not forgotten the awkward moment in 1895 when his political enemies had used against him in debate official documents taken from the Colonial Office at the Pavillon de Flore. He did not care to repeat the blunder of having his own papers used against him.[20]

During his term of office, Delcassé maintained a close contact with his friends in the newspaper world and even with the editors of certain periodicals. A few paragraphs in the diary of Maurice Paléologue, Assistant Political Director at the Quai d'Orsay, show Paléologue going to Delcassé to receive the Minister's instructions before imparting to Francis Charmes the information which the latter used in writing his regular article for the *Revue des Deux Mondes*.[21] Socialist or Monarchist organs might carp at the Minister's policies, but Delcassé's early newspaper associates now stood by him. Nearly all of the Republican papers looked up to him as the great augur. As one contemporary writer says, Delcassé hinted

[18] Combarieu, p. 185.
[19] Combarieu, 185; *Documents Diplomatiques*, 2S., II, 37 and note 1.
[20] See pp. 92 and 97 of this book.
[21] *Revue des Deux Mondes*, June 15, 1931, p. 768.

and was obeyed on the instant. "If a paragraph displeased him patriotism immediately commanded that it should be blue-penciled, or, if already published, apologized for."[22] André Mévil, on the editorial staff of L'Echo de Paris, was Delcassé's personal friend and a staunch defender of his policies. The popular Matin, under the editorship of the intensely patriotic Stéphane Lauzanne, was glad to serve as the mouthpiece of the Quai d'Orsay.[23] The leading French journal of the day, Le Temps, was Delcassé's semi-official organ.[24] The "moderate, conciliatory, and scholarly" Journal des Débats likewise consistently supported Delcassé.[25]

Before going on with our story, let us look at this Minister of Foreign Affairs. Five o'clock in the morning finds him stirring in his modest apartment in the Boulevard de Clichy because, bourgeois to his soul, he has declined to live at the Quai d'Orsay Palace with its magnificent rooms and antique furnishings. Before six, he is on his way to the Quai d'Orsay, which lies on the bank of the Seine, opposite the Palace de la Concorde, between the old Pont de la Concorde and the new Pont Alexander III, then still in the process of construction. The men laboring on this bridge have not yet gone to work, and the few early risers who espy him do not for a moment guess that he is the chief diplomat of the French people because he has never made any attempt whatsoever to assume the diplomatic air or manner. This small, square-headed man with sparkling eyes goes briskly through the lofty grilled entrance of the Quai d'Orsay into the trim garden of the Palace. The guard salutes, so does the porter. Inside the gate, everything is very quiet, the silence being broken during the day only by the champing of the thoroughbred horses drawn up on a broad esplanade for carriages. The Palace is a yellow, brownish-gray structure built in 1845 by Lacornée and adorned in front with graceful pilasters and balustrades.

[22] Jerrold, The Real France, p. 126.
[23] British Documents, I, 175; See O. J. Hale, Germany and the Diplomatic Revolution (Philadelphia, 1931) p. 225.
[24] Hale, op. cit., 226; Deutsche Revue, May, 1905, pp. 131-132.
[25] Hale, op. cit., p. 225.

Delcassé goes inside. The servants, who partake of the majesty of the place, are not overjoyed to see him there at such an undiplomatic hour. Delcassé, though, is a very pugnacious looking figure, and he soon has the whole crowd of them scurrying about to dust up his office. There is a table here used by Vergennes at the time of the peace treaty between Great Britain and the United States. It stands close to a window, having been moved from its sacred position in the center of the room by Delcassé's special order, because he desired to work by a better light. Having assured himself that a squad of well-sharpened pencils are marshaled up against a pad on this desk, Delcassé ensconces himself in a chair used by Talleyrand and gets down to business before the clocks of Paris have struck six.[26]

Such was the usual routine; let us see what was accomplished. First of all, there is the fact that Delcassé's first few weeks at the Quai d'Orsay had a profound effect upon French relations with Germany. On the nineteenth of June, the German Ambassador, Count Munster, had delivered to Gabriel Hanotaux, Delcassé's predecessor in office, a verbal note. This note was in line with a number of other attempts made by Germany with the object of establishing closer and more friendly relations.[27] It referred to Portugal's financial situation, then in such a bad way that it was quite possible that Portugal would have to mortgage her colonies. It was asked that Germany and France take an identical attitude in this business, but the "main object" of the note was a great deal broader: Germany desired to ascertain clearly whether or not all practical coöperation between Germany and France, in every individual question, was possible or impossible.[28] Future German policy would be dependent upon the clearing up of this question in their minds.[29]

[26] Fournol, p. 447; S. Lauzanne, *Great Men and Great Days* (London and New York, 1921) pp. 1-2.

[27] A. Mévil, *De la Paix de Francfort à la Conférence d'Algésiras* (Paris, 1909) pp. 4-14; *G.P.*, XIV, 266; M. B. Giffen, *Fashoda* (Chicago, 1930) p. 143.

[28] *G.P.*, XIV, 266.

[29] Bülow to Munster, June 18, 1898, *G.P.*, XIV, 266.

Hanotaux had been a declared partisan of a Franco-German entente because he thought that Germany could be of assistance to him in his colonial difficulties with England,[30] but the fall of the Cabinet prevented him from answering Count Munster's note. He did, however, make a memorandum of what Count Munster had said and left this for Delcassé.[31]

What happened to this memorandum? Delcassé, speaking in the most categorical manner, declared in the Senate on March 20, 1902, that no such proposition with regard to the Portuguese colonies had ever been made by Germany either to him or to his predecessor.[32] However, although he did not admit the possibility of his being in error, Delcassé said, on this occasion, that he had spoken without notes or previous study. Consequently, it is probable that Delcassé had seen the note in 1898 but had attached little imporance to it at the time. This could happen quite easily during a change of ministry. The new minister is swamped with papers on taking office and can count on little assistance from the old minister, who goes away wounded to the heart and in a bad humor. In any case the note would not have made much of an impression upon Delcassé because he had already decided to orient French policy in a different direction.[33] As his early newspaper articles show, he considered the idea of a rapprochement with Germany to be dangerous and unthinkable.[34] But that was not all. An acceptance of the German proposal would inevitably have embroiled France with England because the English had maintained the closest possible ties with Portugal for centuries, and Delcassé had already decided to come to terms with England, believing that the colonial aspirations of France made it pure folly to balk the

[30] *Ibid.*, p. 266; Giffen, p. 145; Schuman, p. 166.
[31] Mévil, p. 17.
[32] *J.O.*, *Sénat*, March 20, 1902, p. 507.
[33] Delcassé, Jan. 24, 1908, *J.O.*, *Chambre*, p. 106; Lauzanne, p. 2; A. Maurois, *Edouard VII et Son Temps* (Paris, 1933) p. 90, quoting letter of Delcassé, Oct. 7, 1898.
[34] See p. 43 of this book.

nation which controlled the seas.[35] Finally, Delcassé had
never forgotten that peace with Germany could be had only
at the price of surrendering all hope of regaining Alsace-
Lorraine.[36] The note referring to Count Munster's proposal,
if ever noticed by Delcassé, was therefore pushed aside, neglected, and finally dismissed from his mind. No answer was
ever given to the German proposition.

Count Munster had already written his Government on
June 30, 1898, that he feared Delcassé would earn the distrust
of Germany. Delcassé's silence seemed to corroborate this
view. Before many months had passed, the Germans made
up their minds in regard to France on the basis of an expression of the French Ambassador to the effect that, "At
present, opinion forbids the French Government to *bind*
itself in respect to any joint action with Germany; therefore,
between Germany and France, there could be only an acci-
dental agreement—parallel action, so to speak."[37] Bülow declared that the French Ambassador's words had a family resemblance to those once used by Baron de Courcel, French
Ambassador to England, "France has only one enemy, that
is Germany."[38] Thus, by September of 1898, Germany knew
that Delcassé had reversed the policy of Hanotaux.

2. *The Spanish-American Peace Negotiations*

The choice of Paris for the peace negotiations establishes for the
moment the supremacy of French influence in Spain. (Wolff to
Salisbury, Aug. 14, 1898.)

. . . for the future, or at any rate for a long time to come, Spain
will become more or less a dependency of this country [France].
(Monson to Salisbury, Aug. 11, 1898.)

The fact that Delcassé had reversed French policy in regard to Germany did not mean that he was bent upon com-

---

[35] Delcassé, Jan. 24, 1908, *J.O., Chambre*, p. 106; Lauzanne, p. 2; Reynald,
p. 22; Maurois, p. 90.
[36] Delcassé quoted in Paléologue's diary, *Revue des Deux Mondes*, June 15,
1931, pp. 770-771; Mévil, in *National Review*, July, 1908, pp. 712-713.
[37] *G.P., XIV*, 360-361.
[38] *Ibid.*, p. 361.

pletely undoing the work of the man who had preceded him at the Quai d'Orsay. On the contrary, Delcassé won his first important diplomatic victory by carrying out a policy initiated by Hanotaux.

The United States had gone to war with Spain in April 1898. Because of the proximity of France to Spain and because France and Spain were sister nations of Latin background, French sympathies had at once inclined toward the side of the Spanish people.[39] The enthusiastic demonstrations of this sympathy were not always flattering to the United States, and the traditional friendly relations between the United States and France were sadly compromised, in fact had never been so badly compromised since the French expedition to Mexico under Napoleon III.[40]

This animosity engendered between France and the United States seriously interfered with French policy, especially with the commercial policy of Hanotaux which Delcassé intended to continue.[41] Moreover, it interfered with the plans for the French International Exposition scheduled to begin in April 1900, an affair that was expected to involve about 100,000,000 francs.[42] For these reasons, as well as for others to be given later, both Hanotaux and Delcassé were anxious to see the Spanish-American War come to an end as soon as possible.

In addition, there were certain commerical ties which bound France to Spain. Spanish exports per year amounted to from 1,400 to 1,500 millions of francs. Nearly one quarter of this sum—350 millions—went to France. On the other hand, French trade amounted to about 7,544 millions, of which approximately 343 millions went to Spain. Then too, Spanish wines were especially desired in France because they were often used for purposes of dilution with French wines to raise

[39] E. P. Mende, *An American Soldier and Diplomat, Horace Porter* (New York, 1927) pp. 202; 222; *The Independent*, Oct. 6, 1898, pp. 950-951.

[40] *Fortnightly Review*, Jan. 1, 1902, p. 71; Mende, pp. 206-208; 219-220.

[41] J. D. Richardson, *Messages and Papers of the Presidents* (Washington, 1899) X, 183; Porter to Hay, Dec. 1, 1898 U. S. Dept. of State, No. 368, France, Vol. 116.

[42] Mende, 209; *International Year Book*, 1899.

the alcoholic content and thus to facilitate their export.[43] Briefly, both Hanotaux and Delcassé found that the war hampered French commerce.[44]

"Policy, race, commercial relations, mutual esteem and friendship, a thousand diverse and powerful reasons made us wish that this war, which we regarded with regret, should come to an end." This Delcassé publicly avowed in the Chamber of Deputies on January 23, 1899, but the very simplicity and brevity of this statement cloaks much that the diplomat did not care to say. Spain had acquired the habit before the war of calling upon France for most of the capital that she needed. Practically all of the Spanish railroads had been built with French savings. Estimates of French capital invested in Spain ranged from about 3,000,000,000 to 5,000,000,000 francs. The smaller figure was the more probable, and was distributed approximately as follows: 1,500,000,000 in Spanish Government bonds and 1,500,000,000 to 2,000,000,000 in Spanish railroad securities. The investments returned about five per cent or 125 to 150 millions of francs per year.[45] French capitalists were consequently deeply concerned with what happened to Spain. Organized or not, these French holders of Spanish securities were putting pressure on the French Government. Even before Delcassé took office, these gentlemen had already suffered heavy losses. The continuance of the war would further depress their Spanish bonds; every day the situation became worse.[46]

Equally disconcerting to France was the fact that a new military and naval power was coming into being in the West with an appetite for imperialistic expansion little short of alarming. The American President's statement saying that he was opposed to the taking of the Canaries because they were not very valuable and because such a step might create

[43] G. de Molinare, (Editor-in-chief of the *Journal des Économistes*, Paris) in *The Independent*, Oct. 6, 1898, p. 949.

[44] *Annales de la Chambre*, Jan. 23, 1899, I, 146; Mende, p. 210.

[45] Molinare, *loc. cit.*, p. 949.

[46] Mende, p. 210; Porter to Day, June 7, 1898, Dept. of State, France, Vol. 116 (not numbered).

a false impression in Europe was interpreted by *Figaro,* July 25, 1898, as betraying a certain ominous hesitation, and on August 5, 1898, the same paper gave expression to what many French people had been thinking since the latter part of May 1898[47]:

. . . the interest of Spain is not alone at stake. On the other side of the Atlantic a great Power has grown up. Down to the present, North America appeared to us only as a commercial and industrial competitor who was young, full of ardour, and consequently even dangerous. But henceforth, fired by her recent success, intoxicated by her young glory, she is going to raise herself to the first rank of military and naval Powers.

She has the gold and the men. She has the fleet and the army. She has conquered the colonies which she lacked. She will have tomorrow the audacity of those upon whom fortune has smiled; and from the war which is going to be soon terminated will date, for the Old Europe, a new peril: the American peril.

But the most important consideration for Delcassé was the fact that the Spanish-American War had brought up the whole question of Morocco in which both France and Spain were interested.[48] Perhaps America's youthful appetite would not extend to Morocco as well as to Cuba and the Philippines, but the effect of the war necessarily involved the weakening of Spain's position as a great Power, and, accordingly, at the same time, her status in Africa. This interested not only Delcassé, but whetted the palate of John Bull, just across the Channel. There was the fear that, after the loss of Spanish possessions in the New World and the Pacific, Spain might turn her attention to penetrating Morocco, since she considered it her property.[49] Neither Delcassé nor the British Foreign Office cared to see Spain embark upon such a program alone. The supremacy of French influence in Morocco was a cardinal principle in Delcassé's policy; as for Eng-

[47] Mende, p. 207; Porter to Day, May 24, 1898.
[48] *British Documents on the Origins of the War,* 1898-1914, ed. G. P. Gooch and H. Temperley (1926-   ) Vol. II, 253-254; *National Review,* Sept., 1898, p. 30 et seq.
[49] *National Review,* Sept., 1898, p. 31.

land, Morocco was too close to Gibraltar not to have the British look with strong disapproval on Spain's becoming dominant in that area.

As we shall see, the result was a curious effort on the part of France and England to get Spain under their influence. France, however, had the advantage from the start, since at the beginning of the hostilities Spain had charged Jules Cambon, French Ambassador at Washington, to guard Spanish interests in the United States.[50] Perhaps to offset this, a campaign began in the English press which asserted "that French opinion was favorable to Spain and hostile to the United States, and that France was intervening to help Spain in the struggle." The same argument was taken up in the American press immediately after starting in England, and Hanotaux "had to pay ceaseless attention" to this "singular press campaign," which he believed to be of European origin.[51]

The tact and suavity of Hanotaux proved equal to this emergency. He won over the American Ambassador, General Horace Porter;[52] he denied the newspaper accounts; and he discussed frankly and at length possible peace terms which Porter reported to Washington. Delcassé, upon succeeding Hanotaux, continued this same conciliatory policy until it bore fruit.[53] At the last moment, the British Ambassador in Madrid, so we are told by *Figaro,* urged the Queen Regent to choose another than the French Government as mediator, but to no avail.[54]

On July 19, 1898, the Spanish Ambassador at Paris officially requested Delcassé to mediate between Spain and the United States. The Spanish Government desired that the French Ambassador in Washington, M. Jules Cambon, be

[50] *Figaro,* July 27, 1898.
[51] Mende, pp. 202-203, quoting a letter of Hanotaux; "The newspapers of America and France have had quite a scrap, but it was without just cause." Porter to G. M. Dodge, June 22, 1898, quoted in Mende, 374, note 7.
[52] Mende, pp. 202-203.
[53] *Ibid.,* pp. 204; 209-210; State Dept., *France,* Vol. 116, Porter to Day, June 7, 1898 (not numbered), and Nos. 272, 278, 279, and 298.
[54] *Figaro,* Aug. 20, 1898.

authorized to deliver a message of the Queen Regent to President McKinley, the object being the termination of the war. If the American Government would accept this communication, the Spanish Government desired that Cambon should negotiate in its name a suspension of hostilities preparatory to peace negotiations.[55]

This request was but the legitimate fruit of French diplomacy, which had been conducted more skilfully than the English. The diplomatic victory, though, was not yet won; the rôle of intermediary involved grave responsibilities and some dangers: The United States might well have flatly refused the suggestion of peace in order to make Spain drink even the dregs of the chalice of humiliation, and, in that case, damage would have been done to the *amour propre* of France as well as of Spain.[56] Secondly, French intervention, however well disguised it might be, brought France a little way at least into the strife. The rôle of intermediary presupposed always on the part of anybody who accepted the task a certain sympathy toward the one from whom the mandate was held. By being agreeable to one party, France risked wounding the spirit of the other.[57] Nor was that all. France would be placed in a position not unlike that of a confessor to his penitent. The utmost secrecy would have to be kept in regard to the resolutions of the Madrid Cabinet. Any "leak" in the French Foreign Office would be extremely humiliating.[58] Lastly, there had been much talk of collective European intervention; yet, each time the United States had let it be known that it would not tolerate even the shadow of foreign interference.[59] France therefore risked exciting the jealousy of the Powers as well as incurring the ill will of America.

At this critical juncture, the friendship of General Porter

[55] *Documents Diplomatiques, Négociations pour la paix entre l'Espagne et les Etats-Unis*, 1898, p. 5.

[56] *Figaro*, Aug. 20, 1898.

[57] Delcassé, *Annales de la Chambre*, Jan. 23, 1899, p. 146; *Figaro*, Aug. 20, 1898.

[58] *Figaro*, Aug. 20, 1898.

[59] *Ibid.*, Aug. 20, 1898; Delcassé, *Annales de la Chambre*, Jan. 23, 1899, p. 146; *G. P.* XV, 27 and note.

proved to be of considerable importance. He was favorable to the project, and helped to smooth the way.[60] Meanwhile Delcassé sounded out Cambon, and the latter replied that he thought there was a chance of the Spanish proposition being accepted. Accordingly Delcassé transmitted to Cambon the Spanish message, which was delivered by him to President McKinley on the twenty-sixth of July 1898.[61]

Certain English papers at once cast suspicion upon France's neutrality in the conflict;[62] but they were mere voices crying in the wilderness. On the thirtieth, McKinley, Secretary of State Day, and Cambon met in order to discuss the possibility of peace. The French diplomat was especially agreeable to the President who admired his skill and frankness. Ambassador and President discussed the terms of peace point by point, each sustaining his opinion vigorously. Cambon, despite the fact that he had to speak through an interpreter, pleaded his cause well, and proved himself a remarkably able diplomat.

McKinley's terms were immediately forwarded to Spain via Paris. The Spanish were happy to receive a favorable reply, and proposed that the definitive peace negotiations should take place at Paris. To this the United States Government agreed on the fourth of August, since Secretary Day wished to give the Spanish Government a sign of good will and at the same time to give the French Government a guarantee of American confidence.[63] Herein lay one of the diplomatic advantages for which the French had been striving: with the Peace Conference at Paris, Spain would be under the influence of France. That will become evident as this story progresses.

Spain replied to America's terms on August 7. She accepted in general but showed a disposition to haggle over certain points. McKinley and Day, to cut short useless argu-

[60] *Figaro*, Aug. 20, 1898; Mende, pp. 203-204.

[61] *Documents Diplomatiques, Négociations pour la paix entre l'Espagne et les Etats-Unis*, p. 6; Richardson, *Messages and Papers*, X, 173.

[62] *Figaro*, Aug. 20, 1898.

[63] *Documents Diplomatiques, Négociations pour la paix entre l'Espagne et les Etats-Unis*, p. 7.

mentation, decided that the Spanish note was a plain acceptance of the American proposals, and invited Cambon to sign a protocol embodying in precise terms the conditions laid down on July 30. This was a virtual ultimatum. War or the protocol was the choice before Spain! Faced with the ugly alternative, Spain authorized Delcassé to instruct Cambon to sign the protocol, which Cambon did with much ceremony, August 12, 1898.

The protocol provided that the commission which was to draw up the final terms of peace should meet in Paris not later than October first. Between the armistice and the first of October much had to be done, but the duties of France as intermediary were over. Hostilities had ceased, and French diplomacy in behalf of Spain had been successful. France came forth from her intervention with the esteem and respect of both of the former contending Powers. The choice of Paris as the place for drafting the treaty was visible proof that Delcassé had more than satisfied both parties.

The English diplomats were keenly aware of Delcassé's triumph. Sir Henry Drummond Wolff wrote from Madrid to the Marquess of Salisbury to the effect that "The choice of Paris for the peace negotiations establishes for the moment the supremacy of French influence in Spain." He concluded that "Spain, though fallen finally from her station as a Great Power . . . still possesses points likely to attract the ambition of others, especially of France. Her agricultural fertility, unexplored mineral wealth, her numerous ports, and her position on the Straits will make her a valuable adjunct and appendage to her neighbor. . . . The position and influence of Spain in Morocco can be utilised, while her desire for increased territory in Africa to make up for her lost Colonies may render her very susceptible to the overtures of her new ally."[64]

Sir Edmund Monson wrote Salisbury from Paris and attempted to be optimistic, but his letter must have been even more discouraging to the British Foreign Office. He admitted

[64] *British Documents*, II, 254-255.

that Wolff was right in believing that "a great increase in influence over Spain" must accrue to France by the part already taken by her, and by the decision that the final negotiations should take place at Paris. Moreover, he did not see any way to prevent what he considered to be "a certainty," namely "that for the future, or at any rate for a long time to come," Spain would be "more or less a dependency" of France. He was particularly irked because Delcassé had obtained this advantage without compromising good relations between France and America. But, most important of all, Monson said that he feared "the danger" of a "systematic coöperation of French and Spanish policy in Morocco" directed to the detriment of England.[65]

These two letters gauge the extent of Delcassé's diplomatic victory. Obviously, the longer the Conference in Paris lasted, the more advantageous it would be for France.

The work of the Peace Commission was prefaced, September 29, 1898, by a luncheon of twenty-six covers given by Delcassé at the Quai d'Orsay Palace in honor of the Commissioners. The Spanish Ambassador, Leon y Castillo, and General Porter presented to Delcassé the members of the two Commissions: Señores Don Eugenio Montero Rios, José de Garnica, Buenaventura Abarzuza, Wenceslao Ramirez de Villaurrutia, and General Rafael Cerero for Spain, and William R. Day, Senators Cushman K. Davis, William P. Frye, George Gray, and Whitelaw Reid for the United States. The menu was staggering: oysters, lake trout, beef, cutlets *Sévigné àl'Ivoire,* duck, partridges, ham, salads, artichokes *au Champagne,* ices (Russian style), and fruits, to say nothing of the inevitable French wines.[66] After the luncheon, Delcassé entertained the guests with the greatest cordiality in the salons of the Ministry of Foreign Affairs till three o'clock.

Once under way, the Peace Commission met in the Quai d'Orsay Palace in two salons called the Galerie des Fêtes. This gallery adjoined the great dining hall of the Ministry of Foreign Affairs, and was parallel to the gardens. Forty

[65] *British Documents,* II, p. 254.   [66] *Figaro,* Sept. 30, 1898.

years before, in the days of Napoleon III, it had been occupied by the Congress of Paris. The ceilings were of great
height and the walls were hung with red damask, while the
furniture was in the style of Louis XV. The Commissioners
met around a huge table which stood in the middle of the
room. At either end of the table, which was covered with a
green cloth, were the throne-like chairs of the presidents of the
two Commissions, one for ex-Secretary of State Day, the other
for Señor Montero Rios. A nearby apartment contained a
generous buffet, well stocked with French and Spanish bev-
erages which in those days American Congressmen could
afford to appreciate openly.[67]

The work proceeded by joint sessions under dual control,
all secret, and by numerous separate sessions. The separate
American sessions met in the unaristrocratic Hotel Continental, but the Spanish at No. 63 Rue Pierre Charon, near
the Champs Élysées. The negotiations were long and tedious
as the Spaniards hoped to wear out the Americans and thus
to get them to agree to the asssumption of the Cuban and
Philippine debts of Spain. Perhaps they also hoped by delay
to procure assistance in Europe through the influence of
Spanish bondholders. At length, having exhausted all diplomatic resources to get better terms, Spain consented, November 28, 1898, to the hard provisions which she could not
escape. The United States was to pay $20,000,000 for the
Philippines, but was not to be responsible for any Spanish
debts. The formal treaty of peace was signed at Paris, December 10, 1898, and was sealed upon a tricolor ribbon in honor
of France. Delcassé had enjoyed for two months and ten days
those particular diplomatic advantages which Wolff and
Monson had said would inevitably accrue to France as a result of the selection of Paris as the meeting place for the
Conference.

Summing it all up, what had Delcassé gained by his mediation and by this Conference? First of all, Delcassé had bene-
fited politically. The French people, and the people of Paris

[67] *Outlook*, Nov. 5, 1898; *Figaro*, Dec. 11, 1898.

especially, were immensely pleased with the idea of so important a body as the Peace Commission meeting in the French Capital.[68] Even *Figaro,* which was not apt to waste much love on Delcassé, lauded both Cambon and the Foreign Minister. Delcassé was able to declare in the Chamber of Deputies that the choice of France as mediator had a moral effect which could not be exaggerated: a great monarchy had turned to the French Republic as its friend in an hour of need. Concrete evidence had been given that the amity of France was not an object of indifference but that it was worthy of being sought after. Did not that prove the greatness of France under the benign rule of Republicanism? Verily, it is of this sort of material that political fences are made. Only when one realizes how deeply the soul of Delcassé had been wounded by those who jeered at the weakness of France after 1870 can one understand what this meant to him and to all French patriots. The hard-working little fighter in the Quai d'Orsay who had consecrated his life to the restoration of French prestige could now feel that he had contributed something toward that end, and, in this speech which we read with a touch of pathos, he made the most of his diplomatic coup:

. . . do you not find that this [Spanish] call . . . is a victorious answer to those who go about proclaiming that France hardly counts for anything at the present time? Is it not permissible to see in this mark of confidence, given by a monarchy to the Republic, proof that the Republic has established itself in the world as a Government whose friendship is not a matter of little consequence, but whose coöperation is worthy of being sought?[69]

There were also certain gratifying personal considerations. The honor which every diplomat craves, no matter how much of a firebrand he may be—that of being able to pose as the friend of peace—was now the undeniable property of Delcassé. If he and his admirers were not exactly Ciceronian and

[68] Porter to William McKinley, Sept. 6, 1898, quoted in Mende, p. 221; *Outlook,* Nov. 5, 1898, p. 574.
[69] *Annales de la Chambre,* Jan. 23, 1899, p. 146.

did not overwork his late activities on behalf of world tranquillity, nevertheless it served him in a political way on numerous occasions. In November 1899, when there was a lively demand for French mediation on behalf of the Boers, Delcassé, who was then concerned with drawing France and England closer together, turned the demand aside as impracticable, saying that so far as the principle of mediation or abritration was concerned, his attitude toward the Spanish-American War was a sufficient profession of his faith and a sufficient answer to his critics.[70] On July 20, 1909, in a speech forever memorable, the mediation of '98 was one of the facts cited by Delcassé to raise himself from the depths of his disgrace in 1905 and to drive Clemenceau from power.[71] Lastly, in the undignified row in the Chamber of Deputies over Delcassé's funeral expenses, when Delcassé was being branded as one of the criminals who had instigated the World War, M. Herriot came to the dead Minister's defense with the statement that Delcassé's personal intervention had ended the cruel and sanguinary war between the United States and Spain.[72]

Highly valuable as the political consequences were to Delcassé, the diplomatic advantages were even more to be coveted. The Spanish with their fierce pride were deeply grateful for the delicate manner in which Delcassé had helped them out of an undignified situation; and, as has been shown, Spain for the time being was under the dominating influence of France. The way was opened up for Delcassé's accord with Spain and for his far-reaching Moroccan projects. On the other hand, America too was pleased, because the conclusion of the final treaty of peace at so notable a place as Paris was felt to be exceedingly flattering. The French International Exposition of 1900 would profit accordingly. French commerce would profit because the way was smoothed for Delcassé's reciprocity agreement with the United States and for what became a very real Franco-American rapproche-

---

[70] *J.O.*, *Chambre*, Nov. 24, 1899, p. 1941.
[71] *Ibid.*, July 20, 1909, p. 2242.   [72] *Ibid.*, March 9, 1923.

ment. That is to say, Delcassé had auspiciously embarked upon the program which he had outlined for France as early as 1890: to fortify France by making her a center of attraction for other Powers and by being ready at any moment to take the hand of her friends and natural allies.[73] Finally, as we have already seen, the English were fearful lest Delcassé should use his dominance over Spain to inaugurate a systematic coöperation of French and Spanish policy in Morocco directed to the detriment of England. Could not Delcassé use this as a club to bring England likewise into the French orbit? At any rate, *The National Review* carried an article in September 1898, entitled "The Morocco Question and the War" in which it advocated Anglo-French coöperation.

3. The Fashoda Crisis

I am certainly a sincere and enlightened friend of the English, but not so much so as to sacrifice to them the interests of France. . . . Be convinced that the English, good politicians as they are, esteem only those allies who take account of their interests and know how to make themselves respected. (Delcassé, Nov. 6, 1890, quoting Gambetta.)

You cannot desire the hostility of such a powerful State as England when we are still bleeding on our eastern frontier. (Delcassé to Captain Baratier, Oct. 27, 1898.)

Relations with England could hardly have been worse than they were in the summer of 1898. For some years both France and England had been expanding toward the same point in Africa. Both governments momentarily expected an encounter. On the French side, the trouble grew out of the Liotard Mission, which Delcassé had organized as Under-Secretary of State for the Colonies. The purpose of that expedition, it will be remembered, was to give the French possessions in Africa an outlet on the Nile.

Continuing the execution of the old plan in 1896, the French Government sent Captain Marchand to reënforce Liotard and to act as his lieutenant. Marchand made his way

---

[73] *J.O., Chambre*, Nov. 6, 1890, p. 1897.

into the old Egyptian province of Khartoum, and after a
journey of thirty months through the heart of Africa, he
arrived at Fashoda, on the White Nile, July 10, 1898, with
eight officers and subordinates and 120 Senegalese soldiers.
The gallant Captain hoisted the French flag; laid out a camp;
planted a vegetable garden; in short, took possession.

At this juncture, an event occurred which ruined the whole
French scheme. Before the news of Marchand's coup could
reach France via a long trip through African swamps and
jungles, the English General, Kitchener, won a battle at Omdurman, September 2, 1898, which made him master of the
whole country. Kitchener was then five hundred miles north
of Marchand, but even at that distance too close for the latter's comfort.

Immediately after hearing of the great battle of Omdurman, Delcassé became worried. He knew that the English
planned to send their gunboats up the Nile, and that Marchand would be a thousand times outnumbered.[74] Diplomacy
seemed the only way out of the ticklish situation; and, accordingly, he saw the British Ambassador on September the
eighth. Delcassé explained that Marchand was "an emissary
of civilization." He hoped that if Kitchener and Marchand
met, "It would be not as enemies but as champions of the
same idea." The rights of Great Britain and France could
then be settled by their respective foreign offices rather than
by armed force.[75]

Sure enough, as Delcassé had feared, Kitchener advanced
up the Nile with his gunboats, artillery, Sudanese troops,
and Highlanders. Wishing to avoid bloodshed, he sent a letter to Marchand warning the French Captain of his movements and protesting against the French flag at Fashoda.
When the two commanders met, September 19, Kitchener
congratulated the Frenchman on his successful passage
through such hazardous territory, but requested him to haul
down his flag. Marchand was equally polite, but he refused

[74] Delcassé, *Annales de la Chambre*, Feb. 1, 1898; and Jan. 23, 1899.
[75] *Ibid.*, speech of Jan. 23, 1899; Giffen, *Fashoda*, pp. 34-35.

to comply with Kitchener's request until he had orders from his Government. Not to be disconcerted, Kitchener then raised his flag beside that of France.

News of the courteous but grim exchanges at Fashoda reached France in the latter part of September. Delcassé, who was very much relieved on hearing that Kitchener and Marchand had not come to blows, could flatter himself that he had won the first round: the business was to be regulated by diplomacy, the only circumstances under which France had any chance of winning. How glad Delcassé was that he had warned the British Ambassador on September 8 of the possibility of an encounter, and in this way taken the initiative in pourparlers for a peaceful settlement, well in advance of the crisis itself! Yet we know from a private letter of September 28, 1898, that he also appreciated the extreme difficulty of the diplomatic negotiations ahead of him. The superior English force at Fashoda gave the British Government every advantage in the forthcoming discussions. It would not be easy to argue the English out of a piece of territory when they felt perfectly secure in their possession of it.[76]

The French President, Félix Faure, thought that this would be a good opportunity to reopen the Egyptian question and that France might gain something by raising this issue. His consultations with Delcassé left him very confident.[77] And well they might, because as we have already shown in discussing the first speech of Delcassé in the Chamber of Deputies (Nov. 6, 1890), Delcassé considered France to have as much right to Egypt as had Great Britain, and desired to force the English to withdraw from the land of the Pharaohs.

The extent of Kitchener's victory at Omdurman, and the consequent difficulty of Marchand's plight at Fashoda, undoubtedly dampened the enthusiasm of President Faure and Delcassé, but once in the realm of diplomacy, some good for France might conceivably have been extracted from the

[76] A. Maurois, *Edouard VII et Son Temps* (Paris, 1933) p. 88.
[77] M. Steinheil, *My Memoirs* (New York, 1912) pp. 86, 92.

Fashoda affair. The President's continued optimism was an exceptionally fine tribute to the new Minister of Foreign Affairs. "We have no Talleyrand," said the President, "but we have Delcassé, and he possesses both subtlety and audacity, besides a good amount of useful cynicism and sound judgment. And he is as cool headed as he is cautious."[78]

Throughout the trying days of the crisis which followed, Delcassé was dominated by the Gambettist doctrine of how France should deal with England in the Egyptian question. Let us recall the words of Gambetta quoted by Delcassé, November 6, 1890:

I am certainly a sincere and enlightened friend of the English, but not so much so as to sacrifice to them the interests of France. . . . Be convinced that the English, good politicians as they are, esteem only those allies who take account of their interests and know how to make themselves respected.

Delcassé said in 1890 that if Ribot had shown more firmness, if he had convinced England that he knew the strength of France and the value of her coöperation, an important step would have been taken toward the English evacuation of Egypt. More recently, on February 1, 1898, Delcassé had proclaimed that however numerous or important might be the contentions between England and France, none was so vital as to justify a war between the two countries, and he had reiterated the cardinal point of the doctrine expounded in 1890 that if the French resolutely defended their rights, the English would respect them and be inclined to seek the friendship of France. Pursuing this policy, Delcassé aimed to defend French rights and interests vigorously and firmly in the hope of winning the respect of the English by his bold and determined attitude. Only thus could French interests be protected, and only thus could England be made to think of Anglo-French coöperation as a paying investment. The two extremes to be avoided were (1) actual armed hostilities and (2) a supine and tame surrender of French rights which would convince the English that France counted for nothing

[78] *Ibid.*, p. 93.

in international politics. He had the faith that a middle course would bring England to his side.[79]

Delcassé clung to this line of action, but the English took an uncompromising stand. They recalled that Sir Edward Grey, British Under Secretary for Foreign Affairs, had warned the French in March 1895, that Great Britain would regard a French advance toward the Nile as an "unfriendly act"; and while the Foreign Office took the attitude that the matter was beyond the pale of discussion, the English press insisted upon considering the French occupation of Fashoda as an "intolerable affront."[80]

Great Britain claimed Fashoda in the name of Egypt and by right of conquest; Delcassé argued that France had taken formal exception to the utterances of Sir Edward Grey in 1895 and that Fashoda belonged to France by right of prior occupation. The English showed the least possible disposition to listen to reason or to argue the question. "They were not so much like lawyers resting their case upon evidence as like impatient litigants who were prepared to terminate the dispute by pocketing the title-deeds, come what might."[81] The Duke of Devonshire promised that British rights in the disputed region would "not be frittered away by any negotiations, however ably conducted," and the Chancellor of the Exchequer declared flatly that "this country has put its foot down."[82]

On the other hand, Delcassé repeatedly said to the British Ambassador, Monson, that it was his conviction that all outstanding differences between the two countries might be amicably arranged by the exercise of patience and conciliation.[83] In the heat of the controversy he nominated Paul Cambon, known as a warm friend of England, to succeed Baron de Courcel as French Ambassador in London. Delcassé knew

[79] Delcassé, *Annales de la Chambre*, Feb. 1, 1898, p. 430; Jan. 23, 1899, p. 148; Ribot, *Annales*, Jan. 23, 1899.
[80] *Documents Diplomatiques, Haut-Nil et du Bahr-El-Ghazal*, No. 8, p. 8; *National Review*, Oct., 1898, p. 162; Giffen, pp. 66-70.
[81] Giffen, p. 70.
[82] *National Review*, Nov., 1898, pp. 309-310.
[83] *British Documents*, I, 163.

the tact and experience of Cambon, and Cambon promised to dissipate the persistent misunderstandings between the two countries.[84]

In a discussion with Monson on September 28, 1898, Delcassé reiterated that the problem could be solved by an "honest discussion." He stated once more that it was the desire of the French Government to make a friend of England, and said that, just between the two of them, he would much prefer an Anglo-French to a Franco-Russian alliance. He entreated Monson to take account of the excitement in France over the Fashoda crisis. "Do not ask me for the impossible [recall of Marchand without further discussion]; do not drive me into a corner," he said.[85] Yet Delcassé did not forget to wield the one big club at his disposal. If war came, he said, France would not stand alone, meaning, of course, that Russia would help her. Then he added, "But I repeat, I would rather have England for our ally than that other [Russia]."[86]

Delcassé's point of view was that he would not undertake to hold Fashoda in the face of everything, but that he could not abandon it without discussion. There had never been a Marchand expedition, he said, hoping to appease the English. Marchand was but a lieutenant of Liotard, who had been sent out two years before the warning speech of Sir Edward Grey in 1895.[87]

As for the English contention that they were acting in the name of Egypt, Delcassé felt that he had a right to ask by virtue of what mandate and in what way the title invoked by England would be better than his own.[88] Yet he refrained from opening the whole Egyptian question. He was already faced with the prospect of losing Fashoda, and did not care to present his Egyptian claims at such an inauspicious time.

Lord Salisbury, the English Minister for Foreign Affairs, appeared to be uncommonly obstinate; the British Government and the British people seemed determined to force

[84] *Ibid.*, pp. 165-166; *Echo de Paris*, March 1, 1923.
[85] *British Documents*, I, 171.   [86] *Ibid.*, p. 171.
[87] *Documents Diplomatiques*, *op. cit.*, No. 24, p. 18.
[88] *Ibid.*, p. 19.

France either to back down or to fight. Viewed from the outside, the "Fashoda fever" was a most unedifying spectacle.
Speaking to an English writer of note, one keen American
observer remarked:

You may depend upon it, John Bull will take it out of the French
this time, mark my words if he does not. After all, human nature
is human nature, and the old gentleman has stood so much, you
can't blame him greatly if, having got the French in a corner, he
gives them beans. Germany smacked your face in the Transvaal,
Russia wiped your eye at Port Arthur, the Turk has drawn a long
nose at you in Constantinople, the French have been tricking you
in Madagascar and worrying you on the Niger [Delcassé's own
work]—be sure John Bull will pay them out now, if only to set
himself up again in his own conceit. Let the French out quietly—
don't you believe it! They have got to be kicked down the front
doorsteps with full musical honors.[89]

At the beginning of October, Delcassé gave every indication of being as obstinate as Lord Salisbury. Public opinion
in France and England concluded that the diplomatic im-
passe could be broken only by war.[90] Even Delcassé thought
that the British had been on the point of sending him an
ultimatum. Still, Delcassé stood by his old arguments. The
courage of the man was amazing. Everyone knew that the
war would end in a speedy triumph for England. The smaller
French fleet would be swept from the seas almost over night.
Nowhere in Europe could the French count upon assistance
with any reassuring degree of certainty. The Anglo-German
quarrel, for the moment, had the appearance of having been
healed.[91] The value of the Franco-Russian alliance was very
dubious. In the first place, the terms of the alliance were directed not against any and everybody, but against the Triple
Alliance.[92] In the second place, Russia was unprepared for
war, and six weeks after Marchand's arrival at Fashoda the

[89] From *The United States of Europe*, by W. T. Stead, reprinted with permission of Doubleday, Doran & Company, Inc.
[90] *National Review*, Nov., 1898, p. 301; *L'Année Politique*, 1898, p. 361;
Maurois, p. 89.
[91] Stead, p. 97; *British Documents*, I, 162.
[92] *Documents Diplomatiques, L'Alliance Franco-Russe*, No. 95, p. 131.

Russian Czar had issued a manifesto in favor of a Peace Conference which chagrined and "astonished" Delcassé.[93] In the third place, the Russians had seen fit to advertise about Europe their utter indifference to other people's quarrels in Africa, and had made it plain to everybody that Russia would probably not support France in a war with England.[94] No less painful was Russia's unconscionable flirtation with Germany, the arch enemy of the French.[95] The situation on the Italian frontier was also alarming. There was a real danger that the Italian people would throw themselves upon the French as soon as the first French fleet was swept from the sea.[96]

The internal situation in France was likewise woeful enough to dishearten even the stoutest of souls. The Dreyfus scandal had divided society and aroused bitter feelings. An army officer had been court-martialed, disgraced, and imprisoned on the charge of treason simply because he was a Jew; and a long trail of deceit and intrigue had followed on the heels of this initial piece of injustice to cover up the affair.

Lastly, Delcassé's case was rendered hopeless because of Marchand's inability to hold out at Fashoda. The English knew that Marchand was in sore need of ammunition and supplies, and that none could be sent him for months. He was, moreover, cut off from the interior and had inadequate water transport. Finally, he had practically no following among the natives of the country.[97]

The English were consequently perfectly secure in adopting their "back down or fight" attitude; and it is not surprising that about October 10, Delcassé began to show signs of giving in to the English, and that the tone of the Paris press became more moderate, perhaps as a direct result of Delcassé's inspiration. At the same time, Delcassé complained to the British Ambassador of being pressed too hard. A Cabinet crisis was at hand, and Delcassé said that he was injuring his

---

[93] Delcassé, *Annales de la Chambre, Débats*, Jan. 23, 1899, p. 147.
[94] Giffen, pp. 161-171. [95] *Ibid.*, pp. 176-182.
[96] Stead, p. 99; *British Documents*, I, 183, 191.
[97] *National Review*, Nov. 1898, p. 306; *Parliamentary Papers*, Egypt No. 3, 1898, p. 4, Kitchener to Cromer, Sept. 21, 1898.

position in French politics by his friendly attitude toward England.[98]

On October 11, Delcassé told Monson that Baron de Courcel had correctly interpreted the wishes of the French Government in a talk which he had with Lord Salisbury on October 5, 1898. In this conversation Baron de Courcel had stated that the recall of Marchand would have to be preceded by an agreement in regard to its mode of execution and its consequences. He also proposed a "friendly delimitation" of French and British territories in Africa, and added, "Who knows but that at the end of an accord regulating the present difficulty, the long misunderstanding between France and England will be completely cleared up to the great advantage of both countries?"[99]

The truth is that Delcassé was willing to withdraw from Fashoda if the British would make some concession that would serve as a bridge of retreat. A discussion of the frontier between the French Congo and Egypt would have served very well toward this end. "Give me an outlet on the Nile, and I'll recall Marchand," he said. This arrangement he considered honorable and advantageous to both nations. Moreover, in this way he would have accomplished the purpose which he had assigned to himself in 1893 when he first took charge of the French colonies; but the English on the twenty-seventh refused to discuss the question of the frontier so long as the French flag was at Fashoda.[100]

That same day, Delcassé sought to counteract the prevailing idea that Russia was leaving him in the lurch, by showing Monson copies of four alleged telegrams or dispatches from St. Petersburg, promising France the support of Russia in the crisis. Delcassé solemnly stated that he had kept them secret because he did not wish to appear to menace England.[101]

[98] British Documents, I, 175-179.
[99] Ibid., I, 175-179, Documents Diplomatiques, Haut-Nil et du Bahr-El-Ghazal, No. 25, p. 20.
[100] British Documents, I, 181-183, 187; Maurois, p. 91.
[101] British Documents, I, 185.

Two days before, the Brisson Cabinet, of which Delcassé was a member, had fallen during a mad scene in the French Chamber of Deputies. A free fight had ensued between a Laborite and a Boulangist. In addition, Paul Déroulède, the outstanding Chauvinist in France, had escaped a beating at the hands of the Minister of War, General Chanoine, only by virtue of the fact that the diminutive Delcassé had seized the irate General by the coat tails and held him back until Déroulède had safely retired.[102] Finally the whole Cabinet of Brisson had resigned. When Monson saw Delcassé on the twenty-eighth, he found the latter pondering over the question of whether he would be called upon to hold the post of Foreign Affairs in the Cabinet which was to succeed the one that had just fallen. Delcassé told Monson that but for the uncompromising attitude of England, he [Delcassé] would enjoy a long term of office at the Quai d'Orsay. "It is you who make it impossible for me to remain," he exclaimed petulantly. France was the country of sentiment, Delcassé said, and had England chosen, she could have attached France to her by consideration for that sentiment; but, as it was, France would be driven to cultivate the assistance of other powers which would be only too glad to coöperate with her against English colonial policy. Such an one, Delcassé hinted, was Germany.[103]

October 29 found Delcassé in a still more gloomy mood. He told Monson that war was being forced upon France. This, he said, would oblige him to retire from the post of Foreign Affairs because a war between France and England was personally repugnant to him and contrary to his policy.[104]

On November 3, 1898, the new Premier, Charles Dupuy, held a Cabinet meeting. It was decided to withdraw Marchand from Fashoda. Delcassé agreed to remain in office and to take the step decided upon. His decision to remain in office was determined by urgent appeals to his patriotism. He knew

[102] London *Graphic*, Oct. 29, 1898, pp. 566-567; *Le Matin*, Oct. 26, 1898, p. 1.
[103] *British Documents*, I, 185.
[104] *Ibid.*, No. 222, p. 186.

that an order to withdraw Marchand would cost him a certain loss of popularity, and that it would be very disagreeable to defend such action in the French Parliament.[105] After all, Delcassé reflected, Marchand was unable to defend the position; nor did Fashoda constitute the natural outlet that Delcassé had sought in 1893. It would be open only during the season of the highest waters, i.e., about four months in the year. Moreover, Fashoda lay in the province of Khartoum, which, unlike the Bahr-El-Ghazal and the Equator, had not been formally abandoned by the Egyptian Government. Finally, the adventure of Fashoda was inexplicable to the politicians and incomprehensible to the masses—no essential interest seemed to be at stake. On the other hand, Delcassé had sold the national honor as high as he could—six weeks went by from the meeting at Fashoda to the order for the withdrawal of Marchand, which was made public on November 4, 1898.[106]

Meanwhile, Delcassé had been under such a continuous strain that his hair had whitened in the space of a single month. The recall of Marchand was a bitter pill to take, and it left Delcassé in a mood of deep depression. He had adhered admirably to his middle course, but he had seemingly failed to win England to his side. Actually, though there was no evidence of it at the time, he had lost the swamps of Fashoda but gained the ally that he desired.

4. The Modification of the Franco-Russian Alliance

The arrangement of 1891 is solemnly confirmed; but its sphere of action is, however, singularly extended. While in 1891 the two Governments declared themselves concerned only with the maintenance of the general peace, my project states that they are to be especially preoccupied with the maintenance of the European balance of power. (Delcassé to Loubet, Aug. 12, 1899.)

Yesterday, an instrument of security for the two nations; today, a guarantee of liberty of action in the execution of their policy. . . . (Delcassé, March 20, 1902.)

[105] British Documents, I, No. 228, p. 189.
[106] Delcassé, Annals de la Chambre, Jan. 23, 1899.

The credit of the Franco-Russian Alliance was never lower than it was during the Fashoda crisis. Germans and English alike were in exultation when it became apparent that Russia was not going to lift a finger to help her ally. Abroad, and in France likewise, it was conceded that the Franco-Russian Alliance existed merely to preserve the *status quo* and the "German Peace." It would be useful only in the case of an unprovoked attack upon France by Germany, Italy, or Austria. This unsatisfactory character of the Franco-Russian Alliance was summed up definitely in an unsigned article (probably written or inspired by Delcassé) in the *Revue de Paris,* August 1, 1898:

The Russian Alliance, in guaranteeing us against a possible aggression . . . has lessened our worries. It has not, however, put an end to all of them. It in no way changes the armed peace. . . . Contracted by two Powers, both of which have been the victim . . . of Prince Bismarck, one at Sedan, the other at the Congress of Berlin, it will not have proven its fruitfulness until the day when it has definitely checked the continental hegemony of Germany.

At bottom, then, the trouble with the Alliance was that it was too restricted in its scope. It had no practical value as a diplomatic instrument. Neither by France nor Russia could it be used as the basis for a vigorous and determined diplomacy. Fashoda had made that clear.

Briefly, the Franco-Russian agreement provided (1) for a general diplomatic accord which stipulated that the two governments should concert with each other in all questions likely to disturb the peace of Europe; (2) a military convention which came into play in the event of an aggression on the part of one of the Powers of the Triple Alliance. The duration of this military convention was stated to be the same as that of the Triple Alliance.[107]

Delcassé, though, desired not a defensive and passive alliance, but an active one—one that would support a policy of action. The fate of the Russian people did not bother him at

[107] *Documents Diplomatiques, L'Alliance Franco-Russe.* No. 95, Delcassé to Loubet, Aug. 12, 1899.

all. Russia was to him "a diplomatic and military entity."[108] Why, then, should he not turn this "diplomatic and military entity" to account? As he surveyed the political situation in Europe, he foresaw that Austria-Hungary might at any moment dissolve into its component parts, that is, into a number of rival and enemy races. Suppose the German portion of Austria should desire to unite with Germany? What a danger to France! Should not the Franco-Russian Alliance be modified so as to take care of just such contingencies as this? In a letter to President Loubet of France, Delcassé said, August 12, 1899:

> But what would happen if the Triple Alliance should come to be dissolved otherwise than by the will of all of its members; if, for example, the Emperor Francis Joseph, who seems, for the moment, to be the only unifying principle among the rival and enemy races of Austria-Hungary, should suddenly expire; if Austria should be menaced by a disruption *que, peut-être, on souhaite ailleurs, que, peut-être, on favoriserait et dont, en tout cas, on pourrait être amené à vouloir tirer parti?* What subject is more capable of compromising peace in general and of breaking the European balance of power? and what subject merits more that France and Russia should be not only united in a common design, but also ready for its execution?[109]

That this new conception of the Franco-Russian Alliance might come to prevail, Delcassé went to Russia on August 2, 1899. The greatest secrecy was observed on this occasion. The day before leaving for Russia, Delcassé saw Count Munster, the German Ambassador in Paris; yet he said nothing to him of his proposed journey. Out of curiosity, Munster pumped General Galliffet and was told that the "little man" had "only one idea in his head, that of going to shake hands with our friend Nicholas." Prince Radolin, the German Ambassador in St. Petersburg, was completely mystified. He wrote the Ministry of Foreign Affairs at Berlin a long letter with no less than nine separate guesses why Delcassé should be

---

[108] Michon, *L'Alliance Franco-Russe*, p. 302, note (1).
[109] *Documents Diplomatiques, L'Alliance Franco-Russe*, No. 95.

going to Russia. All nine missed the point, except the general suspicion that Delcassé aimed to strengthen the Franco-Russian Alliance.[110] A large part of the French press ascribed the trip to a connection with the Dreyfus affair. Officially, the Government let it be known that it was a matter of a visit rendered by the French Minister of Foreign Affairs to M. Mouravieff, Foreign Minister of Russia, and that its purpose was "to knit more closely the ties of the Franco-Russian Alliance."[111]

Once closeted with the autocrat of all the Russias, Delcassé explained to the Czar the fears that he entertained in regard to the disruption of Austria-Hungary. He said he was particularly concerned because the Franco-Russian Military Convention had a duration limited to the life of the Triple Alliance. He feared that the Alliance would leave France and Russia disunited precisely when their unity could be most useful.

Since our accord of the month of August, 1891, extends to all important questions, is not Your Majesty of the opinion that the Military Convention of 1894, which is the instrument of execution of this accord, should last just as long as the general and permanent interests of the two nations remain the same—?

The Czar agreed, and Delcassé drew from his pocket a projected declaration which he had drawn up that morning. The arrangement of 1891 was "solemnly confirmed"; but "its sphere of action" or "scope" was "singularly extended"; while in 1891 the two governments declared themselves concerned only with the maintenance of the general peace, Delcassé's project stated that they should be preoccupied also with the maintenance of the European balance of power, and the Military Convention was given the same lease on life as the diplomatic arrangement itself.[112] The Czar was pleased. Mouravieff was brought in and given permission to sign the agreement before Delcassé returned to Paris.

[110] G.P., XIII, 273-278; XV, 359-360, No. 4353.
[111] L'Année Politique, 1899, pp. 267-268.
[112] Documents Diplomatiques, L'Alliance Franco-Russe, No. 95.

Delcassé worked all night long elaborating a correct text and, on the ninth of August, 1899, while still in St. Petersburg, he and Mouravieff exchanged letters modifying the Franco-Russian Alliance in the sense agreed upon by Delcassé and the Czar.[113] A purely defensive and passive instrument thereupon became the basis of a larger and more active diplomacy, as Delcassé desired. The expression "maintenance of the European balance of power" was broad enough to cover anything, and had been used by diplomats for centuries to excuse aggressive as well as defensive tactics. Delcassé himself, for instance, contemplated that it might be used by France and Russia to thwart the national will of the German Austrians, should they attempt to join with Germany.[114] Likewise, any modification of the *status quo* in the Balkans could be invoked by Russia to safeguard her interests in the Near East. Thus, in the final analysis, as the historian Mathiez has said, the secret accord of August 9, 1899, constituted a partition: the Balkans against Alsace. The Russians could use the secret accord as a basis for their schemes in the Balkans; by invoking the balance of power at an opportune moment, Delcassé could use the accord to recover Alsace-Lorraine. This is why Mathiez and Michon have declared that the secret letters of August 9 contained the germ of the World War.[115] The importance of the documents was fully appreciated by Delcassé. He brought back the French copy in a manner calculated to foil the boldest robbers, i.e., fastened across his chest and "between underwear and skin"![116]

Obviously the mere signing of papers could not, by itself, transform the Alliance into a policy of action. Accordingly Delcassé introduced new methods into the relations between the two contracting parties. Communications became incessant; ministers consulted each other on almost every subject, and tried to act in accord with each other. In this manner Delcassé obtained a powerful personal influence upon Rus-

---

[113] *Documents Diplomatiques, L'Alliance Franco-Russe*, Nos. 93 and 94.
[114] *Ibid.*, No. 95.
[115] Michon, *op. cit.*, pp. 87-88, quoting Mathiez in *Internationale*, 2, 10, and 26 Aug., 1921.   [116] Combarieu, p. 34.

sian policy and upon the Czar. The confidence of Nicholas in Delcassé was practically absolute. Many times, when difficulties arose, he was heard to remark, "Delcassé will arrange all that."[117]

As a result of his labors, Delcassé was able to say in the French Parliament, February 11, 1901, that during the Boxer Rebellion the action of France and Russia had always been concerted and concordant, and that the Alliance had never functioned with greater mutual confidence and with more delicate respect for the spirit and independence of both parties. He also took this opportunity to urge the politicians of France not to let the Alliance become an object of party strife. "The interests of France require that party spirit should stop where the more serious and dearer interests of France commence."[118]

In April 1901 the Alliance was cemented still more firmly by the visit of the Russian fleet to Villefranche; and, some days afterwards, Delcassé went to visit the Czar a second time. After dinner with their Majesties on the twenty-fifth, Delcassé talked with the Czar in the imperial office until four o'clock. "Count on me; my policy is invariable," said Nicholas. The entire conversation left Delcassé with the impression that the Franco-Russian accord was complete. He was not only entirely satisfied; he was almost overjoyed.[119] Russia was in need of money again. This enabled Delcassé to end a danger to France which had bothered him ever since the days of his newspaper editorials. The particular danger that he had in mind grew out of the slowness of Russian mobilization. As early as November 26, 1887, Delcassé had written in the *Paris* that the German plan of campaign would be to strike a fatal blow at France before Russia could join in the war and then to turn back to deal with Russia at leisure.

[117] Mende, p. 266 (private letter, Porter to Hay, Jan. 17, 1901); Coubertin in *Fortnightly Review*, Jan. 1, 1902; U. S. Dept. of State, Porter to Hay, Sept. 6, 1900, No. 728, France, Vol. 119.
[118] *J.O., Chambre*, Feb. 11, 1901.
[119] *Documents Diplomatiques Français*, 2 S., I, No. 206, p. 246; Combarieu, p. 129.

Shortly afterwards, December 18, 1887, he had written another article for the same journal in which he had pointed out Russia's need of additional strategic railways. It was now agreed that France should arrange a loan of 425 million francs to Russia, and that the proceeds of the borrowing should be primarily devoted to the construction of strategic railroads considered necessary by the French and Russian general staffs and designed to hasten the concentration of Russian troops at the Prussian frontier.[120] Russia promised to take steps permitting her, in case of war, to mobilize against Germany on the eighteenth day instead of the twenty-eighth. But it was considered advisable to shorten the mobilization period by four more days in order to make it impossible for Germany to use all of her troops in an initial campaign against France and to turn back on Russia later. For this purpose, a third line of penetration was to be constructed leading down to the German frontier and placed in between the lines already running down to the German frontier from Moscow and St. Petersburg.[121] Thereafter, if war came, Germany would have to fight on two sides at once. Another dream of Delcassé had been realized.[122]

Early in August 1901, the Czar accepted an invitation to visit France. Delcassé carefully arranged an elaborate reception for him. The program greatly pleased Nicholas, and he decided to take the Empress along. The French President, Delcassé, and most of the Cabinet, met the Russian sovereigns at Dunkirk on September 17. On the eighteenth, the President, Delcassé, and the Prime Minister reviewed the North Fleet from aboard the imperial yacht. After banqueting at Dunkirk the party went to the Château of Compiegne. The Russian guests then assisted at the Eastern military maneu-

[120] *Documents Diplomatiques Français*, 2 S., I, Nos. 159, 239, 251, 263, and 329; H. Feis, *Europe the World's Banker, 1870-1914* (New Haven, 1930) pp. 218-219 and note.   [121] Combarieu, p. 129; Feis, pp. 218-219.

[122] Delcassé's precautions were amply justified. For years, the Germans had planned, in the event of war, to attack Russia first; but in 1898, just as Delcassé had feared in 1887, they adopted the idea of an initial offensive against France. It was retained as a cardinal principle in the plan used by Germany in 1914.

vers, and at a great military banquet served at Fort Witry-les-Reims. Here, at Reims, a toast showed the radical change which had come over the Franco-Russian Alliance: President Loubet, in thanking the Russian autocrats for their visit, said rather significantly that the "aim of the Alliance" was "to serve the interests of France and Russia." The Alliance had indeed become a working diplomatic instrument.[123]

By way of reciprocating the visit of the royal family to France, President Loubet went to St. Petersburg in May of 1902, and Delcassé went with him. The Czar seemed quite anxious to shower exceptional honors upon them. The great dinner given in their honor was long remembered for its brilliance.[124]

During March of that same year, Delcassé consented to a partial extension of the Franco-Russian Alliance to Far Eastern affairs. However, he was careful to stipulate that the Alliance should come into play in the Far East only under exceptional circumstances, i.e., only in the event of an attack on the integrity of China by some other Power or in case of a menace to French interests.[125] This partial extension of the Alliance to the Far East led Delcassé to say in the Senate on March 20, 1902, that the passing of years instead of enfeebling the Alliance had only served to consolidate it and extend its scope; that yesterday it had been an instrument of security for the two nations, but now it was a guarantee of liberty of action for them in the execution of their policy.[126]

A much more notable declaration regarding the Alliance was made by Delcassé, December 26, 1903. On this occasion he told the Senate that the Franco-Russian Alliance was ideal and that it not only gave "complete security" but gave a "fertile security," which permitted the two allies "to act and carry out their affairs."[127] Certainly by this last date, and

[123] Wallier, *Vingtième Siècle Politique*, 1901, pp. 381-387; Coubertin, *Fortnightly Review*, Jan. 1, 1902, pp. 73-74.
[124] Combarieu, pp. 194-197.
[125] Delcassé, *J.O., Chambre*, March 25, 1902, p. 1505; Combarieu, p. 271.
[126] *J.O., Sénat*, March 20, 1902, p. 509.
[127] *J.O., Sénat*, Dec. 26, 1903, pp. 1679-1680.

probably by March 20, 1902, the Alliance was fully consolidated and transformed into a policy of action. The immediate importance of this particular diplomatic triumph is easily overlooked. If we believe the repeated assertions of Delcassé, and there is no reason for not believing Delcassé in these instances, the immediate advantages accruing to him from the consolidation and extension of the Franco-Russian Alliance were almost incalculable: the Alliance became the basis of his whole later policy. The security and liberty of action that he had gained permitted him to strive for, and eventually to conclude, the series of international accords and ententes which was the outstanding achievement of his career.[128] How he accomplished this larger purpose will be seen in the following pages.

5. The Flowering of the Entente System

He was not the first, and doubtless he will not be the last to whom history will render a tardy justice. Later history will say that, elevated above the interests of parties, Delcassé gave his country a policy that was genuinely French; that, thanks to him, France was able to face the field of battle with powerful allies when she was attacked in 1914, and that consequently he, too, was one of the great artisans of victory. (Barrère, in the *Revue des Deux Mondes*, Aug. 1, 1932.)

a. The Italian Rapprochement

A great diplomat is obliged to deal with many matters at the same time. Thus, even while engaged in the pressing affairs just described, Delcassé was patiently dealing with Italy, Spain, England, and the United States, with a view to surrounding France with as many friends and allies as possible. Since 1890 he had preached that France should be ready at any moment to take the hand of her friends and natural allies.[129] As he himself said at a later date, his purpose, now, was "to better without cessation, to fortify with-

[128] Delcassé, *J.O., Sénat*, Dec. 7, 1904, p. 1045; *J.O., Chambre*, Nov. 10, 1904, p. 2381; Delcassé, *Annales de la Chambre*, Jan. 27, 1905, p. 93.
[129] *J.O., Chambre*, Nov. 6, 1890, and Nov. 30, 1891.

out cessation, and to extend without cessation the international situation of France," with a view to restoring a healthy and beneficent European balance of power, and to achieve this end by dissipating the atmosphere of distrust and suspicion which had formed and grown thick between France and certain of her "natural friends." He believed that if he could do away with this accumulation of distrust and suspicion the way would be prepared for frank explanations by which all the misunderstandings would be cleared up.[130]

Delcassé was particularly anxious to restore cordial relations with Italy. After having incorporated herself into the Triple Alliance, Italy had drawn closer to England; and, in the words of Delcassé himself, "a maritime entente ended by establishing what corresponded to a continental alliance . . . France . . . taken between the two sides of this vise, could hardly move or breathe.[131] The questions of the balance of power in the Mediterranean, of the division of the territories in North Africa, of the excessive interest which certain Frenchmen took in the temporal power of the Pope, and of tariffs, still rendered relations between France and Italy so unsatisfactory that during the Fashoda Crisis there was a real fear that Italy might pounce upon France as soon as the English annihilated the French fleet.[132] A cordial understanding with Italy was therefore almost imperative, and certainly would have solid advantages for France.

We already know that since 1887, as a journalist and as a member of the Chamber of Deputies, Delcassé had striven to put an end to Franco-Italian quarrels. Likewise, his old-time associate on the *République Française*, Eugène Spuller, on becoming Foreign Minister of France in the Spring of 1889, had been prepared to do everything in his power to improve relations between the two countries,[133] and Billot was sent in 1890 as Ambassador to the King of Italy with in-

[130] Delcassé's history of his policy, Jan. 24, 1908; *J.O., Chambre*, pp. 104-108.

[131] *Ibid.*, pp. 104-108.

[132] Stead, *United States of Europe*, p. 99; *British Documents*, I, pp. 183, 191, 292-294.

[133] Crispi, *Memoirs*, III, pp. 178-179.

structions to work for a rapprochement.[134] However, very
little came of this attempt, because Billot and the Italian Minister, Crispi, could not get along with each other. Fortunately,
when Delcassé came to power in 1898, cabinet changes in Italy
had brought in men favorable to a termination of Franco-
Italian misunderstandings. The Italian Minister of Foreign
Affairs was now that same Marquis Visconti-Venosta with
whom Delcassé had talked in the spring of 1898, and who
at that time had agreed with Delcassé on the desirability and
possibility of an accord between France and Italy. Moreover,
Delcassé was ably seconded by the popular French Ambassador at Rome, Camille Barrère, who was devoted to the cause
of establishing a Franco-Italian entente, and who systematically courted the Italian press and public with that end in
view.[135]

Pursuing the careful plan of campaign which he himself
had laid out, Delcassé's first step was to put an end to the
atmosphere of distrust and suspicion dividing France and
Italy. This he did by negotiating the commercial accord of
November 21, 1899, which ended the long-standing Franco-
Italian tariff war, ruinous to both countries, and an unending
source of mutual ill humor. Arguing in the French Senate
for the ratification of this accord, January 31, 1899, Delcassé
echoed the idea, already expressed by others, that political
as well as economic reasons dictated the treaty, and spoke of
the reëstablishment of the entente with Italy and the resump-
tion of cordial and confident relations as a higher consideration involved in the agreement.[136]

The negotiations for the commercial treaty had offered
an excellent opportunity to get together and talk about
Franco-Italian relations, and these conversations continued
after the signing of the treaty. If the French were caught in a
vise, as Delcassé said, the Italians had equally sound reasons
for desiring a change for the better. Italy had suffered more

[134] *Revue des Deux Mondes,* Jan. 1, 1899, p. 133.
[135] *G.P.,* XVIII, pp. 597f; *British Documents,* I, pp. 281 and 205.
[136] *Annales de la Chambre,* Jan. 31, 1899, pp. 67 and 73; Cf. Delcassé, in
Paris, July 6, 1888.

than France from the tariff war.[137] An economic crisis in
Germany forced Italy, who needed financial aid, to turn
from Berlin to Paris. The French Capital virtually became
Italy's banker.[138] Then, too, the increasing importance of the
Franco-Russian Alliance and the strengthening of the Franco-
Russian forces in the Mediterranean caused Italy to shift
toward France in self-defense.[139] On the French side, there
was the natural desire to weaken Italy's attachment to the
Triple Alliance in order to avoid the necessity of fighting on
two sides at once in the event of a war between Germany and
France. Finally, Delcassé baited the Italians by holding before
them a tempting slice of Africa. Using words which recall
to mind his newspaper articles of 1886 and 1888, Delcassé
informed Italy through Barrère in the latter part of April
1899, that if she had any designs on Tripoli she would not
find France standing in her way.[140]

Delcassé himself has summarized these conversations for
us: Having exchanged ideas, it was discovered that no grave
cause, no essential interest demanded that France and Italy
remain indifferent, much less hostile to each other, and "that
the Mediterranean, far from inciting them to conflict, should,
on the contrary, serve to draw them together and hold them
together." Once this was understood, and France and Italy
recognized the greater freedom of movement for each of them
in their own sphere, there was nothing to do but continue to
persevere along the same line.[141] Thus, the rapprochement of
France and Italy was effected in the manner predicted by
Delcassé in his newspaper article of February 26, 1887, and
in his talk with Visconti-Venosta in the spring of 1898. To
bring about the desired Mediterranean balance, it was agreed
on December 14, 1900, that France should have priority in
Morocco, and that, similarly, Italy should enjoy Tripoli for

[137] A. Billot, *La France et L'Italie*, 1881-1899, II, pp. 401-402; Cf. *G.P.*, XI,
p. 297; Delcassé, "Guerre de Tarifs," *Paris*, Jan. 27, 1888.
[138] *G.P.*, VII, pp. 128; 133; *Nuova Antologia*, Oct. 1, 1896, pp. 552-553.
[139] Ribot, *J.O., Chambre*, Jan. 23, 1899; *British Documents*, I, p. 204; Cf.
Langer, *Franco-Russian Alliance*, pp. 336-341.
[140] *G.P.*, XIV, p. 435, No. 3953.
[141] Delcassé, *J.O., Sénat*, March 20, 1902, p. 508.

her sphere.[142] In April 1901, the Italian fleet, under the command of the King's uncle, visited the French port of Toulon. President Loubet met the Italian visitors and spoke of France as "the friend of Italy." And, indeed, there was every reason now for friendly relations. Italy had joined the Triple Alliance largely because France had seized Tunis in 1881. Delcassé's exchange of Tripoli for Morocco, by giving Italy a large share of Africa, mitigated Italian resentment, and removed the principal reason for Italy's connections with Austria and Germany.

Delcassé and Barrère reached the climax of their Italian negotiations in 1902, when the time came for Italy to renew once more the Triple Alliance. Their aim was to detach Italy from Germany and Austria, but Italy could not be persuaded to break the connection altogether, so they fell back upon the expedient of making sure that the Triple Alliance, so far as Italy was concerned, should not be in any case directed against France.[143] After some more negotiations, the Italian Ambassador secretly notified Delcassé that in the renewal of the Triple Alliance there was "nothing directly or indirectly aggressive toward France," no engagement binding Italy in any eventuality to take part in an aggression against France, "finally no stipulation which menaces the security and tranquillity of France."[144]

This move was followed on July 10, 1902, by an exchange of letters in which the two Powers declared that no divergence now existed between them as to their respective interests in the Mediterranean, and agreeing further that in the event either was the "object of a direct or indirect aggression," the other would remain neutral.[145]

But what was a "direct or indirect aggression"? Nations frequently took the offensive in self-defense. Hence, a day later "direct" was defined explicitly, the examples being French objection to a Hohenzollern on the Spanish throne

---

[142] Livre Jaune, *Les Accords Franco-Italiens de 1900-1902*, pp. 3-4.
[143] *G.P.*, XII, pp. 730-731; *Les Accords Franco-Italiens*, pp. 4-5.
[144] *Les Accords Franco-Italiens*, No. 4.
[145] *Ibid.*, Nos. 7 and 8; *American Historical Review*, July, 1932. p. 759.

as an indirect provocation, and the Ems Telegram as a direct provocation.[146]

On the basis of these cogent and explicit declarations, Delcassé was able to say in the French Parliament, amid loud applause, on July 3, 1902, that Italy would not in any case or under any form become the instrument or the auxiliary of an aggression against France.[147]

Lest the reader should get the idea that Delcassé met with no obstacles in bringing about cordial relations with Italy, it is well to add that, here again, he had much difficulty. For instance, in the Cabinet with Delcassé was that brilliant but eccentric genius, Camille Pelletan, who on a voyage from Toulon stopped at Ajaccio and declared that the French island of Corsica was a revolver pointed at the heart of Italy, and who later on uttered many other words better left unsaid.[148]

Franco-Italian relations were, furthermore, complicated by the attitude of the extreme anti-clericals in France toward the Pope, and by papal pretensions as well. Delcassé defended those activities of the Church which spread French civilization in distant lands, but accompanied President Loubet when the latter visited the King of Italy in Rome despite the protests of the Pope. Eventually, Delcassé was obliged to break off diplomatic relations with the Vatican altogether.[149] This step was a momentous one. For the first time since 1870, a French Minister of Foreign Affairs had taken a firm stand on the side of the King of Italy as over against the claims of the Papacy.

But, in spite of these troubles, the Franco-Italian entente remained firmly established down to the outbreak of the World War, and must be counted among the greatest of Delcassé's achievements. The reëstablishment of peace between

---

[146] Les Accords Franco-Italiens, No. 9, and p. 9.
[147] J.O., Chambre Débats, p. 2084.   [148] Saint-Cyr, p. 193.
[149] Delcassé, Nov. 26, 1904, J.O., Chambre, pp. 2712-2714; E. Dimnet, France Herself Again, pp. 118-127; J. P. Niboyet, Ambassade de France Au Vatican, 1870-1904, pp. 111-113; 168-169; Documents Diplomatiques, Saint-Siège; Coubertin, La Chronique de France, 1903, pp. 58-67.

the two great nations was, in itself, an end worthy of praise, but the fruits were not harvested until the coming of the World War. Poincaré has told us what the entente then meant to France in words well worth quoting:

in the month of August 1914, she [Italy] immediately informed us that, faithful to the Convention of 1902, she would not associate herself with any warlike enterprise directed against us. Delcassé is one of those who made it possible for us to send our Alpine Chasseurs immediately into Alsace-Lorraine.[150]

b. The Franco-American Rapprochement

The success of the United States in the Spanish-American War opened the eyes of France to this new and growing Power beyond the seas. Frenchmen of all classes who had hitherto sneered at the "dollar-hunting Yankee," vied with each other in an effort to embrace "Uncle Sam." The new attitude was evident as early as July 1898, as one English observer noted in comparing the Fourth of July celebration in France that year with the same demonstration of the previous year.[151]

Among those who had their eyes opened was Delcassé. He saw in the ever growing United States a useful addition to his system of ententes, and systematically set about wooing the new Power. After the "happy mediation" of Delcassé, which put an end to the Spanish-American War, he was able to render Franco-American relations still more close and still more confident.[152] From Delcassé's speech of February 11, 1901, in the Senate, it was evident that he considered this American rapprochement as one of his own achievements, and ranked it along with his Franco-Italian and Franco-Spanish ententes in importance.[153] The author of the *Vingtième Siècle Politique* for 1901 spoke of the *entente* between France and the United States; and, somewhat later, Pierre de Coubertin, in summarizing Delcassé's foreign policies in the

---

[150] Speech of Feb. 28, 1923, in *J.O.*, March 1, 1923, p. 2017; Cf. *Personal Memoirs of Joffre*, I, p. 128.   [151] Stead, *op. cit.*, p. 190.
[152] Delcassé, Jan. 21, 1902, *J.O.*, *Chambre*, p. 102.
[153] *J.O.*, *Sénat*, pp. 295-296.

Chronique de France for 1902, inserted a section on this subject which he entitled "The Conquest of the United States" *(La conquête des Etats-Unis)*.[154] The detailed explanation of how this peaceful conquest was made will show that although it was never reduced to diplomatic documents after the fashion of the Italian or Spanish ententes of Delcassé, and hence had no legally binding character, an entente or a rapprochement did exist between France and the United States, and had its importance in French history at the time of the World War.

Capitalizing the good feeling in France and the United States after his successful mediation in the Spanish-American War, Delcassé wooed the United States as he wooed and won Italy, that is, by negotiating a commercial treaty. He began in November 1898, by proposing to extend to the United States the minimum French tariff in exchange for proposed reductions of certain American differential duties.[155] The negotiations finally resulted in a Commercial Convention, concluded with the United States July 24, 1899, which provided for tariff reciprocity. This treaty Delcassé submitted to the French Parliament with substantial arguments, and secured its ratification after making it a strictly government measure.[156] Although ratification failed on the American side, the United States profited by a clause of the French law of February 24, 1900, authorizing the continuance of the French minimum rates on certain products to countries with which a treaty of commerce was pending. This concession was granted to the United States by decree of the French Government in 1902 and many times renewed, with the result that Delcassé's commercial treaty in part at least achieved its desired results.[157]

Chinese affairs offered the two governments an opportunity

[154] Wallier, *Vingtième Siècle Politique*, 1901, pp. 27-28; *Chronique de France*, 1902, pp. 107ff.

[155] Dept. of State (hereafter to be cited as *D.S.*), France, Vol. 116, No. 368, Porter to Hay, Dec. 1, 1898.

[156] *Ibid.*, Vol. 118, Nos. 601 and 602; Delcassé, April 3, 1900, *J.O., Sénat*, p. 299.

[157] U. S. Tariff Commission, *Reciprocity* and *Commercial Treaties*, p. 498.

to perceive that there existed between them a community of views.[158] The American Secretary of State was interested in the "open door" in China. General Porter wrote him on November 10, 1899, that Delcassé was "exceedingly well informed on the subject of the open door in China, as he is on all subjects pertaining to foreign relations, which he watches closely and studies personally with great care."[159] Delcassé talked "freely" with Porter and said that while the trade of France with China was not large in comparison with that of some other nations, it was one which the French Government constantly aimed to increase, and this fact gave France no small interest in the open door policy. He believed that the self-interest of the several Powers would cause them to continue to follow this policy. "Of course this Government, at present, aims under all circumstances to be in accord with Russia on the matter of foreign relations," said Delcassé, but he made it clear that in such an effort France would not sacrifice any portion of her trade. However, he thought Russia would maintain the open door in China.[160]

Furthermore, on November 24, 1899, Delcassé took the opportunity to indicate his sympathy with the open door policy in a statement before the French Chamber; and on December 16 the American Embassy in Paris was notified by a personal note from Delcassé that France accepted Secretary Hay's general proposal for the open door, but with an omission of "spheres of influence" on the ground that the term was vague and that France had none in China anyway.[161]

Likewise, during the Boxer rebellion, it became evident that the French and American policies were in agreement.[162] At the International Exhibition of 1900 in Paris, every effort was made to give as much space as possible to the "sister Republic" rather than to the Germans or the British, complained W. T. Stead; and was not the Commissioner-General ready to erect a statue of Lafayette on the grounds if only he

[158] Delcassé, Feb. 11, 1901, J.O., Sénat, pp. 295-296.
[159] D.S., France, Vol. 118, No. 559.
[160] Ibid., No. 559.   [161] Ibid., Nos. 591 and 594.
[162] Ibid., Vol. 119, Nos. 690; 725; 803; Vol. 120, No. 965.

could get the space on which to set it up? Then, too, the Minister of Commerce and Delcassé vied with each other in paying exceptional compliments to the commissioners of the United States.[163]

The French soon found other ways of making known their good will toward the United States. In February of 1902 they accepted the American invitation to participate in the World's Fair at St. Louis;[164] they kept hands off during the Venezuela troubles of 1902-3; and at the time of the Panama Canal project, Delcassé declared that he was "decidedly in favor" of the canal being built by the United States, and stated that, so far as he was personally concerned, he would never interfere with the United States in any way. In addition, he put the matter before the French Cabinet and received its assurances to the same effect.[165]

In a very curious maneuver on February 5, 1902, Delcassé told the American Ambassador "very frankly" that he had been approached by Germany for the purpose of ascertaining the disposition of France in regard to a combination of commercial Powers against the United States. The Germans, said Delcassé, desired to learn whether he would join with them and with certain others in a proposed combination of Powers to take united action with a view to counteracting the effect of the commercial prosperity of the United States upon the trade of Europe. Delcassé declared that he gave

. . . a prompt and emphatic refusal, saying that France would not be a party to such action; that the relations between his country and the United States were of the most friendly character, that the trade between them was increasing, and that there was every desire on the part of France to continue her harmonious intercourse with the American Republic.

Finally, Delcassé said he did not object to having this revelation communicated to Secretary Hay, provided it was sent in a confidential dispatch. Porter did, in fact, communicate it, and was grateful to Delcassé, because he reflected that while

---

[163] Stead, *op. cit.*, pp. 190-191.   [164] *D.S.*, Vol. 120, No. 961.
[165] *Ibid.*, Vol. 121, No. 1047, Vignaud to Hay, June 27, 1902.

such action on the part of the European Powers would be "in any case exceedingly difficult," it would be impossible without the coöperation of France and Russia.[166]

Much more important than this bit of telltale diplomacy was another maneuver of Delcassé, one which illustrates the breadth of his genius and exemplifies at the same time the ramifications of the diplomatic art. Down to 1898, America received most of her European news through British agencies or special English dispatches. True, there were interesting letters from the Continental capitals; but long before their arrival or publication the story of any important event had been told from London and had made its impress upon the American mind—an impress which it was not easy to correct.[167] That is, British opinion became in no small degree American opinion. Jules Cambon, the French Ambassador, was much perturbed "because all of the news respecting France came through London and took on a British *nuance*." Luckily he fell in with M. E. Stone, of the Associated Press. Stone wanted the A.P. service expedited, and desired that all of the French Government departments be opened so as to give the news to the Associated Press. Stone said that in return for the more rapid service and for the news, a bureau would be established in France and take all the information respecting France directly from Paris. On Cambon's suggestion, Stone went to France in the autumn of 1902 to take the matter up personally with the Minister of Foreign Affairs.[168]

When Stone arrived in Paris he was cordially received by Delcassé, who evidenced much interest in the proposed plan and sincerely favored it. The business was serious, he said, and he would have to consult his colleagues, particularly the Minister of Telegraphs. By way of preparation, he invited Stone to breakfast at the Quai d'Orsay and introduced him to two or three other ministers. It then became evident that Delcassé would have to work out the problem himself and that it would require time.

[166] Porter to Hay, Feb. 6, 1902, *D.S.*, Vol. 120, No. 960.
[167] M. E. Stone, *M.E.S. His Book*, pp. 125-126.
[168] *Ibid.*, p. 127.

One month after Stone's return to the United States, Delcassé presented his plan. "The French officials would give the representative of the Associated Press all proper information." They would answer any questions that might be "of interest" to the United States, and they would do all in their power to expedite the service. As the plan finally worked out, the French Government issued three forms of telegraph blanks: one marked in red "Associated Press"; the second form "Associated Press, très pressé"; and the third "Associated Press, urgent." When the first form was presented at any telegraph office, the operator sent forward all government messages and then the Associated Press message. In the second case, the news dispatch followed the government message then on the wire; and in the third case it stopped and preceded any government message then on the wire. In return, a press bureau was established in Paris, and a large number of subordinates, some French and some American, were employed.[169]

This was not all. Stone suggested that Paris, and not London, was the natural point of concentration for the Associated Press dispatches from the Latin nations; and Delcassé, "having that in mind," invited Stone to confer with the Italian and Spanish governments. Stone therefore went abroad to pay Delcassé a second visit. We have Stone's account in full of the negotiations on the Italian side. Delcassé issued a letter of instructions to Barrère in Rome, telling him to take the matter up with the Italian Government, and asking him to induce the Italians to expedite the Associated Press service from Italy to the French border, *where the message would be forwarded by the French administration* and rushed on to New York. Barrère entered into the scheme so enthusiastically that the American Ambassador in Rome was not even allowed to give his assistance, as Barrère wanted to make this his own special work. He succeeded admirably, and the system went into effect in Italy on January 1, 1903. When the Pope died, the Associated Press was the first to give the news to the out-

[169] *Ibid.*, pp. 128-129.

side world, a singular tribute to the efficient operation of the plan.[170]

Similarly, Delcassé aided the Associated Press in expediting the German and Russian services, thereby placing the A. P. under still more obligations to the French Government. Although Stone was careful to say that the French should not do anything to influence the character of the service or interfere with its impartiality, it seems clear that Delcassé obtained not only the good will of the Associated Press service, but in addition acquired, as we have seen, a certain measure of control over it in France and in the Latin countries of Europe. The full value of this coup can only be realized when one is aware of the fact that the telegraphic service in France works in close coöperation with the Quai d'Orsay and supplies it with official copies of telegrams,[171] and when one reflects that every Associated Press dispatch was read by one-half of the population of the United States and that Delcassé was feeding it the news![172]

Other contributions to the peaceful "conquest of the United States" were made by the foundation of certain French lectures at Harvard by James H. Hyde; the creation of the Coubertin Debating Prize for the universities of Harvard, Stanford, Princeton, Johns Hopkins, Tulane, California, etc.; the progress of the Alliance Française, founded to propagate the French language in the United States, and the founding at Paris and at other French educational centers of certain institutions designed to aid and attract American students. In 1900 Pierre de Coubertin founded the *Chronique de France*. It was frankly propaganda, being distributed free of charge to American libraries, and was written each year to awaken and stimulate American interest in France and all things French.[173]

The inspiration and the leadership in this cultural rapprochement of the two nations likewise emanated in no small

---

[170] Stone, pp. 129-130; 134; 138.   [171] See above, pp. 112-113.
[172] Stone, *op. cit.*, pp. 127-129; 146.
[173] *La Chronique de France*, 1900, "Avant propos," 1902, pp. 111-113.

measure from Delcassé and his subordinates. At the time of the Rochambeau celebration, in place of a formal representation, France sent General Brugère, generalissimo of the French Armies, at the head of a numerous company representing all the public services in France, the Quai d'Orsay among them, of course. The General visited West Point and Annapolis, and salutes were exchanged which occasioned considerable comment.[174] Jules Cambon proved to be a most valuable agent of the Quai d'Orsay. He succeeded in penetrating different American circles and spent much of his time visiting universities and colleges all over the country, with the result that he did much to modify American opinion of France. His essays and addresses were published in English when he left the United States in November of 1902, and he continued to second the movement as Ambassador Emeritus.[175] Delcassé was also aided by "zealous consuls" who fell into line, and by Cambon's successor, M. Jusserand, a diplomat remarkably well qualified to carry on the work of rapprochment, especially on account of his literary ability.[176]

The tradition of Franco-American amity was therefore kept alive and France was assured of the certain sympathy of the United States.[177] Was the rapprochement unimportant because the two Powers neglected to bind themselves with written documents? Obviously not. When the historians have finally listed all the reasons for America's entry into the war on the Allied side, they will doubtless not neglect to take into account the work of Delcassé which had its part in predisposing the United States to help the French.

One incident will suffice to illustrate the practical value of the tradition of Franco-American amity which Delcassé had laboriously kept alive. In January of 1915, the sailing of the *Dacia,* a German ship recently placed under American registry, might well have involved the United States in war

[174] *Ibid.,* 1902, pp. 112-113.
[175] *Ibid.,* p. 112; Jules Cambon, *Essays and Addresses,* N.Y., 1903.
[176] See J. J. Jusserand, *With Americans of Past and Present Days,* N.Y., 1916.
[177] *Chronique de France,* 1903, p. 51.

with England and consequently with her ally, France. The British were determined to seize the ship in spite of the fact that the United States were just about on the breaking point with England anyway. At the last minute, Ambassador Page suggested to Sir Edward Grey that he ought to let the French fleet seize the *Dacia,* so that the danger of war would be avoided. This was done; the French seized the *Dacia,* and, as Page had expected, there was no serious trouble about it because the memories of Rochambeau and Lafayette still exercised "a profound spell" over the American mind. "It was purely a case of sentiment and psychology," says one writer, and we may add, but nevertheless effective![178]

c. The Ententes with Spain and England and the Foundations of the Triple Entente of France, England, and Russia

It will be remembered, from the section on the Spanish-American Peace negotiations, that one of the much-cherished results of Delcassé's successful mediation was the fact that it gave France a dominating influence over Spain, all of which the English greatly deplored because they feared Delcassé would make use of his advantage to negotiate with Spain over Morocco. The English apprehension was amply justified. Delcassé was the last man on earth to neglect to make the most of such an opportunity. To begin with, he regarded Spain as one of the "natural allies" of France. Moreover, successful negotiations with Spain over Morocco might well have the effect of forcing the English to draw nearer to France in order to protect English interests. This again was right in line with his policy of rapprochement with England.

Delcassé's interest in Morocco certainly dated back as far as 1887. He said then that France, more than any other European Power, ought to be deeply concerned about whatever happened in the Sherifian Empire, and advocated that France and Spain pursue a common policy thereby making Morocco essentially a Franco-Spanish problem.[179] The coun-

[178] B. J. Hendrick, *Life and Letters of Walter H. Page* (New York, 1925) I, pp. 391-395.
[179] *Paris,* Oct. 9, 1887; *République Française,* Oct. 7, 1887.

try allured him from the beginning of his ministry. He realized the value of its resources, the fertility of its soil, and the approximate size of its population, which, he said, was at least that of Algeria and Tunis combined (about 7,000,000). He was also struck by the fact that it was at the very door of Europe.[180] Lastly, he saw that on the state of things in Morocco depended in large measure the security and the regular development of France's North African empire, where France had given so much of her blood, her money, and her genius that it had become "a veritable prolongation of France itself."[181]

Yet we know from Delcassé's speeches in 1904 that he entertained a much larger idea than that of merely annexing Morocco to France. He intended not only to divide up certain stretches of Africa, but at the same time to consolidate, fortify, and aggrandize the position of France in Europe by making such territorial trades as would secure new friends and allies for France. As he himself expressed it:

The problem, in effect, was this: to establish the preponderance of France in Morocco, thereby to augment her power in the Mediterranean, not by alienating, but rather by conciliating the Powers whose position in the Mediterranean brings them to our attention. . . . In considering the positions occupied not only by England, but by Italy and Spain in the Mediterranean, it is evident that if diplomacy succeeds in resolving this problem, it will have at a single stroke fortified and aggrandized the situation of France in Europe by the friendships which it will have procured, and by the rapprochement of interests of which it will have been the creator.[182]

Thus we see that the annexation of a portion of Morocco was part and parcel of Delcassé's European system of diplomacy, that its acquisition was but the means to a much larger end, and that this end was the consolidation and extension of Delcassé's system of ententes which he calculated would

[180] Delcassé, Jan. 24, 1908, *J.O., Chambre*, p. 104f.
[181] Delcassé, March 11, 1903, *J.O., Chambre*, p. 1105.
[182] Delcassé, Nov. 10, 1904, *J.O., Chambre*, p. 2386. Dec. 7, 1904, *J.O., Sénat*, p. 1048

fortify and aggrandize the position of France in Europe. This then, as Delcassé thrice told the French Parliament, was his conscious policy from the beginning of his tenure of office.[183]

This well-conceived plan bore its first fruits at the time of the Franco-Italian rapprochement. Morocco did not touch Italy directly, but the latter was obliged to look after the balance of power in the Mediterranean. Delcassé agreed that Italy should have Tripoli, and thus provided for the balance and at the same time bought out Italy's claims on Morocco.

Next, Delcassé negotiated a treaty and an entente with Spain over Morocco. By the terms of this Franco-Spanish agreement of December 3, 1902, Morocco was divided into French and Spanish spheres of influence. Almost all of the old kingdom of Fez, including the Capital, and Tangier as well, was conceded to be within the Spanish sphere. In short, the best part of Morocco was to go to Spain. Pacific penetration was agreed upon, of course; and France offered to give the Spaniards diplomatic support in the execution of the treaty. Delcassé has been much criticized for the insouciance with which he was willing to give away the richest part of Morocco, but his reasons are not hard to imagine. He understood the utility of a close entente with Spain. Spain would almost certainly recover a good deal of her former strength; therefore it behooved France to be sure of her friendship; but above all, the friendship of Spain would be invaluable in the event of a war between France and Germany.[184]

Actually the treaty of December 3, 1902, was never ratified, because the Spanish Government with which Delcassé had made it fell from power almost at the moment of signature. The incoming Spanish Cabinet feared the consequences of not consulting the English Government in regard to the proposed scheme. In an unlucky moment for Spain, they informed the English of Delcassé's generosity, and the English Government promptly quashed the whole idea of such an arrangement.[185]

---

[183] Delcassé, Jan. 24, 1908, *J.O.*, *Chambre*, p. 104.
[184] Anderson, *op. cit.*, pp. 37-38; M. Sembat, *Faites un Roi Sinon Faites la Paix*, pp. 48-49. [185] Anderson, pp. 38-40.

On the French side, this fortuitous circumstance proved to be as lucky as it was unlucky for Spain; but in order to explain how this came about, it is necessary to describe the negotiations which led to the Anglo-French entente of April 8, 1904.

From the beginning of his career, Delcassé had worked for the rapprochement of England and France. That the entente with England would further the European scheme of diplomacy bequeathed by Gambetta goes without saying; but there was an additional reason for the entente, and on this reason Delcassé loved to dwell. France was a first-rate colonial power, but she could not give to her naval forces all the development befitting the great extent of her empire. How then was it possible not to be struck by the advantages of a colonial accord with the British, who felt that their national existence depended upon control of the seas, and who actually did control the seas?[186] In 1882, Delcassé had bitterly criticized Freycinet for allowing the entente with England to be broken; in his newspaper articles of 1888 he had labored for the triple entente of France, England, and Russia. His speeches in the French Parliament likewise betokened a desire to reconcile the two countries. As Minister of Colonies, the English found him "very combative" because he followed Gambetta's policy of ardently defending French interests; but, at the same time, a willingness to conciliate the English is discernible in his actions.[187] From the first hour after his entry into the office of French Minister of Foreign Affairs, he had worked wholeheartedly for a triple entente of France, England, and Russia.[188] "I do not wish to leave here, I do not wish to leave this armchair, until I have reëstablished a friendly understanding with England." This is one of a number of such statements generally accredited to Delcassé in those early days.[189]

On August 29, 1898, Delcassé told the British Ambassador

[186] Delcassé, Jan. 24, 1908, *J.O., Chambre,* p. 106.
[187] *B.D.,* I, No. 183, p. 158; Reynald, p. 15; Schumann, pp. 103-104.
[188] Delcassé, Jan. 24, 1908, *J.O., Chambre,* p. 106.
[189] V. Bérard, *Revue de Paris,* July 1, 1905, p. 217; Saint-Cyr, p. 217; Personal letter of Delcassé quoted in Maurois, *Edouard VII,* p. 90.

"that he could see no reason why all the supposed divergent interests" of England and Russia "should not be reconciled; just as he thought it possible that every difficulty between England and France could, by patience and by a conciliatory spirit, be peaceably solved." He went on to say that he had always regarded "as eminently desirable a cordial understanding between England, France, and Russia"; and he declared that he was most anxious to coöperate "in smoothing the way both at St. Petersburg and Paris for the attainment of this object."[190]

Not being content with mere words, Delcassé actually began working for the rapprochement of Russia and England as early as September 8, 1898, and his efforts were not without important results.[191] This meant progress toward winning over England, since an entente with England presupposed one between England and France's ally, Russia.

The Fashoda Crisis intervened; but all the ill humor produced by the Crisis, all the repeated failures with which Delcassé met in his efforts to win over the English in the midst of the Crisis, failed to shake him from his purpose, though it must be admitted that he was discouraged and "profoundly depressed" by the uncompromising stand of the British. In witness of his steadfast purpose, Delcassé told his friends that he wished to remain at the Quai d'Orsay until he had restored *la bonne entente* with England.[192] This was all the more remarkable since the shame of Fashoda still glowed, and the British Ambassador wrote home as late as January 1899, that he had heard on every hand expectations of war between France and England.[193] But one of Delcassé's virtues was patience, and he remained firmly attached to the conviction expressed in one of his newspaper articles of 1888 that Germany, rather than France and Russia, was the great opponent of England, and that time, circumstances, and national interests were all on the side of the triple entente of

---

[190] *B.D.*, I., pp. 215-216, No. 262.   [191] *B.D.*, I, p. 37, No. 58.
[192] G. P. Gooch, *Contemporary Review*, p. 449; V. Bérard, 2 March, 1923; *J.O.*, p. 2050.
[193] *B.D.*, I, pp. 199-200; *L'Année Politique*, 1898, p. 405.

France, England, and Russia which he desired. Much of this was reflected in a communication of Monson to Salisbury, December 9, 1898:

I have heard indirectly, but from a very authoritative source, that M. Cambon is empowered to propose to your Lordship that all the outstanding questions in dispute between England and France should be dealt with as much as possible, simultaneously, and a general arrangement come to for a comprehensive settlement.[194] I am assured that the President of the Republic and the present Government are honestly anxious to place the relations between the two countries upon the most cordial footing, and I have certainly no reason to believe that this statement is contrary to the truth.

It corresponds with all that I have heard on several occasions from M. Delcassé's own lips, and especially with what he said in the course of a conversation yesterday. He referred to his declarations of the trend of his policy, and assured me that nothing could change his belief that the best interests of the two countries—most undoubtedly those of his own—demanded its adoption by the Government of the Republic.

The conversation of Monson and Delcassé had then turned on the subject of an Anglo-French war. Monson learned to his surprise that Delcassé was capable of using threats as well as winning words. Delcassé said that if war came, France would not be content to have the support of Russia alone.

He had frequently told me, he said, of the overtures indirectly made by Germany to the French Government. He was convinced that the rival commercial interests of Germany and England would strongly dispose the former to identify her action with that of Russia and France for the purpose of destroying England's maritime and commercial superiority, and he could affirm that recent events had caused in France a very marked turning toward Germany, which might easily be increased to an extent which probably I would not consent to believe. At any rate, I must be aware that public sentiment in Germany is by no means favourable to England.[195]

---

[194] Cambon did in fact raise this subject with Salisbury Jan. 11, 1899, *B.D.*, I, p. 197, No. 240.　　　　　　[195] *B.D.*, I, No. 238, p. 196.

Yet about the middle of January, 1899, Delcassé renewed his offers of settling the outstanding disputes between France and England.[196]

On January 23, 1899, M. D'Estournelles, a former secretary of the French Embassy at London, broke the patriotic silence maintained by the French Chamber of Deputies since the withdrawal of Marchand from Fashoda. He said he did not despair of an entente with England on an honorable and definitive basis. Alexander Ribot also rose and spoke for the entente of England and France. Quoting the words that Delcassé had taught him in 1890, he denied that the French had pursued an anti-English policy, but said that France had merely upheld her just rights as Gambetta had counseled her to do if she wished to gain the respect of the English.

At the psychological moment Delcassé took the tribune and made one of the great speeches of his career.

Conscious of representing what Gambetta had called "the highest moral entity in the world," he said he was trying to create all around France a current of confidence and esteem by pursuing a clear and loyal policy. France was ready, he declared, to examine everything, to discuss everything in a spirit of compromise and conciliation and with the resolution to claim nothing except her rights, but conscious that those rights were not to be denied by anybody.

Closely following these mouth-filling words same others which clearly amounted to holding out olive branches to the British.

. . . however numerous, however important, however powerful may be the differences fated to divide nations which, like France and England, have so many points of contact in the world, I have never seen any of them incompatible with a compromise settlement equally favorable to the two parties; a solution all the more easy to obtain since on both sides they should be persuaded that common and superior interests, political interests, and commercial interests command them to search for it.[197]

[196] B.D., I, Nos. 241 and 243.
[197] Delcassé, 23 Jan., 1899, Annales de la Chambre, p. 148.

The English press devoted long articles to these olive-branch speeches of Delcassé and his friends. The great majority of these journals applauded the tone of the French utterances and saw symptoms of possible rapprochement between the two countries *if France would agree once and for all to concede the preponderance of England in the whole valley of the Nile river.*[198]

On May 12, 1899, Delcassé was partially rewarded for his diplomatic and oratorical efforts when the Chamber ratified an Anglo-French Convention of June 14, 1898, and an additional declaration of March 21, 1899, putting an end to many long-standing disputes between France and England in regard to their African colonies; but as Delcassé had not yet received sufficient compensation, he took care not to bargain away his rights in Egypt. Yet Delcassé considered that the two agreements marked real progress. To use Delcassé's expression, the Gallic cock was given enough room to permit him to scratch at his ease; the English, too, were satisfied, so that there was now no longer any question of war between France and England.[199]

After the convention of March 21, 1899, Delcassé tried to go further and settle all Anglo-French differences. The proverbial instability of French ministries was then found standing in the way. Salisbury said to Cambon, "I have the greatest confidence in M. Delcassé and your present Government, but in a few months time they will probably be overthrown and their successors will do exactly the contrary. No, we must wait a bit."

Those, too, were the days of the Dreyfus scandal, when many Englishmen were estranged from France because of their sympathy for the persecuted soldier, and when many Frenchmen were alienated from England because they considered that John Bull was sympathizing with a French traitor. Another olive-branch speech from Delcassé on November 24, 1899, did much to calm the violent spirits in both

[198] *L'Année Politique*, 1899, p. 47.
[199] Delcassé, May 30, 1899, *J.O., Sénat*, pp. 689-690.

nations. A great section of the English press lauded the French Minister, as did all but the absolutely irreconcilable organs of public opinion in France. *Le Temps* declared: "M. Delcassé's speech struck the right key. . . . He wants peace, and is conciliatory, and yet at the same time is looking after France's real interests." On the other hand, *La Liberté* complained of Delcassé's "policy of the extended cheek," and was displeased that "the entire English press" had praised his utterances.[200]

Just as many Englishmen had complicated Delcassé's task by sympathizing with Dreyfus, so matters were made even more difficult by certain expressions of French sympathy for the Boers, with whom the English were at war. Although Germany and Russia would probably have supported France in some sort of "friendly intervention" on behalf of the Boers, Delcassé carefully avoided displeasing the English by any such action.[201] Interrogated in the Senate by Chaumié on the possiblity of an intervention in favor of the two South African republics, he answered that it was impossible under the circumstances that then existed, because England had shown no disposition to receive such mediation.[202] On November 29, 1900, a Radical deputy asked Delcassé why he did not avail himself of Article Three of The Hague Convention to propose arbitration between England and the Transvaal. Delcassé forced him to withdraw the question as "useless" and "troublesome."

The truth is that Delcassé was still obstinately courting the English. In the midst of the interpellations which would have turned him from his purpose he said:

If . . . the points of contact between France and England are numerous and consequently the subject of dispute, even more numerous and even more forceful to my mind are the reasons for forestalling them or regulating them by a mutual respect for the rights, interests, and dignity of each one; and among these reasons,

---

[200] Porter to Hay, Nov. 28, 1899, *D.S., France*, Vol. 118, No. 577.
[201] Hammann, *Deutsche Welt Politik*, pp. 72-74.
[202] Delcassé, March 15, 1900, *J.O., Sénat*, p. 141.

the clearest to my eyes and the most decisive is the fact that if by mischance a conflict should break out between them, it is not to the victor, whoever he may be, that the principal benefits of the victory will go. (Applause.)

. . . it is time for the irresponsibles on each side of the Channel . . . to cease indulging in gestures which they think are noble, but which are only ridiculous, and in menaces which they think are terrible, but which are perfectly puerile. (New and lively signs of approbation.)[203]

Yet, as late as November of 1900, the English hardly understood Delcassé and his purposes, and the British Ambassador in Paris wrote home that:

Delcassé is an unsatisfactory Minister to us diplomatists in Paris. He is extremely uncommunicative, not to say secretive. Consequently it is very rare that any one of us succeeds in extracting information from him. He has plenty of commonplace conversation, which flows glibly enough, and he will talk eloquently in an academical fashion. But he hardly ever tells one anything in the way of political news, and he has an adroit way of feigning ignorance which took me in at first, until I convinced myself that it was all shamming. He always urges that he is not a diplomat by profession, but he carries the practice of subterfuge to an extent which I have hardly ever met before in a Minister of Foreign Affairs. On the other hand, he does not tell lies systematically, as X did.[204]

A better tribute to Delcassé's skill in mastering the diplomatic arts could hardly be found than this short sketch, but at the same time it shows how far apart Delcassé and the English Ambassador really were even at this date, despite the conciliatory efforts of Delcassé.

Meanwhile the English were beginning to comprehend the disadvantages of their policy of splendid isolation from the affairs of Europe. Queen Victoria was biased in favor of the Germans, as Delcassé had noted in his newspaper articles long before; Salisbury was suspicious of the mercurial French democracy; Chamberlain, the real pilot of the ship of state

---

[203] Delcassè, April 3, 1900, *J.O., Sénat*, p. 298.
[204] Lord Newton, *Lord Lansdowne*, p. 209.

in consequence of Salisbury's age, favored the triple coöperation of England, the United States, and Germany; and Edward VII, then Prince of Wales, supported him in unofficial
overtures to Germany which went on during 1898, 1899, and
1900.[205] Delcassé might desire an entente with England, and
he might wear his heart on his sleeve, but until these negotiations broke down there was little prospect of success for him.

Perhaps the relatively weak position of France in Europe
explains in some measure Delcassé's lack of success in winning
over England by 1900. Germany appeared to be in a more
enviable position, and it was to her that the English were
drawn at first. No one understood better than Delcassé the
weakness of France and the disadvantages of this weakness.
Ever since taking office he had been struggling without cessation to better the international position of France, and to surround her with as many friends and allies as possible.[206] Between 1898 and 1902 Delcassé secured an entente with Italy,
which assured him not only of Italian friendship but also
that in no case would she become a party to, or an auxiliary
to an aggression against France. Similarly, he increased the
power and prestige of France by securing and maintaining
the friendship and sympathy of the United States and Spain.
In 1902 he was ready to seal his entente with Spain by means
of the Franco-Spanish accord over Morocco, which was in fact
all ready for the signatures. Moreover, in 1902, a Franco-
Siamese convention was signed by Delcassé in regard to the
basin of the Mekong river. Finally, during 1899 and 1902,
Delcassé had modified the Franco-Russian alliance so as to
make it a working diplomatic instrument; i.e., one which
would support a policy of French and Russian action in any
part of the world. Consequently, when the Anglo-German
negotiations mentioned above broke down in 1901, Delcassé
was well on the way toward making France a first-rate power.
As the major results of his policies gradually became known

[205] Anderson, pp. 53-54.
[206] Mévil, *Revue Politique et Parlementaire*, June, 1924, p. 389; Delcassé,
Nov. 6, 1890, *J.O., Chambre*, p. 1897.

to the English during 1902, they were forced to respect and to reckon with both the man and his nation. It was clear that Delcassé was going to settle some important world problems in which England was interested, and that if he could not do it with English coöperation, he would do it by himself.

Meanwhile certain changes also came about on the English side. The time and circumstances that Delcassé had said would be on the side of the triple entente of France, England, and Russia had come to pass. Salisbury, the grand old conservative advocate of isolation, disappeared from the Foreign Office in October of 1900, and was succeeded by Lord Lansdowne, whose mother was French. A few days later Queen Victoria died. At the Queen's funeral, both the Kaiser and Edward VII treated the French Ambassador with marked friendliness. Cambon took heart at Edward's advances, but rebuffed those of the Kaiser. Cambon also joyfully wrote Delcassé that the Kaiser was tactlessly hanging around, as Cambon thought, to collect some fifteen million francs loaned to Edward VII by the Kaiser's mother when Edward was a gay Prince of Wales.[207] The disasters and troubles of the Boer War had brought home to the new men in power all the disadvantages of the old English policy of isolation, and by November of 1901 England was becoming more conciliatory even toward Russia.[208] The changeability of French policy and ministries had heretofore been considered by the English to be an obstacle to an Anglo-French entente, but by 1902 Delcassé had been in office four consecutive years, and the tenacity with which he practised his preconceived and "active" and "loyal" policy inspired confidence.[209]

During those same two years, 1900-1902, Delcassé did not give up hope of the entente with England. "Renunciation is abdication" was one of his mottoes. His hour of successful effort came after the consolidation and extension of the Franco-Russian Alliance, which strengthened the position of

---

[207] *Documents Diplomatiques* (hereafter cited as *D.D.*) 2 Serie I, pp. 86-87, No. 67; No. 100, pp. 118-119.

[208] *Ibid.*, No. 523, pp. 616-618; No. 493, pp. 579-582.

[209] See Mévil, *National Review*, July, 1908, p. 716.

France in Europe. Not for nothing, he was fond of saying, had he resisted that current of opposition which would have turned him from the purpose traced for him by his clear insight into French interests.[210] The Anglo-German pourparlers had now broken down, and Delcassé found in Morocco the key and the pivot to the negotiations which brought England into his camp.

In order to understand how Delcassé at last obtained his *entente cordiale* it will be necessary to go back to August 1902 and perhaps to repeat at times certain things already hinted at above. Following his old policy, Delcassé had expressed to, and impressed upon, Cambon his desire to enter into conversations with the British Government.[211] Acting on this general principle, Cambon on July 23, 1902, unofficially made known to Lord Lansdowne his thought that England and France should enter into "frank discussions" in order to be prepared for eventualities which might take place in Morocco. Cambon said he apprehended that England's only real care was in regard to Tangier, but considered that France and England might easily be able to come to some arrangement under which Tangier would be neutralized. In return for the security which the neutralization of Tangier would give to England, Cambon said he thought it fair that in exchange England should recognize the right of France to influence or exercise police in the Moroccan regions to the south. However, he stated that these were his own opinions, but declared that he would willingly ask Delcassé's permission to express them officially. Lansdowne offered to be ready to discuss the subject as soon as Cambon had authority from Delcassé.[212]

Afterwards Lansdowne brought the subject before the Prime Minister, Arthur Balfour, and found him desirous of carrying on the business. Eight days later Cambon put the question to Delcassé verbally in Paris. Delcassé outlined his

[210] Delcassé, Dec. 7, 1904, *J.O., Sénat*, pp. 1045 and 1050.
[211] *D.D.*, 2 S II, No. 369.
[212] *B.D.* II, No. 321, pp. 263-264; *D.D.* 2 S. II, No. 369, pp. 439-440.

views and authorized him to proceed with the scheme officially.[213]

On August 6, 1902, Cambon expounded Delcassé's ideas in a "long and interesting" conversation. Delcassé thought that the French colonial empire was amply sufficient not only for present wants but for years to come. France had no wish to add on more territory. Her colonial policy was conservative, and therefore Delcassé believed that it would be possible for France and England to move in accord with each other. Curiously enough, this is almost the exact language of Delcassé's newspaper articles of 1888.

Concordant action was all the more easy, he opined, because France and England were not competitors in the economic field, nor rivals in the world's markets as were England, the United States, and Germany. Except for the reference to the United States, this, too, is reminiscent of Delcassé's writings in 1888.

So far as Delcassé could see, Cambon went on to say, the position of France was insecure in only two places, viz., Siam and Morocco. In Morocco, France had a long frontier which brought her in contact with turbulent neighbors, against whom she was bound to protect herself—nor could she allow any exterior force to prevent her from doing so.

The case of Siam was identical, except that England likewise had an extensive frontier, coterminous with that of Siam on the side of Burma and in the Malay Peninsula.

Delcassé proposed to settle the Siamese matters by reading into an already existing treaty two spheres of influence in Siamese territory—one English, one French.

As for Morocco, Delcassé thought that France and England should frankly discuss the action which they might be constrained to adopt in the event of Morocco passing "into liquidation." This contingency should be provided for in advance. Delcassé offered to neutralize Tangier and to "reckon with Spain." England would then have no interest in Morocco, the entrance to the Mediterranean being secure.

[213] D.D. 2 S. II, No. 369, p. 440.

Lansdowne replied to Cambon that England was also trying to consolidate rather than extend her colonial territory. He proposed to round out the conversation by dealing with the long-standing Anglo-French dispute over the Newfoundland fishing rights of France. Cambon replied that France could not abandon her rights without territorial compensation, and that on this subject the English had never answered him. "I told you," said Lansdowne, "that we cannot give you Gambia; but if you wish to search well, and ask something else of us, we shall see." It was evident that Lansdowne was pleased. He promised to take the matter up that very day with the Prime Minister, but said that the consent of the ministerial council would have to wait until after the council's vacation. Cambon did not insist upon hurrying up matters because he knew Delcassé wished to complete his agreements with Spain first.[214]

About the middle of October, 1902, Delcassé's Franco-Siamese negotiations became known to the British. Cambon admitted that the proposed Franco-Siamese treaty pinched England somewhat, but invited her to make a treaty herself along the same lines. The Anglo-French negotiations over Siam then hung fire because Lansdowne refused to go ahead with them until the French treaty with Siam had been ratified. Unhappily for Delcassé, his treaty aroused much opposition in the French Parliament, which refused to ratify it as it then stood.[215]

The Moroccan negotiations, however, continued. By December 1902 Chamberlain was added to the list of Englishmen who judged that the jealous avidity and rapid development of German commerce rendered all rapprochement with Germany impossible for a long time to come. Even he considered the time opportune to negotiate with France.[216] The obstacle to be overcome now was the English dread of binding themselves by formal treaties. It did not take long to find

[214] B.D. II, No. 322, pp. 264-267; D.D., 2 S II, No. 369.
[215] B.D. II, Nos. 325; 327; 329; and 340.
[216] D.D., 2 S II, No. 524, pp. 653-654.

a way out. In a conversation of December 17, 1902, Cambon remarked that England and France might find themselves surprised by revolution or grave disorders in Morocco. The sooner they talked over the Moroccan situation the better it would be. He added that they were assuredly not able to make a treaty in form (*en forme*) but that they could first agree on the *status quo,* and then plan for the eventual preservation of their interests in case they should be menaced. Lansdowne was pessimistic. Granted that he and Delcassé did agree, how could they provide for the future? Neither of them would be in office forever—perhaps not even the next day. Cambon replied that it was precisely because they would not always be in office that it was important to establish right away their respective situations in such a manner as to avoid a conflict in the future. "Without making a formal convention," he said, "we can enter into an exchange of views which will be embodied in dispatches and we shall thus be beyond chance." Lansdowne seemed inclined to adopt this view—yet afraid of going too far. Perhaps he was then being held back by the Cabinet.[217]

On the French side, Delcassé, like Cambon, would have found the above arrangement just as good as a formal treaty. As early as November 6, 1890, Delcassé had given utterance to his conviction that formal treaties were unnecessary. To him the forms and signatures of alliances were unimportant. The important fact was that two nations with identical international interests should preserve as long as possible an identical attitude in international affairs. That is, Delcassé appreciated the truth borne out at the time of the World War that a well-established friendship, based upon recognized common interests, is superior to a formal treaty or alliance.[218]

The next important step in these negotiations was the deliberate attempt of the French Government to exclude Germany from Morocco. The published documents seem to

[217] *D.D.*, 2 S. II, No. 529, pp. 660-661.
[218] Delcassé, Nov. 6, 1890, *J.O., Chambre*, p. 1897.

indicate that Cambon was largely responsible for this bold move—that perhaps he went far beyond Delcassé's instructions. On the other hand, there is good reason to think that Delcassé shared the responsibility equally with Cambon. For the sake of greater secrecy, the latter repeatedly went back and forth between London and Paris during the Anglo-French negotiations, with the result that Cambon and Delcassé were almost continually in verbal communication, and each one must have known the thoughts of the other.[219]

As has already been observed, the object of these conversations was secrecy, yet some written instructions were occasionally necessary. These were conservatively phrased lest they fall into the wrong hands, but Cambon only needed a cue. So it was that on December 30, 1902, Delcassé instructed Cambon that one of the constant preoccupations of the Quai d'Orsay was the maintenance of a privileged position for France in Morocco, and advised him it was desirable that the exchange of views be limited to those Powers "principally interested." He was cautioned not to open the door to the intervention of other Powers in his interviews with Lansdowne.[220] The following day Cambon repeated these ideas to Lansdowne, who asked what was meant by limiting the matter to the "interested Powers." Without hesitation Cambon answered that he had Germany in mind and that the French Government would like to exclude this Power. Germany should be told that she had no *locus standi*.[221] While agreeing that it was desirable to exclude third Powers, Lansdowne remarked that a partition of Morocco would invite competitors and that it would be very difficult not to give the Kaiser his morsel. How could such intervention be declined? he asked. Cambon replied that it could be done by an immediate exchange of views between France, England, and Spain, providing for all eventualities and for quick action in case of danger. That is, Germany should be confronted with an established entente and with accomplished facts. Lansdowne prom-

---

[219] *B.D.*, II, No. 370, p. 317; 373, p. 320; 378, p. 329; 382, p. 336; 390, p. 343; 398, p. 352; 408, p. 360.
[220] *D.D.*, 2 S II, No. 548, p. 683.   [221] *B.D.*, II, No. 330, pp. 274-275.

ised to talk this over with Balfour because the scheme required reflection.[222] The English were endeavoring to ascertain Cambon's exact relations with Delcassé. The British Ambassador in Paris believed Cambon played his own hand and counted upon being approved and supported later on by Delcassé. He also thought there was no definite intimacy or sympathy between them. Doubtless the British uncertainty as to Cambon's status explains in part their hesitation.[223]

The English learned definitely on February 13, 1903, that Delcassé had meanwhile been forging ahead of them in his Moroccan projects. On that date the Spanish Government informed the British of Delcassé's proposed Franco-Spanish treaty of 1902, giving Spain a relatively large share of Morocco. In much trepidation the Spanish Government promised not to sign the treaty until England had expressed her opinion of it.[224]

The Franco-Spanish treaty of 1902 was consequently lost, but Delcassé had now progressed so far in his negotiations with England that Spain alone suffered by the fiasco. By way of reassuring the English of his loyal intentions, Delcassé hastened to say in the French Chamber of Deputies, March 11, 1903, that

Whatever may be the interior condition of Morocco, whether the present organization maintains itself or not or whether the future imposes upon it some modifications, one point, it seems, should be beyond all discussion, that is that no change can be made along the Moroccan Mediterranean Coast which would be of such a nature as to affect in any degree whatever the necessary freedom of the Strait of Gibraltar.[225]

This speech was also in all probability intended to prepare the minds of parliamentarians and of the public for the approaching accord with England. Delcassé was asked categorically in this session whether he had "at any time" or "in any degree" tied the question of Morocco to Egypt. Delcassé answered, "That would be in my sleep" (*ce serait en dormant*).

[222] *D.D.*, 2 S. II, No. 552.
[224] *B.D.*, II, No. 336, p. 279.
[223] Lord Newton, *op. cit.*, 270.
[225] Delcassé, *J.O., Chambre*, p. 1105.

As late as March 11, 1903, therefore, the Anglo-French negotiations had not reached the vital problem dividing the two nations. On both sides they were saving up their Egyptian claims. Yet much solid progress had been made. Public opinion was soon brought into line, partly by the speeches of Delcassé and his friends, and partly through the work of Sir Thomas Barclay, an English lawyer practising in Paris, who interested the British Chambers of Commerce in better Anglo-French relations. This last group popularized the idea of an Anglo-French arbitration treaty. Delcassé thought their schemes too far reaching, but considered their propaganda useful to his own cause; therefore he took the initiative in diplomatic negotiations for an arbitration treaty of limited scope.[226] Since many of the people behind the treaty were commercial men, Delcassé in his public speeches employed economic arguments, and pointed out that a settlement of economic difficulties between France and Italy had led to a complete Franco-Italian entente. He argued that so far from being rivals or in absolute opposition to each other, France and England by virtue of the differences of their productions complemented and fortified each other.[227]

Edward VII also did a great deal to popularize the *entente cordiale*. In May 1903 he made a trip to France. By the third day in Paris he had achieved a triumph. His success paved the way for the entente both in France and at home.

The success of King Edward in France led to a return visit on the part of the French President in July of 1903. Delcassé accompanied the President to England, as did certain other Frenchmen interested in promoting the *entente cordiale*. Among them was Eugène Etienne, an old Gambettist whom Delcassé had known since 1891, and now the head of the colonial group in France. Delcassé and Loubet included him in the party that he might discuss territorial trades point by point with members of the English Government. Etienne's most important interview was with Lansdowne on July 2,

[226] *B.D.*, II, No. 319, pp. 261-262; No. 352, p. 289.
[227] Delcassé, Dec. 26, 1903, *J.O., Sénat*, p. 1680.

1903. After a discussion of all the subjects in dispute except Egypt, Etienne expressed his belief that the most serious menace to the peace of Europe lay in Germany, that a good understanding between France and England was the only means of holding German designs in check, and that if such an understanding could be arrived at, England would find that France would exercise a salutary influence over Russia and relieve Great Britain of many of her troubles with that country.[228]

Delcassé also interviewed Lansdowne personally, and with momentous results. The preceding conversations between Cambon and Lansdowne had touched upon the position of France and England in Newfoundland, Morocco, Siam, the New Hebrides, and other parts of the world except Egypt. The ground had been cleared, but there had been no definite settlement.[229] Delcassé's talk with Lansdowne laid the basis of the entente. In the course of the conversation Delcassé repeated his earlier idea that France had ceased to desire new colonial territory, and only wanted to consolidate what she had and to remove future sources of trouble along the borders. Lansdowne replied that the same view prevailed with his Government. Delcassé then said that the French interests in Newfoundland were largely "sentimental." The possibility of reaching an understanding in regard to them really depended upon the English attitude toward France in Morocco. France wanted to make Morocco a French protectorate under the Sultan. If England agreed, the Newfoundland question would be solved—or at least made easy. Later the conversation turned on Siam and there was much cynical laughter over the clever way in which Delcassé had read "zones of influence" into the old treaty of 1896. When Lansdowne brought up the opposition of Australia to a partition of the New Hebrides, Delcassé again replied that it all depended upon the English attitude toward France in Morocco. After he had held out for compensation in return for certain frontiers in the region

[228] *B.D.*, II, No. 356, pp. 292-293; Etienne, Nov. 8, 1904, *J.O.*, *Chambre*, p. 2335.   [229] *B.D.*, II, No. 357, p. 294.

of Lake Chad, Lansdowne brought up the Egyptian question. England would never withdraw from Egypt, he said, but he admitted that France could cause her no end of trouble under the guise of protecting French holders of Egyptian securities. Delcassé answered that the Egyptian question was part of the larger African question, and could be settled if England would come to an agreement in regard to Morocco.[230]

The English were surprised that Delcassé had included Egypt in the larger African question; in fact, they were inclined to believe that he had made a slip of the tongue, but saw no reason for not taking him at his word. From that time forward, Lord Cromer, the British Consul General and agent in Egypt, became one of the staunchest supporters of the entente. He had found that French interference in Egyptian affairs created an intolerable situation, and consequently when he learned of this opportunity to put an end to it, he never tired of urging Lansdowne to rush through the negotiations before Delcassé changed his mind. After all, Morocco was falling into anarchy and must go to somebody. England didn't want it. France could have it, and along with it the expense of restoring order. All the commercial and political rights of England in Morocco were being guaranteed by France. The French were not yet in possession of Morocco and might never be. On the other hand, England was actually installed in Egypt, and the concessions she demanded were positive and immediate. In fact, the whole bargain seemed so one-sided to Cromer that he looked beyond the terms of the agreements to their larger implications and wrote Lansdowne that he fancied Delcassé's main purpose in the whole scheme was based on the hope that after she came to terms with France, Great Britain would make her peace with Russia, too, and thus isolate Germany.[231]

There was much truth in what Cromer had written. The possibility of an Anglo-Russian rapprochement had been raised while Delcassé and Loubet were in England. The far-

---

[230] *B.D.*, pp. 294-297.
[231] *Ibid.*, II, No. 359; Lord Newton, *op. cit.*, pp. 284-285.

sighted Cambon had arranged that during a dinner at the French Embassy in London, Delcassé should sit between Lansdowne and Chamberlain. As the meal progressed, Chamberlain rather abruptly turned to Delcassé and asked him if he would not like to do something really "astonishing," to wit, lead Russia to the side of England! Delcassé thought that his head would burst. "It was exactly my dream," he said later to his friend Paléologue. However, he knew that if this dream were to come true, Russia would have to be courted with extreme care, and he therefore answered Chamberlain with a word of caution: "No. If I put pressure on the Russians I shall have the appearance of having sold them to the English. The offer must come from them."[232] As a matter of fact, negotiations for a rapprochement actually began just after Delcassé's return to France and at the instigation of Delcassé himself, though, in order to avoid offending his ally, he was content to serve only as a medium for drawing the two nations together. Thorny problems arose and, to make the Anglo-Russian negotiations a success, Lansdowne had to call upon Delcassé to get him to intercede when Count Lamsdorff came to Paris in October of 1903. Delcassé was able to secure from the Russian diplomat a public expression of satisfaction over the Anglo-French and Franco-Italian rapprochements.[233] More progress was therefore being made toward a triple entente of France, England, and Russia than Cromer even suspected.

The conclusion of the Anglo-French agreements themselves still required a great deal of time. Since the English were in a hurry, Delcassé saw his advantage and began to bargain. He tried without success to avoid giving up his Egyptian claims; and held out for compensations here and there. At one time the negotiations reached a deadlock, but after a while the business of give and take was resumed. War broke out between Russia and Japan in February of 1904 and proved a considerable embarrassment because England was allied to Japan and France to Russia; but it was quickly seen

[232] Maurois, *Edouard VII*, pp. 193; 204-205.
[233] Anderson, pp. 95-97.

that an Anglo-French entente was now all the more necessary if the spread of the war to Europe was to be prevented. On April 8, 1904, England and France signed the agreements, which became the foundation stone of the *entente cordiale*.

The accord of April 8, 1904, consisted of three documents: 1. A convention settling Anglo-French disputes in Newfoundland, and West and Central Africa. 2. A declaration in regard to Siam, Madagascar, and the New Hebrides, the most important provision of which was that marking out two spheres of influence in Siam. Delcassé took the basin of the Mekong, and England took her sphere in the region of the Malay peninsula. 3. A declaration in regard to Egypt and Morocco. The portion of this document given to the public press declared that there was no intention of altering the status of Morocco, but secret articles provided for changing the status of either Morocco or Egypt. In short, in return for giving Great Britain a free hand in Egypt, France was given a free hand in Morocco. The Moroccan agreement also contemplated that France would make a separate treaty with Spain to buy out her interests.

Delcassé had already signed a new treaty with Siam, February 13, 1904, which was calculated to supplement his main accord with England. The agreement with Spain was signed October 3, 1904. In this treaty, Spain gave her formal adhesion to the Anglo-French declaration of April 8, 1904. The secret clauses, like those of April 8, frankly contemplated a partition of Morocco,[234] but Spain now had to be content with a smaller share of Morocco than Delcassé had promised her in 1902.[235]

Having signed the accords, Delcassé was faced with the problem of securing their ratification. The difficulty in this connection lay in the fact that some of the secret articles were precisely those which made the agreements most worth while for France. A knowledge of these secret articles would therefore in all probability have facilitated ratification on the French side, but Delcassé intended to make the French Parliament "buy a pig in a covered basket," that is ratify the agree-

[234] S. B. Fay, *Origins of the World War*, p. 164.
[235] Anderson, p. 40.

ments in ignorance of the secret articles attached to them.

From the start, Delcassé had exhibited a desire to handle the whole business himself and to keep it as secret as possible. As late as January 8, 1904, he had not consulted his colleagues in the Cabinet even on the general question involved in the accord of April 8, and, in spite of the fact that the whole arrangement was intimately connected with colonial questions, as late as March 2 he had still not taken the French Colonial Minister into his confidence.[236] Moreover, there is good reason to believe that Delcassé never acquainted the majority of the Cabinet with the secret articles.[237]

The diminutive autocrat in charge at the Quai d'Orsay was therefore depending to a considerable extent on his own personal prestige and influence to secure ratification. During the last six years cabinets had come and gone, but Delcassé had remained at the post of Foreign Affairs, having preserved himself in the midst of the Dreyfus case, the first Nationalist crisis, the Déroulède affair, the campaign against his staunch friend, President Loubet, the burlesque conspiracy and the High Court Trial, the Church and State quarrel, and many other minor political convulsions. France had grown accustomed to the prospect of Delcassé's permanent reign. So well entrenched was he in his position that most people were willing to concede that he was the only living man who understood or was capable of disentangling the threads of France's diplomacy. He had become practically indispensable to his country, and he knew it. The most excitable legislative body in Europe listened to him with quiet awe and timid acquiescence whenever he deigned to favor them with the carefully prepared bits of "diplomatic reticence and patriotic fervor" which went for answers to interpellations.[238] That is to say, in spite of the occasional protest of a Socialist, in the Chamber and in the Senate, the words of Delcassé were regarded as law.

---

[236] Lord Newton, pp. 287-289; *B.D.*, II, No. 394, pp. 347-348.
[237] Lord Newton, pp. 341-342; Morel, *Diplomacy Revealed*, p. 54; L. Jerrold, *The Real France*, pp. 133-134; London *Times*, June 7, 1905.
[238] Halgan, *J.O., Sénat*, March 20, 1902, p. 509; Cochin, *J.O., Chambre*, March 25, 1902, pp. 1505-1506; *Manchester Guardian*, Feb. 23, 1923, p. 13.

He incarnated France, his voice was the voice of France, and all true Frenchmen bowed their heads as they listened to the oracle.[239]

These circumstances made Delcassé reasonably sure that his accords would be ratified, but suddenly an event occurred which threatened to ruin everything by precipitating a war between Great Britain and France's ally, Russia. During the night of October 21-22, 1904, the Russian Baltic fleet, en route for the Far East, sighted some vessels off Dogger Bank. There had been rumors of Japanese torpedo boats, and in a moment of panic the Russian fleet opened fire upon the suspicious-looking objects near them, which after all turned out to be only a number of harmless English trawlers. When these English boats put into the port of Hull with their dead and wounded, there was a storm of indignation in England. The British Channel fleet, Mediterranean fleet, and Reserve fleet joined forces and took up a position threatening the Russian fleet. The situation was exceedingly dangerous even for the French. If England intervened, France would be drawn into the war against her. Delcassé offered to act as mediator and, after moving heaven and earth, he persuaded both parties to settle the Hull affair by means of an international commission of inquest at Paris. The successful mediation of Delcassé in this Hull incident is perhaps the capital act of his career. He used his position as mediator not only to relieve the extreme tension of the moment but to draw England and Russia closer together and to propose an extension of the *entente cordiale* so as to include Russia and Italy as well as France and England. To be sure, he did not then and there create the Triple Entente of France, England, and Russia, but he had certainly prepared the way for it.[240]

The mediation in the Hull affair, coming as it did just before the senators and deputies took up the question of

---

[239] Jerrold, *The Real France*, pp. 126-127.
[240] M. de Taube, *La Politique Russe d'Avant Guerre* . . . (Paris, 1928) pp. 29-30; Michon, *Franco-Russian Alliance*, pp. 129-130; Lord Newton, *Lord Lansdowne*, pp. 339-340; Delcassé, *Annales de la Chambre*, July 20, 1909, p. 1526.

ratifying Delcassé's Anglo-French agreements, smoothed the path for parliamentary approbation, because it was, in the minds of the French people, a visible proof of the worth of the Anglo-French accord in securing the peace of Europe.[241] During the critical debates of November and December, Delcassé was ably supported in the first instance by Etienne, who said he would vote for the Anglo-French entente with both hands raised, and urged his friends in the Colonial Group to do the same. He admitted that the accord wounded certain "very respectable [colonial] interests" of France, but said that . . . "we desire to fortify our entente" with England, "because we have the feeling, the hope, that one day our country will be persuasive enough and perhaps strong enough to bring about in turn the entente of England and Russia."[242] In one of his own speeches, Delcassé told the Senate that it had under its eyes all the results of a foreign policy perfectly conceived, and executed during the past six years with method and stubbornness in spite of frequent difficulties and crises. He declared that this policy increased and fortified Indo-China by the establishment of the power of France in the basin of the Mekong; that it opened Morocco to the regenerative actions of France and had made Spain the neighbor and friend of France in Africa as she was neighbor and friend of France in Europe; that the policy carried with it the assurance that Italy and France would not be found in opposition to each other, but on the contrary that France would sympathetically view the development of Italian prosperity; and that, finally, it left both France and England happy because of the elimination of so many grave causes of suspicion and conflict, and led England to see in France, the ally of Russia, only a proven artisan of concord and peace.[243]

Nevertheless, those portions of the accord relating to Newfoundland and Egypt awakened a great deal of lusty opposition in the Chambers, and Delcassé felt obliged to promise

[241] Anderson, p. 108; Gooch, *Contemporary Review*, April, 1923, pp. 451-452.
[242] Etienne, Nov. 8, 1904, *J.O., Chambre*, pp. 2335 and 2339.
[243] Delcassé, Dec. 7, 1904, *J.O., Sénat*, p. 1050.

that he would reopen negotiations on the Newfoundland question. Jaurès, the socialist, supported the measures as likely to bring peace between France and England; but he was troubled in spirit because he heard the excited whispers of those who were planning to use the *entente* for less worthy purposes. Dragging the skeleton out of the closet, as was his wont, he showed that the new grouping of Powers could be used by the British to bring about the ruin of their German commercial rival, and that it could be used by the advocates of *Revanche* to win back Alsace-Lorraine. His speech was a clear warning to Delcassé to see the wisdom of rapprochement with Germany. He urged that the accord of April 8, 1904, be not used as an instrument of *Revanche,* but that the process of surrounding France with friends be extended to Germany too, and the peace of the world assured. In closing, he cautioned Delcassé not to follow a policy of spite and of non-coöperation with Germany.[244]

Amidst much patriotic language and some warnings, then, the accord of April 8, 1904, passed in the Chamber of Deputies on November 10, 1904, by a vote of 435 to 105, and in the Senate on December 7, 1904, by 215 votes to 37. On the English side, one member of the House of Commons prophesied that Germany would send in her bill, yet the English Parliament ratified the accord even before France, and the public received it with almost general applause.[245]

Ratification by both countries forged the last link in what was a visible sign and the first product of an *entente cordiale.* All of the outstanding disputes between England and France were settled or provisions made for their settlement. Anglo-French colonial friction ceased, because the French and the English were no longer rivals but friends. England had taken the first steps in the abandonment of her traditional policy of splendid isolation from the Continental Powers, and she had thrown her influence into the scales on the side of France.

---

[244] Jaurès, Nov. 10, 1904, *J.O., Chambre,* pp. 2376-2378.
[245] Anderson, pp. 105-106; *Cambridge History of British Foreign Policy,* III, 340; *D.D. S* 2, V, 22.

After doggedly making his way against innumerable and seemingly insuperable obstacles since 1898, Delcassé was at last rewarded by the realization of his long-desired entente with the greatest naval and colonial Power in the world! Thanks to the skilful diplomacy of the French Foreign Minister, this victory did not involve the sacrifice of any previous alliance or friendship. On the contrary, his supplementary accord with Spain guaranteed the continuance of amicable Franco-Spanish relations, and opportunity had been found to draw England and Russia closer together, thereby laying the foundation of a triple entente of France, England, and Russia. This was the outstanding diplomatic achievement of the Third Republic; and since the diplomacy of France was virtually the personal diplomacy of Delcassé, it was also, in a measure, his personal triumph.

IV

THE FALL FROM POWER
1898-1905

1. *Delcassé at the Height of His Power—His Achievements
and Political Position*

IT IS due to France's great Foreign Minister, and probably to him
alone, that the Republic has been safely guided through the
mazes of European politics . . . and that his country has again
taken the place in the world's councils to which her history, her
wealth and her position entitle her. . . .

. . . He has made himself well-nigh indispensable to France
and his place would be exceedingly difficult to fill. (*Philadelphia
Public Ledger,* April 23, 1905.)

WHEN Delcassé surveyed the political horizon of Europe
on December 8, 1904, the morning after the Senate
had ratified his accord with England, he could flatter himself
that he had been the chief author of a diplomatic revolution.
England had promised to give diplomatic support to the
French Government the moment any controversy arose in
Europe over Morocco. By the accord of April 8, Delcassé had
therefore gained a great deal more than the friendship of
England—he had the promise of English assistance in a matter
that could easily become a major European problem. In the
new balance of power, England was henceforth definitely
lined up on the side of France. Since Delcassé's mediation in
the Hull affair, Russia could be expected to become a third
member of this entente, after a little time and after the exercise of a little patience. Italy would be obliged to gravitate
in the same direction. With her long, defenseless coast lines
projecting out into the Mediterranean, she could not afford
to be hostile to the combined naval power of France and
England. The arrangements which Delcassé had made with

Italy in 1902 were therefore not only consolidated but guaranteed. Virtually the same thing was true of Spain. The naval power of France and England, the successful mediation of 1898, and the secret agreement giving Spain a portion of Morocco, enabled Delcassé to feel perfectly sure of Spanish friendship. In addition, the Franco-Russian Alliance had meanwhile been consolidated and transformed into a policy of action. The weakening of Russia by the Russo-Japanese War was to be deplored; but there were opportunities for compensation in the Balkans. The revolution which Delcassé had seen brewing in Serbia as early as 1887-88 occurred in 1903. The pro-Austrian rulers were slain and the new Serbian Government drew closer to Russia and also, on several occasions, sought to draw closer to France. Delcassé, with much graciousness and charm, welcomed these advances and won the gratitude of Serbia.[1] Lastly, thanks to his peaceful "conquest of the United States," Delcassé was assured of the friendship and good will of the greatest Power in the New World.[2] Of the alliances and ententes which had been recommended by him in his newspaper articles, all but the entente of France and Austria had been realized, and even that had seemed to be in the realm of posssibility in 1900 and 1901. During those years, a group of Hungarian patriots had offered to create a Franco-Russophile party in Hungary and to work for a Franco-Russo-Austro-Hungarian Alliance. Delcassé had listened to their plans, but suddenly broke off the consultations in 1901 when it became apparent that the scheme was going to involve the expenditure of French money and dangerous meddling in the internal politics of another country. The patriots, however, were undaunted and continued their agitation on their own account.[3] Moreover, as late as 1905, Delcassé

[1] Tardieu, *Questions Diplomatiques de 1904* (Paris, 1905) pp. 204-207; M. Boghitschewitsch, *Die Auswärtige Politik Serbiens 1903-1914* (3 vols., Berlin 1931) III, 13.

[2] Coubertin, *Chronique de France*, 1903, p. 51; *Revue de Paris*, July, 1905, pp. 218-223.

[3] J. Rimler, (a Hungarian diplomat) *De la nécessité de l'alliance Franco-Russo-Austro-Hongroise, pourparlers diplomatiques secrets entre M. Delcassé et des patriots Hongrois, 1899-1901* (Paris, 1901) pp. 1-111.

noted with satisfaction that Austria was an unsteady member of the Triple Alliance.[4] If the Franco-Austrian entente was not yet realized, Delcassé could nevertheless afford to be well satisfied with his accomplishments. Taken as a whole, he had brought into being a sympathetic grouping of France, Russia, Great Britain, Italy, Spain, Serbia, and the United States. Bismarck's vast diplomatic structure was crumbling. Germany was no longer the pivot of European politics; the states of Europe were beginning to gravitate around France instead. Unable to count with absolute assurance even upon Austria-Hungary, Germany was faced with the specter of diplomatic isolation and encirclement. Delcassé had accomplished a "moral *Revanche!*"[5]

Defending the policy of regulating the affairs of Europe by means of two opposing alliance systems, Delcassé said to the French Parliament that the maintenance of the balance of power had been the traditional policy of France and the principal object of his own diplomacy. The alliance system, he said, was the inevitable consequence of the formation of great, powerful national States which were approximately equal in strength, and which therefore found it increasingly difficult to execute their own particular policy or to make their will prevail in Europe. He believed that, since the profound transformation of Europe in the second half of the nineteenth century, it was no longer sufficient for a nation to be exceedingly strong itself: allies were necessary. Bismarck, although he had won the War of 1870, was the first to feel the need of outside assistance, and he was the founder of the alliance system. This gave Delcassé a talking point upon which he loved to dwell. If the victor of 1870 found allies necessary, how much more imperative was it for France, who had been weakened in 1870, to surround herself with powerful allies? The ideal alliance, said he, was that founded on (1) solidarity of national interests, (2) popular sympathy, (3) skill of the governments to put this sympathy to use, and (4) on the willing-

[4] Combarieu, pp. 303-304.
[5] The expression actually used by Coubertin in *Chronique de France*, 1903, p. 51.

ness of the two governments to persevere along the same line. It is significant that Delcassé did not mention signed documents. Essentially a realist, he believed that documents were superfluous if the above desiderata could be had. It was for this reason that he frequently said that he preferred a well-established entente to a formal alliance.[6]

With this philosophy of the European alliance system no one could find fault; but one may well ask if Delcassé had not done more than build up a counter alliance to the Triple Alliance. His sympathetic grouping of France, Russia, Great Britain, Italy, Spain, Serbia, and the United States was immeasurably stronger than Germany supported half-heartedly by Italy, by a tottering and uncertain Austria-Hungary, and by a not too certain Rumania. In his attempt to restore the balance of power in Europe, Delcassé had himself thrown it out of balance in favor of France. The result was a diplomatic triumph of the first magnitude, but one replete with danger because Germany could hardly be expected to resign herself to the new alignment of the Powers.

Delcassé had likewise enjoyed certain minor triumphs, of which we can enumerate only a few. He had proclaimed before all Europe the protectorate of France over the Catholic Christians of the East. He took the initiative with Russia in securing the freedom of Crete and, with the aid of England and Italy, made this freedom a reality. His note of September 30, 1900, during the Boxer crisis, was accepted in the main by all of the other Powers and became the basis of their settlement with China. At the expense of a little "treaty ink," he had extended the French color on the map of Africa to include vast regions many times greater than France in area. Moreover, the influence of France in the Moslem world, particularly in Morocco, had been greatly increased.[7]

All of this had been accomplished by Delcassé, working

[6] J.O., Sénat, March 20, 1902, pp. 508-509; Dec. 26, 1903, pp. 1679-1680; J.O., Chambre, Nov. 6, 1890, p. 1897; March 11, 1903, p. 1108; Paris, Nov. 21, 1888.

[7] L'Année Politique, 1899, pp. 38-39; same for 1900, pp. 116-117; J.O., Chambre, Jan. 21, 1902, p. 100; March 11, 1903, pp. 1107-1108; A. L. P. Dennis, Adventures in American Diplomacy, 1896-1906, (N.Y., 1928) pp. 235-236 (Boxer affair.)

virtually alone and often against contrary currents, but always with the sober approval of the great majority of French people. The masses gave little thought to diplomacy, but were impressed by the Paris Peace Conference, by the sojourn of the Italian fleet at Toulon, by the visits of the Russian royal family and the kings of Sweden, England, and Italy, and by Delcassé's own trips to the courts of St. Petersburg, Copenhagen, and London. To the man in the street, this was tangible evidence that Delcassé knew his business and that he was capable of looking after the best interests of France. The vanity of democratic France was also a little flattered by the thought that the French Minister of Foreign Affairs was the personal friend of numerous European monarchs, notably King Edward VII and the Czar of Russia, and besides everyone realized that these friendships gave him added authority in his negotiations with other Powers. In short, most Frenchmen were inclined to agree with the opinion of King Edward, who on one occasion turned toward Delcassé and said, "Just now the Concert of Europe has a good orchestra leader."[8]

Delcassé's popularity was all the greater because his meteoric rise had made no change in his outward appearance. His contacts with European sovereigns had brought him membership in innumerable orders of knighthood and, if the occasion demanded, he could decorate his chest with an enviable display of badges and ribbons; yet he remained approachable and easy to address and kept his air of bonhomie as well as his democratic habits, believing that a man honored himself in remaining true to his origin. He wanted his fellow townsmen and constituents to enjoy his good fortune. The mayors of Ariège were received at the palace of the Quai d'Orsay in 1900 and regaled and honored like sovereigns of great European states. Already, as Minister of Colonies, he had recruited "battalions of colonists and colonial officials" from Ariège, and many a fellow member of his Department owed his prosperity to Delcassé. Mindful of the struggles of his own youth, he retained a sympathy for those who, like himself, had to make their way in the world unaided, and he was always willing to lend them a helping hand. The people of Ariège followed his fortunes with affectionate attention, proud of the glory which he shed upon his native Department. He in turn thought constantly of his provincial friends. Of the three trans-Pyrenean railways which were to be built, Delcassé reserved two for Ariège, and it was near one of them at Ax-les-Thermes that he built the home to which he re-treated during the parliamentary vacations. A conversation between Delcassé and the Czar of Russia illustrates the same point. The Czar compared the people of his own country with those of France and, recognizing the shortcomings of the Russians, he said to Delcassé, "France is strong because she has men." Delcassé replied, "Napoleon, speaking of our Ariège, did not express himself differently."[9]

The affability of Delcassé, and perhaps even the oddities of his physique, endeared him to the cartoonist, the comic writers, and the journalists generally. He was stocky now and this, together with his small stature, caused the writers to allege that he had been a little crushed in from the top or folded up like an accordion. This "gnome" was the expression habitually used in speaking of him. Others were struck by the fact that Delcassé could look exceedingly combative at times, and likened him to a diminutive Vercingetorix. His steel-gray hair was unparted, cropped close and plastered down over his flat cranium in a manner which suggested the helmet of the Gallic chieftain. His long moustaches, iron constitution, resolute air, quickness and energy, likewise served to carry out the resemblance to the redoubtable Gallic warrior of Caesar's day. But, underneath this pugnacious exterior, the man Delcassé was quite different: good humored and gentle, a lover of flowers and dogs and quiet walks. The reporters liked him because, after all, he was one of them. He still looked more like a "supple, suave, keen-witted journalist" than like an old-style statesman. Then, too, he willingly gave them information, but at the same time they were forced to respect his

[9] Pérés, *J.O.*, March 2, 1923, p. 2049.

perfect mastery over his own tongue. He could not be inveigled into saying more than he wanted to say. Briefly, never before did a Minister have the friendship of so many journalists, and, as has been aptly remarked, this was one of the secrets of his political strength.[10]

The great majority of the ambassadors accredited to Paris appreciated him in the highest degree, captivated for the most part by his loyalty and by the largeness and justice of his views. The Spanish Ambassador was particularly fond of singing his praises.[11] This popularity was maintained in spite of the fact that the state dinners given by Delcassé were celebrated not for their pomp but for the excellent way in which the servants of the Quai d'Orsay were organized, for the careful manner in which the menus were planned and served, and for the great quantity of flowers in evidence on such occasions. The last was a reminder that the Minister of Foreign Affairs loved to cultivate flowers himself and that he had a special fondness for roses. The Minister also strove to be popular with the members of his own diplomatic corps. He maintained a close personal relationship with every one of them and often invited them to dine. At all of his dinners, the service was business-like and rapid. M. de Mohrenheim, French Ambassador to Russia, and an intimate friend of the Foreign Minister, complained that at Delcassé's one had to eat too fast; but Mohrenheim's criticism was generally taken to be a compliment, because he was a noted gourmand. Delcassé, on the other hand, was too much of a man of affairs to waste time in prolonging the pleasures of the table.[12]

Everybody admired his punctuality and his methodical habits. He still rose at five o'clock in the morning, and usually finished his day's work at the Quai d'Orsay before most people began theirs. Just before the midday meal, he would take a walk—ordinarily by himself—and preferably toward the Bois

[10] Recouly, Rev. Pol. et Parl., Dec., 1905, p. 539; Nuova Antologia, Vol. 185, p. 31.
[11] G.P., XX, 316-317; Comte de Maugny, Cinquante Ans de Souvenirs, 1859-1909 (Paris, 1914) pp. 275-276.
[12] Reynald, p. 37; Nuova Antologia, Vol. 185, p. 32.

de Boulogne because this son of the Ariège was still an ardent lover of natural beauty. After *déjeuner,* he was entirely free to devote himself to Parliament and to the exactions of the political situation. His sense of duty was strong. It is said that even on the occasion of very late sessions of the Chamber of Deputies, he would habitually return to the Quai d'Orsay to affix his signature to important diplomatic documents. As a rule, however, he was in bed by nine o'clock.

He was no less orderly and methodical in his work, and was capable of sustained application. When his family was absent from Paris, or when affairs were of a pressing nature, he would scarcely leave his desk at all. Often, on hot summer nights, he toiled there until his bedtime hour of nine. He was impatient at interruptions. The story goes that one day during his mediation in the Hull affair, he had the happy idea of stimulating the pourparlers by writing a personal letter to the Prime Minister of England. While he was writing it, an attaché burst into his office to apprize him of an exciting disturbance going on in Parliament, a sort of "boxing match" with General André as the center of interest. "Oh I don't give a damn!" said Delcassé, "I only want my dispatch to produce its effect!"[13] In truth, whenever Delcassé did anything, he put his whole soul into the work and for the time being had no thought for anything else.

President Loubet and Delcassé were warm personal friends. Both men were staunch defenders of the Franco-Russian Alliance. They had the same modest family background and the same democratic habits. On great state occasions they were wont to dress and act alike. For instance, at Toulon, during the reception of the uncle of the King of Italy and the Italian fleet, the President and Delcassé made one concession to the circumstances of the day—they each borrowed a cap from an officer in the French Marine.[14]

In short, Delcassé seemed well established at the Quai d'Orsay. The diplomatic service, his constituents in Ariège,

[13] *Nuova Antologia,* Vol. 185, pp. 31-32.
[14] Combarieu, VIII, IX, 124-125.

the Republican press, the President of France, and a majority
of the French people were all devoted to him. Only in one
quarter was there any serious danger to his political position.
There was a growing antagonism between Delcassé and certain members of Parliament, especially those in the Cabinet.
The Minister of Foreign Affairs had withdrawn into the
Quai d'Orsay like a god to Mount Olympus, and there he
serenely took counsel only with himself. Businesslike to the
nth degree, he was never seen loafing around at the Palais
Bourbon. He would not concede more than a few minutes to
its halls or conference rooms at the most, and this aloofness
inevitably excited ill-feeling in the hearts of certain men.
This feeling of dislike was intensified by the fact that Delcassé
hardly disguised his contempt for both Parliament and the
Cabinet. In the early days of his ministry, he openly avowed
that he had never been able to understand the abominable
pleasure which some parliamentarians took in continually
agitating that "scum," the Dreyfus case.[15] As early as October
of 1900, he was complaining that the members of Parliament
as a whole, and without exception, were the daily obstacles
to the pursuit of a national policy. The best of them were
impatient or indiscreet—compromisers, who too often forgot
national interests when elections were near at hand. Revert-
ing to his old idea of reforming the executive power, Delcassé
desired to reduce Parliament to its proper function of control
and to give the initiative in finance and legislation to the
Cabinet.[16] A bitter quarrel broke out between Delcassé and
the Colonial Group in 1902. Delcassé's system of territorial
trades was designed to establish French influence in Siam,
Morocco, and in Europe; but Etienne and his followers overlooked the gain and saw only what France was giving away.
They attacked Delcassé's Franco-Siamese Treaty of 1902 with
especial fury. Delcassé called in a host of journalists—"both
the light cavalry and the heavy cavalry"—to combat Etienne
and his cohorts and to prove to them that they were wrong,
but even so, the treaty of 1902 was lost.[17] This, together with

[15] *L'Année Politique*, 1899, p. 46.   [16] Combarieu, p. 93.
[17] Combarieu, pp. 217-220; Recouly, *Rev. Pol. et Parl.*, Dec., 1905, p. 539.

certain other happenings, caused Delcassé to become extremely pessimistic by February of 1903. He was convinced that Parliament had given itself over to the lowest appetites. Those who stirred up the Church and State quarrel and the quarrel with the Vatican seemed heedless of the effect it might have upon French prestige and diplomacy. Camille Pelletan, the Socialist Minister of Marine, seemed to be blithely on the way to scuttling the whole French navy. The budget of the War Department became the subject of a most degrading discussion. One group demanded the purchase of wines for the army from the south; another that the ciders should come from the west; no one thought of the army itself. In a conversation with Combarieu, President Loubet's Secretary, February 22, 1903, Delcassé denounced both Parliament and his colleagues in the Cabinet in no uncertain terms. The Ministry was for the most part composed of fanatics and imbeciles, he said. It was impossible to work with them for the general interest of the country.[18]

Combarieu received the impression that Delcassé wanted to close up the Chamber of Deputies and the Senate, and appeal to the people to support a government which would be responsible to the President of the Republic. He said that he was too tired to engineer this *coup d'état* himself, but thought that the President ought to try it. Finally he said that if no one else would undertake the enterprise, he himself would do his best at the instance of the President. Delcassé's pessimism could go no further—the program was Déroulède's, but "without Déroulède!"[19]

A state of acute tension between Delcassé and his colleagues existed throughout 1904. The untiring zeal displayed by Prime Minister Combes in keeping the Church quarrel alive exasperated and disgusted Delcassé. The Minister of War was preparing to reduce compulsory military service from three to two years, and was heedless of conditions in the army which destroyed the morale of the soldiers. The eccentric Minister of Marine was still playing havoc with the navy. "All

[18] Combarieu, pp. 228-230.   [19] *Ibid.*, pp. 228-230.

this is the very negation of my policy," Delcassé complained bitterly to Paléologue on March 29, 1904. However, when the Foreign Minister expressed the desire to give up office, his friend showed him that to do so would be very unwise. "The whole network of ententes and friendships which you have so patiently built up would be immediately destroyed. . . . Under present circumstances, your resignation would be a diplomatic disaster. You do not have the right to retire," he said.[20] In July 1904, the situation became almost intolerable. Delcassé offered to bring about the fall of the Combes Ministry, and to form a new Cabinet of his own; but President Loubet would not give his consent because the Premier had too strong a following in the Chambers and throughout the country.[21] Meanwhile the religious quarrel continued its devastating effect in dividing French society, and the army and navy remained in a state of weakness and unpreparedness.

Combes and his Cabinet fell on January 18, 1905. Delcassé's political position had become increasingly unsteady. A number of his friends, including Barrère, advised him to relinquish the reins of power. They reasoned that French diplomacy had achieved all of its objectives. The Foreign Minister had been in office six and a half years but, in the unstable political life of France, he could not possibly hope to remain in charge of the Quai d'Orsay forever. It would therefore be prudent for him to take this opportunity to retire before his policy became involved in his own political downfall.[22]

The task of forming a new Cabinet was confided to Maurice Rouvier. This man had begun his political career at Gambetta's side in 1867, had served in the *Grand Ministère* of 1881 as Minister of Commerce and Colonies, and had sustained the active colonial policy of Jules Ferry. He became Premier of France, and it will be remembered that Delcassé had congratulated him on keeping Flourens in office in 1887.

[20] Paléologue, *Un Grand Tournant de la Politique Mondiale (1904-1906)* pp. 44-46; Combarieu, pp. 285-287.

[21] Combarieu, pp. 286-287.

[22] Barrère, interview already cited, and in *Revue des Deux Mondes*, Aug. 1, 1932, pp. 611-612.

More recently, as Minister of Finance in the Combes Cabinet, he had quarreled with Delcassé over the question of joint French and German participation in certain financial projects in the East. Rouvier was anxious to coöperate with Germany; but Delcassé held out for positive guarantees to French interests, and so seemed to be placing obstacles in Rouvier's way. Then matters were made even worse by the fact that Rouvier approved a new Russian loan without first consulting Delcassé as to political conditions.[23]

As a result of this persistent antagonism between the two men, Rouvier was at first minded to give Delcassé's place at the Quai d'Orsay to someone else. He actually offered the post to a diplomat well qualified to hold it, but this gentleman, instead of accepting, warned Delcassé of Rouvier's unfriendly action. Delcassé and Rouvier therefore had no illusions about each other. Yet, in the end, political circumstances were such that Rouvier felt obliged to invite Delcassé to become a member of the new Cabinet. The other members were to be Etienne, who had led the opposition to Delcassé's Siamese Treaty of 1902 and who had been lukewarm toward Delcassé ever since; Bienvenu-Martin, whom Delcassé had dropped from the Colonial Office in 1894 and who was now known as a militant anti-clerical; Chaumié, whom Delcassé had disobliged in the question of intervening on behalf of the Boers; Gaston Thomson, a former editor of the *République Française* who had supported Gambetta and Jules Ferry in Parliament; and five other Republicans of lesser note, four of whom belonged to the left wing of the Republican party: Gauthier (Right), Ruau, Clementel, Berteaux, and Dubief. Of these last, Ruau had been a supporter of Combes, Berteaux was a believer in separation of Church and State, and Clementel was committeed to the idea of reducing compulsory military service to two years. On the whole, this was strange company for Delcassé to keep, particularly when his friends had urged him to retire, yet his decision to remain in

[23] *Documents Diplomatiques* 2 S., Vol. III, 27, 46, 102-104, 450-454, 469-492, and pp. 240, 413.

office was natural enough. He had grown accustomed to carrying on the foreign affairs of France without reference to the political opinions of his colleagues in the Cabinet and without having much contact with the other Ministers. If he had very little sympathy for Rouvier's Cabinet, it could also be argued that he had had just as little sympathy for Combes and his followers. In the second place, after the hard labor and disappointments of the early years, his diplomacy was just beginning to bear its first fruits. How disagreeable it was to contemplate resignation when in a few more months he might be able to reap the golden harvest himself; How tempting it was to remain in office to consolidate his ententes and, above all, to draw England and Russia still closer together![24] But, in any case, did not the personal character of French diplomacy from 1898 to 1905 make retirement difficult if not impossible? The Delcassé system of ententes might collapse altogether under a less able successor. Finally, Delcassé's name was inseparably connected with this system. If he did not remain in office to defend it, would he not be open to the charge of shirking his responsibilities?[25]

The Rouvier Cabinet was formed, January 23, 1905, with Delcassé as Minister of Foreign Affairs. Four days later, Delcassé was called on to defend his policy toward Russia. The failure of Russian campaigns during the Russo-Japanese War intensified political disturbances at home. Retaliating against strikes and disorders, the Russian Government shot down a number of workers and some women and children. These "massacres" created a storm of protest in France against the Franco-Russian Alliance. Maurice Allard interpellated Delcassé in the Chamber of Deputies and asked if France should remain coupled with such a nation. For the sake of the Alliance, Delcassé mounted the tribune in an effort to smooth over French opinion. He was greeted by loud and prolonged applause from a great number of benches, but the Left declaimed against him in excited tones. For a moment nothing

[24] B.D., III, No. 96, p. 78.
[25] Barrère, Revue des Deux Mondes, Aug. 1, 1932, p. 612.

could be heard but this uproar. At length the Chamber quieted down sufficiently for Delcassé to begin speaking. The Left, however, continued to jeer and heckle. The interruptions came with such frequency that Delcassé had to speak in half sentences or even single phrases. He argued that instead of judging Russia, they should think of French interests. Jaurès denounced the Foreign Minister for defending a government which had steeped its hands in blood. Delcassé replied that he only defended the interests of France. He pointed out that Russia was engaged in a serious war and that strikes in Russia weakened her in this moment of danger. Finally, he reminded them that the Franco-Russian Alliance gave security to France, and said that it had permitted him to strive after, and achieve, a series of invaluable international accords and to look properly after French affairs in all parts of the world.[26] These arguments satisfied the Chamber, but Clemenceau kept the subject alive by carrying on the attack in the *Aurore*.

Meanwhile Delcassé became involved in other difficulties on Russia's account. Anxious to help his ally in every way possible, he violated the spirit but not the letter of international law while the Russian Baltic fleet was en route for the East. The Russian men-of-war, to the great indignation of Japan, sojourned an uncommonly long time in French waters at Nossi-Be, Kamranh Bay, and Saigon. Energetic opposition to the irregularity of Delcassé's actions developed in France under the leadership of F. de Pressensé, parliamentarian and journalist; and not content with intervening in Parliament during the month of January, this group in the first part of April took up their cause with the French Premier. They maintained that Delcassé was criminally playing with fire and that the Russo-Japanese War might be spread to Europe.[27]

This growing opposition to Delcassé was coeval with a long series of Russian reverses culminating in the disastrous defeat

[26] *Annales de la Chambre*, Jan. 27, 1905, pp. 92-93.
[27] A. S. Hershey, *The International Law and Diplomacy of the Russo-Japanese War* (N.Y., 1906) pp. 193-198; Pressensé, *Monthly Review*, July, 1905, p. 25.

at Mukden, March 1905. The battle greatly weakened the prestige of Russia, and the value of the Franco-Russian Alliance sank accordingly. Since Delcassé prided himself on being the man of the Franco-Russian Alliance, his political position was in the same measure undermined. Equally awkward was the fact that, until the last minute, Delcassé had refused to believe in the possibility of a Russo-Japanese War and had prophesied that if it came, Russia would be victorious.[28] The battle of Mukden did not provoke an immediate political crisis in France, but Delcassé was cast in the rôle of a bad prophet at a time when he could least afford to play such a part. It was as though the Delphic Oracle had been in a measure discredited, or the Pope caught on a delicate point involving infallibility at a time when the Papal throne was none too secure.

Nevertheless, Delcassé might well have remained in office to reap the rich harvest of his system of ententes. It mattered little that the Socialists and men of the extreme Left disliked him, that Nationalists, Royalists, Moderates, and men of the Right were unfriendly, and that many Radicals, Radical Socialists, colonial jingoes, and anti-clericals tolerated him with a bad grace. In the ordinary course of French politics, these conflicting, and even antagonistic, groups could never hope to coöperate with each other or meet on a common ground. Storm clouds were certainly gathering on the horizon in opposite points of the compass, but there was no necessary reason why they should coalesce over Delcassé's head. For instance, the collapse of Russia might have been used as a common meeting ground for a concerted attack upon Delcassé, but the dissatisfied elements allowed the Foreign Minister to go seemingly unscathed.[29] The real weakness of Delcassé's position did not become apparent until Germany attempted to check him in the midst of his vigorous penetration of Morocco; but, in order to understand this German

[28] *J.O.*, *Sénat*, Dec. 26, 1903; *G.P.*, XIX, 165-167; Paléologue, *Un Grand Tournant* . . . , pp. 8, 14, and 22.
[29] Schuman, p. 156.

attack upon Delcassé, it will be necessary to summarize the latter's relations with Germany from 1898 to 1905.

2. *Delcassé and Germany, 1898 to March 31, 1905*

What intimacy would you like to have between France and Germany so long as the gulf of Alsace-Lorraine separates the two countries? (Delcassé to Paléologue, May 10, 1905.)

Since Delcassé had reversed Hanotaux's policy toward Germany, Franco-German relations had been characterized by coldness and misunderstandings on both sides. German diplomacy and French diplomacy were alike to blame for the failure to reach a Franco-German rapprochement.

During the most critical period of the Fashoda Crisis, Delcassé had hinted to the British that he might come to terms with Germany in an arrangement directed against England if the British did not take a more compromising stand. This was not an idle threat. In the latter part of November 1898, he talked for more than an hour with Arthur Huhn, Berlin correspondent of the *Koelnische Zeitung*. Delcassé expressed great indignation at the way in which he had been treated by the English. They made him "swallow a toad frog every day," and the end wasn't even in sight, he complained. Then, coming to the subject of his conversation, he carefully avoided the word alliance but said to Huhn that France and Germany ought to pursue a common policy in the face of English encroachments. By a mutually friendly attitude, the gulf which separated the two countries could be overcome. Practical means to this end could be found in French colonial policy. France was already over-supplied with colonial territory and hence could look kindly upon German expansion, particularly in China. "It is necessary to go back to the policy of sixteen years standing," he said. The *Revanche* idea had lost many partisans in the last few years; and, in the arrangements entered into by Germany and France, Russia would stand in between as a guarantee, and would give additional weight to the engagements undertaken by the French Government. When the question of political opposition to a Franco-German rapprochement came up during the conversation, Delcassé said that he saw no reason why any minister should not avow the policy before Parliament. "I shall do it tomorrow if you wish!" he declared.[30]

News of this unofficial overture reached the German Foreign Office early in December 1898, but the German Government did not follow up the French move. On December 20, 1898, Prince Radolin, then German Ambassador at St. Petersburg, informed Hohenlohe that he had learned from Russian sources that France desired nothing more ardently than to come to terms with Germany, and that it was possible to effect a Franco-German rapprochement which would serve as a basis for a pacific entente of all of the Continental Powers. In his opinion, it was only necessary to be polite and to flatter the vanity of the French in order to obtain this end. The German Foreign Office and the Kaiser again remained unresponsive. The Kaiser felt that the French overtures had come too late. To his mind, they should have been made three years sooner, during the Transvaal controversy. Any arrangement that Germany and France might make at this time, when the Fashoda fever was still alive, would have its point directed against England; but just now the Kaiser did not care to antagonize England.[31] Moreover, the German diplomatic service despised Delcassé on the ground that he was not a professional diplomat. They saw in him a mere politician who knew nothing about diplomacy, and who ought to have disavowed Marchand from the very beginning, but who had created embarrassing difficulties for himself and for his country "by climbing up on such a high horse."[32] In any case, the Kaiser had not the slightest desire to extricate Delcassé from the Fashoda Crisis. In the first place, he wanted just such conflicts between France and England because they tended to force England into the arms of Germany. In the second place, he believed that these French advances were inspired

[30] G.P., XIII, 247-254.
[31] Ibid., XIII, 196-198; XIV, pt. 2, pp. 391-393 and notes.
[32] Ibid., XIII, 238-242; XIV, pt. 2, pp. 391-393 and notes in both cases.

by nothing more nor less than fear of England and that as soon as the danger was over, France would turn her back on Germany at the first opportunity. He was determined that Germany should not be naïve in her relations with France and that Germany should not be imposed upon so easily.[33]

On the French side, the problem of Alsace-Lorraine was the chief obstacle. A conversation between Delcassé and Adolph Rey, an Alsace-Lorrainer, throws much light on this aspect of the Franco-German question. Delcassé and Rey conversed freely with each other in the first part of February 1899.

"How goes it in Alsace-Lorraine?" queried Delcassé.

"Very well," replied Rey.

"What is the sentiment of the people there?" asked the French Foreign Minister.

Rey answered that it was very difficult to summarize the opinion of so many people. Delcassé saw the reasonableness of this view, but continued his questioning.

"Do you believe that the German Kaiser would come to an understanding with France on the ground of a retrocession of Alsace-Lorraine in return for a French colony?"

Rey answered, "Do you wish me to tell you the truth, freely and openly, and without empty phraseology?"

"Yes," said Delcassé, and he explained that he was anxious to have the opinion of a cultured man who was neither a diplomat nor a German official but who, at the same time, knew France and Germany equally well. He urged Rey to speak frankly and openly, and said that he would be grateful to him. Rey promised to do so and said that the German Kaiser would never cede a piece of German territory to another Power, never under any circumstances, because the legacy of his fathers was holy to him and he would defend it with his own person. But, said Rey, even if the Kaiser were willing to abandon a portion of his territory, the German people would not let him. Alsace-Lorraine was holy to them too, and they would give their last drop of blood for it.

Delcassé interrupted, saying, "Yes, doubtless that is the way

[33] *Ibid.*, XIII, 196-198, 238-242 and notes of the Kaiser; XV, 164-165.

the officials in Alsace-Lorraine speak—they who do not wish
to leave this beautiful land, this garden!"

On the contrary, such was the opinion of all Germany, said
Rey, and he reminded the Foreign Minister that he knew the
feeling of the German people because he traveled all over
that country. Delcassé then asked him point-blank for the
opinion of the Alsace-Lorrainers. In reply to this, Rey said
that at the age of sixteen he had fought on the French side in
the War of 1870, that he had been wounded in the right arm
and still suffered from the wound. He declared that he had
loved his French Fatherland, and wished France to be great
and happy, but said that Alsace-Lorraine had been more or
less Germanized since 1870 and was content. Alsace-Lorraine
still had a deep sympathy for France, but did not desire a war
of liberation. She only desired that France and Germany
should be friends. Delcassé was deeply moved, and gave Rey
both hands as he thanked him. The conversation had confirmed Delcassé's conclusion of 1888 respecting the problem
of Alsace-Lorraine: Germany would never give it back until
she was forced to do so.[34]

Shortly thereafter, Delcassé concentrated more than ever
on winning the friendship of England. News of this, too, was
reported to the German Foreign Office. The Kaiser refused
to believe that Delcassé would ever be successful. On the
margin of the German diplomatic document which informed
him of Delcassé's latest tactics, he wrote, "The poor man!
He doesn't know John Bull."[35]

Relations with Germany were therefore still anything but
cordial when the First Hague Conference met (May-July,
1899). Delcassé's attitude toward this conference was cynical
and ironical in the highest degree. When he spoke of the
forthcoming disarmament conference on January 23, 1899,
he said that French sympathy for the Emperor Nicholas' proposal was acquired in advance because the idea of disarma-

[34] Hohenlohe-Schillingsfürst, *Denkurdigkeiten Der Reichskanzlerzeit* (Stuttgart, Berlin, 1931) pp. 483-485; Delcassé, *Paris*, March 6, 1888; also March 21,
1888.
[35] *G.P.*, XIV, pt. 2, pp. 423-425 and note 1.

ment was its own recommendation. Everybody would save great sums of money. France had never before been in such complete accord with Russia or relations more confidential. France herself, at divers periods of her history, and notably just before the War of 1870, had conceived and wished to execute the same magnanimous design that Nicholas II now contemplated. (This was not far from the truth. The Czar's proposal originated in the Russian War Office and was calculated to place Austria at a disadvantage as over against the superior man-power of Russia; the chief concern of Napoleon III in 1870 seems to have been to retard the unification of Germany.[36]) Toward the end, Delcassé promised that, at the international conference, the French representatives would "work with all the other Powers for the realization of the humanitarian proposal of the Emperor Nicholas."[37] Nevertheless, just before the Hague Conference began its deliberations, Delcassé joined with Germany in wrecking the disarmament proposal. He seems never to have had any real faith in either peace conferences or disarmament,[38] and said to the German Ambassador, Count Munster, in the latter part of April, 1899:

We have quite the same interest in this Conference that you have. You do not wish to limit your power of defense at this moment nor to have anything to do with proposals for disarmament. We are entirely of the same opinion.

We both wish to spare the Czar and to seek a formula for side-stepping this question, but not to have any part in anything which could weaken our power of defense.

In order to avoid a complete fiasco, we shall possibly be able to make some concessions with reference to arbitration. But these must in no way limit the complete independence of the Great States.

[36] E. J. Dillon, *The Eclipse of Russia* (London, 1918) pp. 272-278; Chas. A. Beard, *Harpers Magazine*, Jan., 1929; H. Oncken, *Napoleon III and the Rhine* (New York, 1928) pp. 113-122; 144-149.

[37] *Annales de la Chambre*, Jan. 23, 1899, p. 119.

[38] *Paris*, July 22, 1888, and May 16, 1899; *J.O., Chambre*, March 11, 1903, p. 1107: "In this world, as it is organized today, I doubt if disarmament will ever be capable of realization. . . . I doubt if people will ever be willing to give themselves guarantees of their own existence."

. . . Besides the Czar, we must also spare the public opinion of Europe, since this has been aroused by the senseless step of the Russians.[39]

Even in this matter Germany and France were not in complete harmony. The Kaiser vetoed Delcassé's suggestion that they work for a high-sounding but innocuous arbitration clause.[40] Concordant action with France in the Portuguese question would have been a pleasure; but, in this instance, Delcassé's enthusiastic support had the appearance of inviting Germany to cut her own throat. The Kaiser remained suspicious.

By August of 1899, the ill-feeling between Bülow and Delcassé had grown considerably. The French Foreign Minister "ostentatiously" avoided Berlin on his trip to Russia in August of that year, and during the same month, Bülow felt called upon to caution the German Foreign Office that he did not desire Russia to act as *"honnête courtier"* between France and Germany. Relations between the two countries were normal from the point of view of diplomacy, he said, and all questions could be treated directly between Berlin and Paris. But, before many months had passed, Bülow was hearkening to Mouravieff, who told him that Delcassé was quite obsessed with the idea of revenge for 1870. "Delcassé," said Mouravieff, "is a maniac, who subordinates everything to the idea of *Revanche.* He sees only Strasbourg, without thinking of the superior interests of Europe or of the monarchical interests, which for you as for us should be the first consideration and which should unite our two countries."[41]

At the beginning of March 1900, the German Ambassador in Paris reported with no little satisfaction that Delcassé was not getting along very well in his attempt to win over the English. Like the Kaiser, this German diplomat refused to believe that Delcassé would ever effect an entente with Great Britain or that Russia and England could be reconciled. "The

[39] *G.P.*, XV, 186.   [40] *Ibid.*, p. 186 and notes.
[41] Bernhard von Bülow, *Memoirs of Prince von Bülow, 1897-1903* (Boston, 1931) I, 354; *G.P.*, XIII, 278.

French know nothing about foreign policy and have eyes only for what they desire," he said. He went on to say that popular hatred of England manifested itself in France with greater strength than formerly and that it would be possible to arrive at a Franco-German entente by gradual steps.[42] In order to refute the idea that Alsace-Lorraine stood in the way, the Kaiser quoted a telegram of Delcassé to Noailles, which stated that the French Government recognized "without mental reservations" *(sans arrière-pensée)* the frontiers of Germany as they were established by the Treaty of Frankfort.[43] Whether Delcassé really meant this and whether or not he had put his heart into it, it is difficult to say. Diplomacy is not a perfectly straightforward game. As expressed in his newspaper article of 1887, Delcassé's feeling on this subject was that France, in her relations with Germany, would respect the Treaty of Frankfort to the letter, since it was a legal obligation, but yet would never consent to think of it as being beyond revision.[44]

At any rate, Franco-German relations did not improve but grew steadily worse. When the question of intervention on behalf of the Boers came up in 1900, the Kaiser's suggestions and actions made Delcassé profoundly suspicious.[45] Five months later, both Delcassé and President Loubet were angered by the aggressive manner in which William II pushed the candidacy of Count Waldersée as commander of all the foreign troops in China during the Boxer uprising. At this time, the attitude of Delcassé was "correct" but "cold." In October of 1900, Delcassé and the Kaiser were again in disagreement over the questions of punishing the Chinese rebels and of the demands which should be made upon China.[46]

Yet, at this very moment, Spain was making earnest efforts to bring Germany and France together. Spanish fear of England, during the Spanish-American War and immediately

---

[42] *G.P.*, XVIII, pt. 2, pp. 765-766.

[43] *G.P.*, XV, 519-520 and note 6. "Le Gouvernement reconnaît sans arrière-pensé les frontières de l'Allemagne comme elles sont délimitées par le Traité de Francfort."

[44] *Paris*, July 29, 1887.

[45] Combarieu, p. 52.   [46] Combarieu, pp. 83-85; 92-93; 96-97.

after that conflict, caused certain Spanish leaders to work for a defensive alliance with France, Germany, and Russia. From 1899 until 1902, the Spanish Ambassador, Leon y Castillo, acted as a would-be mediator between France and Germany. For the sake of his Moroccan accord with Spain and for the sake of cordial relations with the Spanish Government, Delcassé allowed these mediation attempts to drag on year after year, but he did little or nothing on his own account to encourage them. He declared himself willing to converse with Germany on certain points and to reach an understanding, but said that he represented the nation which had been defeated in 1870 and that consequently Germany would have to take the initiative in the discussions.[47] Leon y Castillo then urged Germany "to strike while the iron was hot," but the German response was that the *sine qua non* of such an arrangement must be found in a mutual guarantee by Germany and France of each other's territorial integrity[48]—a requirement that made the Spanish mediation hopeless, because Delcassé had warned Leon y Castillo that the French Government had an eye to public opinion in France and was not in a position to speak of renouncing Alsace-Lorraine.[49]

On another occasion when this question of a mutual territorial guarantee had arisen, Delcassé said privately:

They ask us to sign the Treaty of Frankfort a second time. France cannot give up the Alsatians.

.   .   .   .

A nation is not dishonored when she is beaten, or when, with an enemy's knife at her throat, she signs a disastrous treaty. But she is dishonored when she ceases to protest, when she gives assent to her ruin. Misfortune is not defeat, but renouncement is.[50]

Since this was Delcassé's real attitude toward Germany,[51] it is probable that he did not seriously desire a rapprochement,

---

[47] *G.P.*, XV, 125-127; XVIII, pt. 2, pp. 772f., 775, and 777f.
[48] *Ibid.*, XVIII, 778ff.   [49] *Ibid.*, XVIII, pt. 2, 774-777.
[50] S. Lauzanne, *Great Men and Great Days*, pp. 8-9.
[51] A similar statement by Delcassé is to be found in M. Paléologue, *Un Prélude à l'Invasion de la Belgique, le Plan Schlieffen, 1904*, (Paris, 1932) pp. 80-81. Poincaré, *J.O.*, March 1, 1923, p. 2017: "Delcassé had guarded in his heart the wound of 1870." Victor Bérard (a close friend), *J.O.*, March 2, 1923,

but only wished to seem accommodating to his Spanish colleagues with whom he was negotiating over Morocco.[52] The suspicious and cautious nature of German diplomacy enabled Delcassé to go a long way in obliging Spain. Urged on by the Spanish and Russian governments, Delcassé in October of 1901 expressed a desire to meet Count Bülow and to speak to him in person. If Bülow would come to Paris secretly, he promised to make a public visit to Berlin in return. Bülow refused to take the risk. The French people and the French Government were not yet sufficiently desirous of a German rapprochement, in his opinion, and he therefore put off the matter until a more opportune moment. Thus the sincerity of Delcassé's overture was never tested, and this attempt at rapprochement failed like all the others.[53]

In March 1902, France officially proposed a certain hand-in-hand policy between France and Germany regarding East Asiatic questions, and in June made similar proposals with regard to Siam. Inasmuch as this was the first time since 1870 that France had officially proposed working together with Germany, the Secretary of the German Foreign Office, Baron Richthofen, thought that the matter was of considerable importance, but his superiors in the Foreign Office did not see fit to take advantage of the French suggestions, which therefore came to naught.[54]

The Spanish Ambassador was again trying to promote a rapprochement of France and Germany in October of 1902 and, with that object in mind, talked long and earnestly with both the German Ambassador in Paris and Delcassé. He reminded the German Government that on the occasion of two

---

p. 2050: "Delcassé was convinced that, after thirty years of insolence, the days of Prussian Germany were counted and that France could and should appear to the West . . . not only as the claimant of the Provinces which had been taken away and those sons of hers placed under subjection, but also as the champion of the dignity and liberty of humanity." See also the view of André Mévil (another close friend) in *Echo de Paris*, Feb. 28, 1923.

[52] W. Mommsen, *Archiv für Politik und Geschichte*, Dec., 1924, p. 590; Combarieu, p. 52.

[53] *G.P.*, XVIII, 782ff. and 785.

[54] *G.P.*, XVIII, 794-796; also 802ff.; Anderson, p. 49.

former mediation attempts by Spain, Delcassé had been dis-posed to treat with Germany; and, at the same time, he told Delcassé that France was committing a fault in not resigning herself to the loss of her provinces.[55] Delcassé replied:

> But I do not believe that Germany wishes to come to terms with France. . . . Four years ago it was said to M. de Noailles at Berlin that the two countries might be able to come to an accord on certain points. I found the matter to be so important that I went immediately to the President of the Republic and the Premier. I was authorized by them to telegraph Noailles that we were dis-posed to treat with Germany on all points on which the two countries would be able to agree. He answered that they had sig-nified to him at the *Wilhelmstrasse* that the question was impor-tant enough to deserve study. That was four years ago! In all these four years, not a word more has been said on this subject to Noailles. Our Ambassador is still waiting for a response. I am still disposed to discuss the question, but they must [first] speak to me. Let the reply come to me from Berlin![56]

When this assertion was reported to Bülow, the German Chancellor flatly denied that any such advances had ever been made by Delcassé. The French Ambassador had never dis-cussed the matter except in an "academic way"—no concrete propositions had ever been made to Germany.[57]

Bülow's denial was reported back to Delcassé early in De-cember 1902. His comment was, "Then M. de Noailles must be crazy!" The incident referred to by Delcassé and Bülow seems to have occurred in the latter part of October 1899. According to Stephane Lauzanne, Delcassé's friend, who cites a dispatch alleged to be in the archives of the Quai d'Orsay in Delcassé's own handwriting, Bülow proposed that France and Germany come to an understanding; but Delcassé suspected Bülow of trying to trap him. He feared that the Chancellor wanted him to enumerate the terms of a possible Franco-German treaty only so that he could inform England, Italy, and Spain of those parts of the French proposal likely to be

---

[55] *G.P.*, XVIII, 782f., 797ff. [56] *G.P.*, XVIII, 797ff.
[57] *Ibid.*, XVIII, 799-800.

offensive to them. Thus France would be trapped again as Bismarck had trapped her in the time of Emile Ollivier and Napoleon III. Lauzanne says that, after consulting the President and the Premier (Waldeck-Rousseau), Delcassé sent the following dispatch to Berlin on October 30, 1899, and Noailles officially communicated it to Bülow on the thirty-first of the same month:

. . . That, since France had asked for nothing, she should not take the initiative in laying down the conditions of which M. von Bülow had spoken; that she was waiting until Germany should formulate the proposals she intended to make, and that these proposals would receive a most careful examination on the part of the French Government, with the single reservation that, in any case, they should not be of such a nature as to disturb the Franco-Russian alliance.[58]

If Lauzanne's account is correct, Delcassé's reply to Berlin lacked concreteness because Delcassé feared a trap. He preferred to make Bülow state his propositions first, but this Bülow would not do. Mutual suspicion and distrust ruined this attempt at rapprochement in the first instance; the ill-humored discussions of 1902 which resurrected the dead negotiations only increased the bitter feeling between Berlin and Paris. Delcassé and Bülow had avoided calling each other a liar only by making a scapegoat of Noailles.

By April of 1903, it was reported to the German Foreign Office that Delcassé's attitude toward the German Ambassador in Paris, although outwardly correct, was nevertheless verging on impoliteness. He would converse with other foreign ambassadors by the hour, but he regularly dismissed the German Ambassador after a five-minute chat. This discrimination wounded the pride of the German Ambassador and convinced Bülow of Delcassé's "ingrained hatred" of Germany.[59]

During that same year, Delcassé reversed his attitude on the question of the Bagdad railway. Rouvier, then French

[58] Lauzanne, *Great Men and Great Days*, pp. 10-11. See Delcassé to Bihourd, June 1, 1905, *D.D.*, 2 S., VI, 569 (summary of the letter).
[59] *G.P.*, XVIII, 799f., 801-802.

Minister of Finance, and the French bankers strongly favored participating with Germany in this undertaking. Delcassé at first gave his consent provided France was accorded absolute equality with Germany in the management of the road. But Russia absolutely disapproved of the Bagdad railway being built, and, in the meantime, Delcassé became suspicious of the guarantees that Germany was offering to French interests, and consequently began to oppose the project with all his strength. He also turned against a proposal for consolidating the Ottoman debt which he feared would hasten the construction of the road by liberating Turkish funds.[60]

Meanwhile the success of Delcassé's diplomacy had been very disquieting to Bülow. At first he attempted to make light of Delcassé's triumphs. Upon the conclusion of the latter's entente with Italy, Bülow put on his accustomed air of optimism and nonchalance, and said to the Reichstag, January 8, 1902:

> The Triple Alliance still enjoys the best of health. . . . I would not consider it proper if even a small part of the German Press should show any uneasiness over Franco-Italian agreements. In a happy marriage the husband must not become jealous if his wife dances an extra round with someone else. The main thing is that she does not run away with him, and she will not do so if she is best situated with him. . . .[61]

Delcassé, though, was not content with one "extra round." After the conclusion of the accord with Italy, he and Barrère carried on an active courtship of the Italian Government with the intention of drawing Italy completely out of the Triple Alliance and over into the camp of France and Russia.[62] With this in mind, Barrère did everything he could to create friction between Italy and Austria.[63] In the spring

---

[60] *D.D.*, 2 S., III, 27, 46, 102-104, 450-455, 469-471, 479-480, 487-492; S. B. Fay, *"Documents Diplomatiques Français"* in *American Historical Review*, April, 1933, p. 556.

[61] Anderson, p. 27.

[62] *D.D.*, 2 S., IV, 191-203, 309f., 385-389, 404f., 408, 416, 429f., 510f.; 2 S., V, 111. G. Giolitti, *Memoirs of My Life* (London, 1923) p. 183.

[63] *B.D.*, V, 74; Anderson, pp. 143-145.

of 1904, German resentment reached critical proportions when Italy and her King insisted upon drinking toasts to France and President Loubet (then visiting in Italy with Delcassé) without mentioning the existence of the Triple Alliance. Germany demanded that no more such toasts be made; yet, at Naples, the King of Italy again exchanged toasts with Loubet without speaking of the Alliance.[64] Bülow thought of dissolving the German connection with Italy, but gave up the idea for the sake of appearances. "One would say that our policy since the retirement of Bismarck has lost us first the alliance with Russia, then good relations with England, and finally the Triple Alliance itself."[65]

As we have seen, William II, Bülow, and Holstein for a long time remained untroubled by Delcassé's efforts to create an entente with England and a triple entente of France, England, and Russia. They argued that such combinations, if possible at all, lay far in the future. When Russia announced verbally that she approved of the Anglo-French and the Franco-Italian rapprochements, and when the Anglo-French agreement was actually signed, the three erst-while optimists received a most unpleasant shock. Bülow and Holstein became concerned for German prestige, and William II began to suffer from the "nightmare" of anti-German coalitions.[66] Bülow at once saw that the Anglo-French entente increased the drawing force of France on Italy,[67] but when he rose to calm the fears of the more thoughtful members of the German Reichstag on April 12 and 14, 1904, he assumed his usual air of indifference: "We have no reason to suppose that the Anglo-French colonial accord is directed at any other Power . . . from the standpoint of German interests we have nothing to object," he said, though he promised to protect German economic interests in Morocco. He scoffed at the idea that Germany was diplomatically isolated and added: "If we keep our sword sharp, we need not fear isolation very much. Ger-

---

[64] Anderson, pp. 144-147; *D.D.*, 2 S., V, 103-104; 111.
[65] *G.P.*, XX, 78; Anderson, p. 146.
[66] Anderson, pp. 135-143; 159.   [67] *Ibid.*, p. 143.

many is too strong not to be able to make alliances. Many combinations are possible for us."[68]

Faced with the collapse of German prestige and security, Bülow endeavored to strike back at Delcassé in the latter part of April 1904, when the French Minister of Foreign Affairs was making his supplementary accord with Spain over Morocco. Delcassé was bent upon making Spain accept a smaller portion of Morocco than he had offered her in his earlier treaty of 1902. Spain appealed to Germany for aid in the hope of getting a larger share. Bülow willingly went to the assistance of the Spanish Government but soon found that he could make very little headway and that in any case there was not apt to be much profit for himself in these negotiations.[69] After this additional failure, Holstein saw the handwriting on the wall. Germany's enemies were on the point of "encircling" her with a coalition of hostile states. Characteristically, he attempted to use his quarrels with Baron Richthofen as an excuse to retire from the German Foreign Office. Bülow smoothed over the personal differences between the two men, and Holstein continued in charge of his old functions. It had not been as easy to dodge his responsibilities as he had at first imagined.[70]

Delcassé was even then capitalizing his successes by rapidly bringing Morocco under the influence of France. This process had been going on for some time to the increasing uneasiness of the German colonial group and of other Germans, too.[71] Germany carried on a considerable commerce with Morocco, and in the carrying trade was exceeded only by England.[72] Bülow headed the list of Germans who coveted at least a share of the disintegrating empire. The portion of Morocco which he was particularly anxious to have was the southern area along the Atlantic Coast. He believed that an

[68] Anderson, pp. 141-142, quoting Bülow, Reden II, 74, 84, 90f.
[69] Anderson, pp. 152-154.   [70] Ibid., p. 159.
[71] G. Saint-René Taillandier, Les Origines du Maroc Français, Récit d'Une Mission, 1901-1906 (Paris, 1930) pp. 13-15, 130-139, 209, 242; Fay, 157-160. D.D., 2 S., V, 566.
[72] Schuman, p. 176; Fay, p. 157 n.

Anglo-French settlement of Morocco to the exclusion of Germany would weaken and discredit Germany, and that consequently his country could not possibly accept such a settlement. As Holstein expressed it, "If we permit our toes to be trodden upon in Morocco without saying a word, we encourage others to do the same thing elsewhere."[73]

As a matter of fact, Bülow had been disposed to treat with Great Britain for a Moroccan accord as early as 1900, but met with poor success at that time. In April of 1900 he became alarmed when Delcassé sent French troops into the eastern frontier of Morocco, ostensibly to pacify that region. Bülow instructed his Ambassador in Paris to take the first opportunity to say to Delcassé that the activity of French troops in this region was a cause of anxiety among many Powers, but cautioned the Ambassador not to mention Germany's name. He should only say that he (Bülow) had tried to calm the fears of those foreign ambassadors who had spoken to him about the French action.[74]

The German Ambassador carried out these instructions. Delcassé had just returned from the Pyrenees where he had gone during the parliamentary vacations. He admitted that the French advance toward Touat had somewhat worried Spain and perhaps England and Italy, but said he had assured the Spaniards that he was not meditating an attack of any sort upon Morocco. The French Government intended to open the Sahara and protect commerce and caravans. For this purpose the oasis of Touat would have to be occupied, he said, and he left the German Ambassador with the impression that France would not go beyond that point.[75]

For a few weeks thereafter, Bülow felt reassured. Germany had never before asked France for explanations about Morocco, hence he thought that his recent request for information must have a certain gravity about it which French diplomats could not fail to perceive. Delcassé by saying "so clearly" that he did not intend to go beyond Touat, appeared to have

[73] G.P., XX, 207-209; Anderson, pp. 63-64.
[74] G.P., XVII, 299-301.   [75] Ibid., XVII, 301-302.

caught the significance of the German move, and Bülow did not expect him to take any further action on the Moroccan frontier. From the standpoint of German interest, the Chancellor thought it an awkward time to open the Moroccan question because England was occupied elsewhere and the English Prime Minister was then not especially favorable to Germany. Bülow hoped to postpone settlement of the problem until Germany could be sure of English support.[76]

Instead of improving, Anglo-German relations became worse. At the end of 1901, the Anglo-German negotiations for an alliance, which had been going on intermittently since 1898, broke down entirely. Bülow's hope of English support in the Moroccan question vanished at the same time.[77]

While Bülow failed to get a share of Morocco for Germany, Delcassé continued to make rapid progress in his attempt to bring the Sherifian Empire under the exclusive control of France. The French Foreign Minister aimed to accomplish his purpose in two ways: first, by making the Sultan increasingly dependent upon France for loans, military aid, and protection; and second, by obtaining the assurance of the disinterestedness of other Powers.[78] The weakness and incompetence of the Moroccan ruler facilitated Delcassé's task. Abd-el-Aziz shocked his fanatical subjects by riding on bicycles and in automobiles, and by wearing European garments. New taxes to pay for his extravagant and unpopular mode of living caused disorders, and France took advantage of these disturbances to accustom him to French military aid in pacifying and governing his people. Heavy French loans began to be made in 1903-4, and Frenchmen proceeded eagerly to the economic conquest of the country.[79] A particularly outrageous act of banditry in May 1904 became an excuse for sending two French warships to Moroccan waters and for securing the appointment of French and Algerian officers over the Tangier police.[80]

[76] G.P., XVII, 302-303. [77] Ibid., XVII, 318-321.
[78] Taillandier, op. cit., pp. 13-15, 124, 130.
[79] Ibid., pp. 22, 79, 90, 130, 137-139, 160-161, 168; Anderson, pp. 130, 132.
[80] Anderson, pp. 131-132.

While the pacific penetration of Morocco proceeded auspiciously along these lines, Delcassé secured the "disinterestedness" of Italy and England in Moroccan affairs and arranged an agreement with Spain by which France would eventually get most of Abd-el-Aziz's dominions. During these negotiations, and afterwards too, Delcassé exercised considerable care in excluding Germany from the discussions. When in March 1904 the German Ambassador could control his curiosity no longer and indiscreetly asked Delcassé about the reported negotiations for an Anglo-French accord, the Foreign Minister told him in an informal manner that they concerned Newfoundland, Egypt, Morocco, Sokoto, and Siam. He stated that he wished to maintain the existing political and territorial status of Morocco, but that improvements would have to be made. France did not wish to have any special interests there, he said, but it was her task to put an end to the anarchy in this neighboring state. This would benefit all nations carrying on trade in the Sherifian Empire, he pointed out, and promised that German commercial liberty would be "rigorously and entirely respected."[81] Radolin appeared to be satisfied. Later, however, Delcassé learned that, while Germany asked only for assurances of commercial liberty in Morocco, she desired to be given every possible guarantee of this last.[82]

Shortly after April 8, the French Ambassador in Berlin warned Delcassé that the Germans felt much more deeply on the subject of Morocco than their words were apt to imply, and quoted the English Ambassador there as saying that he thought it not improbable that Germany would seize the first opportunity to leave her position of isolation and to have her say in the regulation of the Moroccan question.

In spite of this warning, Delcassé neglected to send the Wilhelmstrasse a complete and regular notice of the Anglo-French accord. When Radolin observed in passing that he

[81] *G.P.*, XX, 5-7; Livre Jaune, *Affaires du Maroc*, I, 122, 167f., 196f.; *D.D.*, 2 S., IV, 509-510, V, 5; Anderson, 126f.
[82] *D.D.*, 2 S., V, 5.

did not have a reliable copy of the agreement, Delcassé said to him, "You can see it in the Yellow Book."[83]

The news soon spread throughout Berlin that Delcassé was snubbing the German Government. Bihourd, the French Ambassador, reported to Delcassé on the seventeenth of April that his colleagues were asking him if Germany had really been kept in complete ignorance of the accord of April 8. Realizing that he must not push matters too far, the French Foreign Minister then authorized Bihourd to make to Richthofen the same declarations which he himself had made to Prince Radolin three weeks before, i.e., that France had sought to serve her own interests in Morocco without damage to the existing interests of other Powers. Bihourd, though, had already promised that, in delivering this message, he would be careful not to give the Germans a chance to ask questions.[84] In other words, Germany was to be notified of the Anglo-French accord, but in such a way that she would be unable either to make suggestions or get an opening wedge for herself in Morocco.

Quite in contrast to the above measures, the French Minister of Foreign Affairs, on that very same day, sent the text of the Anglo-French accord to Jules Cambon in Spain and advised him that France was willing to enter upon discussions with the Spanish Government with a view to defining their respective spheres of influence in the Sherifian Empire.[85]

Subsequent despatches from Berlin indicated that it was hazardous to attempt to exclude Germany from the negotiations going on over Morocco. It was reported that numerous German papers were complaining about the accord of April 8 and urging the German Government to defend its interests. Bülow was described as impatient to reëstablish his credit in the eyes of Parliament and the Emperor. His soft, reassuring speeches were declared to be insincere and nothing more than a mask to hide his profound discontent. As for the Kaiser, it was said that he was fairly burning up with the desire to do something that would restore German prestige.[86] Fi-

[83] G.P., XX, 266n.   [84] D.D., 2 S., V, 32, 36.   [85] Ibid., V, 37.
[86] Ibid., V, 38, 51-53, 72.

nally when, in accordance with Delcassé's instructions, Bihourd spoke to Richthofen about the Anglo-French accord on April 26, the latter maintained an icy silence that left no doubt of the fact he was very angry.[87]

Nevertheless Delcassé informed Germany of the conclusion of the Franco-Spanish Moroccan accord of October 3, 1904, in the same casual and incomplete manner in which he had notified her of the Anglo-French agreement. On October 7, Bihourd laid before Richthofen a brief but empty notice of the accord. Asked if he were at liberty to tell what effect it would have on German commercial interests in Morocco, Bihourd replied that he had not received any communications on that subject, but supposed Germany's commercial interests were amply covered by the accord of April 8 and would not be modified by the new arrangements with Spain. Then, on October 12, 1904, Delcassé instructed Bihourd to tell Richthofen that the Spanish agreement was conceived in the same spirit as the Anglo-French accord, "In obtaining Spain's adhesion to the principle of commercial liberty expressed in the declaration of April 8, we have augmented still more the guarantees which international commerce will enjoy in Morocco."[88]

The German Government, however, did not care to let the matter come to an end in a manner so unsatisfactory to themselves. The next day Prince Radolin endeavored once more to insinuate Germany into the Moroccan discussions. While he admitted that Delcassé had spoken to him of the Anglo-French accord early in March, he said that since then the situation had "developed somewhat." In the course of the same conversation, he made vague references to a possible German coaling port on the coast of Morocco, but Delcassé, who already knew the ambitions of the German colonial party, did not respond to this broad hint.[89]

If the French Foreign Minister had notified Berlin of the

[87] *Ibid.*, V, 72, 77-78.
[88] *Ibid.*, V, 435, 440-441, 445, 447-448.
[89] *Ibid.*, V, 448.

above Moroccan accords, not only officially, but fully and regularly, he would have invited comments and suggestions from Germany and given her an opportunity to present her claims; but, as we have already seen, Delcassé was anxious to exclude Germany from Morocco and intended to let her know that she had no *locus standi* in that country.[90] If Germany were invited to discuss the Moroccan problem, she would almost certainly ask France to make concessions, but so far as Delcassé could see, Germany was not in a position to be able to make any substantial concessions in return. In short, he deliberately refrained from discussing the Moroccan question with Germany because he could not see any profit for France in such a discussion.[91] On the other hand, he felt safe in confronting Germany with a *fait accompli*. The Anglo-French entente was the crowning achievement of his diplomacy, and his diplomatic position in view of his sympathetic grouping of France, Russia, England, Italy, Spain, and Serbia, as over against a Triple Alliance of dubious solidarity, seemed so overwhelming that he felt he could go to extremes in his relations with Germany without any risk to France.[92] He furthermore based his policy on the fact that Germany was not a Mediterranean Power and hence not directly interested in Morocco.[93] In making this assumption, Delcassé ignored the fact that although Germany was not a Mediterranean Power, she was a great European Power with colonial ambitions, and that as a signatory to the Treaty of Madrid, 1880, she had exactly the same legal status in Morocco as France, Great Britain, Italy, and Spain.[94]

[90] *B.D.*, II, 274-275.

[91] Letter of Delcassé to Luzzatti, June 29, 1905, in *Revue des Deux Mondes*, May 1, 1931, p. 96 note 2. "By the acceptance of the Conference, the door was opened at Morocco to interferences which I had carefully sought to keep out," Delcassé, *J.O., Chambre*, Jan. 24, 1908, p. 105.

[92] Delcassé, *J.O., Chambre*, Jan. 24, 1908, pp. 104-108, especially 104 col. 3 and 107 cols. 2 and 3. Tardieu, *France and the Alliances*, pp. 178-182; Anderson, p. 127 and notes.

[93] Delcassé, *J.O., Chambre*, Jan. 24, 1908, p. 104; *Paris*, Oct. 9, 1887; *B.D.*, II, 274-275.

[94] J. S. Ewart, *The Roots and Causes of the War, 1914-1918* (2 vols. N.Y., 1925) II, 757-758; Cf. Tardieu, *La Conférence d'Algésiras*, p. 38, quoting Bülow on this point. His effort to explain it away is not very convincing.

Delcassé's disinclination to negotiate with Germany over Morocco caused the German Government to feel humiliated and slighted.[95] Germans felt that Delcassé was treating them as a "negligible quantity" in world affairs.[96] This feeling naturally became intensified as months went by and still Delcassé did not ask for German recognition of France's special position in Morocco.

While they were waiting, the Germans attempted to patch up relations with Russia. The Kaiser wrote numerous letters to "Dear Nicky," and the German Government did its best to get the Czar to sign a Russo-German treaty of alliance aimed at England and contemplating the ultimate adhesion of France. The Kaiser knew that Delcassé would not approve of this scheme but thought that the combined power of Russia and Germany would oblige France to become a member of the proposed coalition.[97] The advantage to be gained by Germany was evident. In this proposed grouping of the Powers, Germany rather than France or England would be the center of gravity about which the diplomacy of Europe would revolve.

Delcassé heard of the German design almost at once.[98] Through Edward VII, he learned that the Kaiser still longed to visit Paris and be acclaimed by the French people. From other sources he was informed that William II had boasted that he would force France into the Russo-German combination.[99] As for the Kaiser's desire to proclaim a rapprochement with France by visiting Paris, Delcassé said privately to Paléologue (July 1904) that the idea was foolish and puerile. He went on to say that he would be willing to have the Kaiser come to Paris in order to consummate the political reconciliation of the two peoples, but that one did not begin a

[95] Fay, p. 178; Anderson, p. 154.
[96] "Die Marokkanische Frage und Herr Delcassé" in *Deutsche Revue*, May, 1905, p. 131; also *D.D.*, 2 S., VI, 448, statement of Monts to Luzzatti, April, 1905.
[97] Anderson, pp. 166, 171; "Willy to Nicky," 17/11/1904, in *Letters from the Kaiser to the Czar* (New York, 1920) pp. 131-136; *G.P.*, XIX, 305-307, 313-315.
[98] *D.D.*, 2 S., V, 38f., 103, 107, 119, 139-140.
[99] M. Paléologue, *Un Prélude à l'Invasion de la Belgique le Plan Schlieffen, 1904* (Paris, 1932) pp. 48-50; 73-76.

rapprochement with the beating of tom-toms and so much band music. If William II sincerely desired to draw France and Germany closer together, he would have to begin more modestly. He ought to refrain from remarks which were insulting to France, such as his recent references to the battle of Sedan in a speech at Carlsruhe, and he must give up his habitual "rodomontade" for a few months. Finally, he should instruct his Chancellor to address to France positive and concrete proposals which Delcassé said he would examine without prejudice. Otherwise the French Minister failed to see any chance of a Franco-German rapprochement for a long time to come.[100]

On the subject of joining in the Russo-German combination of Powers, Delcassé expressed himself emphatically and vehemently on November 5, 1904. As was his custom when deeply moved, he breathed hard and sniffed, and paced the floor of his office. Then halting in front of Paléologue he said that he would not for a minute entertain the idea of entering into the German combination. As for the threat to force France into it, Delcassé declared that he would do anything before he would permit France to be towed around by Germany: . . . "So long as the Treaty of Frankfort stands unrevised, no intimate collaboration is possible between France and Germany. To affiliate ourselves with German policy would be equivalent to nothing less than irrevocably sanctioning the loss of Alsace-Lorraine." And he said again, November 8, 1904, "I shall never—never—trail behind Germany, and I shall have all France with me."[101]

In the last part of December 1904, the German scheme seemed to have failed, because the Franco-Russian Alliance proved to be stronger than the German diplomats had supposed.[102] The Kaiser, though chagrined, continued on good terms with the Czar, and seems not to have given up hope of ultimately winning over that monarch. Bülow felt the rebuff more keenly and became willing to take desperate measures

[100] Paléologue, *Un Prélude à l'Invasion de la Belgique*, pp. 50-51.
[101] *Ibid.*, pp. 80-81; 98.   [102] Anderson, p. 180.

to check Delcassé and to secure a diplomatic victory for Germany.

Bülow's idea was to inaugurate a more active German policy in Morocco. Even before the Russo-German negotiations had broken down, he had made preparations to block Delcassé's Moroccan projects and perhaps to get a portion of the Sherifian empire for his own country. Unhappily for the Chancellor, his imperial chief was not interested in Morocco and during an interview with the King of Spain, March 16, 1904, he had disclaimed any desire for territorial acquisitions in that region.[103] From the start, therefore, Bülow was in a quandary. How could he get a share of Morocco without violating the Emperor's explicit statement to the King of Spain? But at the same time that he had disclaimed any desire for territory, William II had declared that Germany aimed at the maintenance of the open door in Morocco. Bülow was consequently free to pose as the protector of German commercial rights in the Sherifian Empire. He decided to use this as an opening wedge.

Bülow's decision came at a moment when the Sultan was already becoming restive under the French system of pacific penetration of his dominions. His Sherifian Majesty was particularly uneasy and suspicious because he had not been consulted in the making of the Anglo-French and Franco-Spanish accords dealing with his country. He naturally inferred from this that the conclusion of the accords in question augured ill for his own personal interests.[104] Then, too, in December 1904, the French sent a special mission to Fez under M. Saint-René Taillandier to urge upon the Sultan the necessity of far-reaching reforms in policing the country, in spreading the French language, in transportation and communication, and, inevitably, in financial matters; but the Moroccan people were already showing their hostility to Christian influences and foreign control.[105] Under these cir-

[103] G.P., XVII, 362-363; Anderson, pp. 151-152.
[104] Taillandier, pp. 201-202; Anderson, pp. 128-129.
[105] Anderson, pp. 128-129, 133.

cumstances, Abd-el-Aziz turned to Germany for support, and Bülow quietly and unofficially encouraged the "Commander of the Faithful" to resist France, and aimed to strengthen his backbone and his will power whenever necessary. If the Sultan continued to yield to the French, the German Government planned to confine itself to a defense of German economic interests.[106]

Instead of inaugurating the French "reforms" at once, the Moroccan Government convened an assembly of notables and forced M. Saint-René Taillandier to explain the French program. At the same time, Germany prompted the Sultan to resistance by expressing the hope that no changes would be made which would alter the equal rights and freedom of all nations in Morocco, and by stating that Germany strongly disapproved of the French plan.[107] Shortly afterwards the German Government was informed that M. Taillandier had told the assembly of notables that he had the assent of the other foreign representatives at Tangier to his program of reforms. This the French Government later denied; but, meanwhile, the German Foreign Office remained under the impression that M. Taillandier had misrepresented his case in order to overawe the Moroccans. More determined than ever to frustrate the designs of Delcassé, Bülow, in a speech to the Reichstag, intimated that he was going to defend German economic interests in Morocco, and then decided to have the Kaiser, who was cruising in the Mediterranean, stop at Tangier and intervene personally. He wrote to the Emperor, "Your Majesty's visit to Tangier will embarrass M. Delcassé, thwart his plans, and be of benefit to our economic interests in Morocco."[108]

William II disliked interfering in the Moroccan question, partly because of his lack of interest in Morocco, and partly because he had other ideas on how to improve the position of Germany. He therefore found numerous plausible excuses

[106] Anderson, pp. 183-184; G.P., XX, 243.
[107] Taillandier, pp. 244-247; Anderson, pp. 184-185.
[108] G.P., XX, 262; Anderson, p. 186.

for not landing which he cabled back to Bülow.[109] In the end, his hand was forced. A lively Franco-German press war took place in the semi-official journals of Bülow and Delcassé after it was reported on March 19 and 20 that the Kaiser would land at Tangier.[110] Furthermore, the Chancellor made a speech to the Reichstag in which he announced that Germany would open relations with the Sultan of Morocco in order to defend German interests in that country. Finally, Bülow warned the Kaiser that if he did not carry out the program, Delcassé would exploit his failure to land as another diplomatic victory for France.[111] He also cajoled the Emperor with the thought that if the visit turned out as desired, Delcassé with his anti-German policy would "stand there as a disgraced European," and would probably then be overthrown by his enemies in France.[112]

3. Intrigue—the Resignation of Delcassé

. . . M. Drumont has written: "In thirty-five years, Delcassé is the only Minister of Foreign Affairs who has dared to look Germany squarely in the face." I shall be proud, later on, to show these few lines to my children. (Delcassé, quoted in *La Libre Parole*, Jan. 31, 1906.)

May the end be attained that the independence of our foreign policy be preserved. (Delcassé to Lauzanne, Oct., 1905.)

Having landed at Tangier on March 31, 1905, the Kaiser received the members of the German colony and the diplomatic corps. He said to the French representative that his visit signified that Germany was interested in the freedom of trade in Morocco. He also spoke of the Sultan as a free and equal sovereign of an independent country. He emphasized this last point when he spoke to the Sultan's uncle and plenipotentiary, and expressed the view that Moroccan reforms should be in accordance with the Koran and Mohammedan tradition and that European customs should not be blindly adopted.[113]

[109] *G.P.*, XX, 263, 279; XIX, 497.
[110] O. J. Hale, *Germany and the Diplomatic Revolution*, pp. 101-104.
[111] *G.P.*, XX, 264-265.   [112] Anderson, p. 190.   [113] Fay, p. 184.

Delcassé took careful note of the Kaiser's landing at Tangier, but he did not become unduly alarmed. He concluded that the move was primarily the result of German dissatisfaction over his Anglo-French accord and that Germany aimed to tear up the agreements which he had made with other Powers concerning Morocco. He had already received assurances that Great Britain, Italy, and Spain would hold loyally to their agreements, and he now reflected that it was to their interest to abide by them. The economic competition of Germany, which each day became more menacing to England, would prompt Great Britain to support France. Italy, although allied to Germany, felt that she was her rival in the Mediterranean. Finally, Delcassé counted on the fact that even Austria feared the covetousness of Germany.[114]

With these ideas in mind, Delcassé began to consolidate his position in view of the coming struggle with Germany. He mediated strenuously in an attempt to bring the Russo-Japanese War to a close in order that Russia might once more become a useful ally to France in Europe, and made preparations to affirm the solidarity of the *Entente Cordiale* by an exchange of visits between the French and English fleets.[115] Saint-René Taillandier was instructed to warn the Sultan against hearkening to the proposal of the German press for an international conference on the subject of Morocco, and the Italian Government was likewise informed that such a solution was inadmissible to France.[116]

While Delcassé remained relatively calm, many other people became greatly excited. The Continental press played up the story of the Kaiser's visit to Tangier until it assumed the proportions of the first act in a major international quarrel. Indeed, the first of the great Moroccan crises which did so much to deepen the hatreds of Europe and to drag Europe down into the abyss of war had been precipitated and was to last like a nightmare for many months.

The French became all the more worried because the Ger-

[114] Anderson, p. 197; Combarieu, pp. 303-304.
[115] Anderson, pp. 197-198 note 7; Combarieu, p. 304.
[116] Anderson, p. 198.

man Government adopted a policy of "sphinx-like silence" and remained cold and reserved and even "wooden-faced" toward Delcassé.[117] This policy seemed to confirm the view of those Frenchmen who interpreted the Tangier episode as a menace to France. The average Frenchman was dumbfounded. For years he had paid very little attention to foreign affairs. Now he suddenly awoke to find France and Germany seemingly on the verge of war. The threatening attitude of Germany was all the more alarming because the people of France suddenly became conscious of their unpreparedness. The Radicals, who had been in power for years, were pacifists and had permitted the French navy to be reduced to the fourth or fifth rank.[118] The French army was disheartened and the French people had lost confidence in it.[119] No appreciable military aid could be expected from Russia. For months, Frenchmen had seen the millions which they had loaned to that country, as a security to themselves, being used up on the battlefields of the Far East. The battle of Mukden had made it quite evident to all that for the time being Russia was useless to France. Had the public, like Delcassé, been fully informed concerning the alignment of the Powers, the French people might have had more confidence in their ability to defend themselves, but of course they did not know the real situation. They only knew that their one sure ally was *hors de combat*. This idea of the utter helplessness of France was largely responsible for the abnormal state of mind which gradually developed in France as the crisis dragged on week after week.

Delcassé said in 1908 that if the first Moroccan crisis had been left entirely in the hands of qualified diplomats, it would have been better for everyone concerned.[120] Actually, the questions at issue in the crisis became badly tangled with

[117] G.P., XX, 271 and 278; B.D., III, 76.
[118] J. Tramond and Reussner, Eléments d'Histoire Maritime et Coloniale Contemporaine (published under the direction of the historical service of the Chief of Staff of the French Marine, Paris, 1924) pp. 710-711.
[119] Tardieu, France and the Alliances, pp. 180-181; P. Fontin, Guerre et Marine (Paris, 1906) p. 197n. D.D., 2 S., VI, 602; 607.
[120] Delcassé, J.O., Chambre, Jan. 24, 1908, p. 105.

French politics. It soon became apparent that Delcassé should never have remained in the Rouvier Cabinet. Representing high financial circles, Rouvier, in forming his Cabinet, had drawn heavily upon the Right, yet had not drawn enough support from that quarter to command the allegiance of the Nationalist groups. At the same time, he failed to hold the support of Combes and the Left Bloc—a combination of Socialists, Radicals, and Radical Republicans. Rouvier's Ministry was therefore subject to a cross-fire from the extreme Right and Left. After the landing at Tangier, this deadly cross-fire was concentrated upon Delcassé as the weakest member of the Rouvier Cabinet.[121] The result was that he was caught on the horns of a double set of charges, often contradictory in character, but no less effective in undermining his position on that account. The Nationalists, who should logically have favored a spirited foreign policy, attacked him in these words: "For thirty-four years we have refrained from a war against Germany for the recovery of Alsace-Lorraine. Does M. Delcassé wish to go to war for Morocco?" The Socialists attacked his policy of ententes because he always had the air, when he concluded an alliance or entente, "of concluding it against someone." Combes denounced Delcassé's Moroccan policy as adventurous, and other parties and politicians on Right and Left joined in the chorus that Delcassé had blundered in not foreseeing and guarding against the probable attitude of Germany.[122]

Interpellated in the Senate, March 31, 1905, by M. Decrais on the attitude of the German press with regard to French foreign policy in Morocco, Delcassé assured the Senate that he planned to maintain freedom of commerce in Morocco and that consequently other nations need not be alarmed. Significantly enough, his reply ignored the press controversy and even the name of Germany.[123] Next day Clemenceau sarcastically remarked in the *Aurore* that Delcassé had made a "declaration" but had declared nothing.

[121] Hale, pp. 107-108.   [122] *Ibid.*, p. 109.
[123] *Annales du Sénat*, March 31, 1905, p. 641f.

In the midst of these attacks in the Chambers and in the press, Delcassé, through the medium of two influential journalists, made unofficial overtures to the German Government with a view to reaching an understanding on the subject of German economic interests in Morocco.[124] Meanwhile, the German Government was pondering over the question of what its next move should be, because, incredible as it may seem, Bülow and Holstein had opened the Moroccan question and engaged the entire prestige of Germany without having in mind any definite plan of action for settling the crisis.[125] It was not until the third or fourth of April that the' two men agreed upon the course that they should follow. They decided to hold out for an international conference of those Powers signatory to the Convention of Madrid, 1880, and to refuse to enter into any direct negotiations or separate agreements with Delcassé. The unofficial overtures of the French Foreign Minister consequently fell upon deaf ears.

Numerous persons interpellated Delcassé in the Chamber of Deputies on April 7. The Foreign Minister, who found Parliamentary interference in his affairs to be irksome, made only a short speech in reply. He did say, however, that he was' willing to clear up any misunderstanding which might still exist between France and Germany. Jaurès congratulated him on being willing to clear up all misunderstandings, but denounced him for dodging the point of the interpellations and for refusing to give the Chamber the assurances for which it had asked. He charged that Delcassé was attempting to proceed as though there had been no change in the state of international affairs—that he appeared to be officially ignoring the difficulties in his way.[126] After the speeches of April 7, a number of Republican journals which had hitherto supported Delcassé began to desert him. Clemenceau went so far as to say that public opinion in France was almost unanimous in demanding that the Minister of Foreign Affairs repair his mistakes.[127]

[124] G.P., XX, 282f., 305n.   [125] Hale, pp. 117-119.
[126] Annales de la Chambre, April 7, 1905, pp. 1569-1570.
[127] Hale, p. 111.

Until April 7, the German press had complained that Delcassé had wounded the pride of Germany by not officially informing her of the Anglo-French accord over Morocco. This German campaign had effectively weakened the political position of the Foreign Minister. Otto Hammann, the director of the German press, wrote Bülow on April 7 that:

. . . the principal argument of Jaurès, Lanessan, Clemenceau, and Cornély against Delcassé is the cold and stiff attitude of the German press, and the conclusion drawn from the declaration of the Chancellor to the Reichstag that the legitimate self-respect of Germany had been uselessly and dangerously wounded by the arrogance of Delcassé. [Note of Bülow on the margin of this document: "Quite right."] For the direction of the press tell us how we should now receive the advances of Delcassé . . . should they be rejected in favor of a conference, or should we be ready to accept the French propositions? [Note of Bülow: "Wait calmly without committing ourselves irrevocably to any policy."][128]

At that very moment, Delcassé was attempting to draw out the German Government through the medium of *Le Matin*. Hedemann, acting on behalf of the great Parisian journal, asked Hammann for a friendly word for Delcassé. Called upon to decide this question, Bülow answered, "No. Delcassé must be made to learn his fate other than through the medium of a Parisian journalist;" and he instructed the German press as follows: "Say nothing against the Anglo-French entente . . . that only fortifies it. All the criticism and all the attacks should be directed against the arrogant, clumsy, and systematically anti-German policy of Delcassé."[129]

By the ninth of April, even the diplomatic corps in Paris, English and Russians excepted, grew anxious over the press campaign and because of the silence of Germany. Radolin, the German Ambassador, wrote on April 9 that his colleagues persistently sought to force him to depart from his attitude of reserve. They asked him point-blank why he did not speak to Delcassé, and they would add that the French Foreign Minister was only waiting for a sign that Germany was will-

[128] G.P., XX, 312.   [129] Ibid., XX, 310-313.

ing to begin conversations. Conformable to his instructions from Germany, Radolin refused to give any such sign. Delcassé, however, seemed to have a way of getting the diplomatic corps into his confidence, so much so that most of the diplomats in Paris adopted the version that he had notified Germany of the accord of April 8. This made it very difficult for Radolin to maintain his attitude of reserve. His position was all the more awkward because Delcassé greeted him in a manner that was friendly enough. In fact, Radolin himself seems to have felt that Bülow was carrying the punishment too far. "At a dinner with the President of the Senate, April 6, everyone must have noticed how depressed and preoccupied Delcassé was," he wrote Bülow, but the Chancellor was adamant: "It is very much to be desired that Radolin remain calm toward his colleagues, particularly that there should be no nervousness and no ill humour. With a face of brass and a smile one can get anywhere, said Talleyrand—Radolin is his grandnephew."[130]

Before retiring from a dinner at the German Embassy on April 13, Delcassé saw Radolin and said to him in a voice which betrayed considerable feeling, "Will you let me have a moment for an interview? I should have asked it of you yesterday if you had come to see me." Radolin answered with a tone of indifference that he did not wish to make him waste his precious time since he had nothing to say to him. "This deplorable press battle," continued Delcassé, "gives me the impression that the Imperial Government is offended." Radolin interrupted with icy coldness, "I cannot talk to you on this subject; I have no instructions. What you think fitting to say to me, I can take only *ad referendum*." "I am determined to declare to you formally," said Delcassé with evident emotion, "that if there is any misunderstanding whatever, in spite of all the declarations I have made . . . I am ready to dissipate them. I ask that you make this known to the Imperial Government. I for my part will ask M. Bihourd, French Ambassador at Berlin, to do the same." Delcassé then

[130] *G.P.,* XX, 316-317.

launched into a defense of his own policy. M. Taillandier had not sought to speak in the name of the other Powers represented at Tangier. He knew this because he had telegraphed M. Taillandier and received his assurances that such language had never been used. Delcassé declared that the Anglo-French accord having been concluded at London was at once published. "I confess," he continued, "the idea never occurred to me to communicate to the Imperial Government this paper which had been immediately given publicity." Radolin looked at Delcassé with astonishment and could hardly refrain from laughing, but Delcassé went on with his explanations. He declared that he had communicated the Franco-Spanish accord to the German Foreign Office before publication. This treaty guaranteed the absolute liberty of foreign commerce and was therefore an additional guarantee of German interests. "By the communication of the Franco-Spanish treaty—which emanated from the Anglo-French Convention—I thought to have advised you of everything." Radolin listened in ominous silence, evidently unimpressed. Delcassé then admitted to Radolin that the conversation of March 23, 1904, on the subject of the proposed Anglo-French accord, did not constitute an official communication of that accord to Germany. Referring to this admission, Radolin said, "I take note of the fact, because your official press has sustained just the contrary thesis."[131] In short, Delcassé did not get any comfort from Radolin at all, but, by taking the initiative, the French Minister had prepared the way for direct diplomatic negotiations if Germany cared to engage in them.

When Radolin reported the conversation of April 13 to his home Government, he remarked that two courses were open to German diplomacy. First of all, they could refuse to accept the rapprochement offered by Delcassé in the hope that the French Government would drop their Foreign Minister and replace him by a man more acceptable to Germany. With regard to this first course of action, Radolin said it

---

[131] G.P., XX, 328-330; Contrast Delcassé's own account in the Yellow Book, *Affaires du Maroc, 1901-1905,* pp. 211-212.

was doubtful that Delcassé would be dismissed because Loubet was known to be supporting him, but nevertheless Radolin thought it a possibility because the Combes-Jaurès clique was working for the downfall of the Foreign Minister. Secondly, said Radolin, Germany might accept Delcassé's explanations and deal with him directly, keeping in mind the dictum that he gives twice who gives quickly.[132]

Bülow chose Radolin's first alternative. He charged his Ambassador to say to the French Minister that separate Franco-German negotiations were not apropos; and, when Bihourd went to the German Under-Secretary of State in Berlin to lay before him the main points of Delcassé's conversation with Radolin, the Secretary answered shortly that the visit was superfluous because the German Ambassador had already reported everything.[133] Delcassé's overture of the thirteenth for a direct diplomatic settlement therefore failed. This was primarily because Bülow and Holstein had now determined upon an international settlement and had not only pressed the Sultan to speak for a conference, but had sought to win over the European Powers to the same idea. They felt sure that the Powers would accept the German plan and that the conference would refuse to let France carry out her penetration of Morocco. The German argument ran something like this: Germany had a good case in international law. Austria would be a loyal ally to Germany. Russia was occupied with revolution at home and war in the Far East. Spain was of no importance. Italy could be held in check by hinting to her that Austria might be willing just now to settle the Irredentist troubles. England would not stir; and Roosevelt was not only known to favor the open door, but was suspicious of Delcassé, because Delcassé's desire to act as mediator between Russia and Japan conflicted with the President's own plans for bringing the Russo-Japanese war to a close.[134]

[132] G.P., XX, 331.
[133] G.P., XX, 334; Affaires du Maroc, 1901-1905, p. 214.
[134] Anderson, pp. 203-204; the German diplomats continued to feed the vanity of Roosevelt and to sow the seeds of suspicion, with the result that Roosevelt eventually concluded that Delcassé was an "unbelievable scamp"

While Delcassé had been waiting for the German response to his overture, excitement had been running high in Paris. Serious men in important positions asked if Europe were not drifting into war. Diplomats in many cases were of the same mind. One of them, Count Khevenhüller, deplored the press campaign as particularly dangerous. He had seen the War of 1870 start in much the same way, he declared. At the same time, the politicians hostile to Delcassé continued to attack him. Clemenceau, a master of sarcasm and ridicule, said in the *Aurore*, April 17—

It is not in his personal efforts that I put my faith. The man who guaranteed the maintenance of peace to M. Rouvier the very morning the Russo-Japanese War broke out; the man who thought Germany was a "Mediterranean Power" when we acquired Tunis, but that she had no interest in Morocco in 1904; the man who lost an entire week refusing to negotiate with Berlin only to change his mind when he found his portfolio at stake—that man might make, perhaps, an excellent undersecretary or minister of agriculture. He is not a minister of foreign affairs.[135]

The nineteenth of April was signalized by a general debate in the Chamber of Deputies on Delcassé's foreign policy. The orators of the Right and Left, from Archdeacon and Boni de Castellane to Jaurès and Pressensé attacked the Foreign Minister without mercy, while the Center remained ominously silent. Not a voice was raised in Delcassé's defense as the speakers denounced him for not having consulted with Germany before he proceeded to the realization of his Moroccan projects. Delcassé, in defending himself, dealt in generalities and sought to take refuge in the assertion that, as Minister of Foreign Affairs, he would have to guard his secrets of state and could not talk with impunity in the Chambers.[136] He said that he had already declared to the German

---

who was carrying on an "underhand game" to make the American negotiations fail so that England and France might step in and bring the warring nations together. T. Dennett, *Theodore Roosevelt and the Russo-Japanese War* (New York, 1925) pp. 60, 77-79, 87, 174-177; note in Rhodes and Howe, *James Ford Rhodes American Historian*, pp. 122-123.

[135] *Aurore*, April 17, quoted in Hale, p. 112.
[136] *Annales de la Chambre*, April 19, 1905, pp. 1931 et seq.

Ambassador that if any misunderstandings still existed, he was willing to clear them up, and he reiterated this promise before the assembled Deputies. At one time during the debate, he interrupted Jaurès to say that while Foreign Minister of France, he had never refused to respond to an invitation addressed to him by another Power. Jaurès curtly replied that it was not now a question of Delcassé responding to invitations made to him by other Powers. Since he had taken the initiative in a policy tending to modify the *status quo* in Morocco, he should also have taken the initiative in explanations to Germany. The Chamber took up the cry, "You should have taken the initiative," and Rouvier, seeing the life of his Cabinet in danger, was driven to defend his Minister of Foreign Affairs. The Premier attempted to calm the Chamber by saying that Delcassé had taken the initiative and that France was waiting for the German reply. Retention of Delcassé as Minister of Foreign Affairs was made a Cabinet question, but Rouvier promised that in the future he would himself supervise the foreign policy of France. Since the Chamber did not wish to overturn the whole Rouvier Cabinet, no vote of confidence was taken. Delcassé had been saved, momentarily at least. However, since it was obvious that he did not have the confidence of the Chamber, Delcassé went to President Loubet shortly afterwards and stated that he would like to resign.

The debate of April 19 and the announcement of Delcassé's intention to resign (ostensibly on account of ill health) occasioned widespread comment in the French press, but only a few journals came to the aid of the Minister of Foreign Affairs. Clemenceau wrote on April 20 that "Thanks to the intervention of the President of the Council," Delcassé was still officially the Minister of Foreign Affairs, but that if Rouvier wished to stay in power, "he should begin immediately to look for a successor to M. Delcassé."[137] On the other hand, President Loubet begged Delcassé not to give up his position. "Under the present circumstances, this resignation

[137] Hale, pp. 114-115.

would only serve the enemies of France," he said.[138] Rouvier also asked the Foreign Minister to remain at his post, and many of Delcassé's friends appealed to him to reconsider. Delcassé having officially tendered his resignation on April 22, therefore withdrew it the same day.[139]

Delcassé resumed his functions at the Quai d'Orsay on the afternoon of the twenty-second of April, but with his authority diminished, since Rouvier had promised the Chamber of Deputies that he would supervise the foreign affairs of France. One of Delcassé's first steps was to send Paléologue to Berlin to study the situation there carefully and to bring back a report.

Meanwhile the English people and the British Government displayed their sympathy for Delcassé. The English could not believe that Germany had stirred up all this excitement in order to preserve the open door in Morocco or that it was based on a desire to restore German prestige. They imagined that Germany wished to obtain a port on the Atlantic coast of Morocco, and were determined to support Delcassé in resisting this German design.[140] While German and French newspapers attacked the French Minister of Foreign Affairs, the English papers praised him inordinately. Some of them even went to the extreme of lecturing the Chamber of Deputies on the lack of patriotism which it had displayed on the nineteenth of April. This English press campaign helped Delcassé very little and may even have worked against him, because the extreme enthusiasm of the English press raised the suspicion that it was prompted by English hostility to Germany rather than by love for France.[141] Anyhow, there was much solid truth in Clemenceau's observation: "The Foreign Minister of France needs the confidence of the Chamber of Deputies, and not that of the House of Commons."[142]

[138] Combarieu, p. 305.
[139] Paléologue, *Revue des Deux Mondes*, June 15, 1931, p. 763; Anderson, pp. 201-202.
[140] H. Nicolson, *Sir Arthur Nicolson, Bart., First Lord Carnock* (London, 1930) p. 163; Anderson, p. 210.   [141] Hale, pp. 115-116.
[142] *Aurore*, April 20, 21, 1905, quoted in Hale, p. 115.

Had Clemenceau known of a somewhat unusual step taken by King Edward VII, he might have written a similar line. The English King was yachting in the Mediterranean when he learned of Delcassé's intended resignation. He sent a telegram to Delcassé in which he urgently requested him to retain his portfolio. This seems to have reached Delcassé on the twenty-third, the day after his resignation had been withdrawn.[143]

Of much more value to Delcassé was an official overture of the British Government. On April 25 Sir Francis Bertie, the English Ambassador in Paris, gave Delcassé written assurance that the British Government considered the actions of the German Government "most unreasonable" and offered to give Delcassé "all the support in its power" if Germany tried to get a port on the Moroccan coast.[144] Delcassé thanked the Ambassador warmly for this support and promised to communicate with the British Government if the contingency contemplated by them actually arose.[145]

Paléologue returned from Berlin on the afternoon of April 26 and said that in his opinion Germany would fight unless Delcassé changed his ground. Since the German Government had refused direct negotiations, he advised the Foreign Minister to try to reach Germany indirectly through Russia, England, or Italy.[146] Paléologue noticed that Delcassé looked careworn. Suddenly the telephone rang. Delcassé answered it and came back smiling. "The President of the Council is going to dine this evening at the Germany Embassy. He asked if I had any new suggestions to give him in case Prince Radolin should speak to him about Morocco. . . . You see by this simple detail that Rouvier and I are precisely in accord with each other."[147]

During the dinner that evening, Rouvier said to the German Ambassador that there was no reason for France and

---

[143] Maurois, *Edouard VII*, p. 215. Delcassé's daughter seems to have given Maurois a copy of the telegram.
[144] *B.D.*, III, 72ff. Nos. 91-93; *D.D.*, 2 S., VI, 414-415.
[145] *B.D.*, III, 74f.
[146] Paléologue, *Revue des Deux Mondes*, June 15, 1931, p. 764.
[147] *Ibid.*, p. 764.

Germany to quarrel, and he promised that the *status quo* and freedom of commerce in Morocco would be maintained. "We will do everything that is possible to give you the explanations and satisfaction that you desire," he declared. He also said that the French people liked the Germans more than they liked the English. If a few patriots wearing the cap of office still preached *Revanche,* that was only "foolish prating." In his opinion, France ought to resign herself to the realities of the situation in order to have friendly ties with Germany. If the two nations came to an understanding, the peace of the world would be assured. He ended by saying that it would be criminal for two nations "intended to agree" to become embroiled over Morocco. Radolin, for his part, coldly suggested an international conference as the best solution of the problem before them. Just before the dinner began, he had learned from a confidant of the French Premier that the latter had said that he in no way identified himself with Delcassé because he knew that the British navy did not have wheels. Radolin's informant also left him with the impression that Rouvier would willingly allow Delcassé to fall.[148]

Next morning, Radolin telegraphed a full account of these conversations to his home Government. Following its usual custom, the French telegraph bureau sent a copy of the telegram to the Quai d'Orsay where it was deciphered that same afternoon. Delcassé, who had concluded from Rouvier's telephone call that the Premier was in accord with him, was cruelly shocked. Indeed Rouvier's conversations, as reported in the German telegram, seemed to Delcassé to be treacherous and infamous in the extreme.[149]

A more charitable view of Rouvier's actions is possible. By his promise of April 19 to supervise the foreign affairs of France, Rouvier had become in a sense jointly responsible with Delcassé for the success of French policy. He differed radically with Delcassé on the subject of Franco-German relations. Delcassé was counting on English support in the

[148] *G.P.,* XX, 344-345.
[149] *Ibid.,* XX, 344-345; Paléologue, *Revue des Deux Mondes,* June 15, 1931, pp. 766-767.

emergency which had arisen, but Rouvier suspected the motives of England and, in any case, felt that it was not safe to rely upon her because, to his mind, the English fleet would be of little use in a land battle between France and Germany. Consequently, when it became apparent that Germany was not going to respond to Delcassé's offer of April 13 to clear up all existing misunderstandings, and when the German Government continued to take a theatening attitude at the same time that it refused to deal with Delcassé, Rouvier decided to open negotiations with Germany himself.[150] His first steps were taken on the evening of the twenty-sixth at Radolin's dinner. He did not succeed in opening direct negotiations between Germany and France, nor did he succeed in improving Franco-German relations, but he was able to keep in communication with the German Government through intermediaries. These intermediaries were his own friends and, like himself, financiers and business men but not in any sense qualified diplomats. The consequence was that Rouvier gave the appearance of negotiating with the German Government behind the back of the French Minister of Foreign Affairs. Delcassé did not remain ignorant of what the Premier was doing. Thanks to the cryptographic service of the Quai d'Orsay, he was able to follow Rouvier's movements day by day in the telegraphic correspondence between the German Foreign Office and the German Embassy in Paris.[151] In order to confirm the information gathered by his cryptographic service, Delcassé had one of Rouvier's intermediaries trailed and found him going from the Premier's office to the German Embassy.[152] Such was the situation. Rouvier attempted to succeed where Delcassé had failed, and used his friends as in-

---

[150] Anderson, pp. 212-213 .

[151] Paléologue, *Revue des Deux Mondes*, June 15, 1931, pp. 765-767; *Un Prélude à l'Invasion de la Belgique*, pp. 85-86. Paléologue was himself an expert at deciphering the diplomatic correspondence of other nations. During the Dreyfus controversy, Delcassé sent Paléologue before the Court of Cassation to decipher a dispatch of Major Pannizardi, Military Attaché of the Italian Embassy at Paris, the Quai d'Orsay having intercepted it some time before. In 1905, the intercepted dispatches were served up on Paléologue's desk and by him communicated to Delcassé. (*Ibid.*, p. 765.)

[152] Mévil, *Echo de Paris*, March 28, 1922.

termediaries; Delcassé considered this little short of treason.[153]

On the twenty-seventh, Rouvier proposed, in his indirect way, to the German Ambassador that the best settlement of the Moroccan question could be found in an exchange of notes between France and the other Powers. If the Powers disapproved, France would not carry out her Moroccan reforms. However, the German Government did not reply to Rouvier on this occasion because they preferred to delay their answer until their special agent en route to Fez, Count Tattenbach, could get the ear of the Sultan and persuade him to accept the idea of an international conference.[154] That same day, rumors of war caused a panic on the stock exchange. Very much frightened, Rouvier told Radolin when the latter came to extend to him Bülow's thanks for the personal declarations of the twenty-sixth, that an international conference (humiliating to France) was extremely difficult but that a way out of the present tense situation would have to be found. He suggested a Franco-German agreement similar to the Anglo-French accord, "where all doubtful points," including the question of Morocco, would be settled. Since it was obvious that Delcassé might oppose this solution, Rouvier added that he had clipped Delcassé's wings and was in control of French foreign affairs himself.[155]

While Rouvier maintained his indirect contacts with the German Government, Delcassé worked out his own diplomatic campaign. He was in a much more favorable position than Rouvier because he had at his disposal the telegraphic instructions and correspondence of the German Ambassador and could shape his policy accordingly. On the twenty-seventh, he decided to try to open negotiations with Germany through the medium of Italy. Barrère was moving heaven and earth in Rome to save his chief, and M. Luzzatti, the Italian Minister of Finance, was likewise anxious to help, and actually spoke to the German Ambassador, Count Monts, on Delcassé's

[153] *Revue des Deux Mondes*, June 15, 1931, p. 769.
[154] Anderson, p. 213; *G.P.*, XX, 346-348.
[155] *G.P.*, XX, 360-361.

behalf. However, Luzzatti's efforts proved unavailing.[156] Meanwhile, on the thirtieth, King Edward came to Paris. He had long conversations with Delcassé. As a sincere friend, the King advised him to use all of his skill in an attempt to lessen the tension in Franco-German relations. He promised that the British Government would aid in this task. France might suddenly find herself in a grave situation, he said. This advice and the warning somewhat sobered Delcassé.[157] On the other hand, Paul Cambon and Barrère counseled him to resist the demands of Germany. Cambon argued as follows: Germany was only bluffing. The Kaiser cared little about Morocco. His real aim was to force the resignation of Delcassé and to break up the *Entente Cordiale*. The Kaiser rightly attributed to Delcassé the rapprochements of France with Italy, Great Britain, and Spain, rapprochements which were all the more remarkable because they had been brought about without alienating Russia. The Emperor could not conceive of so many ententes being made without German participation and was profoundly soured by hearing people speak of the isolation of Germany. Just what Germany wanted at this particular moment, no one could say. The German Government seemed to be ignorant of its own intentions. Cambon advised that Delcassé remain calm—offer to open conversations with the German Government and then to wait tranquilly for a German reply, like one who was certain of his rights and sure of being supported by the public opinion of Europe. A display of nervousness or weakness would be the death of the *Entente Cordiale*; Italy, "virtually detached from Germany," would hasten to go back to her old ally; the Spanish would not fail to manifest their disdain, and even Russia might be led to listen to overtures from Berlin.[158] Loubet and Delcassé had reached most of these conclusions as early as

[156] Paléologue, *Revue des Deux Mondes*, June 15, 1931, p. 764; *G.P.*, XX, 362; Barrère, *Revue des Deux Mondes*, May 1, 1931, pp. 96-101; *D.D.*, 2 S., VI, 447-451; 477-478.
[157] Paléologue, *Revue des Deux Mondes*, June 15, 1931, pp. 768 and 773.
[158] *Ibid.*, p. 764; Cambon to Delcassé, May 8, 1905, in *D.D.*, 2 S., VI, 489-493.

April 1.[159] Barrère's opinion was the same as that of Cambon: if France permitted herself to be victimized by the German threats, she might lose the respect of the world as well as her alliances and her ententes.[160] Furthermore, both Barrère and Cambon agreed with Delcassé that, in spite of the feebleness of France's Russian ally, Germany would not press the issue to the point of war, because Germany herself was not prepared.[161] The conclusion finally reached by the three men was that, fortified by her "allies" and her friends, France ought to resist Germany and resolutely maintain all of the French positions in the controversy. That is, Delcassé was willing and ready to make commercial concessions to Germany if she were minded to discuss the subject of Morocco, but was determined not to yield anything politically or territorially.[162]

Rouvier continued to be greatly worried by the attitude of Germany. During the first week in May, he sent his friend William Betzold (an international financier) to interview Holstein, and also persuaded Baron Eckardstein to speak directly to Count Bülow. They were to say that the French Cabinet disapproved of Delcassé and hoped to find some domestic reason for dismissing him from his post within the next three or four weeks. They were also to say that, in case of war, England would side with France, but that the whole French Cabinet, Delcassé excepted, preferred not to seek this support. Finally, they were empowered to offer Germany a coaling station or a strip of the Atlantic coast of Morocco.[163] Tempting as this offer was, the German Government could not accept it because the Kaiser's declaration to the King of Spain at Vigo prevented Germany from taking any Moroccan territory at this time. Unable to accept the territory which he coveted, Bülow determined to "hold the future free" until he could accept it. A conference seemed to him to be the best

[159] Combarieu, pp. 303-304.
[160] Barrère, Revue des Deux Mondes, Aug. 1, 1932, p. 614.
[161] Ibid., pp. 615-616; Combarieu, pp. 303-304; Delcassé, Jan. 24, 1908, J.O., Chambre, p. 105.
[162] Barrère, Revue des Deux Mondes, Aug. 1, 1932, p. 615; B.D., III, No. 96, p. 78.
[163] Anderson, p. 219.

means of achieving his purpose.[164] Betzold and Eckardstein therefore failed in their missions. Holstein told Betzold that for the time being, he saw no possibility of direct negotiations with France. The German Government did not trust Delcassé enough for that because the French Minister's policy toward Germany had been "dishonest," "hostile," "insidious," and in the recent affair "disrespectful." He advised slow tempo, temporary truce and the "setting aside" *(Beiseitigung)* of Delcassé.[165] Eckardstein was treated more roughly. He informed Bülow on May 5 that Rouvier and Etienne had no sympathy for Delcassé and wanted to disembarrass themselves of him. The German press should therefore cease attacking the French Foreign Minister because such attacks only strengthened his position. Rouvier wanted the Emperor and the Chancellor to declare that, while they could not permit France to keep Germany on the outside in the Moroccan question, they nevertheless desired friendly relations with France. This would lead to the fall of Delcassé. Rouvier was absolutely in accord with the German desire to go slowly in the Moroccan affair. Eckardstein then stated that he personally thought that if war came, England would support France. King Edward's actions left no doubt of it at Paris. Bülow replied gruffly that the English acts of incitement did not impress Germany at all. In case of war, the conflict would be between France and Germany, and the latter was in a position to await further developments with composure.[166]

Delcassé now began to be more accommodating to Germany, thereby making it increasingly difficult for Rouvier to get rid of him. Moreover, Delcassé clung very tenaciously to his portfolio and would not let go of it of his own accord. Since it was not easy to drop Delcassé, Rouvier promised the German Government that he would find an excuse for giving the Minister of Foreign Affairs a leave of absence. That, however, might take weeks or even months, he said, because

[164] *Ibid.*, pp. 216-217.
[165] Anderson, pp. 219-220; *G.P.*, XX, 357-359.
[166] *G.P.*, XX, 369; Anderson, p. 220.

Delcassé had assumed the task of bringing about peace between Japan and Russia. If there should be an armistice, Delcassé could not be removed at once. But Rouvier assured the German Government that in the future Delcassé would be careful to act as the Premier desired. "I am emancipated," said Rouvier, "Delcassé no longer runs things to suit himself. The entire Ministry now prescribes exactly what is to be done."[167]

This was the state of affairs when Prince Henckel von Donnersmarck arrived in Paris. The Prince posed as an emissary of William II, and the French statesmen with whom he associated accepted him as such.[168] Since his spectacular movements of March 31, the Kaiser had taken little or no part in the Moroccan Crisis. Assuming that Von Donnersmarck really was an emissary of the Kaiser, his utterances lead one to suspect that William II, without consulting the German Foreign Office,[169] had at last decided to fish in troubled waters on his own account and for the sake of his long-desired Continental coalition against England. This coalition necessitated the coöperation of France and Russia, which could not be had so long as Delcassé remained in charge of the Quai d'Orsay; therefore the main burden of Von Donnersmarck's message was the demand that Delcassé be dismissed from office. But, whether authorized to meddle in the Moroccan crisis or not, this much is certain, Von Donnersmarck materially contributed to the fall of Delcassé and did a great deal to embitter Franco-German relations.

The Prince lunched on the eighth of May with Rouvier, Etienne, Jean Dupuy, Francis Charmes, and a few others. He exposed to them what he alleged to be the opinions of the Emperor. His Majesty thought that France and Germany should sincerely and cordially effect a rapprochement and live united, both for their own good and for the preservation of the peace of the world. The Emperor considered the

---

[167] G.P., XX, 375-376.
[168] Combarieu, pp. 306-308; Paléologue, *Revue des Deux Mondes*, June 15, 1931, pp. 768-771.
[169] See G.P., XX, 390n.

Moroccan question to be intrinsically of little importance. It could be arranged in five minutes. The real question was that of France's relations with Germany. France was friendly toward all other Powers, but would not have anything to do with Germany. She entertained many foreign sovereigns in Paris, but not the Emperor William. France was represented in all of the Continental capitals by men of distinction, except in Berlin, where she was represented by a man with whom conversation was impossible. The Emperor asked that all of this be changed. Delcassé's actions clearly put him into the discard, and William II demanded that this enemy of his be sacrificed. Similarly, the French Ambassador in Berlin would have to be succeeded by another man. Furthermore, the Kaiser wished to come to Paris, "like other sovereigns," and be given the Grand Cross of the Legion of Honor. Finally, Germany wanted intimate relations with France, because otherwise France would ally herself to the English. Germany could not permit an Anglo-French alliance. "We have already let you make the Franco-Russian Alliance. That is enough!"[170]

A more tactless and bunglesome method of drawing France and Germany together could hardly have been devised than this conversation. Perhaps, as Paul Cambon suspected, the real purpose of German diplomacy was to divide the French Cabinet by frightening its more timid members. Thus Delcassé's position might be undermined and the *Entente Cordiale* wrecked.[171] At any rate, news of Von Donnersmarck's conversation spread rapidly about Paris and created varying degrees of apprehension according to what portions of it were emphasized. President Loubet was "distressed" and "confounded" by the Emperor's "proposals." He wrote his Secretary on the twelfth that it was a dream to expect France to break the entente with England when nothing was offered in return. As for Delcassé, wrote the President, he was too much attached to the continuation of that Minister's policy

[170] Combarieu, 306-308; Paléologue, *Revue des Deux Mondes*, June 15, 1931, pp. 768-771. For Paul Cambon's comments on Von Donnersmarck's conversation, see *D.D.*, 2 S., VI, 521-522 and notes.
[171] *D.D.*, 2 S., VI, 521-523 and notes.

to think of his dismissal.[172] Francis Charmes concluded that the Emperor offered France the alternative of "intimacy or war." He asked Paléologue to urge Delcassé to resign at once, lest France find herself in a perilous situation.[173] Delcassé heard of the Von Donnersmarck utterances from several sources. He marched around his office in great excitement, violently denouncing Rouvier—"This traitor who has dared to say to the German Ambassador: 'I don't give a d—n about Alsace-Lorraine. Do you wish me to sacrifice Delcassé?' " . . .[174] When Paléologue gave him Francis Charmes' version of the Von Donnersmarck conversation, Delcassé said:

What you have just said to me, my dear friend, is full justification of my policy. It is just this that I have always raised as an objection to those who have adjured me to be more communicative and more confident with Germany. . . . Francis Charmes has very well summarized Von Donnersmarck's language: The Emperor William offers us either intimacy or war. . . . But what intimacy would you like to have between France and Germany so long as the gulf of Alsace-Lorraine separates the two countries? Or at any rate, there is no possibility of intimacy today except on one condition and that is that the French people say to the German people as the President of the Council said to His Excellency, Prince Radolin: "I don't give a d—n now about Alsace-Lorraine. . . . Let us forget the past! . . . Let us embrace each other!" . . . Ah well! France has not yet fallen so low. William is fooling himself! . . .[175]

For some days after the eighth of May, strong pressure from various sources was brought to bear upon Rouvier to overthrow Delcassé. Betzold reported that the banks, the press, the Parliament, and the Rothschilds had all turned against the Foreign Minister. The war scare continued in Paris unabated. Delcassé himself spread around the rumor that Germany was trying to oust him from office. "He has played on that chord," wrote Radolin to the German Foreign Office, May 15. Bülow, though, had not yet come to the point of asking for Delcassé's

---

[172] Combarieu, 307-308.
[173] Paléologue, *Revue des Deux Mondes,* June 15, 1931, p. 770.
[174] *Ibid.,* p. 769.
[175] *Ibid.,* pp. 770-771.

head. He noted on Radolin's dispatch: "We do not dream of overthrowing Delcassé. On the contrary, he doesn't bother us at all."[176] That is, since Rouvier had "clipped Delcassé's wings" and was thought to be in control of French foreign affairs, Delcassé no longer mattered. But the next day, May 16, in response to Radolin's observation that German trust in French policy was lacking, Rouvier offered to sacrifice Delcassé, and asked only that he be given time in which to find some internal crisis as an excuse. Bülow himself did not press the issue until after Count Tattenbach telegraphed him on the seventeenth from Fez, saying that Delcassé had issued veiled threats of violence against Morocco if the Sultan agreed to the German proposal for a conference.[177] Then Bülow telegraphed Radolin that Delcassé was two-faced—that he spoke one way and acted in another. While Rouvier was saying that the Foreign Minister would be conciliatory in the future, Delcassé had sent instructions to Fez which contradicted Rouvier's statements. This apparent duplicity confirmed the Kaiser and Bülow in the opinion that so long as Delcassé remained Minister of Foreign Affairs, Franco-German relations would only go from bad to worse. His latest actions could not long be kept secret, and Bülow was unwilling to accept responsibility for the repercussions on public opinion when they should become known. Consequently, the Chancellor determined to warn Rouvier once more of the dangerous consequences of maintaining Delcassé in office. He decided to instruct Von Miquel, Councilor of the German Embassy in Paris, to inform Rouvier officially of Germany's dislike for Delcassé.[178]

Von Miquel carried out Bülow's instructions on April 30. He told Rouvier that Germany had made advances to the French on five different occasions, viz., in the case of the Portuguese Colonies in 1898, the Shanghai affair, the Bagdad railway, the Haiti question, and now in Morocco, but that Delcassé had compromised all of these German efforts.

[176] G.P., XX, 378.
[177] Ibid., XX, 380; Anderson, p. 223.
[178] G.P., XX, 388-389; Anderson, p. 224, Memoirs of Prince Bülow, II, 121.

Rouvier was now not so easily convinced that he ought to discard his Minister of Foreign Affairs. He argued that Delcassé might still be useful in Franco-German relations after Von Tattenbach had oriented himself at Fez. Von Miquel replied that he didn't think this possible. Delcassé had about used up all of his credit in Germany. Rouvier again demurred. Delcassé could render great services in the peace negotiations between Japan and Russia. "I cannot cause Delcassé to fall just because Germany frowns. I should be reproached always —always." He added that the Moroccan Crisis was incomprehensible to him, since no German interest there was in danger. Von Miquel then explained how serious Bülow considered the situation to be. Rouvier thanked him but said the question "turned on persons of extraordinary difficulty." Von Miquel was therefore left with the impression that Delcassé would not be turned out of office for some time to come.[179]

Toward the last part of May, the Sultan freed himself from the restraining influences of the French representative at Fez, rejected the French proposals, and approved the plan of calling an international conference. Bülow at once warned Rouvier through Betzold that, since the Sultan had accepted the German idea of a conference, Germany "would follow up the consequences" if France continued the policy of "intimidation and violence" in Morocco "hitherto pursued by M. Delcassé."[180]

In the meantime, Delcassé and his diplomats had been very busy. Paul Cambon, Barrère, and Delcassé were agreed that, once the material support of England was acquired, Germany would give up all thought of making war on France. They felt all the more certain of this because Berlin was obliged to know the attitude of Italy toward a war provoked by Germany in which France and England appeared as allies.[181] Barrère was able to give Cambon and Delcassé absolute assurance that Italy, in accordance with the agreement of 1902, would

[179] *G.P.*, XX, 394-398.
[180] *Ibid.*, XX, 392f., 407; Anderson, p. 225.
[181] Barrère, *Revue des Deux Mondes*, Aug. 1, 1932, pp. 615-616; Combarieu, pp. 303-304; Delcassé, Jan. 24, 1908, *J.O., Chambre*, p. 107.

maintain a benevolent neutrality and reserve her liberty of action with regard to the German Empire.[182] Cambon was exceedingly optimistic about English support, but it was decided that he should press the English Government for definite assurances.[183]

On the seventeenth of May, Lord Lansdowne and Cambon had a discussion concerning the attitude assumed by Germany in Morocco and in other parts of the world. Cambon stated that while Delcassé did not regard the situation as particularly dangerous, it was nevertheless "sufficiently serious" to cause him "much preoccupation." Lansdowne replied that the French and British Governments "should continue to treat one another with the most absolute confidence, should keep one another fully informed of everything which came to their knowledge and should, so far as possible, discuss in advance any contingencies by which they might in the course of events find themselves confronted," and as an example of what he meant, he cited the communication recently made by Bertie to Delcassé[184] when the English feared that Germany might demand a port on the Moroccan coast.[185]

In an effort to avoid misunderstandings, Lansdowne and Cambon exchanged notes verifying the above conversation. Cambon, in his note dated May 24, referred to Lansdowne as having said that

. . . if the circumstances demanded it, if for example we had serious reason to expect an unprovoked aggression on the part of a certain Power, the British Government would be ready to concert with the French Government on the measures to be taken.[186]

Lansdowne, in his note dated May 25, sought to avoid such a broad commitment, and said that it was the British desire

. . . that there should be full and confidential discussion between the two Governments, not so much in consequence of some acts

---

[182] Barrère, *loc. cit.*, pp. 615-616.
[183] *Ibid.*, p. 616; Paléologue, *Revue des Deux Mondes*, June 15, 1931, p. 771; *D.D.*, 2 S., VI, 523 and note 3.
[184] See above, p. 241.
[185] *B.D.*, III, 76, No. 94; *D.D.*, 2 S., VI, 522-523.
[186] *D.D.*, 2 S., VI, 538-539.

of unprovoked aggression on the part of another Power, as in
anticipation of any complications to be apprehended during the
somewhat anxious period through which we are at present passing.[187]

When Cambon transmitted this note to Delcassé, he remarked that the wording of the note had been very carefully
studied by the British Government and certainly had the
approval of the Prime Minister, Arthur Balfour, and that it
constituted recognition of the fact that Lansdowne had spon-
taneously offered to discuss in advance measures to be taken
in view of every contingency. As Cambon interpreted this
note, Lansdowne intended it to apply not only in the case of
an unprovoked aggression, as in the French version, but to
every possible contingency. He concluded that Lord Lansdowne had deliberately rectified the French communication
of the twenty-fourth in order to propose an immediate examination of the general situation. This meant that if France
accepted the English proposal, she might be led into a general
entente which would be in reality an alliance.[188]

Delcassé and his advisers in the diplomatic service seem to
have insisted upon giving this broad interpretation to Lansdowne's note.[189] Having received the British message and
Cambon's comments upon it on May 30, Delcassé at once
telegraphed Cambon as follows :

Say to Lord Lansdowne that I am also of the opinion that the
two governments should more than ever give each other their
entire confidence and that I am ready to examine with him all
aspects of a situation which does not fail to be a little disquieting.[190]

Cambon did not act upon these instructions. Instead, he
wrote Delcassé "a personal letter," which for the sake of
greater secrecy was addressed to Paléologue, who had charge

[187] D.D., 2 S., VI, pp. 558-559; B.D., III, 77, No. 95.
[188] D.D., 2 S., VI, 557-558; also Maurois, *Edouard VII*, pp. 220-221; Paléologue, *Revue des Deux Mondes*, June 15, 1931, p. 778.
[189] Maurois, p. 222; Paléologue, *loc. cit.*, pp. 778, 781-782; Barrère, *Revue
des Deux Mondes*, Aug. 1, 1932, p. 616.
[190] D.D., 2 S., VI, 563-564; B.D., VI, 747-748.

of the ultra-secret files of the Quai d'Orsay.[191] It will be remembered that since April 19, Rouvier had been jointly responsible with Delcassé for the foreign affairs of France. In his letter to Delcassé, Cambon explained that he was unable to enter into further discussions with Lord Lansdowne without Rouvier's consent. The President of the Council had specifically warned him in Delcassé's presence not to concert with England. Unless Rouvier had completely changed his mind, Delcassé could not on his own account undertake to respond to overtures which would strengthen and extend the English understanding with France and which might even lead to an alliance. The English might desire to bring together the chiefs of staff of the French and English armies and navies. "You would certainly not be followed by your colleagues in the Cabinet nor by public opinion and you would be accused of bringing on war," was Cambon's conclusion.[192]

The King of Spain visited Paris from May 31 to the evening of June 4. During the festivities in honor of the King, Delcassé's political enemies made ready for his dismissal. The German Ambassador was promised that as soon as the King left the French Capital a Cabinet meeting would be held on Franco-German relations and, if necessary, the question would be carried before the Chamber where a majority for Rouvier could certainly be expected. This was reported to the German Foreign Office by Radolin on the third; and, since the German correspondence was being read by the Quai d'Orsay, Delcassé knew even before the evening of the fourth that he was a doomed man.[193] When the reception given by Delcassé in honor of the King of Spain was over, the King shook hands with Delcassé warmly, expressed pleasure at the entertainment, and spoke of the satisfaction he would have in receiving him personally in Spain. His words cut Delcassé like a knife, because he knew that in forty-eight hours he would cease to be Minister of Foreign Affairs—that the will of his colleagues in the Cabinet was fixed on that score and that everything was

[191] *D.D.*, 2 S., VI, 573; *B.D.*, VI, 747-748.
[192] *D.D.*, 2 S., VI, 573.   [193] *G.P.*, XX, 400-403.

arranged in consequence.[194] That night a telegram arrived from Barrère in Rome. It stated that Count Monts had said to the Italian Government that the French Minister at Fez had threatened to invade Morocco if the Sultan agreed to Germany's plans, but that Germany was determined to send her troops into France the moment French troops crossed over into Morocco.[195] Delcassé refused to be worried by this alleged German declaration, which he characterized as "absurd," but admitted to Paléologue that the other French Ministers would take it seriously and that consequently it would be harder than ever to win over the Cabinet to his own policy of a strong stand in the face of Germany.[196]

Barrère's telegram was communicated to Rouvier on the following morning. It fitted in with Radolin's declaration that Germany could not remain indifferent if Delcassé's policy of "intimidation and violence" in Morocco were continued.[197] Rouvier became almost frantic with excitement. He burst in upon President Loubet with the tale that France was on the verge of war and that within two days after the war broke out, revolution would be unchained in Paris and in the larger cities. He laid the blame squarely upon Delcassé and declared that, next day, the Cabinet would have to decide between Delcassé's policy and his own, and that one or the other of the two men would have to leave the Ministry.[198] President Loubet himself informed Delcassé of Rouvier's decision. Delcassé replied that he too would oblige the Cabinet to choose between his policy and that of Rouvier: "Tomorrow, one or the other of us will have to give up office," he said.[199]

If Delcassé knew that his colleagues in the Cabinet were determined upon his dismissal, why did he bother to attend the famous meeting of the Cabinet on June 6? Delcassé has himself answered this question:

I knew in advance what was going to happen [at the Cabinet

---

[194] Lauzanne in *Le Matin*, Oct. 7, 1905; Paléologue, *Revue des Deux Mondes*, June 15, 1931, p. 783.

[195] *D.D.*, 2 S., VI, 585-586; Taillandier, p. 308. Taillandier denies that he presented the Sultan with an ultimatum, either directly or indirectly (p. 309).

[196] Paléologue, *loc. cit.*, pp. 782-783.   [197] *G.P.*, XX, 392-393.

[198] Combarieu, pp. 314-315; Paléologue, *Revue des Deux Mondes*, June 15, 1931, p. 783.   [199] Paléologue, *loc. cit.*, p. 783

meeting of June 6]. I knew that I was condemned even before being heard, and that it was simply a formality of the execution. I went not to defend my person because my person is of little consequence. It is not even anything. But I wished to defend my policy and especially to sound a cry of alarm and to give the danger signal to those who had the Government of France in their hands.[200]

In a note written for his own guidance, Delcassé said:

... Are we going to go back on those who, in their own common interest, are desirous of supporting us? Look out! The English will not lose their time in weeping over the ruins of the French entente; they will turn away and we shall remain alone because neither Italy nor Spain will proudly maintain a dangerous fidelity to a cause which we ourselves have been the first to abandon.[201]

He believed that the Germans wanted to force his resignation because they regarded him as an obstacle to their own schemes in having negotiated the Anglo-French accord and in desiring to encourage the idea of an English understanding with Russia.[202] As he saw it then, it was not a question of personalities, but a question of a whole policy and perhaps of a whole future. He attended the meeting of June 6 to defend that policy which he had pursued for seven years and which now seemed to be in serious danger.[203]

While Delcassé selected a number of secret documents to use in defense of his policy, and prepared his speech to the Ministerial Council, Rouvier conferred with political leaders in the Chamber. The Premier's own concern for the safety of France soon became an almost universal alarm. Rumors spread from one group to another, and as has been aptly remarked, a rumor in one group reappeared in another group as an established fact.[204] Insignificant mattérs became portentous in their meaning. William II had telegraphed congratulations to King Alfonso on his escape from an anarchist's bomb, but Loubet, who had been at Alfonso's side, had not

[200] Lauzanne in *Le Matin*, Oct. 7, 1905.
[201] Maurois, p. 222.
[202] Conversation of Delcassé and Bertie, June 10, 1905, *B.D.*, III, p. 78, No. 96.
[203] Lauzanne in *Le Matin*, Oct. 6, 1905.
[204] Hale, p. 129.

been similarly congratulated. At the wedding of the German Crown Prince, General Lacroix, who represented France, was not seated at the first table of honor. Von Flotow arrived late at Delcassé's diplomatic reception. Then there was a frontier incident. In short, France was verging on a state of panic that rendered Delcassé's position virtually hopeless.[205]

At ten o'clock on the morning of June 6, all of the Ministers assembled at the council chamber except Rouvier and Delcassé who conferred with the President for more than an hour. At last, about eleven o'clock, the *huissier* announced the President of the Republic, who entered the room with Rouvier, followed closely by Delcassé. The Ministers took their proper places. Anguish was written on the face of every one of them. Rouvier and Delcassé were both very pale. The session was opened. Rouvier stated that he thought Delcassé should give his colleagues the explanations which he had just given in the office of the President.[206]

For more than an hour, Delcassé expounded his policy. He declared that he had not followed a diplomacy which was vexatious to Germany, but that he had notified Germany of the Anglo-French accord in a conversation with Radolin, on March 23, 1904; that Germany was not a Mediterranean Power and her interests in Morocco were not in danger.[207] As for the German proposal for an international conference, Delcassé's views on this point were very clear. The best procedure would be to have France, Great Britain, and Spain send identical notes to the Sultan declining the conference.[208] It was only necessary to say to the Sultan that, so far as France was concerned, the Moroccan question was regulated by the Franco-Moroccan accords of 1901 and 1902 and by the Anglo-French accord of April 8, 1904, of which the Sultan himself had already made use to obtain French military and financial aid. If Germany should interrogate France in this matter,

[205] Hale, p. 129.

[206] Procès verbaux of Chaumié, Minister of Justice, dated Paris, June 6, 1905, printed in *Le Temps*, March 19, 1922; and in *D.D.*, 2 S., VI, 601ff.

[207] Combarieu, pp. 315-316; Lauzanne in *Le Matin*, Oct. 7, 1905; Maurice Saurraut in *Dépêche de Toulouse*, Oct. 14, 1905.

[208] *B.D.*, III, 91.

France need only communicate to her the declarations made
to the Sultan and indicate at the same time the motives which
inspired her to hold to them.[209] The attitude of Germany was
menacing, but Delcassé said that, personally, he considered
this to be nothing but bluff and that France ought to resist
Germany. He insisted that Germany would not declare war.
This was the conclusion drawn from certain information
which had come to him and the conclusion of all of his ambassadors in foreign countries.[210] One thing or the other was
true, either Germany was bluffing, or, contrary to all of his
previsions, Germany really was anxious for war. In the latter
case, the coöperation of the English fleet would be invaluable
to France. The French could count on English support, he
said, and to prove it he read from Lansdowne's note of the
twenty-fifth to Cambon. The English offer could easily lead
to an alliance, he said, and he pointed out all of the advantages to be obtained.[211] France's Russian ally was weakened
by defeat; England could be all the more of a bulwark to
France because her own interests drove her to act as a counterpoise to Germany.[212] In closing, he said that France ought to
reject the conference, accept the English offer of support and
conclude the accord which the British had proposed.

> Weigh carefully the decision that you are about to make. To-
> day, England boldly espouses our cause. But tomorrow, if she sees
> us weaken or tremble, . . . she will no longer take any stock in us.
> And, turning around her batteries, she will negotiate a reconcilia-
> tion with Berlin at the expense of our Colonial Empire. . . .[213]

Rouvier then stated his side of the case. He said that he had
information which proved that the German threats were not
vain but were very serious, that Germany was not bluffing but
would push matters to extremes if France continued to pur-

---

[209] Delcassé, Jan. 24, 1908, *J.O., Chambre,* p. 105.

[210] *Ibid.,* p. 105; Chaumié's account, *Le Temps,* March 19, 1922; Delcassé,
letter in *Figaro,* March 24, 1922.

[211] Paléologue, *Revue des Deux Mondes,* June 15, 1931, p. 785; Delcassé,
letter in *Figaro,* March 24, 1922; *Dépêche de Toulouse,* Oct. 14, 1905.

[212] *Dépêche de Toulouse,* Oct. 14, 1905.

[213] Paléologue, *loc. cit.,* 785; Chaumié's account in *Le Temps,* March 19,
1922; *D.D.,* 2 S., VI, 603.

sue the policy of Delcassé. He also stated that Germany knew of the negotiations going on between France and England. At this point, Delcassé interrupted him: "How could such a secret offer be known to Germany? At London, only three persons know of it—the King, Balfour, and Lansdowne; here, I have not spoken to anyone except the President and yourself!" Rouvier did not explain how Germany had learned of the Anglo-French pourparlers, but insisted that he had been solemnly warned that if the English negotiations were concluded, Germany would soon know about it and would make war on France.[214] The French people would not understand going to war over Morocco, he said, and he refused to accept responsibility for a policy which might provoke Germany to armed conflict. He therefore urged that France give up the idea of relying upon England.[215]

After a short general discussion, each Minister was called upon in turn to decide between Rouvier and Delcassé. They were unanimously for the Premier and his policy of declining to accept English aid. This was tantamount to the dismissal of the Minister of Foreign Affairs. President Loubet remained silent. Delcassé offered his resignation. Rouvier accepted it, and then added that the manifest divergence of views on that day did not obliterate the memory of the great services which the Minister had rendered while in charge of the Quai d'Orsay.

The session broke up at 12:45 P.M. The "tragic hour" was over. Delcassé had been forced out of the office which he had held for seven consecutive years. The question now was, would the broad lines of his policy remain? Could his system of ententes stand the strain of the German attack, now that Rouvier was alone at the helm?[216]

[214] According to Paléologue, this threat had been made to Rouvier by Isaac R—., "an emissary of Bülow," about the same time that Von Miquel interviewed the Premier. Paléologue, *Un Grand Tournant de la Politique Mondiale*, pp. 349-352.

[215] Chaumié's account in *Le Temps*, March 19, 1922; Delcassé, letter to Jean Bernard, in *Figaro*, March 24, 1922; Paléologue, *Un Grand Tournant . . .*, pp. 351-352.

[216] *Le Temps*, March 19, 1922; Paléologue, *Un Grand Tournant . . .*, pp. 351-352; Combarieu, pp. 316-317.

V
THE RETURN TO POWER AND
INFLUENCE
1905-1923

1. The Consequences of Delcassé's Fall

. . . do you not remember this cry, which, without provoking contradiction, was raised in the Reichstag, "It would have been better for Germany if the Conference had never met." (Delcassé, Jan. 24, 1908.)

THE fall of Delcassé was commensurate with the unprecedented heights of personal power to which he had risen in the short space of seven years. Three months before, he had enjoyed the confidence of a majority of the French people and the friendship of numerous European monarchs. Under his able direction, France was rapidly becoming the pivot of international politics. The strings of European diplomacy which, in 1882, he had desired to see in the hands of France, were actually at his own finger-tips. Yet, when he fell on June 6, almost the entire French press was against him. In the panic of June 6-7, only one of the newspapers in Paris, the *Journal des Débats,* kept a cool head and reserved its judgment. The other papers, including those formerly eulogistic of Delcassé and his policies, seemed to be dominated by only one idea—that of rending the fallen Minister. At any rate, they denounced him without mercy, the usual charge being that he had followed a blind and mistaken policy.[1]

Le Matin recovered from the general fright on June 8, and printed an article by the intensely patriotic Stephane Lauzanne, which read in part as follows:

Delcassé has rendered great services to his countrymen which,

[1] Excerpts from fourteen of these papers were reprinted on March 2, 1911, by *Figaro.* See also Lauzanne in *Le Matin,* June 8, 1905.

later on, when no one has need of his skin or his post, they will perhaps recognize. He has signed treaties which, whatever one may do or say, have changed the orientation of French policy in Europe. In every instance, he has represented France with dignity . . .

The former Minister, who had searched the newspapers of the preceding day in vain for a word of sympathy,[2] was deeply moved. That evening, Lauzanne found Delcassé's card on his desk with the word "Thanks" written upon it.

In the camp of Delcassé's political adversaries, Rouvier and his supporters were not long in exploiting the Minister's fall for their own benefit. Said Rouvier, "M. Delcassé had dug a mine from the Quai d'Orsay to the Wilhelmstrasse. If I had not stepped on the fuse just in time, all Europe would have blown up."[3]

Across the Rhine, Bülow announced that the resignation of Delcassé could be the first step toward better Franco-German relations. He alleged that the former French Minister of Foreign Affairs had followed an anti-German policy which tended to "isolate" Germany. The Chancellor therefore considered that Delcassé's retirement from office marked real progress toward peace and a common understanding between the two countries. He even made it clear that the way was now open for a Franco-German rapprochement.[4]

The story of what went on in the Cabinet meeting of June 6 could not long be kept secret. As *Figaro* observed on October 15, 1905, "Ten ministers heard the terrible dialogue between Rouvier and Delcassé. How many friends could ten ministers have? and how many of them [coufld] have [had] the strength to remain silent?" Moreover, Delcassé himself had disclosed certain facts to Stephane Lauzanne, and had also given an account of the Cabinet session to his close friend Paléologue and perhaps to others. On October 6 and 7, Lauzanne, acting

[2] Even *Le Matin* had carried an article on the 7th which bitterly reproached him for carrying on what was alleged to be an anti-German policy. Lauzanne was then at Toulon.

[3] Quoted in *La Libre Parole*, Jan. 23, 1906.

[4] *Le Matin*, June 9, Oct. 4-5; *Petit Parisien*, Oct. 4; *Le Temps*, Oct. 5, 1905. See Hale, pp. 194-195.

on his own responsibility and without Delcassé's consent,[5] created a sensation in France, and in Europe, by publishing in *Le Matin* an account of the famous session of June 6 and of the events which led up to it. He stressed the activities of Henckel von Donnersmarck and left the reader with the impression that Delcassé had been forced out of office largely as the result of German pressure. He also stated that, in the council meeting, Delcassé had informed his colleagues of an English offer to make an alliance with France. Worse still, Lauzanne added in a footnote that England had offered, in the event of a war between France and Germany, to mobilize the English fleet, to land 100,000 men in Schleswig-Holstein, and to seize the Kiel Canal. The *Matin* "disclosures" occasioned lively protests and denials from various sources; and, for more than a week, the newspaper story of Delcassé's fall was edited, revised, and reëdited. André Mévil published in *L'Echo de Paris* a series of articles similar to Lauzanne's, and one of the fullest accounts appeared on October 14 in the *Dépêche de Toulouse*. No subject had been quite so well advertised since the Dreyfus quarrel.[6]

Naturally, the Anglo-German feud was intensified. Many English journals questioned or denied the fact that the British Government had offered armed assistance to France, but freely admitted that, in the case of a German attack, England would have given all the aid in her power to the French.[7] On the other hand, the German newspapers declared that an "assassin's plot" had been revealed: England had been using Delcassé as a tool to precipitate a war between France and Germany. This conviction stimulated anti-English feeling in Germany, and caused a demand for greater armaments on land and sea.[8]

In France, the newspaper "revelations" had the effect of hardening the French antipathy to Germany. Internal French politics as a contributing cause to Delcassé's dismissal was

---

[5] *Le Matin*, Oct. 11, 1905.
[6] *Le Matin*, Oct. 6-15; *Echo de Paris*, Oct. 7-26; *Dépêche de Toulouse*, Oct. 14, 1905.
[7] Hale, p. 197.   [8] *Ibid.*, pp. 198-199.

largely obscured by the effort of the press to expose the sinister intrigues of Germany and the brutality of German policy as over against the loyalty with which England had supported France in the crisis.[9] Many French people were left with the idea that France had thrown out her patriotic and unselfish Minister of Foreign Affairs at the brutal command of Germany. This was a national humiliation and an insult which they could not easily forget or forgive. A French history designed to be read by the average citizen and written in 1910 carried this paragraph:

Whatever one may think of Delcassé, the man of Fashoda and the servile executor of the English will, it is certain that to disavow him and force him out of office at such a moment was to capitulate before Germany. It meant inflicting on our country the most cruel humiliation.[10]

The Belgian Ambassador in Paris wrote his Government on October 24, 1905:

. . . resentment is deeply rooted in the hearts of Frenchmen, and will live on there. Those who reveled in dreams of peace have suffered a frightful disillusionment: the national jingoism has revived; people are discussing the efficiency of the French defensive power as compared with the formidable organization of France's eastern neighbors, and seem ready to make fresh sacrifices in order that the army and navy may be prepared for any emergency . . .[11]

The injury to French pride was felt all the more keenly because the Imperial Government appeared to celebrate Delcassé's fall as a German triumph. Frenchmen were quick to note the fact that Bülow was raised to the rank of Prince on the very day that Delcassé fell from power.[12]

As we see it now, France need not have felt humiliated. Delcassé would have fallen in any case, though perhaps not

[9] Hale, p. 196.

[10] L. Hosotte, *L'Histoire de la Troisième République, 1870-1910* (Paris, 1910) p. 713; Lord Newton, *Lord Lansdowne*, p. 342, says much the same.

[11] Leghait to Favereau, Oct. 24, 1905, published in Morel, *Diplomacy Revealed*, p. 22f.

[12] For instance, see Tardieu, *France and the Alliances*, p. 185.

so soon if there had been no German pressure.[13] Yet, in spite
of contradiction at various times, the legend that Delcassé
had been removed at Germany's bidding persisted and was
vigorously propagated down to the outbreak of the World
War, at which time it became quite generally accepted as
history.[14] That the legend was based upon the error of neglect-
ing to take into account the strength of those political forces
within France which were likewise working for the Minister's
downfall does not alter the influence of the story upon French
history and upon the tragic course of European events. The
important fact is that for the next ten years a school of very
influential French journalists and writers taught that the
resignation of Delcassé was a grave humiliation to France
forced upon her by direct German intervention.[15] After the
press war of October 1905, the name Delcassé therefore took
on a new significance. In the minds of many French people
it stood not for the man Delcassé but for a policy and for an
unforgettable moment in French history. He was the man
who had been "sacrificed" to Germany, because, for an instant, France had been unable to throw down the gage of
battle.

In the midst of the press quarrels centering about his name,
Delcassé maintained a dignified silence. Seven years of office
and the nerve-racking experience of the last few months had
been a terrific strain upon him. He now sought to restore his
health through rest and exercise. By ten o'clock, he had gal-
loped all over the Bois de Boulogne and had returned to his
apartment at 11 Boulevard de Clichy, which was then decorated with such souvenirs as a marble bust of Nicholas II
and a portrait of Edward VII. A considerable amount of time
was spent in quiet study in his library—"That alone mitigates
or does away with sorrow," he was wont to say. Occasionally,
he conversed with some friend who came to visit him. Time
was also found to call upon those diplomats in Paris who had

[13] Bertie to Lansdowne in Lord Newton, *Lord Lansdowne*, pp. 341-342.
[14] Hale, p. 132.
[15] Notably Mévil, Tardieu, Lauzanne, Bourgeois and Pagès, Hosette; see
Hale, p. 107 and note, also p. 132.

been particularly friendly to him when he had been at the height of his power. Moreover, he wrote to Lord Lansdowne, thanking him for his recent coöperation. Yet he by no means despaired of regaining office. Certainly, he remained a conscientious and assiduous attendant of the Chamber of Deputies.

As soon as practicable, he traveled southward to "Les Cascatelles," his retreat at Ax-les-Thermes. This country estate lay halfway up the sides of the Pyrenees on a bend of the road leading into Spain. Here, in perfect quiet and in full view of the mountain peaks, he gave himself over to complete rest or mingled familiarly with his friends in the nearby town. It is hardly necessary to say that he did not neglect to rebuild his political fences. In the midst of the controversy provoked by the so-called "*Matin* revelations," he was acting as president of a congress of three thousand persons interested in a trans-Pyrenean railway from Ax-les-Thermes to Puigcerda and Ripoll.[16] A year later, at the time of the local elections for the Chamber of Deputies, he was able to poll 10,327 votes as over against 4,182 votes of his nearest competitor.

His attitude toward the newspaper war raging about the story of his fall was one of impressive disdain. During the second week in July 1905, an article appeared in *Le Gaulois* purporting to be the substance of an interview with the former Minister of Foreign Affairs and attributing to him some highly incendiary utterances. Moreover, many people generally assumed that Delcassé had deliberately inspired the "*Matin* revelations." In fact, men like Clemenceau, who had reproached him the day before as a monster of iniquity for maintaining an irresponsible reserve and silence while at the Quai d'Orsay, now denounced him as a traitor for exposing secrets of state.[17] Delcassé, however, refused to issue statements to the press or to contradict the newspaper accounts. He desired the veil of forgetfulness to fall as rapidly as possible upon a past so painful to all those who had gone through it. He said to Lauzanne, "Explanations would be equivalent to

[16] *Le Matin*, Oct. 21, 1905.   [17] *Œuvres de Jean Jaurès*, II, 373.

pleading the case. . . . It is better to let the facts speak—they express themselves with sufficient eloquence."[18]

Poincaré tells us that Delcassé had "an instinctive horror of denials and rectifications," and that he preferred to wait patiently with unshakable faith in "the power of truth and the sovereign impartiality of history."[19] But this policy of silence was not altogether instinctive. It was based on sound judgment and experience. Delcassé once said in giving advice to a young man:

"My dear friend, never deny anything. Profit by the experience of one who has been in the Ministry for seven years. Don't take the trouble to answer!"

"But," said the youth, "the story was false!"

"It was ridiculous, that is enough," said Delcassé, and he added with a smile, "besides, with journalists one can never have the last word. I know because I used to be one myself."[20]

The apocryphal "*Gaulois* interview," mentioned above, was brought to Delcassé's atttention by President Loubet's secretary, who took the trouble of sending the newspaper to Delcassé at Ax-les-Thermes. In thanking him, Delcassé said in his letter:

. . . this gentleman [the author of the "*Gaulois* interview"] knew nothing and had not asked anything of me, knowing full well what sort of a reception he would receive. Those who really know me have not found my style [in the article]. As for the others, what on earth could make them change their opinion?[21]

Only on one occasion did Delcassé lose patience. On October 11, 1905, he wrote a short, indignant note to the editor of *Figaro* protesting against the credence which the latter had seemingly given to the "absurd" charge that the former Minister of Foreign Affairs had given away a secret of state.[22]

---

[18] *Le Matin*, Oct. 5, 1905; *Echo de Paris*, Feb. 28, 1923.

[19] Poincaré, Feb. 28, 1923, quoted in *Le Matin*, March 1, 1923.

[20] *Annales Politique et Littéraires*, March 4, 1923, pp. 212-213.

[21] Combarieu, p. 318. For the apocryphal character of the *Gaulois* article, see Mévil, *Rev. Pol. et Parl.*, June, 1924, p. 372, citing a letter of Delcassé dated July 17, 1905.

[22] A charge based on the premise that Delcassé had inspired the "*Matin* Revelations."

This note was published the next day, but the wording was so equivocal that no one could deduce any reliable conclusion from it.[23]

If Delcassé had chosen to speak, he would have had plenty of documents with which to support his statements. Anxious to avoid the error which he had committed upon leaving the Ministry of Colonies, he had carefully supplied himself with valuable evidence before leaving the Quai d'Orsay.[24] However, he was forced to choose between personal disgrace[25] and the interests of France. It would have been easy to expose the secret negotiations between Rouvier and the German Government as found in the telegraphic correspondence of the German Embassy in Paris. By so doing, Delcassé might have provoked a reaction of public opinion in his own favor. Many times he said to Mévil, "Ah! If I wanted to have my say! The paving stones of Paris would rise up under the popular indignation!"[26] But the scandal would have damaged the prestige of France and weakened her in the face of Germany. This Delcassé was unwilling to contemplate. Moreover, by a disclosure of this sort, France would obviously lose the advantage of being able to keep on reading the German telegrams in the future. For seventeen years, therefore, Delcassé guarded his secret and his precious data. Rather than injure France in any way, he told his friends that he would even go so far as to give his own support to his triumphant political opponents if the interests of the nation required him to do so. This was not idle talk. A year later when the act of Algeciras was laid before the Chamber of Deputies, Delcassé smothered his feelings and voted to ratify the work of the Conference rather than weaken the Government by his opposition and criticism.[27]

The truth is that Delcassé was more concerned for his foreign policy than for his own political welfare. He said to

[23] *Figaro*, Oct. 12, 1905; Hale, p. 197.
[24] Combarieu, p. 325; See also Mévil, *Echo de Paris*, Feb. 28, 1923.
[25] So called by Combarieu, p. 333; Mévil, *Echo de Paris*, Feb. 28, 1923.
[26] Mévil, *Revue Hebdomadaire*, June, 1923, pp. 133-134.
[27] Combarieu, p. 325; Delcassé, *J.O., Chambre*, Jan. 24, 1908, p. 105.

Lauzanne (or his friends) during the controversy provoked by *Le Matin*, "May the end be attained that the independence of our foreign policy be preserved";[28] and he remarked to Mévil, "All that matters is that my policy should remain undisturbed. I am convinced that it is strongly cemented. Sooner or later justice will be done to me."[29]

During the following months, it became apparent that the policy of Delcassé had not been materially affected by his resignation. There were good reasons for this. He had pursued a double end during 1904 and 1905. His basic aim had been to consolidate his great system of ententes. Then, because his diplomatic position seemed so powerful, he had attempted to exclude Germany from Morocco and thus to make a diplomatic triumph at Germany's expense. The system of ententes was sound to the core and rested upon the common interests of the Entente Powers, but the effort to exclude Germany from all discussions concerning the Sherifian Empire was something of an adventure, and an unnecessary one at that.[30] France repudiated this last as a useless departure from Delcassé's basic program, but retained the other features of his policy. Then, too, Germany got rid of Delcassé but did not succeed in getting rid of the permanent staff of the Quai d'Orsay. For instance, Paléologue, who was a sincere admirer of Delcassé's diplomacy, remained in charge of his old functions. Similarly, Bülow did not succeed in removing the career diplomats who had shared Delcassé's ideas on the subject of foreign affairs. M. Barrère said to his British colleague in Rome, June 13, 1905:

. . . that the leaders of French diplomacy, the two Cambons, Jusserand, and himself, were firmly united in sympathy for the policy of their late Chief and considered that there was no cause for alarm; the French position was a sound one in harmony with England and others."[31]

[28] *Le Matin*, Oct. 17, 1905.
[29] Mévil, *National Review*, July, 1908, p. 717.
[30] Delcassé, however, strongly maintained in 1908 that it was a necessary part of his policy. See Delcassé, *J.O., Chambre*, Jan. 24, 1908, pp. 97 and 103-108. It is difficult, though, to agree with his view.
[31] *B.D.*, III, 95.

Finally, German policy overreached itself. Rouvier, the new French Minister of Foreign Affairs, hoped that the Imperial Government would take a more compromising stand now that Delcassé was no longer in office. He insisted that France could hardly agree to an international settlement of the Moroccan dispute, because public opinion was opposed to it; but, in spite of all of his arguments and entreaties, Bülow persisted in his determination, and dragged France into the Conference of Algeciras. The tension between France and Germany therefore continued, as did the danger of war. In January of 1906, when the quarrel over Morocco was particularly acute, the chiefs of staff of the French and English armies and navies, with the approval of the ministers of state of their respective countries, carried on conversations and consultations regarding steps which could be taken to render military assistance to France in the event of an unprovoked attack on that Power by Germany. This involved an exchange of military information and the drafting of plans for transporting English troops and supplies across the Channel. Since it was foreseen that Germany might attack France through Belgium, the Belgian Chief of Staff was also persuaded to enter into the consultations, and plans were made for landing English troops on Belgian soil and for transporting them on Belgian railways.[32] Bülow's unwillingness to meet Rouvier halfway merely succeeded in forcing the new Minister of Foreign Affairs to adopt Delcassé's policy, and he adopted it with a vengeance—the military conversations between France, England, and Belgium leave no doubt of that!

In other respects, too, the Chancellor's victory over Delcassé was worse than a defeat. At the Conference of Algeciras, Bülow found to his amazement that he could not count on the support of any Powers other than Morocco and perhaps Austria. Great Britain, Russia, Spain, Portugal, and the United States generally gave their assistance to France, and

[32] B.D., III, 179, 186-187; Lt. Col. C. A. Repington, The First World War, 1914-1918 (London, 1920) p. 14; D.D., 3 S., II, 267-271; Collected Diplomatic Documents Relating to the Outbreak of the European War (London, 1915) pp. 354-360.

even the Italian delegation took sides against him. There can be but one conclusion. In the contest with the French diplomats, Bülow lost every round. He had attempted to break up the French system of ententes, but the *Entente Cordiale* had been cemented by the military and naval conversations mentioned above; and, at the Conference of Algeciras, the friends and allies of France had loyally supported her against Germany. He had tried to obtain a material interest in Morocco, but signally failed to accomplish his purpose, because the Powers decided to leave the Sherifian Empire in the tender care of France and Spain, subject only to a number of entirely inadequate provisions for international supervision.[33] Bülow succeeded in getting rid of Delcassé the man, but the Delcassé policy remained to plague him; and meanwhile French hatred of Germany had been increased by the Chancellor's own ill-considered actions. Finally, Bülow himself had pointed out to Delcassé the fact that the French system of ententes was weak on the military and naval side; and, as we shall see, the former Minister of Foreign Affairs immediately devoted all of his energy to remedying this defect, which might otherwise have escaped his notice until too late.

After the Conference of Algeciras, as Delcassé surveyed the European situation, it became apparent that, on the diplomatic side, his work was virtually finished. The same French statesmen who had denied his policy for a moment were rapidly carrying it to completion. Kaiser William II likewise noted this and was disgusted. "Fine prospects!" he remarked in September 1906. "In the future, we can count on the Franco-Russian Alliance, Anglo-French *Entente Cordiale* and the Anglo-Russian Entente, with Spain, Italy, and Portugal as appendages thereto in second line!"[34] The Anglo-Russian Entente, which completed the Triple Entente, was in fact sealed by a series of Anglo-Russian agreements regarding their respective interests in Persia, Afghanistan, and Thibet on August 31, 1907.[35] About two years later, October 24, 1909, Italy and Russia definitely made their peace in the Racconigi

---

[33] Anderson, pp. 394-402.   [34] *G.P.*, XXV, 23.   [35] *B.D.*, IV, 618-619.

Agreement dealing with the Straits, the Balkans, Tripoli, and Cyrenaica.[36] Diplomatically, France was in an exceptionally strong position. Her one weakness, at home and abroad, lay on the military and naval side—the first Moroccan Crisis had made that very clear. In June 1905, Delcassé had desired to call the German bluff, but France had not been strong enough to take the risk. A pacifist movement was in full swing; André and Pelletan had been allowed to throw the army and navy into confusion; even ammunition was lacking; and, in March 1905, compulsory military service had been reduced to two years.[37] Then, too, at that time, plans had not been made for receiving aid from the other side of the Channel. More than most Frenchmen, Delcassé perceived this fact as the chief lesson of his fall—that foreign policy and strategical preparedness would have to go hand in hand. Failure of such harmony meant military disaster or humiliating retreat.[38] Henceforth, we shall find him working to build up the fighting strength of France and the armed forces of those Powers in his system of ententes. This necessitated not only the creation of a stronger French army and navy, but assisting or encouraging Russia and England to build larger armies and navies. Finally, it was essential to coördinate the war plans of all three of these Powers. What a task! Nevertheless Delcassé was to apply himself to it wholeheartedly. Decidedly he was more dangerous to Germany now than he had ever been. It was not necessary to return to the Quai d'Orsay, where his work was approaching completion. He could best serve his system of ententes by playing this new rôle. How well he played it will be seen in the succeeding portions of this book.

2. Minister of Marine

. . . do not cease to improve and to tighten our alliance and our ententes, and at the same time to look after the army of our ententes and our alliance. (Delcassé, Jan. 24, 1908.)

[36] R. Marchand, *Une Livre Noire: Diplomatie d'avant Guerre d'après les Documents des Archives Russes* (2 vols., Paris, 1922) I, 357-358.

[37] Fontin, *Guerre et Marine*, p. 197; H. W. Wilson, *The War Guilt* (London, 1929) p. 99.

[38] *B.D.*, VI, 110.

The fact that M. Delcassé now aspires to control the French army or navy, seems to show that he now sees the nature of the great error into which he had fallen, of shaping a foreign policy without making sure that there was enough force to carry it through. (Minute in the British Foreign Office, signed by E.A.C., Jan. 28, 1908, C.H., and W.L., and subscribed to by E.G.)

The man who had decided to undertake this great task of strengthening the armed forces of France and of improving the fighting ability of those Powers in the French entente system, was already well prepared for this important work. As Minister of Foreign Affairs, he had maintained a close contact with the Chief of the General Staff of the French army and was informed of much of the secret military information concerning other Powers gathered by the army intelligence service and by the French spy service. For the same reason, he was acquainted with some of the features of the plan of campaign of the French and German general staffs. He also carried in his mind figures relative to the size of the standing armies of France and Germany.[39] Similarly, the Quai d'Orsay had been in close touch with the Chief of Staff of the French Marine, and Delcassé was perfectly aware of the deplorable condition of the navy: ". . . thanks to Camille Pelletan, we no longer have a fleet," he had remarked in November 1904.[40] Moreover, M. Barrère had warned him in the latter part of July 1904, that the German Government was cognizant of the decadence of the French navy. The French warships were not of a uniform type, and many of them were outmoded; the personnel was divided, and bad discipline reigned in the ranks. According to M. Barrère, Germany was counting upon this condition of the French marine, and on her own program of rapid naval expansion, to give her control of the sea by 1912. In this way, Germany hoped to maintain her hegemony in Europe in spite of all of her recent diplomatic defeats.[41]

[39] Paléologue, Un Prélude à l'Invasion de la Belgique, pp. 21-25; 53; 60-61; 79; 100-101; 107-108.

[40] Ibid., pp. 79; 106-107.

[41] Barrère to Delcassé, July 27, 1904, published in Revue des Deux Mondes, February 1, 1932, pp. 637-640.

In addition, M. Barrère learned that, during the Moroccan Crisis, the German Ambassador to Italy, Count Monts, had said, "There can be no question of our making war over the Moroccan affair. England would almost certainly take part in it and Germany would at one blow lose her fleet and her colonies, but in 1914, we shall be ready," meaning that by that date the German naval program would be complete.[42]

The most pressing need of France after 1905 was therefore a strong navy, and it was this problem which first engaged Delcassé's attention. However, the return to power lay through a long, hard road. He was still in partial disgrace, and many of his friends had left him.[43] An effort to exploit the French feeling for *Revanche* and to pose as a Nationalist was not received with any degree of enthusiasm.[44] Although the temptation to retire from politics must have been great, since Delcassé was counted a wealthy man, nevertheless he remained true to his purpose and did not despair of ultimately obtaining his object of serving the French marine. His perseverance was to some extent rewarded early in March 1906, when King Edward visited Paris. The English Monarch especially sought Delcassé and invited him to lunch. After such a signal honor, Delcassé's friends began to come back to him.[45] Moreover, Delcassé visited England, and was not only warmly welcomed there but was accommodated on the steps of the throne in the House of Lords.[46] Meanwhile, in March 1907, he was selected to be president of a parliamentary commission charged to investigate the explosion of the French warship *Jéna*. This indicated that he was at last beginning to regain the confidence of the Chamber of Deputies. It also marked his first success in his determination to restore the fighting strength of France.

While working for the favor of the Chamber, the distin-

[42] Barrère in *Revue des Deux Mondes*, Feb. 1, 1932.

[43] *Annales Politiques et Littéraires*, March 4, 1923, p. 212.

[44] *La Libre Parole*, Jan. 31, 1906; E. Judet, *Ma Politique* (Paris, 1923) pp. 37; 141.

[45] *Annales Politiques et Littéraires*, March 4, 1923, p. 212; Leghait to Favereau, March 6, 1906, in Morel, *Diplomacy Revealed*, pp. 42-43.

[46] Lord Newton, *Lord Lansdowne*, pp. 342-343.

guished Deputy from Ariège had maintained a discreet silence. On January 24, 1908, Jaurès referred to Delcassé's "rash" policy of 1905, and demanded that France abandon the whole Moroccan venture. All eyes turned toward the former Minister of Foreign Affairs. Delcassé saw his opportunity and asked to be allowed to say a few words. The presiding officer agreed to let him speak as soon as the others already on the schedule had finished their interpellations. Extraordinary excitement and movement at once prevailed throughout the Chamber and even in the street. So great was the curiosity and speculation as to what the gentleman from Ariège would have to say that deputies and journalists flocked in from everywhere. When the time came for Delcassé to defend his policy and to uphold the Moroccan enterprise, the house was packed.[47] Clemenceau, who had been one of the bitterest enemies of the Minister of Foreign Affairs in 1905, was there, too, and listened with arms crossed.

In defense of his Moroccan policy, Delcassé said that it had been inextricably bound up with his whole system of diplomacy, i.e., with his system of ententes. He declared that France ought not to liquidate her interests in the Sherifian Empire, but should continue to bring that valuable territory under French influence. In spite of Jaurès' protest against linking the name Delcassé to the Anglo-French rapprochement then so popular in England and France, Delcassé insisted that the *Entente Cordiale* was his handiwork and showed how he had gained the friendship of England without damaging the Franco-Russian Alliance. He also pointed out that he was chiefly responsible for the fact that France then enjoyed cordial relations with Spain and Italy. Guarded references to the intrigue which had caused his downfall, and the expression of the opinion that Germany would not have gone to war in 1905, provoked outbursts of indignation from two former members of Rouvier's Cabinet, but Delcassé did not elaborate his argument and did not permit himself to expose the whole secret of his dismissal. As a rule, his speeches

[47] Mévil, *Rev. Pol. et Parl.*, June, 1924, p. 393; *Le Temps*, Jan. 26, 1908.

were notable for their cogent reasoning and for their factual content rather than for eloquence, but on this day he stirred the patriotic feelings of his audience with such moving language as:

Messieurs, rappelez-vous! Il y a trente-sept ans, une nation gisait à terre, mutilée, saignée à blanc, seule, Oh! bien seule! Qui la pouvait craindre? Quelles appréhensions pouvait-elle inspirer? C'est le vainqueur pourtant, qui jugea utile et qui crut légitime de s'entourer d'alliés et d'amis. Il fit alliance avec une première puissance, puis avec une seconde, puis il contracta une contre-assurance avec une troisième, puis il gagna à son système les sympathies d'une quatrième, si bien que l'Europe entière finit par graviter autour de lui. Qui donc, alors, trouvait enviable la situation de la France? Qui donc alors n'aurait pas souhaité, autour de la France, des alliés et des amis? Et si une politique prévoyante avait déja pu les lui procurer, quel Français aurait eu l'idée de lui jeter la pierre?[48]

One deputy said later that, since the days of Gambetta, the Chamber had never heard words "*si belles et plus reconfortantes*," a tribute that must have gladdened Delcassé's heart.[49]

In closing, Delcassé urged France to improve further the Franco-Russian Alliance and to tighten the bonds between those Powers in the French system of ententes at the same time that she watched over the armies of her friends and allies. These preparatory measures, he maintained, would not only discourage aggressors, but would preserve and increase the security and prestige of the French Republic.[50]

As the speaker returned to his bench, the Chamber gave him a veritable ovation, the Socialists alone abstaining. In France, Delcassé's words produced "the great effect anticipated by his friends." The former Minister received more than four thousand telegrams, letters, postcards, and other communications from all parts of his native country, many of them being from distinguished literary men, artists, and

[48] *Annales de la Chambre*, Jan. 24, 1908, p. 132.
[49] Mévil, *Rev. Pol. et Parl.*, June, 1924, p. 393.
[50] *J. O., Chambre*, Jan. 24, 1908, pp. 97-108.

scientists.[51] The debate of January 24, 1908, was therefore an important step in his return to political power. Outside of France, the incident contributed materially to the hardening of the antagonism between the Entente Powers and Germany. In England there was a concert of praise for Delcassé as the Minister who had "conceived and realized" the *Entente Cordiale*.[52] Italian journals likewise reacted favorably to the speech, especially to those passages in which Delcassé had spoken of cordial relations between France and Italy. Some Italian papers quoted him *in extenso*.[53] On the other hand, German papers manifested a strict reserve, inspired perhaps by the Government, yet one of them replied to Delcassé's assertion that France and Germany would not have come to blows in 1905, by citing a speech of Prince Bülow, in which the latter had said that Germany would not have made war over Morocco any more than over the Hohenzollern candidacy to the throne of Spain in 1870, but that both controversies were capable of becoming for Germany an occasion for defending her honor, her prestige, and her position in the world. On the whole, the tone of the German press indicated that considerable tension existed between France and Germany, that mutual resentment divided the two nations, and that the Moroccan problem was still a very live issue.[54]

For about eight months after January 24, 1908, Delcassé sank back into his accustomed silence as he busily investigated the *Jéna* catastrophe and the condition of the French marine. He discovered that Pelletan had left the navy in a state of chaos. When Gaston Thomson became Minister of Marine at the time of the formation of the Rouvier Cabinet, improvements might have been expected, because he had been an editor of the *République Française* and an old disciple of Gambetta. However, after three years of office, the best that

[51] Mévil, *National Review*, July, 1908, p. 718.
[52] London *Times, The Globe, Westminster Gazette*, Jan. 25-27; *Le Temps*, Jan. 27, 1908.
[53] *Le Temps*, Jan. 27, 1908.
[54] *Le Temps*, Jan. 27, 1908; The German paper referred to was the *Cologne Gazette*.

could be said for Thomson was that he had created a school
for target practice at sea, bettered the powders and projectiles
somewhat, and made a good choice for the command.[55] Yet
the French navy remained fourth or fifth in rank, and the
old chaos and abuses continued. Worse still, the advent of
Thomson was attended by a long series of unprecedented disasters. A submarine and fourteen men were lost on July 5,
1905. An explosion on board the *Couronne* in April 1906,
and on the *Jules Ferry* in July, cost the lives of eight men.
In October, another submarine was lost with sixteen persons
on board. The *Algésiras* burned up in the harbor of Toulon
in the month following. This cost a million and a half francs
and the lives of three men. Nine others were killed in an
explosion at Quiberon, February 8, 1907; and, four days
later, the *Jean Bart* went aground on the Barbary coast, thereby entailing a loss of five and a half million francs. Then, on
March 12, 1907, the warship *Jéna* blew up at Toulon. The
Captain, seven officers, and 110 men were killed. This time
the bill amounted to thirty-five million francs. The French
people were at last aroused. A commission was appointed to
investigate the cause of the explosion and, as we already
know, Delcassé was made president of this commission. While
the commissioners labored, other accidents occurred. Two
ships ran into each other; a cruiser and a transport were
stranded; and thirty lives were lost in explosions or other
mishaps on five different occasions.[56]

As a result of the above circumstances, Thomson was bom-
barded with embarrassing interpellations on October 19,
1908. For more than an hour he strove to answer those who
angrily criticized his administration; but before he could recover from the first onslaught of his opponents, Delcassé came
forward to give him the fatal thrust. The debate was perhaps
all the more to Delcassé's liking because Thomson had been
one of those who had voted for Rouvier in the Council meeting of June 6, 1905. At any rate, Delcassé's attack was un-
usually violent. He asserted that during Thomson's adminis-

[55] C., Bos, *Refaisons une Marine* (Paris, 1910) pp. 86-87; 121.
[56] Hosotte, *Histoire de la Troisième République*, pp. 804-806.

tration there had been more destruction in the French navy than would have been occasioned by the loss of a major battle in wartime. Such a long and persistent series of accidents could be explained only on the ground of gross negligence on the part of the Minister of Marine, who had failed to heed the repeated warnings afforded by the accidents themselves. He declared that the *Jéna* catastrophe would never have occurred if Thomson had acted upon a report of August 1906, on the care of explosives. The marine as a whole, and the Commander of the *Jéna*, had awaited the Minister's authorization for safety measures all through 1906 and until the *Jéna* blew up on March 12, 1907. Delcassé then showed that Thomson had been unconscionably slow in reading and replying to the reports sent in to him as Minister of Marine. He had taken from April 20, 1905, until January 4, 1906, to read and reply to certain requests made after an inspection of the *Jéna*; yet, fourteen months later, he had still done nothing to improve conditions on board that ship.[57]

Delcassé's indictment of Thomson was very long, but when the speaker offered to rest the case, the Chamber cried, *"Parlez! Parlez!"* He continued, saying that negligence and heedlessness had spread from the top rank in the marine through the whole service and had resulted not only in confusion but in general discouragement as well. Hence the long list of accidents which had been accompanied with such horrible loss of life. Conditions in the French marine, he said, brought to mind the words of Marcellus, "Something is rotten in the State of Denmark." In conclusion, Delcassé said that there was no rational organization either in the marine service as a whole or in any branch of it. Harmony and coördination of effort simply did not exist. The basic ideas essential to military preparedness were also lacking. In short, the defects in the French navy were both moral and material. Reforms would have to be made at once, he said, and he called upon the Chamber for instant action.[58]

Thomson, who was now a very pathetic figure, attempted

[57] Delcassé, *Annales de la Chambre,* Oct. 19, 1908, pp. 81-85.
[58] *Ibid.,* pp. 85-86.

to reply to Delcassé; but the Chamber grew impatient when
the Minister argued that the situation was not as bad as it
had been described. "Do you want us to put our heads in a
bag so that we can't see?" cried one deputy. Meanwhile the
Chamber considered a motion by Delcassé censuring the
Government. The Premier, who happened to be Clemenceau,
was forced to intervene. He saved himself and all of the members of the Cabinet except Thomson, who was, of course,
beyond salvation. Indeed, the Minister of Marine had to
undergo the humiliation of resigning in front of the whole
Chamber.[59]

Thomson's post was given to Alfred Picard, who certainly
did not reform the marine and may have made it even worse,
if indeed that were possible.[60] On March 25, 1909, M. Brousse
reported on scandals in the service during the period 1902-
1907. The exposé was so astounding that Delcassé asked that
the Chamber appoint a commission of inquest to look into
the state of the marine and to report in time for legislative
action that session. He argued that a strong navy was necessary, first, to act as a sort of bridge between France and her
possessions in Africa, and, secondly, to strengthen the hold
of France upon those Powers in the French system of alliances
and ententes. The Chamber acceded to Delcassé's demand
and voted a commission of inquest, but it refused to go any
further. A motion censuring the Clemenceau Government
was lost by a vote of 316 to 267.[61]

A few days later, Delcassé was named to act as the president
of the new commission. He at once began a thorough investigation. Even the French ports in Algeria and Tunis were
visited. The verdict was that the French navy was unprepared
and that the naval administration and organization were both
scandalously vicious and even ridiculous. This report was
drawn up on the twenty-fourth or twenty-fifth of May. After
the reporter for the commission had described the situation
to the Chamber, Delcassé commented at length upon the con-

[59] Delcassé, Annales de la Chambre, Oct. 19, 1908.
[60] Bos, op. cit., p. 87.
[61] Annales de la Chambre, March 25, 1925, pp. 1018-1035.

clusions to be drawn from the report.[62] The climax was reached on July 20, 1909, when Delcassé turned his critical eye upon Picard and the whole Clemenceau Cabinet. The French marine had been the prey of fashion and caprice, he asserted. First of all, torpedo boats had been in vogue. No doubt such ships were useful, but they would have to operate close to the shore. Meanwhile, France had neglected to supply her men-of-war with proper cannon. The Russo-Japanese War showed that modern naval warfare was apt to be a long-range artillery combat. French warships would therefore have to be built to take the offensive and be armored according to the penetrating power of the enemy's guns. As the French navy actually stood, the fleet would be sunk long before it could get within reach of its foe, he declared. That is to say, if a war had broken out, the French ships would have had to run in order to escape destruction. But why, asked Delcassé, should France build heavy and expensive battleships which could do nothing more than beat a retreat?

Continuing his theme, Delcassé exposed the fact that there was an incredible slowness in the process of constructing a French warship. The machines in the shipyards were "archaic," anywhere from twenty-five to forty years old. By the time a man-of-war was finished, it was virtually out of date. It took seven years to build a French battleship. In that length of time England could build three. Equally amazing, however, was the fact that, even after the ships had been built, they were not adequately equipped with war materials and supplies, and were unable to fight for lack of ammunition. Moreover, there was only one place in France to repair a ship damaged in battle. In case of war, the French battleships would have to go in and out of this dock one at a time! Warships said to be in service were actually laid up in port in a hopeless condition. Anarchy reigned in the marine arsenals; confusion and disorder in the central administration.

Delcassé's final conclusion was that the Clemenceau Government had failed in the task of regenerating the French

[62] *Ibid.*, July 20, 1909, pp. 1385; 1510-1528.

marine. All of its reforms were plans laid in the future. In 1904, two years before Clemenceau came to power, he had presided over a commission of inquest into the marine. Why had he neglected to institute reforms upon becoming Premier? Was not the French navy a matter of concern for the Government? It followed that Clemenceau and his Cabinet were criminally responsible for the loss of the *Jéna* and for the deplorable condition of the French navy. They had done absolutely nothing to stop the forces of disintegration which had been at work in the French marine. Since the Cabinet had failed, it was time for the Chamber to do its duty, said Delcassé. The country demanded immediate action. The marine must be given a program and made capable of executing that program. The navy would have to be built up again from its very foundations, and it would have to be given an entirely new organization. Coördination of effort must be restored and directed toward preparedness for war. Construction should be speeded up; the quality of the ships improved; and provision made for wartime repairs. Such were the essentials of a marine worthy of the confidence of the French people, said Delcassé.

Delcassé's charges were so stupefying, so damning, that this time Clemenceau was at a loss to defend himself. The allegation that he had stifled the inquest of 1904 threw him into a blind rage. He decided to reply with a personal attack upon the former Minister of Foreign Affairs.

Delcassé says that I was president of the 1904 Commission of Inquest into the Marine. True; but it occurs to me that at the same time, Delcassé was a Minister and that he might well have applied to himself the excellent counsel which he has given to me today. . . . That was all the more necessary since he was planning in his mind the great piece of European diplomacy which was to conduct us to Algeciras. Remember those days and ask yourself if it is right that the man who led us to Algeciras should call ministers to account and accuse them of negligence in the preparation of the national defense![63]

In reply, Delcassé cited his own accomplishments as Min-

[63] *Annales de la Chambre*, July 20, 1909, pp. 1524-1526.

ister of Foreign Affairs. He had never been Minister of Marine, nor Premier, and preferred never to be Prime Minister, he said. During his term of office at the Quai d'Orsay there had not been any serious naval disaster. The same could not be said for Clemenceau, whose inaction as president of the commission of 1904, and as Premier, was inexcusable. The Chamber should do its duty and throw him out of office.

Then Clemenceau committed one of the supreme blunders of his political career. In answering, he said:

> Delcassé has singled me out personally and said, "You were president of the commission of inquest. You knew all the facts. Why have you done nothing?" What did I answer? I said, "You were a minister and you carried out a policy which involved us in the greatest humiliation we have ever undergone."
>
> You brought us to the doorsill of war, but you had not made any military preparation. You know full well—all the world knows, all Europe knows, that when the ministers of war and marine were interrogated they answered that we were not ready. . . .
>
> I have not humiliated France, but I say that Delcassé has humiliated her.[64]

The Chamber was thrown into a tumult. Was the Tiger crazy? Did he not realize that the fall of Delcassé, like the loss of Alsace-Lorraine, was a subject to be always kept in mind but never mentioned in public! *"Aux voix!"* "To the ballot!" cried the outraged deputies. The vote was taken. Clemenceau and his whole Cabinet were forced to resign immediately. As the former ministers were seen leaving the Chamber in a body, the Marquis de Pomereu exclaimed, "There is a justice!"

After overturning the Clemenceau Cabinet, Delcassé might reasonably have expected to return to power. Instead he found himself ostracized. He not only failed to get a portfolio, but he was not even called into consultation at the Elysée.[65] Justice had seemingly deserted him as abruptly as she had come to his aid.

[64] *Annales de la Chambre*, July 20, 1909, pp. 1527f.
[65] Mévil, *Revue Hebdomadaire*, June, 1923, p. 138.

If Delcassé did not benefit personally from his recent success in the Chamber, he at least had the satisfaction of seeing his hard labors result in the beginning of positive reforms in the marine. Briand formed the new Ministry, and the incompetent Picard was succeeded by Admiral Lapeyrère, who, between July 24, 1909 and March 2, 1911, gave new chiefs to the marine service, bettered conditions in the arsenals somewhat, and worked out a program of construction calling for twenty-eight new warships.[66] These measures were the first signs of a renaissance in the French navy, but most of the work still remained to be done when the Admiral and the Briand Cabinet fell from power in March 1911. It was still necessary to determine the probable allies and enemies of France, to give the French navy a clearly conceived strategy, to map out plans for concentration in peacetime and in wartime, to make arrangements for provisioning, coaling, and repairs, and to do away with those abuses in the service which Admiral Lapeyrère had been unable to remedy.

The stupendous task of completing the regeneration of the French navy fell to Delcassé, who became Minister of Marine in the Cabinet of Earnest Monis. It is clear that Delcassé occupied a very influential position in this Ministry, which was formed on March 2, 1911. Together with Monis and Minister of War Berteaux, he selected the other members of the Cabinet. Moreover, he completely overshadowed the Minister of Foreign Affairs, M. Jean Cruppi, who had, in fact, been chosen at the dictation of Berteaux and Delcassé.[67] Cruppi was a Radical Republican from Toulouse who had been Minister of Commerce in Clemenceau's Cabinet. He was wholly untrained in diplomacy. As *Le Figaro* said, *"Et Cruppi aux affaires étrangères? C'est parfait. Il y sera tout à fait étranger."*[68]

As an indication of how thoroughly Delcassé dominated

[66] Bos, pp. 87-88; Vice-Admiral De Cuverville, *La Marine Française* (Paris, 1911), p. 58.

[67] *Manchester Guardian*, March 2 and 3, 1911.

[68] *Le Figaro*, March 2, 1911; *Le Matin*, March 2; *Manchester Guardian*, March 3, 1911.

the situation, we need only point out that M. Monis was anxious to be in accord with Delcassé on questions of foreign policy,[69] and that, characteristically, one of the first acts of the new Cabinet was to pay a visit to the English Embassy. This last took place on the third of March. All of the French ministers expressed their satisfaction at the friendly understanding which existed between their country and England. Bertie, the English Ambassador, voiced his regret that Delcassé had not returned to the Quai d'Orsay, but added that doubtless M. Cruppi, who had only a short and indirect experience in foreign affairs, would find the Minister of Marine a valuable counselor. Delcassé replied that he would have preferred to remain out of office, but that the vote of the Chamber and the appeal of M. Monis had obliged him to heed the call of duty. He knew that, for the time being, he could not hold the office of Foreign Minister, yet he feared that, in addition to his onerous labors as Minister of Marine, he would be constantly appealed to in regard to foreign affairs. As for French relations with other Powers, M. Cruppi would tell the Ambassador that the Monis Ministry intended to continue the policy which he, Delcassé, had initiated and which had been followed ever since by successive French Governments. Moreover, Delcassé declared that his own presence in the Cabinet was the best proof possible that France desired to have the most intimate relations with England.[70]

M. Monis spoke next and said that he intended to be very correct in matters of foreign policy in order to avoid giving the German Government any pretext for complaint. He had been glad to avail himself of Delcassé's services for the navy, and had incurred the risk of offending Germany by including him in the Cabinet, he said, but it was a risk which he had felt obliged to take in the interest of a better French marine.[71] M. Monis concurred with Bertie in thinking that Delcassé's experience in foreign affairs would be very valuable to the other ministers, but went on to say that the foreign

---

[69] *Manchester Guardian*, March 2, 1911.
[70] *B.D.*, VI, pp. 596-597.
[71] *Ibid.*, VI, p. 596f.; *G.P.*, XXIX, p. 74, No. 10523n.

policy of France would be decided not by one man but by the whole Cabinet. M. Delcassé would have his say, and his opinions would carry great weight, but he would have his own work to attend to, and it would be quite sufficient to occupy all his energy.[72]

However, Delcassé seems to have been much more influential than the Premier was willing to admit. For instance, Bertie's conversation with the French Minister of Foreign Affairs turned almost exclusively on commercial topics; but the English diplomat was careful to have another general discussion with Delcassé on such important subjects as the Potsdam interviews, Persian affairs, the Bagdad Railway, and Turkey. He also proposed to make a return visit to Delcassé and to ask him to confer with the Minister of Foreign Affairs on the subject of an aerial conference.[73] Moreover, we know that Cruppi "loudly and emphatically" echoed all that Delcassé felt and said with regard to Franco-Russian relations.[74] and that he was completely dominated by Delcassé's advice when, in the latter part of May 1911, questions arose with regard to the secret Franco-Spanish Moroccan treaty of 1904.[75] These facts appear to corroborate the opinion prevalent at the time, that Delcassé would inevitably influence the activity of M. Cruppi because the latter was so poorly versed in foreign affairs.[76]

As Minister of Marine in the Caillaux Cabinet, which lasted from June 27, 1911, until January 14, 1912, Delcassé continued to follow the course of European events from a double point of view, the one military and the other diplomatic, and unsparingly devoted his interest and vigilance to both the navy and questions of foreign policy.[77] At this time, the Foreign Minister was De Selves, who, like Cruppi, was without experience in diplomacy.[78] The outstanding

[72] B.D., VI, p, 596f.   [73] Ibid., VI, p. 596f.
[74] B. de Siebert and G. A. Schreiner, Entente Diplomacy and the World (N.Y. and London, 1921), p. 560.
[75] B.D., VII, pp. 272-273; 277.
[76] F. Stieve, Isvolsky and the World War (N.Y., 1926), p. 24; Fay, I, p. 281.
[77] Mévil, Revue Hebdomadaire, June, 1923, p. 139; Le Matin, February 21, 1913.   [78] Schuman, op. cit., p. 190.

diplomatic event was the second Moroccan Crisis, which was precipitated on July 1, 1911, when the German gunboat *Panther* anchored at the Moroccan port of Agadir in protest against the French occupation of Fez. Delcassé's acquaintance with Morocco and experience in the earlier crisis obviously qualified him to give useful suggestions to the Caillaux Cabinet, yet he was forced to be very circumspect. His return to power in March as Minister of Marine had been received with enthusiasm in England, where naval matters were of such import and where opinion was hostile to Germany. In Russia there had been similar rejoicing because he had assured the Russian diplomats that his entry into the Ministry was a guarantee of the special care which would be bestowed upon the military power of France. In fact he had promised "redoubled activity" in that respect.[79] On the other hand, his appointment, and the extravagant eulogies in the English and Russian press, had occasioned widespread distrust and discontent in Germany. Although newspapers in that country attempted to be indifferent to Delcassé's political successes, yet it was admitted that his return to power brought up memories of a bitter conflict and that the very name Delcassé stood for a program which, needless to say, was characterized by hostility to Germany.[80] Then, too, since the second Moroccan Crisis followed closely upon the heels of Delcassé's return to high office, it was natural that there should have been a tendency to connect his name with the controversy. Some Germans insisted that Delcassé was the true originator of French Moroccan policy, and a cartoon entitled "The Moroccan Comedy" appeared in Munich on September 11, 1911, showing France under the mask of Delcassé with sword raised.[81]

[79] R. Marchand, *Un Livre Noire* (Paris, 1922), I, 43, 45; Siebert-Schreiner, *Entente Diplomacy and the World*, pp. 558-559.

[80] *Vossische Zeitung; Post; Kölnische Zeitung*, March 1-3, 1911.

[81] *Simplicissimus*, Sept. 11, 1911; Siebert-Schreiner, *op. cit.*, pp. 580, 582; "Delcassé und Marokko," in *Blatter Historisch-Politische, für das Katholische Deutschland* (Munich), 1911, pp. 794-800; "Delcassé und Delcassismus," in *Monatschrift, Konservative*, 1911, pp. 1085-1093; Boden, C. F., *Zur Psychologie der französischen Diplomatie* (Brauschweig, 1912), pp. 32-35; 40; G.P., XXIX, p. 127, reference to the press.

During this trying period, Delcassé remained upon his guard, but gave advice freely, as he considered it his duty to do, to both the Premier and the Minister of Foreign Affairs. Moderation and sound sense best describe his counsel, and Caillaux, at least, appears to have been swayed by it. When the suggestion was made that France might respond to the German coup at Agadir by despatching a French warship to Mogador, Caillaux insisted that Delcassé must be consulted because, as Minister of Marine, he would have to send the ship, and moreover because "his knowledge of foreign affairs and particularly his insight into the Moroccan question gave him a special authority" in this matter.[82] With his usual quickness of perception, Delcassé saw that a French expedition to Mogador was hardly apropos, and he strongly opposed the idea. Such action would only be an indication of weakness, he said. It would give the impression that France did not dare send her man-of-war to Agadir where the German battleship was anchored. On the other hand, France would seem to be inviting a conflict if she did order her ship to that port. Delcassé therefore concluded that it would be best to interpret the *Panther* incident as a German request for conversations on the subject of Morocco. If, in the course of these discussions, Germany should make demands which were not acceptable, then, and then only, should the French Government consider retaliatory measures.[83] After some trouble with De Selves and after Great Britain declined to send a ship to a Moroccan port, Delcassé's wise solution of the problem came to prevail, and the Franco-German conversations which he had envisaged took place.[84] The negotiations were long drawn out, and in the successive Cabinet meetings and conferences of ministers and ambassadors Delcassé was given an opportunity to exert an important influence as the "arch-apostle of prudence and moderation."[85]

[82] J. Caillaux, *Agadir, Ma Politique Extérieure* (Paris, 1919), p. 108.
[83] *Ibid.*, pp. 108-109; Sir Geo. Arthur (translator), *The Memoirs of Raymond Poincaré* (N.Y., 1926-   ) (hereafter to be cited as *Memoirs of Poincaré*), Vol. I, 8; Mermeix, *L'An 1911*, pp. 91-94.
[84] Caillaux, *Agadir*, pp. 109-111; *Memoirs of Poincaré*, I, 8.

Although he had become the champion of cautious measures, Delcassé did not believe that war with Germany could
long be postponed. More than ever he was convinced that
France must get herself in readiness for an armed conflict
with her great eastern neighbor. In a conversation that illustrates his mental attitude toward Germany and toward the
impending struggle, he said to his friend André Mévil, September 13, 1911, when the Agadir Crisis was at its height:

> I think that this time an agreement will be reached, but it will
> not settle anything, because war is inevitable. No durable arrange-
> ment can be concluded with Germany. Her mentality is such that
> one can no longer dream of living in lasting peace with her. . . .
> Paris, London, and St. Petersburg should be convinced now that
> war is, alas! inescapable and that it is necessary to prepare for it
> without losing a minute.[86]

According to Delcassé, in case of an immediate war with
Germany, France and her allies would have a slightly better
chance of winning, the odds being about fifty-five to sixty
out of a hundred in their favor. In six months or a year the
French chances of success would be even greater. The war
would take place not in Lorraine but on the Belgian frontier,
he prophesied; but the English would come to the assistance
of Belgium and France. Five days after the declaration of war,
England could send over to the Continent an expeditionary
force of 100,000 men under General French. That excellent
officer had just watched the military maneuvers in both Germany and France, and considered that the French army was
not inferior to its German adversary. He even believed the
French army superior in some respects. Finally, said Delcassé,
France would have command of the Mediterranean, and so
Spain need not be feared. Moreover, Italy would remain'
neutral.[87]

Delcassé's assertion that in six months or a year France

---

[85] Caillaux, *Agadir*, pp. 110, 210, 229; Mermeix, *L'An 1911*, pp. 145-155;
Memoirs of Poincaré, Vol. I, 8.

[86] A. Mévil, *Revue Hebdomadaire*, June, 1923, pp. 140-141, from a written
memoir of the conversation made immediately afterwards by Mévil.

[87] *Ibid.*, pp. 140-141.

would have a better chance of winning the next war with Germany was not an idle boast. He was at that very moment taking measures which would greatly increase the efficiency and strength of the French navy; and, as if to make doubly sure of the neutrality of Italy, he figured in the prelude to the Turco-Italian War which broke out in the last days of September 1911. Cruppi had promised the Italians some time before that if Italy went to war, France would loyally abide by the engagements which Delcassé had concluded with the Italian Government in 1902. Later, when the time came for the Italians to act, Cruppi's successor, De Selves, agreed to give unconditional diplomatic support, and Delcassé himself assured the Italian Ambassador that every French wish and sympathy was with Italy.[88]

Upon the fall of Caillaux, January 14, 1912, Delcassé might easily have formed a Government of his own. Poincaré promised his support, and, for more than an hour, urged him to accept the double post of Premier and Minister of Foreign Affairs.[89] Even the Germans would have had no objection to make,[90] but Delcassé considered that his oratory was quite inadequate to do justice to a Prime Minister's rôle in Parliament, and so refused to accede to the wish of Poincaré. However, when the latter offered to take charge of the Quai d'Orsay and to form a Cabinet, Delcassé agreed to remain in office as head of the French navy.[91] Since the two men were united by a friendship which dated from 1889, and since they saw eye to eye in matters of foreign policy, they were able to work together in the closest harmony from January 14, 1912, until the dissolution of the Ministry on January 18, 1913. As we shall see, during this period the principal achievements of Delcassé as Minister of Marine had vast diplomatic consequences.[92]

Before describing Delcassé's reform of the marine, it is

[88] G. Giolitti, *Memoirs of My Life* (London, 1923) p. 265.
[89] *Memoirs of Poincaré*, Vol. I, 8.   [90] *G.P.*, XXIX, 447, No. 10793.
[91] *Memoirs of Poincaré*, I, 8.
[92] Poincaré's speech of Feb. 28, 1923, quoted in *Le Matin*, March 1, 1923; Poincaré, *J.O.*, March 1, 1923, pp. 2017f.

also necessary to say that he regularly attended the meetings of the Supreme Council of National Defense. This body was formed July 28, 1911, in order to coördinate the work of the General Staffs of the army and navy with that of the various ministries devoted to the national defense, such as war, marine, and foreign affairs. The Council first met in October 1911, and held secret sessions at regular intervals thereafter.[93] At such meetings, Cabinet ministers and military and naval experts exchanged ideas and information and carefully made their plans for concerted action in wartime. Among the questions discussed by Delcassé was that of the initial action of the French army in the event of a war with Germany, the transport of North African troops to France after the outbreak of hostilities, the place where the French fleet should be concentrated, and the first objectives of the French navy after the declaration of war.[94]

Such were the varied activities of Delcassé as Minister of Marine from March 2, 1911, to January 18, 1913. The navy itself, however, was that branch of the national defense most in need of his energy and his genius. As he said in the Senate on June 22, 1911:

What conclusions were drawn from the exposé of the condition of the marine in 1909? They were two in number: First, that France did not have a fleet capable of supporting her foreign policy. . . . Second, that the fleet which we did possess in 1909, on account of the lack of munitions and on account of the absence of supplies and dry docks, was scarcely capable of being used.[95]

In reforming and strengthening the French marine, Delcassé's first step was to map out a plan of action. Briefly, he proposed to make sure that the French navy was strong enough to play the rôle that it ought to play in the French system of alliances and ententes which he himself had built up and which had been consolidated into the Triple Entente

[93] T. B. Mott, *Personal Memoirs of Joffre* (2 Vols., N.Y. and London, 1932), I, 37-38, 49-52, 99f.
[94] *Ibid.*, pp. 49-52, 99f.
[95] *Annales du Sénat,* June 22, 1911, p. 1079.

by his successors. Taking into consideration existing alliances and understandings and the sources from which France could expect enemy attacks, he planned to have the French fleet act either as an auxiliary to some friendly or allied fleet, or, if necessary, to act alone, but always to have a superior force at those points where the vital interests of France would have to be defended.[96] As time went on, one feature of this plan came into special prominence. Written naval agreements were necessary to insure the French fleet of assistance from Great Britain and Russia, and these commitments had the effect of tightening the bonds between the Entente Powers.

Moreover, it was Delcassé's opinion that, above everything else, France must have control of the Mediterranean in order to obtain supplies and troops from Africa. In the intimacy of his office at rue Royale, he said to his subordinates:

> You know whence the danger comes; without Africa, without the marine to make a *bridge,* France cannot resist Germany. The fate of our colonies is tied to that of the mother country, but the existence of France also depends upon the maintenance of her Mediterranean communications.[97]

Having clearly defined the purpose and the needs of the French marine, Delcassé carried on a strenuous fight in the Chambers to secure an organic naval law which would place the navy beyond the reach of transient political majorities and thus make it a permanent force. He asked that Parliament sanction a complete building program to which a schedule for the replacement of each ship after a definite period of service should be attached. This was the salient feature of his great naval law of March 30, 1912, which called for twenty-eight warships by 1919, and for fifty-two torpedo boats, ninety-four submarines, and a great number of other craft to be used as transports, mine layers, scouts, etc. The law gave each ship a definite term of life and provided for replacement. It also went into details on such matters as armament and the size of the crew. Provision was made for spare can-

[96] G. Durand-Viel, Capitaine de Vaisseau, *Delcassé et la Marine* (Paris, 1923), pp. 5-6, reprinted from *Revue Maritime,* May, 1923.
[97] *Ibid.,* pp. 6-7.

non, munitions, food, and supplies of all sorts, as well as for the construction of works in France and at Bizerte where the fleet could be received and given necessary repairs. Moreover, Delcassé began to organize an aviation service.[98]

While the naval program was being successfully carried through the mazes of parliamentary politics, Delcassé was also doing his utmost to hasten ship construction and naval preparation. In order to enlist the sympathy and coöperation of all Frenchmen in this work, he decided to name the first two ships *Paris* and *France,* and to call the later ones after the great maritime provinces, i.e., *Bretagne, Provence, Normandie,* and *Gascogne.* Likewise, in the very midst of the Agadir Crisis, he staged the great naval review of September 4, 1911, which was attended by the President of France, the Premier, six ministers of state, twelve admirals, twelve thousand sailors, ninety-three war craft of various descriptions, and a great crowd of visitors, both French and foreign. During this celebration, Delcassé hugely enjoyed himself on board the *Edgar Quinet.* He knew that the newspaper men would vie with one another in describing the review and that the attention of the French people would be focused upon naval questions, and also that assembling so many warships at Toulon would have its effect upon foreign affairs. "The French marine is particularly sneered at in Germany," said the *Echo de Paris,* September 4, 1911. "It is well that our amiable neighbors should be able to perceive that it still has very much life." Maneuvers took place immediately after the review, and, in order that the French people might remain "marine conscious," Delcassé took the unusual step of permitting the press to follow the operations of the fleet. He even ordered the visiting journalists to be shown every attention upon the warships themselves. In return, the newspapers devoted long articles to the French navy and its problems.[99]

[98] *Annales de la Chambre,* Feb. 13, 1912, pp. 436f., 394-438; Tramond and Reussner, *Éléments d'Histoire Maritime* (published under the direction of the Historical Service of the Chief of Staff of the Marine, Paris, 1924) pp. 719-720; Durand-Viel, *op. cit.,* pp. 5, 9-11.
[99] *Echo de Paris,* Sept. 4, 9, 11-13, 16-19, 22-23, and throughout the year; Durand-Viel, *op. cit.,* p. 11.

Delcassé also remained for the first part of the battle practice. Before leaving, he eulogized the fleet and its spirit and made the significant remark, "I insist upon this, that our war material be ready for all emergencies which may arise in any place at any time."[100]

But even while he was attempting to inspire throughout France a patriotic interest in the French navy, a dangerous spirit prevailed among the workers in the shipyards and in the arsenals. Strikes and other troubles among these laborers had been looked upon as almost normal under preceding ministers of marine; but Delcassé determined to put an end to such disorders. Just before the *Jean Bart* was to be launched on September 22, 1911, it was reported that the workers were planning hostile demonstrations. While the "Marseillaise" was being sung in honor of the new ship, they were to come together and sing both the "Carmagnole" and the "Internationale" and to prevent the launching if possible.[101] In order to handle this problem, the Minister of Marine decided upon a twofold policy. First of all, he resolved to suppress labor disturbances by taking a firm stand with the aid of soldiers and police. Gendarmes were to protect government property; and workmen who insisted upon being unruly were to be summarily dismissed from their jobs. Secondly, he purposed to make an appeal to the patriotism and self-interest of the laborers. This double plan was carried out at once. Energetic police measures prevented disorders during the christening of the *Jean Bart,* which took place under the towers of the old fortress of the Borda at Brest on September 22, 1911. However, it was not necessary to take unusual precautions when the *Courbet* was launched without disturbance the day following at Lorient, where the whole town rejoiced in fête attire. In each case, after the ship had glided into the water, Delcassé made a patriotic address to the engineers and workers. He informed them that he desired to speed up construction, but that in order to succeed, greater regu-

[100] *Echo de Paris,* Sept. 11, 1911.
[101] *Echo de Paris,* Sept. 16, 17, 20, 1911.

larity was needed on the part of the laboring men and mechanics, and that, consequently, he must have their coöperation. He announced that he had already taken steps to improve their lot considerably by providing for promotions and for an annual two-weeks vacation with pay. He intended to do even more for them, he said, but if they wished to see these additional improvements made, they must give him an argument to use before the budget committee of the Chamber of Deputies. This they could best do by increasing the quality and quantity of their work. At Lorient, where most of the men had been loyal to the Government, Delcassé decorated and embraced many of the mechanics. By giving them the honors of *Chevalier du Mérite Agricole,* he sought to wean them away from strike leaders.[102]

On the whole, Delcassé's twofold policy succeeded admirably well. The big warships which Admiral Lapeyrère had expected to complete by 1922 Delcassé was able to promise three years sooner. By January of 1913, the activity in the French shipyards became intense. Officials in charge of building operations, and even most of those in the lower ranks, made it a point of honor to deliver the finished product as soon as possible, and often did so sooner than the date mentioned in the contracts. Henceforth, units were to be constructed and ready for service in three years, though twice as large as those formerly exacting five or six years under previous ministers. The speed with which France constructed her men-of-war was then equal to the best foreign records, and excited the admiration even of the English naval authorities.[103] The Minister of Marine could afford to be satisfied. The size of the building program and the speed with which the ships were built were both in keeping with his ideal of giving France a fleet corresponding to her foreign policy. France was guaranteed a position of influence in the councils of her friends and allies.[104]

[102] *Echo de Paris,* Sept. 16-17, 20, 23-24, 1911.
[103] *Echo de Paris,* Sept. 29, 1912; Jan. 11, 28, 1913; *British Navy League Annual,* 1913-1914, pp. 233; 242.
[104] Durand-Viel, *Delcassé et la Marine,* p. 10.

The above result was not obtained without a tremendous nervous strain upon Delcassé. Something was radically wrong with the gun powder then in use, and the Minister of Marine was plagued by a series of disastrous explosions, the most notable of which completely destroyed the battleship *Liberté* on September 25, 1911. This was the finest warship in the French navy, and for a while it was feared that the whole French fleet might be sunk by its own munition supply. Whereas Thomson had allowed matters to drift, Delcassé applied himself with almost superhuman energy to the task of preventing the recurrence of such accidents. His difficulty was all the greater because of the tense European situation during 1911 and 1912. He could not dump all the old ammunition overboard because France would have been left unarmed at a moment when there was a serious danger of war. He was obliged to work feverishly far into the night consulting technicians and experts, and reading the reports and recommendations of his officers. Next morning, he would be at his desk as early as usual. At times he reached his office long before anyone else had arrived, and had to enter the Ministry of Marine by way of the rear entrances and fire escapes. Mévil thinks that the strenuous labors of this critical period brought on the heart trouble from which Delcassé died many years later.[105] The necessity of viewing and investigating the wreck of the *Liberté* was a particularly harrowing experience for Delcassé He was at first unable to go on board the ruined hull of the ship and returned to the cabin of his launch, where he lay prostrate for some time. In the end, however, he summoned all his reserve strength and went through the ordeal.[106]

Delcassé's ultimate solution of the gunpowder problem was to take all of the safety measures possible. The older munitions on each ship were ordered debarked and the remaining supplies were to be replaced gradually by a new explosive containing the "diphenylamine stabilizer" in use

[105] *Revue Hebdomadaire*, June, 1923, pp. 138f.; Reynald, p. 6.
[106] *Echo de Paris*, Sept. 26 and 28, 1911.

in the American navy. He planned to accomplish this by the end of 1912 but, at the same time, to carry on studies designed to effect further improvements in the French explosives. Success crowned the Minister's efforts here as elsewhere. Though he did not succeed in getting a perfect powder, there were no more major disasters in the service.[107]

Two more reforms connected with the building of a strong French navy should be mentioned before passing on to other aspects of Delcassé's work. In July 1912, he laid before Parliament his plans for reorganizing the technical section of the Ministry of Marine. This body of men prepared the building plans and watched over the construction of the ships. Delcassé declared that he wanted permission to expand or reduce this department according to the needs of the mo-ment, as in private industry. Just then he desired to augment its staff, he said. He also proposed to house the men in more sanitary and healthful surroundings. Then, too, it was Delcassé who introduced the practice of having future captains and lieutenants go to the shipyards to supervise the completion of the warships which they were slated to command. The Minister first tried this scheme in connection with the officers who were to be in charge of the torpedo destroyers then being built, and the results were so happy and so immediate that he applied the system at once to the larger ships also.[108]

Obviously, the creation of a new and larger fleet necessitated a more numerous and a more efficient personnel. When Delcassé took charge of the marine, the officers and sailors were discouraged by the decadence of the French navy and were still under regulations which were better suited to navies of the eighteen nineties than to those of the twentieth century. Moreover, the recruiting and training services were so far behind the times that they could not enlist and train men fast enough to furnish officers and sailors for the fleet which was being built in accordance with the law of March

---

[107] *Echo de Paris*, Sept. 28, 1911; *Navy League Annual* (British), 1912-1913, p. 243; Durand-Viel, *op. cit.*, pp. 25-27.
[108] *Echo de Paris*, July 8 and 20, 1912.

298 Théophile Delcassé

30, 1912.[109] In the course of ninety-five sessions of the great committee of inquest, Delcassé had interviewed every man qualified to tell him what ought to be done to remedy this condition. His reforms included modernizing the instruction in the naval academy, which was to be given new quarters and new equipment. Better training was also provided for all of the officers of lower grade. Men in all ranks were asked to specialize and were ordered to be employed in that branch of the service for which they were best qualified by their intensive training or education. Specialization was to be encouraged, particularly in the field of naval aviation. By way of increasing the number of seamen in the humbler ranks (aside from the conscripted men to be used under the two-years' service law), Delcassé arranged for a system of reserves. Then, too, the sailor's life was made more attractive by providing for retirement after a period of fifteen years. Moreover, alluring posters were printed and displayed in order to draw adventurous and ambitious young men into the navy, or into some branch of it where they might become skilled mechanics, electricians, or designers. New methods were also instituted for the recruiting of workers in the arsenals. Formerly they entered upon government employment at the age of thirteen or fifteen as apprentices and had been instructed at state expense. The system had two disadvantages. It was costly and, besides, such persons were apt to be the children of those workmen already employed by the Government. This last meant that, like their fathers, they were discontented and given to strikes. Delcassé proposed to take in new blood. The doors of the arsenals were opened to young men between the ages of sixteen and eighteen who had graduated from the practical industrial schools and who were to be given places as workers' assistants. Then, as a final measure in the reform of the personnel of the marine, Delcassé infused his own energy and patriotic spirit into all branches and ranks of the department. He was frequently seen inspecting the shipyards and arsenals and speaking to the workers or

[109] Durand-Viel, *op. cit.*, 13.

ordinary sailors. He loved to mingle with the men on board ship, to watch the call to the colors at evening, and to follow the regular naval maneuvers. At such times, the aides who accompanied him found that it was necessary to be alert, because they had to answer a multitude of questions accurately. Delcassé had a remarkable memory for detailed information, and more than once astonished a young officer by citing facts and figures relative to the armament of the ships which were passing in review. The naval administration was impressed particularly by the Minister's wholehearted devotion to his duty. It was long remembered that one day when a messenger arrived at the Ministry of Marine with the news that the gallant Jacques Delcassé had been dangerously wounded in an aeroplane accident, the Minister, although visibly grieved, insisted upon signing and commenting upon the day's despatches before proceeding to the bedside of his injured son. Such unselfish patriotism on the part of the Chief necessarily inspired something of a like spirit throughout the whole marine organization.[110]

A great navy, if it was to be an effective fighting instrument, had to be properly commanded. Moreover, under modern conditions, war plans and preparations had to be carefully made in time of peace in order to avoid wasted effort after the outbreak of hostilities. Finally, an up-to-date and well-organized central administration was needed to read and act upon the reports and recommendations which came in to the Ministry of Marine from the inspectors of the fleet and from those who reported on the state of the training schools, the construction works, and the repair shops. When Delcassé first took over the marine, great confusion reigned in these particulars. For the purpose of the maneuvers, it was customary to select a commander-in-chief of the naval forces, but his office terminated with the close of the exercises. There was no assurance that the man who commanded and trained the navy in time of peace would also lead it into

[110] Durand-Viel, op. cit., pp. 13-16; 27-31; Echo de Paris, Aug. 28, 1912; Sept. 26, 27, 29, 1912; Jan. 13, 1913.

battle. In addition, the fleet was scattered in different parts of the world and hence necessarily under separate officers. The French navy therefore lacked cohesion and unified training. Equally harmful was the fact that since there was no permanent chief commander, there was likewise no permanent staff for the high command, and consequently no continuity of ideas in that important quarter. The staff, like the office of commander-in-chief, was provisional and changed completely as each new admiral took charge. There was a Chief of the General Staff of the navy, but an old law of January 21, 1892, made him director of the Ministry of Marine and vested him with absolute authority over all branches of the service. This meant that in addition to his normal occupation of making war plans, he was expected to look after the central administration; but unhappily the magnitude of the task rendered it an impossible one. Certain directing officials in the marine were therefore given an autonomy which resulted in an absence of responsibility and a lack of coördinate action in administrative matters.

Even before Delcassé took office, there had been a reaction against these anarchical conditions. Admiral Lapeyrère, by grouping around him men used to working together under his command, had achieved more unity than his predecessors, but the same institutions remained in operation as before and threatened to restore the old chaos the moment he was succeeded by another Minister. Here again, Delcassé made sweeping reforms. Although he insisted upon the responsibility of the Minister of Marine for coördinate and efficient action in his department, he saw that a complete reorganization of the central administration was necessary. He wisely decided to "give the marine to marine," i.e., to men who made the navy their profession. This he did by having the President of France place the central administration under the direction of two admirals who were to look after both the fleet and the various construction and repair works on shore. Being in close touch with the other naval officers, these two admirals would be in a better position than anyone else to make decisions and to give the orders seen to be necessary after reading the reports of the inspectors and other experts. Moreover, under this arrangement, the Chief of the General Staff of the marine would be left free to concentrate upon his proper function of preparing war plans and signals.[111] As for the supreme command of the French navy, that also occupied Delcassé's attention. The French warships were concentrated in the Mediterranean and placed under the orders of Admiral Lapeyrère, who was also given the assurance that he should be the commander-in-chief in the event of war. Finally, Delcassé instituted new regulations which provided for a reasonable degree of permanence in the staffs of both the commander-in-chief and the other high officers in the service. This last gave stability to the high command and made possible that continuity of ideas which was indispensable to a good military organization and to military preparation.[112]

There remained the task of coördinating the war plans and preparations of the French navy with those of England and Russia. The disturbed state of Europe in 1912 occasioned by the Turco-Italian War and its repercussions in the Balkans caused uneasiness among the great Powers. Austria and Germany drew closer to each other at the same time that Germany expanded her naval program. The Powers of the Triple Entente also increased their solidarity and sought to quicken their own preparations. In July 1912, Vice-Admiral Prince Lieven, Chief of the General Staff of the Imperial Russian navy, came to Paris, took up his residence in a hotel near rue Royale and went daily to the Ministry of Marine where he had long conversations with Admiral Aubert, Chief of the General Staff of the French navy. The object of their concern was the fact that although the Franco-Russian Alliance provided for coöperation and exchange of information between the French and Russian armies in time of peace,

[111]Durand-Viel, pp. 16-19; *Echo de Paris*, Dec. 19, 1912; *Navy League Annual* (British), 1912-1913, p. 244.
[112] Durand-Viel, pp. 16-22; *Echo de Paris*, Nov. 3, 1912; Dec. 19, 1912; Jan. 28, 1913; *Navy League Annual* (British), 1912-1913, p. 244.

there was no similar agreement respecting the navies of the two allied Powers. It was now proposed that the coöperation of the French and Russian naval forces be worked out in time of peace and that the Chiefs of Staff be authorized to correspond directly, exchange information, study all hypotheses of war, and prepare strategic plans. It was also thought advisable for the French and Russian Chiefs of Staff to meet at least once a year to discuss important questions, and it was further agreed that a written account of these meetings should be kept. On July 16, 1912, a naval convention embodying these principles was signed by Admiral Aubert and Delcassé on the one hand and by Prince Lieven and the Russian Minister of Marine on the other. This naval agreement was expected to supplement the military and diplomatic accords of the Franco-Russian Alliance, and Article Four specifically gave to it the duration, effectiveness, and secrecy of the Franco-Russian military convention of August 17, 1892, and all subsequent Franco-Russian agreements. Poincaré, Premier and Minister of Foreign Affairs in France, and the Russian Minister of Foreign Affairs joyfully gave their consent to this arrangement, and, when the former went to Russia in August of the same year, an exchange of letters between the French and Russian Ministers of Foreign Affairs placed the naval convention on an absolute par with the Franco-Russian diplomatic accord and the military convention referred to above.[113]

Until Delcassé's advent to the Ministry of Marine, France did not have any naval understanding with England equivalent to that which had for some time existed between the General Staffs of the French and English armies. Since 1906, careful plans had been made for landing British troops on the Continent in support of France, but regarding naval matters there had been only an "occasional exchange of views, and these at long intervals."[114] Under the ægis of Delcassé

[113] D.D., 3 S., tome III, pp. 270, 303, 344-345; L'Alliance Franco-Russe, Nos. 102 and 103. The original documents are in the French Ministry of Marine. See also Memoirs of Poincaré, I, 204, 212; and Mévil in Echo de Paris, Aug. 2, 1912.   [114] Memoirs of Poincaré, I, 110.

and Winston Churchill, Anglo-French naval conferences began to be held during 1912, and plans were made for the concerted action of the French and English fleets.[115] On February 21, 1912, in a meeting with the other members of the
Supreme Council of National Defense (Poincaré, Millerand,
Paléologue, General Joffre, and Admiral Aubert) Delcassé
explained the plan for common action then being considered
by the British Admiralty and the French Naval Staff. All
operations in the North Sea, English Channel, and Atlantic
were to be carried on by the English fleet, while France was
to guard the Mediterranean.[116] The scheme had many advantages but the British were not quite ready to abandon
their traditional naval policy of guarding all of the principal
trade routes of the world. However, a new German naval law
was passed in May 1912. The time then seemed to be rapidly
approaching when Great Britain would have to recall her
Mediterranean fleet in order to protect her own coasts. The
prospect was a disheartening one to the British, who knew
that Cyprus, Egypt, and the route to India would be left at
the mercy of Austria-Hungary and Italy. It was of course
possible to confide the defense of English Mediterranean interests to some friendly Power, such as France, and this was
proposed many times in the Conservative press and in diplomatic and naval circles, but the idea was a humiliating one
to a people who had prided themselves on their ability to
rule the seas. Nevertheless, German naval competition became so keen that the English soon became more receptive
to the plan of calling upon France for aid.[117]

During July 1912, the question of drawing up a naval accord
was considered in earnest by both the English Cabinet and the
French Government. The initiative in these pourparlers seems
to have come from the English side, a fact which put the
French in a very strong position throughout the negotiations.
However, Delcassé at length proposed to Sir Francis Bridge-

---

[115] *Ibid.*, I, 94; *Personal Memoirs of Joffre*, I, 49-50.
[116] *Personal Memoirs of Joffre*, I, 40, 49-50.
[117] *D.D.*, 3 S., III, 78-79, 176-181.

man, the English First Naval Lord, that France should concentrate her Third Squadron in the Mediterranean, thereby forming a naval force in that quarter superior to the combined fleets of Austria and Italy. Bridgeman, upon assurances that the French fleet would be strong enough to maintain this supremacy until 1914 and that Delcassé was planning to build more ships, promised to have his Chief of Staff study the problem and formulate the terms of a naval agreement which would then be submitted to Delcassé for approval.[118] During the same month, the English Government decided to withdraw their ships from the Mediterranean and to station them in home waters. Indeed, there was hardly anything else to be done. The German navy was almost as strong as that of England and lay so near to the English coast that it was capable of delivering a sudden and decisive blow at the British Isles.[119]

In the first week of September 1912, before the question of an Anglo-French naval accord had been settled, and while Delcassé was at his home in Ariège, a staff officer prematurely forwarded an order to the Third French Squadron off Brest commanding it to proceed to the Mediterranean. This blunder imperiled the naval agreement, because the British seemed to be in a fair way to get what they desired without having to make any promises to the French. Paul Cambon, however, wisely informed the English Government that the Third Squadron was only going south for maneuvers, and made it clear to the British Foreign Office that France could not concentrate her fleet in the Mediterranean permanently without a substantial guarantee from England.[120]

Meanwhile Delcassé, in conjunction with the British Admiralty, had made detailed arrangements for the joint cooperation of the French and English fleets in the event of war. Moreover, the English Government drafted a proposed naval convention regarding these preparations. It was stipulated that while the French fleet should be concentrated in the Mediterranean, virtually all of the English naval forces

[118] D.D., 3 S., III, 235-236.   [119] Ibid., pp. 285, 290.
[120] Ibid., pp. 523-525, 530; Memoirs of Poincaré, I, 112; Le Temps, Sept. 11; Echo de Paris, Sept. 11-14, 1912.

were to be withdrawn from that locality and stationed nearer home. However, the English were wary of committing themselves to a strict military alliance and carefully inserted into the convention a number of clauses designed to maintain their liberty of action. For instance, it was stated that the agreement related solely to a contingency in which Great Britain and France should be allies in war and that it did not affect the political freedom of either government as to entering upon such a conflict. It was also declared that the disposition of the French fleet in the Mediterranean and of the English fleet in home waters proceeded from the individual interest of each Power and had been made independently, without any naval arrangement or agreement. In communicating this English document to Poincaré on September 17, 1912, Delcassé remarked that since England had been the first to propose these conversations, she should be made to give her naval arrangements the character of a firm engagement. He was categorically opposed to much of the wording in the English draft and wrote out a new text which stated more clearly the English obligations to France.[121]

Negotiations for an Anglo-French naval agreement continued into the month of October and were perhaps accelerated by the outbreak of the Balkan wars which raised the specter of a general European conflict. Finally the two governments decided that in place of a naval convention there should be an exchange of letters between Sir Edward Grey, British Minister of Foreign Affairs, and Paul Cambon, French Ambassador at the Court of St. James. In order to give the letters additional sanction, it was agreed that the wording should first be approved by the English Cabinet in its October session.[122] The Cabinet gave its consent on October 30, and the correspondence between Grey and Cambon took place on November 22 and 23, 1912. It was again declared that the respective disposition of the French and British fleets was not based upon an engagement to coöperate in war; but it was also agreed that:

[121] D.D., 3 S., III, 503-508. [122] Memoirs of Poincaré, I, 113.

... if either Government had grave reason to expect an unprovoked attack by a third Power, or something that threatened the general peace, it should immediately discuss with the other whether both Governments should act together to prevent aggression and to preserve peace, and, if so, what measures they would be prepared to take in common. If these measures involved action, the plans of the General Staffs would at once be taken into consideration, and the Governments would then decide what effect should be given to them.[123]

By this time, Delcassé had concentrated the French fleet in the Mediterranean and the English fleet had been withdrawn to home waters. The moral obligations thus created were far beyond the legal ones expressed in the shifty and ambiguous Grey-Cambon formula. According to Winston Churchill:

From the moment that the Fleets of France and Britain were disposed in this new way our common naval interests became very important. And the moral claims which France could make upon Great Britain if attacked by Germany, whatever we had stipulated to the contrary, were enormously extended. . . .[124]

He had warned Grey on August 23, 1912, that it was the fact of concentrating the French fleet in the Mediterranean and the English fleet in the North Sea which was important rather than the language of any written agreement:

But [consider] how tremendous would be the weapon which France would possess to compel our intervention, if she could say, "On the advice of and by arrangement with your naval authorities we have left our Northern coasts defenseless. We cannot possibly come back in time." Indeed [I added somewhat inconsequently], it would probably be decisive whatever is written down now. Everyone must feel, who knows the facts, that we have the obligations of an alliance without its advantages, and above all, without its precise definitions.[125]

[123] Collected Diplomatic Documents Relating to the Outbreak of the European War (London, 1915) p. 80.

[124] Winston Churchill, The World Crisis, 1911-1914 (New York, 1928) pp. 114-115, reprinted with permission of Charles Scribner's Sons.

[125] Ibid., p. 116, reprinted with permission of Charles Scribner's Sons. See also Viscount Morley's Memorandum on Resignation (N.Y., 1928), p. 17f.

Accordingly the French authorities in drawing up Plan XVII, upon which their plan of campaign in 1914 was based, counted definitely upon British naval assistance. They were not entirely sure of military aid on land, but stated that "On the sea, however, we can count without risk upon the effective support of the British fleet."[126]

With the approach of January 1913, Delcassé concluded that his work as Minister of Marine was finished.[127] He had desired to give France a powerful navy, equal to the demands of her foreign policy, and ready for action at the first call to arms. This double end had been accomplished. The organic naval law permanently assured France of a strong and efficient navy. The fleet was concentrated in the Mediterranean and occupied in time of peace the very position foreseen for it in time of war, with the natural result that its action, in the event of armed conflict, could be instantaneous, sure, and completely effective. The whole fleet was under the supreme command of Admiral Lapeyrère, who understood that the first goal of French naval strategy should be the conquest and mastery of the Mediterranean, and that it was his duty not only to train the navy in peacetime but also to command it if war should break out. In the Ministry of Marine itself and in the central administration, where chaos and darkness had formerly reigned, Delcassé had brought order and light and had infused new life and vigor into the whole organism. Construction of warships and war materials had been modernized and expedited. Drydocks appropriate to the needs of a twentieth-century navy had been built at Cherbourg, Brest, Lorient, Bizerte, and Toulon, and adequate arrangements made for resupplying and reprovisioning the fleet. Naval aviation had been commenced, and experiments with flying machines were being carried on both upon land and on the high seas. Plans for the surveillance of the western basin of the Mediterranean, the Channel, and the North Sea by dirigibles and aeroplanes had been elaborated. Moreover,

[126] *Les Armées Françaises dans la Grande Guerre*, I, 47ff., quoted in Fay, I, 324. [127] *Le Matin*, Jan. 19, 1913.

Delcassé had secured laws which placed this powerful marine and its organization above petty politics and beyond the reach of the arbitrary action of successive ministers of marine, an achievement all the more remarkable since it ran counter to the selfish interest of politicians and of certain localities. Finally, the war plans and preparations of the French navy had been coördinated with those of the English and Russian navies, and in consequence thereof written understandings had been exchanged which strengthened the solidarity of the Triple Entente. True, these accomplishments had been made possible by the firm support which the Minister had received in Parliament, but Delcassé must be given credit for having been able to inspire this support by creating in the Chambers and throughout the country a spirit of interest in maritime matters and in forcing upon his countrymen the conviction that a strong war fleet was indispensable to a powerful and "respected" France.[128]

Accordingly, as President Fallières' term of office drew to a close, Delcassé decided to stand on his record as Minister of Marine and present himself as a candidate for the presidency of France. In addition to desiring the great honor which this position would confer, Delcassé was motivated perhaps by one other consideration, namely by the fact that in accordance with the French Constitution, the President of France is able to exert an important influence upon foreign affairs. The hope of securing this high office in 1913 was not an altogether vain one for Delcassé. Politically, he was a person to be reckoned with very seriously each time that a ministerial crisis occurred. Since 1911, whenever a new Ministry was to be formed, he had been regularly called into consultation by the President because his personal worth, his competency in resolving the problem of foreign policy, and the rôle which he played in French politics, qualified him to give valuable advice. He had many loyal followers. In those days, a

[128] *Echo de Paris*, Nov. 3, 1912; Jan. 28, 1913 (a very able summary of Delcassé's work by Sauvaire Jourdain); Mévil, *Rev. Pol. et Parl.*, June, 1924, p. 396; Durand-Viel, pp. 1-31.

dinner was periodically held by "the friends of Delcassé," a body of deputies and other statesmen who admired his sincere and amiable temperament and who were perhaps also attracted to him in some cases by the thought that he might one day succeed to the highest office in the state.[129] These political supporters might have elected Delcassé to the presidency of the Chamber of Deputies upon the death of Brisson in April 1912, but the Minister of Marine had hesitated in presenting himself for election and his friends had voted without knowing whether he was a candidate or not.[130] Deschanel had therefore been chosen to succeed Brisson. During the contest for the presidency of France, Delcassé did not make the same mistake, but promptly announced his candidacy and, on election day, appeared at Versailles wearing a high silk hat in place of his well-known derby.[131] However, after several days of balloting, it soon became apparent that Pams and Poincaré were the favored nominees, and on the seventeenth of January, 1913, Poincaré won by a large majority. It was a triumph of a national idea rather than of a man or a party, aptly remarked the *Echo de Paris*. France had declared definitely for military preparedness.[132] Delcassé did not hold a grudge against Poincaré because of his success, but was one of the first to greet him at the Elysée Palace on January eighteenth. Nor did the newly elected President have any hard feeling toward Delcassé. On the twenty-fourth, he visited him at the bedside of Jacques Delcassé, and remained for a long time with his old friend, who was much affected by the ill health of his wife and son.[133]

Poincaré's Cabinet was necessarily dissolved after its Chief had been elected to the presidency. Briand was asked to form a new Ministry. Delcassé at once announced that he desired to leave the Marine because his work there had been com-

---

[129] Fournol, *Revue Politique et Littéraire*, July 16, 1921, p. 448; Roland de Marès, "L'Artisan de la Triple-Entente, M. Delcassé, Ministre et Diplomate," in *Je Sais Tout* (Paris), November 15, 1915, pp. 456f.
[130] Mévil, *Revue Hebdomadaire*, June, 1923, p. 141; *Memoirs of Poincaré*, II, 136. [131] *Le Matin*, Jan. 16-17, 1913.
[132] *Echo de Paris*, Jan. 18, 1913. [133] *Ibid.*, Jan. 19, 24, 1913.

pleted. However, he intimated that, on account of the dangerous international situation, he might be willing to accept the portfolio of the War Department formerly held by Millerand. On January 20, Briand offered Delcassé the post of Minister of Marine, and, upon the latter's refusal, asked him to become Minister of War; but, during the night, Delcassé had changed his mind about accepting office. He declined Briand's overtures on the ground of weariness and family cares. Madame Delcassé's illness had been aggravated by worry over Jacques Delcassé. The young aviator, in consequence of his aeroplane accident, was about to undergo a second operation.[134] Delcassé therefore retired from office, but did not obtain the rest which he so richly deserved after the intensive labors and worries of the last two years. He was soon called upon to execute a new and extremely difficult undertaking.

3. Ambassador to Russia and Minister of War

After having been the architect [of the Triple Entente], I shall also be the builder. (Delcassé, on his nomination as Ambassador to Russia, February, 1913.)

... in all the offices which have been confided to him [Delcassé], he has had his eyes obstinately fixed upon the same ideal; Minister of Colonies, Foreign Affairs, Marine, and Minister of War, he has had only one thought, to save France from the peril of German hegemony and from the mortal risk of a new aggression. (Poincaré, February 28, 1923.)

Turkey and the allied Balkan states came to blows on October 8, 1912, and peace was not made until May 30, 1913. Almost immediately, the victorious allies began fighting among themselves. The fear that these conflicts might spread to Western Europe caused a lively race in military preparations between the Triple Entente and the Central Powers. Germany knew that in a European War she would have to fight France and Russia simultaneously. For this reason, in January 1913, she felt obliged to expand her effectives by the immedi-

[134] *Echo de Paris*, Jan. 18-21, 1913; *Le Matin*, Jan. 19, 1913; Mévil, *Revue Hebdomadaire*, June, 1923, p. 141.

ate application of an army law passed in 1912. At the same time, she contemplated other additions to her land forces. The French nation, which had in a moment of patriotic enthusiasm elected Poincaré President, turned to the idea of a reintroduction of the three-years' service law.

Besides an increase in their military strength and renewed activity in their own preparations, the French naturally desired corresponding measures on the part of Russia, and above all, that the Russian troops, upon the outbreak of hostilities, should be mobilized and concentrated on the German frontier with all possible speed. For the purpose of spurring Russia on to greater military effort no one was so well qualified as Delcassé. Georges Louis, who was then in St. Petersburg as French Ambassador, was a hard worker, but better suited to hold a position in the Quai d'Orsay at Paris than to handle the delicate negotiations which were to be undertaken. Moreover, Louis was disliked in certain influential Russian circles and could not maintain the close relationship between Paris and St. Petersburg with the French Government desired.[135] On the other hand, Delcassé had regulated the Hull incident with such consummate skill that he had been able to draw England and Russia closer together. He had negotiated the accords of 1899 and 1912 complementary to the Franco-Russian Alliance, and in addition he enjoyed the confidence and esteem of Nicholas II. Finally, in France and in Russia, Delcassé was regarded as the personification of the Franco-Russian Alliance, and was therefore the very diplomat that the circumstances required.

When this background is taken into consideration, it would seem to be natural enough that the French Government should have recalled Georges Louis and replaced him by Delcassé. Yet an air of mystery still surrounds this episode in pre-war history. We now know that Delcassé was charged with a special military mission. Who conceived his instructions? And who first thought of him as successor to Georges Louis? Certainly grave difficulties seemed to stand in the way of

[135] *Memoirs of Poincaré*, I, 166; *D.D.* 3S., III, 1, 75, 173, 209, 230f., 341.

Delcassé's acceptance of the post. His election as President of the Gauche-Radical was a foregone conclusion, and he was expected to play an important rôle in politics as head of this influential party. Madame Delcassé was still confined to her bed and Jacques was just beginning to convalesce from his aeroplane accident. A journey to Russia therefore involved considerable sacrifice on the part of Delcassé.[136] Such historical sources as we now have do not make clear the answers to these questions. All we can say is that when the recall of Georges Louis had been decided upon, Foreign Minister Jonnart, President Poincaré, Briand, Louis Barthou, and other ministers urged Delcassé to go to St. Petersburg as French Ambassador. It is said that Delcassé hesitated before accepting, but finally agreed after his friends had assured him that he was the logical man—that this was not a diplomatic post they were offering him, "it was a service which they asked him to render to his country." "A statesman was needed who could inspire in the Czar, in the Russian Government, and in the Russian people, a feeling of absolute confidence."[137] Since Delcassé could not very well abandon his legislative mandate one year before the general elections, it was arranged that a special decree should nominate him *"ambassadeur en mission temporaire."* This decree could then be renewed as often as desired. Briand asked that he leave for St. Petersburg by March eighth. Later on, his family could join him in Russia.[138]

On February 21, just before Poincaré read his presidential message, the news that Delcassé would soon go to Peterhof spread through the Chamber of Deputies and created considerable surprise on every hand. Since Poincaré in his speech spoke of the army as "the most effective auxiliary of diplomacy," Delcassé's return to active participation in foreign affairs caused grave apprehension in some quarters. Jaurès particularly was given to pessimism, but the official press and

[136] *Le Matin* and *L'Echo de Paris*, Feb. 21, 1913.
[137] *Le Matin* and *L'Echo de Paris*, Feb. 21, 1913; *Memoirs of Poincaré*, II, 32-35; Mévil, *Rev. Pol. et Parl.*, June, 1924, p. 397.
[138] *Le Matin*, Feb. 21, 1913.

the chauvinistic journals paid long and flattering tribute to both Poincaré and Delcassé. *L'Echo de Paris* began its leading article on the subject with the first sentence in English, "The right man in the right place," and declared that the nomination of Delcassé as Ambassador to Russia "wiped out the last trace of France's abdication before Germany in 1905."[139] At St. Petersburg and in Russian diplomatic circles a most favorable impression was created.[140] Among the Pan-Slavs in the Balkans, the news was received with an outburst of joy as being an added sign that France would henceforth serve as a *point d'appui* for Slavism in its struggle against the Germanic Powers. Serbian patriots especially were gladdened. Was not Delcassé "the man of *Revanche* whose very name inspired terror in Germany?"[141] In England, the editor of the *Manchester Guardian* frowned upon Delcassé's return to foreign affairs as likely to disturb the peace of Europe, but the majority of the English papers hailed the new Ambassador with enthusiasm. *Le Matin* was able to say that in England Delcassé was "without doubt one of the best known and most popular of French statesmen," that he was "more than popular; he was loved."[142] Consequently, it was believed that his mission to Russia would consolidate the ties between all three of the Powers in the Triple Entente. Needless to say, the Germans were embarrassed by Delcassé's appointment, yet hardly dared to give any evidence of their discontent.[143] Some journals said, "M. Delcassé is one of the most ardent partisans of *Revanche.* . . . We shall have then a period of tension worse than that which we have had for forty-two years." Others put on an air of optimism and remarked that Delcassé was no longer the man of German encirclement. During the Agadir Crisis, they said, he had acted as though he had "put water in

[139] *L'Echo de Paris, Le Matin,* Feb. 21, 1913; *Le Figaro, Manchester Guardian,* Feb. 21-24, 1913.
[140] *L'Echo de Paris, Le Matin,* Feb. 21-22, 1913; Schuman, p. 203.
[141] *D.D.,* 3S., V, No. 457; *Berliner Monatshefte,* Sept., 1933, p. 901, note 1, quotations from Balkan newspapers.
[142] *Le Matin,* and *Manchester Guardian,* Feb. 21-22, 1913.
[143] R. Marchand, *La Condamnation d'un Régime* (Paris, 1922), p. 117.

his wine."[144] However, financial circles were very much concerned. Stocks fell on the Berlin Boerse and the Paris market was weak.[145]

Russian ceremonies and diplomatic etiquette deferred the recall and replacement of Georges Louis until March nineteenth. On that date Delcassé took train for St. Petersburg at the Gare du Nord. Among the friends who went with him to the station were Izvolski, the Russian Ambassador, Pams, Reynald, Constant, and Fournol. When the train pulled out, they gave him a warm send-off.[146]

Upon arriving in the Russian capital, Delcassé instituted new methods at the French Embassy. He locked himself in his office and wrote out his despatches and cipher telegrams in his own handwriting so as to keep his negotiations secret even from his own collaborators.[147] Inasmuch as social vanities and formalities often appeared to him to be a waste of time, he endeavored to cut them to the minimum. He was the bourgeois ambassador *par excellence*. He was out of bed at six and insisted upon his usual quiet walk along the banks of the Néva. In a country devoted to nocturnal life, he seldom went out after dark, and usually retired promptly at ten o'clock. Yet his prestige and authority in Russia were so great that these oddities of temperament in no way interfered with the success of his mission. On the contrary, he was left free to expend all of his energy upon the important task before him.

The nature of Delcassé's work in St. Petersburg can be gathered from the correspondence between the Russian Ambassador in Paris and the Russian Minister of Foreign Affairs, and from a special letter of Poincaré to Nicholas II.

[144] These German opinions were summarized by Jules Hedeman in *Le Matin*, Feb. 22, 1913, and in the *Echo de Paris* of the same date. See also *Vossische Zeitung* (Berlin) and *Berliner Tageblatt*, Feb. 21-23, 1913. For the existing tension, see *Kölnische Zeitung*, March 10, 1913.

[145] Schuman, p. 203; *Berliner Tageblatt*, Feb. 21, 23, 1913.

[146] *Le Matin*, March 20, 1913. The other friends present were Michel, Vermorel, Bluysen, Dalimier, Massé, Leboucq, Lecherpy, Maunoury, Guernier, Milliaux, Chevillon, and Fayssat.

[147] Mévil, *Revue Hebdomadaire*, June, 1923, p. 142; Marchand, *Condamnation d'un Régime*, pp. 129-130; see also *D.D.*, 3S., VII, 564, No. 521.

Izvolski wrote Sazonov on March 13, 1913:

As you are aware, M. Delcassé is particularly competent, not only in questions of foreign policy, but also in all that concerns military and especially naval matters. After information obtained by our military attaché he has been given as his special mission the task of convincing our War Department of the necessity of increasing the number of our strategic railroads, so that our army can be more rapidly concentrated on the western frontier. M. Delcassé is so well informed on this matter and so familiar with the views of the French General Staff that he can discuss the question quite independently with our military authorities. He is also empowered to offer Russia all the financial assistance required, in the form of railway loans.[148]

Poincaré said in his letter to the Czar, March 20, 1913:

I did not wish to content myself with the credentials given Delcassé.

By sending a statesman especially versed in international affairs as its ambassador to Russia, the Government of the Republic has sought to strengthen the Franco-Russian Alliance and to maintain a close and permanent contact between the French Government and the Imperial Government.

It is not necessary for me to inform Your Majesty that, recently, as Minister of Marine in my Cabinet, M. Delcassé interested himself in all the problems of foreign affairs occasioned by the Balkan Crisis and that he has attentively followed the march of events, He is *au courant* with the smallest details of these matters and is in a better position than almost anyone else to concert with M. Sazonov and to insure harmony in French and Russian diplomacy.

Last year, when I had the honor of being received by Your Majesty at Peterhof, I called your attention to the fact that, according to the opinion of our General Staffs, it was advisable to hasten the construction of certain railroads on the western frontier of your Empire. The great military effort which the French Government proposes to make, in order to maintain a balance in European forces, renders it at this time particularly urgent for Russia to take the corresponding measures agreed upon by the General Staffs of our two countries. M. Delcassé will discuss these

---

[148] Marchand, *Livre Noire*, II, 49; *Condamnation d'un Régime*, pp. 116-117.

important questions with Your Majesty and with the Imperial Government, and will also talk over all other matters pertaining to the functioning of the Alliance, or which should permit us to preserve peace more effectively.[149]

Without loss of time, Delcassé interviewed Nicholas II on the subject of proposed increases in the size of the French and Russian armies. He observed that it was indispensable for France and Russia to act simultaneously and concordantly if their military efforts were to be efficacious. The Czar promised that the number of Russian effectives would be substantially increased by the autumn of that year. Delcassé in his despatches to Paris then urged the French Government to proceed in a determined manner toward the fulfillment of plans for enlarging the French army, by which he doubtless meant the three-years' service law, which was presented to the Chambers early in March 1913. An augmentation of the French forces would be necessary, he hinted in his despatches, because Russia was watching France closely and was anxious to see the French projects put into execution.[150]

Delcassé also spoke to the Czar about completing the strategic railways considered necessary by the two general staffs. In so doing, he never lost an opportunity to call attention to the delicate European situation and to insist upon the necessity of having Russian equipment in good condition so that, when war came, the Russian army might take the offensive simultaneously with the French army and thus oblige Germany to divide her forces. Nicholas II was favorably impressed, and not only agreed to the construction of new lines, but also promised to improve and reconstruct other railways serving the western frontier. Afterwards, Delcassé carried on detailed negotiations with the Czar's ministers and with subordinate Russian Government officials and succeeded in obtaining enough improvements to assure a gain of four days in Russian concentration. Then, in order to make his work permanent, he exchanged letters with the Russian Minister of Foreign Affairs. This correspondence constituted a veritable

[149] *D.D.*, 3S., VI, 62-63.   [150] *D.D.*, 3S., VI, 66, 81f., 94.

convention between France and Russia relative to strategic railroads and other military matters, and was designed to give the finishing touches to the military accords of the Franco-Russian Alliance.[151]

The conclusion of the accord of 1913 was another triumph for the perseverance of Delcassé. As early as December 18, 1887, in an article for the *Paris*, he had called the attention of the French people to the need for more Russian lines. While Minister of Foreign Affairs, he had put new life and vigor into the Franco-Russian Alliance and had made a special trip to Russia in 1901 in order to arrange for the construction of the railways considered necessary by the French and Russian General Staffs. Now finally in 1913, he had accelerated both the improvement of the old roads and the building of the new ones, and, in addition, he had obtained written assurances which gave certainty and permanence to this important phase of French and Russian military preparation.

Delcassé's long interest in this problem, and his continued assocation with it, suggest that he had more to do with the origin of the Russian mission of 1913 than is commonly supposed. The older view, expressed in the newspaper of the period, was that Delcassé went to St. Petersburg only after he had been persuaded by both his friends and the President of the Republic.[152] But the early careers of Briand, Jonnart, and Barthou lead one to believe that they knew very little, if anything, about Russian strategic lines. Moreover, until 1912 the President was without experience in diplomacy, and his previous Cabinet posts had been concerned with education and finance rather than military affairs. Almost certainly, Delcassé was more acutely aware of the need for the railroads than Poincaré could have been at that time. Doubtless the railway question had been discussed by the Poincaré Cabinet during 1912, and the subject must have come up in the sessions of

[151] *D.D.*, 3S., VI, 82, 94; VII, 555, 563-564, VIII, 881-884; Marchand, *Condamnation d'un Régime*, pp. 118-121. cf. G. Dupin, *M. Poincaré et la Guerre de 1914* (Paris, 1931), p. 21.

[152] *L'Echo de Paris*, and *Le Matin*, Feb. 21, 1913.

the Supreme Council of National Defense, but Delcassé was also present on these occasions and he was probably among those who impressed Poincaré with the need for quick action. A man who had taken special care in 1901 to induce Russia to begin the construction of these roads would naturally wish to see them completed as rapidly as possible. The conclusion then is obvious. Instead of being the tool of others, as many persons would have us believe, it is more likely that Delcassé was the master of his own fate, that he was indeed the mind and the stimulating force behind Poincaré and the Nationalist Government in 1912 and 1913.

Not content with an accord on the subject of railways, Delcassé, as a final measure of preparedness, arranged to have General Joffre and twenty-five other French officers come to Russia in August of 1913 in order to attend the Russian maneuvers and that they might collaborate with the Russian military authorities on technical matters. In this way, too, Delcassé helped make the heavy and complicated Russian military system more prompt, more practical, and consequently more useful to France.[153]

While busily engaged in improving the war machinery of Russia, Delcassé was attending to other duties purely diplomatic in character. As a consequence of the First Balkan War, Rumania and Bulgaria quarreled over the southern boundary of Dobrudja, but about the middle of March 1913, they agreed to settle their differences through the mediation of the Great Powers. St. Petersburg was selected as the meeting place for these negotiations, and Delcassé became one of the mediators. His chief preoccupation was to remain in complete accord with Russia and England in the questions which were to be settled. More particularly, in accordance with instructions from Paris, he favored a solution of the dispute which would be sufficiently favorable to Rumania to win that Power over to the Triple Entente and yet not so one-sided as to wound

[153] D.D., 3S., VI, 88; VII, 602, 634; VIII, 864; 882; P. Albin, *D'Agadir à Sarajevo, 1911-1914* (Paris, 1915), pp. 72-73; Mévil, *Rev. Pol. et Parl.*, June, 1924, p. 397; Michon, *Franco-Russian Alliance*, p. 271.

the feelings of Bulgaria.[154] The ambassadors of Germany, Austria, and Italy supported Rumania's claims and proposed that she be allowed to annex Silistria. Austria also suggested that Bulgaria might be given Salonika as a *quid pro quo* for abandoning her rights in the above territory. Delcassé, however, would not permit Salonika to be wrested from Greece, and Sazonov also declared that the Rumanian demands were excessive.[155] In the end Rumania was given Silistria, but it was agreed that she should give up certain other pretensions and indemnify any Bulgarian inhabitants who wanted to leave the town.[156]

In the days preceding the Second Balkan War, Delcassé was especially active in determining French policy. On June 9, 1913, he informed the Government at Paris that Russia had decided to intervene in Balkan affairs in order to prevent the Balkan League from being destroyed by internal strife. In reporting this Russian decision, Delcassé added for the edification of the French Minister of Foreign Affairs: "We are ourselves, from a European standpoint, too much interested in the maintenance of the Balkan Union not to wish that Russia may succeed and not to do all that we can to aid her."[157]

Subsequently Delcassé did his best to persuade the Balkan Powers to keep the peace, and the Quai d'Orsay adopted the same policy, but the war itself finally put an end to these efforts.[158]

Meanwhile the Turks, having learned the lesson of their military disasters, decided upon reforms. A Frenchman and an Englishman were employed to take charge of Turkish financial affairs; an English admiral was asked to reorganize the navy; and a German general, Liman von Sanders, was invited to train the Turkish army and to improve the defenses of Constantinople. When, in November 1913, Sazonov

---

[154] *D.D.*, 3S., VI, 78, 145, 187, 332f.   [155] *Ibid.*, VI, 185-187, 283.
[156] *Ibid.*, VI, 363f.; *Memoirs of Poincaré*, II, 45.
[157] *D.D.*, 3S., VII, 66.
[158] *Ibid.*, VII, 168f., 172, 181f., 238f., 282, 292f.

learned of the German military mission to Turkey, he became quite worried. Perhaps he nourished the hope that Russia might one day control Constantinople and the Straits, and feared that General Liman would make it more difficult, if not impossible, for Russia to realize this age-old dream. He may also have been afraid that the Germans might use their advantageous position to make themselves masters of Constantinople. Delcassé fanned the suspicions of the Russian Foreign Minister. The French Government had long been concerned lest the occasionally friendly relations between Russia and Germany should damage the solidarity of the Entente. Delcassé seems to have seized upon the Liman von Sanders mission as a convenient opportunity to drive Germany and Russia further apart and "to cut for all time" the bridges between them.[159] Be this as it may, much that Delcassé said to Sazonov sprang from honest conviction. The proof is found in Delcassé's despatches to Paris, which, like his warnings to the Russian Foreign Minister, were filled with gloomy predictions. On one occasion he wrote his Government that "The falling to pieces of Turkey has already begun, or is about to begin, and Germany will occupy a position guaranteeing to her all the advantages of a partition."[160]

In view of the seeming imminence of a general European war, Delcassé "very often and very thoroughly" discussed French war aims with the Russian Minister of Foreign Affairs and made perfectly clear the expectations of France with regard to Alsace-Lorraine.[161] He found Sazonov a sympathetic listener, and it was discovered that the aims pursued by France and Russia were "identical."[162] Whether or not Delcassé promised to give Constantinople to Russia in return for Alsace-Lorraine is a point which cannot be settled definitely at this time, but it is known that he subsequently favored this

[159] Marchand, *Condamnation d'un Régime*, pp. 123-129; Nicolson, *Lord Carnock*, p. 404; Fay, I, 499-500.

[160] Fay, I, 501. See also *D.D.*, 3S., VII, 528f., VIII, 658-659; 777.

[161] H. Lutz, *Lord Grey and the World War* (N.Y., 1928), p. 189; F. Stieve, *Isvolsky and the World War* (N.Y., 1926), pp. 141-142; 248.

[162] Lutz., *op. cit.*, p. 189.

policy, and hence he may well have assured Sazonov in 1913 that Russia could rely upon the sympathy of France in the Straits question.[163]

Early in January 1914, Delcassé refused to accept a renewal of his nomination as French Ambassador. He did not give any reasons for declining to remain at his post, but evidently felt that his temporary mission was completed and therefore wished to return to France.[164] One of his last acts was to assure Sazonov that in the effort to keep Liman von Sanders from obtaining control of the Turkish army, Russia would have the active support of the French Government, which would go just as far as Russia might wish in this matter.[165] Delcassé's final audience with the Czar took place on January twenty-ninth. The parting was warm and friendly. Nicholas was in a communicative mood and talked a great deal about the Liman von Sanders episode and about Russian distrust of Germany.[166] Obviously the Delcassé mission of 1913 had been a huge success. His chief objectives had been embodied in the accord relating to strategic railroads and other military matters. Joffre and his corps of experts had been able to increase the efficiency of the Franco-Russian war machine. The relations of France and Russia were much more cordial and confidential than they had been when Georges Louis was at St. Petersburg; and Russia and Germany were more estranged than formerly.[167]

While an old friend and former collaborator, Maurice Paléologue, took over the French Embassy in Russia, Delcassé engaged in a political struggle in France to maintain the three-years' service law. This measure was one of the chief

---

[163] Marchand, *Un Livre Noire*, III, No. 497, Izvolski to Sazonov, Sept. 30/Oct. 13, 1914. Sazonov to the Russian Ambassador at Paris, March 18, 1915, printed in the *Manchester Guardian*, Dec. 12, 1917. Michon, *Franco-Russian Alliance*, p. 254, refers to Leon Bourgeois to prove that Delcassé offered Constantinople to Russia.

[164] *Memoirs of Poincaré*, II, 104; Paléologue, "La Russie des Tsars," in *Revue des Deux Mondes*, Jan. 15, 1921, pp. 227f.

[165] Lutz, *op. cit.*, p. 178.   [166] *Memoirs of Poincaré*, II, 104, 109.

[167] For the last point, *see Memoirs of Poincaré*, II, 109; and *D.D.*, 3S., VIII, 783f.

issues in the general elections of April-May, 1914. With Delcassé, the national defense took precedence over every other consideration, and he espoused the cause of three-years' compulsory service with all of his accustomed ardor. His efforts proved very fruitful in his own Department. Six-sevenths of the constituency of Ariège rallied to his support at the polls. After the elections were over, the struggle for the maintenance of the statute continued in the houses of Parliament. The question was still a very much debated one when the Doumergue Government resigned in the first days of June 1914. The political situation seemed to demand that Delcassé hold office in the new Cabinet which was to be formed. Realizing the strategic position which he then held in French politics, Delcassé announced on June 2 that he would not give his political backing to any Government which was even suspected of contemplating the abrogation of the existing military law.[168] Many persons desired a Delcassé Government, and on June 3, the veteran diplomat conferred for a long time with the President. However, as in 1912, Delcassé declined the Premiership. Yet it was made evident that he intended to dictate the policy of the new Cabinet, because, next day, the *Echo de Paris* stated that Delcassé and Poincaré had discussed general internal politics and problems of foreign policy and had agreed that the international situation was such as to forbid all tampering with France's army laws. Indeed, the maintenance of three-years' service had been recognized as "vital" and "absolutely indispensable" to the safety of the country.[169] Moreover, Delcassé himself appeared before the *Gauche-Radical* group and with all the high authority of a former Minister of Foreign Affairs, Minister of Marine, and former Ambassador to Russia, exposed the "incalculable and disastrous consequences" of abandoning three-years' compulsory service.[170]

On the sixth and seventh of June, friends were again urging

[168] *Echo de Paris*, June 2, 1914; *Manchester Guardian*, Feb. 23, 1923.
[169] *Echo de Paris*, June 4 and 7, 1914; *Memoirs of Poincairé*, II, 135-136.
[170] *Echo de Paris*, June 5, 1914.

Delcassé to form a Ministry, but he was too ill to comply with their wishes. At the same time, Poincaré again summoned him to the Elysée. M. Clementel, Delcassé's personal friend, was then sent with a message which explained to the President that Delcassé would have to decline to form a Government because of ill health.[171]

A few days later, Alexander Ribot announced his firm resolution to maintain the existing military requirements and called upon Delcassé and other noted patriots to support him in forming a Cabinet. Delcassé was glad to aid his old friend and consented to take over the portfolio of the War Department, from which point of vantage he could personally look after the military measures which were so dear to his heart. The decree nominating him Minister of War appeared in the *Journal Officiel* on June 10, 1914. He was too ill to go to his new offices, but promised that, sick or well, he would be at his bench to defend the Cabinet when it presented itself to the Chamber. He was among those who voted for the Ribot Ministry when it fell on June thirteenth.[172] As a result of this vote, Delcassé ceased to be Minister of War before he had time to clear the first papers off his desk! However, the principle of three-years' service had nevertheless been saved. Most of the members of the succeeding Cabinet (Viviani's) were pledged to uphold that legislative enactment.[173]

For a short while Delcassé rested at Ax-les-Thermes, but in July 1914 he was again in Paris and unofficially attached to the Government in the absence of Viviani (Premier and Minister of Foreign Affairs) who had accompanied Poincaré on his visit to Russia. In those critical days after the assassination of the Austrian Archduke, the responsible chiefs of the

---

[171] *Ibid.*, June 7-8, 1914.   [172] *Ibid.*, June 8-14, 1914.
[173] It is a curious fact that, in spite of the short life of the Ribot Government, Delcassé could say that he rendered service as head of the War Department. In the summer of 1912, when Millerand went on vacation, Delcassé, while attending to his own duties as Minister of Marine, also took charge of the Ministry of War. Grave questions arose over Lyautey's campaigns in Morocco. Delcassé appointed a committee to investigate the matter and was later sustained in this action by Millerand, who thanked him warmly. See *Echo de Paris*, Sept. 4, 1912.

French Government were glad to get the advice of a seasoned diplomat and statesman. Thus, on June 28, 1914, Delcassé attended the ministerial council which met under the presidency of Bienvenu-Martin.[174]

The outbreak of the World War did not surprise Delcassé. Ever since his return from Russia, he had realized that the European situation was desperate.[175] He gloomily told his friends that from the French standpoint a long struggle was more to be desired than a short one, because then the superior man power and greater resources of the Entente would come into play.[176] The first few months of the war were a triumph for Delcassé's policies in national defense and foreign affairs. The Russian army was mobilized much more rapidly than the Germans had expected, and it constituted a grave menace to East Prussia until stopped at Tannenberg, August 26-31, 1914. On August 2, 1914, Paris ordered the torpedo boats and submarines in the Channel to block the passage of the German fleet at the Pas de Calais. The Light Squadron steamed forward to defend the position indicated, but the German ships were never sighted, because, in accordance with the agreement of 1912, the English fleet lay between them. At the same time, and without an hour's delay, the great French squadrons began moving out from Toulon in order to protect the Mediterranean interests of France and to guarantee the passage of the Nineteenth Army Corps from Africa. In short, the French navy of 1914 performed swiftly and efficiently a double duty for which the fleet of 1909 would have been utterly unprepared.[177] Meanwhile, Delcassé's system of ententes proved their real worth. It was not necessary for France to guard the Pyrenees. Thanks to Delcassé, King Alfonso of Spain was devoted to the French cause[178] and had

[174] Berliner Monatshefte, June, 1934, p. 525, citing Le Temps, July 29, 1914. London Times, Feb. 23, 1923, p. 11.
[175] Mévil, Revue Hebdomadaire, June, 1923, p. 142; Durand-Viel, Delcassé et la Marine, pp. 24-25.
[176] Mévil, Revue Hebdomadaire, June, 1923, p. 142.
[177] Durand-Viel, p. 25.   [178] D.D., 3S., VI, 73.

assured the French Government in March 1913, that France need not station troops near the Spanish frontier. "You have need of your soldiers elsewhere," he had said. Indeed, the King was almost "more French than the French."[179] The Franco-Italian border was equally secure. Loyally abiding by Delcassé's agreement of 1902, Italy informed the French Government on August 2 that the Italians would remain neutral. As a result, the French soldiers who otherwise would have had to hold the Alpine frontier, were immediately available for opposing the German armies.[180] England came into the war on the French side. The ties of interest and friendship created by Delcassé's entente of April 8, 1904, by the Anglo-French military and naval conversations, and above all by the fleet agreement of 1912, were powerful factors in the English determination to come to the assistance of France.[181] The support of this great naval and colonial Power practically guaranteed victory to France if the war proved to be of long duration. Finally, as a result of Delcassé's peaceful "conquest" of the United States, American sympathy, from the very beginning of the struggle, inclined toward the side of the French people,[182] a matter of great significance when one considers how valuable American credit and American supplies were to the Allied cause.

Since Delcassé's life work had been of such supreme importance to France, it was natural that his countrymen should desire to honor him and that they should restore to him his beloved post at the Quai d'Orsay. Indeed he was, in any case, the man best fitted for that position inasmuch as he had been the principal organizer of the coalition which was now fighting Germany. Accordingly, on August 27, 1914, he was named Minister of Foreign Affairs in Viviani's Ministry of National Defense.

[179] *Ibid.*, VI, 65, 73.

[180] *Memoirs of Poincaré*, II, 278; *J.O.*, March 1, 1923, p. 2017.

[181] Sir Edward Grey, speech of August 3, 1914, *Parliamentary Debates, Commons*, 5th series, Vol. 65, 1914, pp. 1821f.

[182] *Memoirs of Poincaré*, III, 109.

4. The Wartime Diplomacy of Delcassé, His Post-War Opinions, and His Death

. . . Winston [Churchill] derides any scruples as born of perverted sentiment, and remarks with truth, "the great thing is to win the war." (H. H. Asquith, Prime Minister of England, note dated Dec. 31, [1914].)

France cannot do without security and reparations. The Rhine is our security. The provinces on the left bank by an annual contribution of three to four billions to the national budget would mean the rebuilding of our ruins. It should always be deplored that they did not make this one of the conditions of the armistice. [Delcassé, January or February, 1923.)

Shortly before Delcassé returned to the Ministry of Foreign Affairs, the suggestion had been made that the Entente Powers should promise in writing that they would not make separate peace with Germany. His first care was to push these negotiations to completion, and a pact was signed at London, September 5, 1914, containing the above provision. It also contained a paragraph which could be interpreted to mean that France, England, and Russia might formulate peace conditions among themselves prior to opening negotiations with the enemy. Moreover, the general language of the document was such as to have the effect of transforming the Entente into a wartime alliance.[183]

Before the Pact of London had been signed, Delcassé began laboring to bring Italy into the war on the Allied side. He himself had laid the basis for these pourparlers just before his return to the Quai d'Orsay. At that time he had made certain declarations to the *Corrière della Sera* of Milan which are well worth quoting:

The present crisis, the gravest in history on account of the large number of men engaged, will doubtless involve vast alterations in the map of Europe. It is my opinion that these changes will endure for a century. The next Congress will have to accomplish a task more serious and more heavy than that of the Congress of Vienna.

---

[183] *Collected Diplomatic Documents Relating to the Outbreak of the European War* (London, 1915), p. 264; H. M. Ehrmann, "The Pact of London, September 5, 1914," in *Berliner Monatshefte*, March, 1935, pp. 231-241.

The distribution of the war gains will be proportionate to the sacrifice of each State. Everyone will share according to his effort or contribution. It is therefore to the interest of every Power arriving at the Congress to be able to say that it has taken an active part in the struggle. More than ever before it is necessary to think of the future and to be mindful of the definitive arrangement of Europe.

How will Europe be apportioned after this formidable crisis? One of the surest results is as follows: England and France will remain friends. . . . Their colonial possessions are so extensive that their only concern is to guard and administer their Empires. What could Italy have to fear from France and England? Nothing, absolutely nothing. . . . Italy will be useful to them in preserving the balance of power in the Mediterranean. The French and English are not opposed to the aspirations of the Italian people. But let us be specific. I am certain that neither France, England, nor Russia would stand in the way of the cession of the Trentino to Italy. As for the annexation of Trieste, the consent of France and England is already acquired, and it is my impression that Russia will not object. Concerning the rest of the Adriatic, let us speak frankly. Neither France nor any other Power of the Triple Entente will argue with you about Valona. Do you think that anyone could say the same thing of Germany?

Suppose that Austria should be unable to keep all of her present territory. Do you think that Germany, who has an intense longing for access to the Adriatic, would permit herself to be barred from that sea if she were able to prevent it? Manifestly, no. Germany therefore stands across your path, thwarting the realization of your legitimate ambitions.

Where, then, does the interest of Italy lie? On one side, she sees a group of Powers able to help her in obtaining what she desires. On the other hand, she sees two Powers blocking the way to all Italian expansion. It is not up to me to draw the conclusion. . . . Certainly a great deal is at stake. . . .[184]

The above declarations of Delcassé are important because they indicate that as early as August 24, 1914, he was willing to make substantial sacrifices in order to bring Italy into the

[184] *Le Temps*, August 24, 1914, declaration of Delcassé, reprinted at length from the *Corrière della Sera* of Milan.

war on the French side. Fully conscious of the value of their aid, the Italians did not at once respond to Delcassé's overtures, but from December 1914 until May 1915 bargained with both the Allies and the Central Powers in order to see which would offer the better reward for Italian participation in the conflict. On the Allied side, Delcassé seems to have been disposed to deal more generously than either the British or Russian diplomats, because he believed Italian intervention would involve that of Rumania, Bulgaria, and Greece, and thereby hasten the end of the war considerably.[185] On the other hand, Germany and Austria were loath to offer all that Italy demanded, as was natural, since much of the territory that the Italian Government wished to have lay within the boundaries of Austria-Hungary. The result was that Italy finally agreed to give her support to the Allies. By the secret Treaty of London, signed by France, England, Russia, and Italy on April 26, 1915, the Italians were to receive as their price the Trentino, the Cisalpine Tyrol as far as the Brenner Pass, Trieste, the Counties of Gorizia and Gradisca, and all of Istria as far as the Quarnero. In addition, they were to get northern Dalmatia, Valona, and a large number of islands in the Adriatic as well as full sovereignty over the Dodecanese Islands which Italy was then occupying. Nor was this all. Italy was also promised a share of the German colonies, part of the prospective war indemnity, and a portion of southwestern Asia Minor.[186]

Before this agreement had become generally known to European diplomats, Wickham Steed, who had heard of it, asked Delcassé for an interview and was received on Saturday, May 1, at eight o'clock in the morning. Steed protested against the folly of giving way to Italian demands. He declared that the treaty played into the hands of the Habsburgs, who could henceforth say that they were fighting to save Southern Slav territory from the grasp of the rapacious Italians. Delcassé listened patiently, then said:

[185] Marchand, *Livre Noire*, III, 92-93, 95-96.
[186] Great Britain, *Parliamentary Papers*, 1920, Vol. LI, Cmd. 671.

We may have done wrong, but we were placed in a terrible position. Italy put a pistol at our heads. Think what it means. Within a month there will be a million bayonets in the field, and shortly afterwards 600,000 Roumanians. Reinforcements as large as that may be worth some sacrifice, even of principle. But I ask you, was there ever a moment in the history of the world when decisions were so difficult, or the responsibility of statesmen so heavy?[187]

While Italy was still on the auction block, Delcassé had been extremely anxious to bring the Japanese into the European theater, but was restrained by the Russians and by the British, who disliked offering Kiaochow and other necessary inducements to Japan.[188] However, he reached an agreement with Russia regarding war aims. More than once he promised to support the Czar's right to annex Constantinople and the Straits; and, in return, he asked that his ally take the same kindly attitude toward the French desire to rectify certain colonial boundaries and to recover Alsace-Lorraine. He also demanded the greatest possible weakening of the military and political power of Prussia as well as the destruction of the political and economic power of Germany.[189]

After France and Russia had made their purposes clear to each other, and immediately after Italy joined the Allies, Delcassé concentrated his attention on the Near Eastern States. France, Great Britain, and Russia were very much interested in these little countries and aimed to revive the Balkan Entente with the idea of adding Rumania, Bulgaria, and Greece to the Allied forces in Europe. The scheme was ambitious and daring, but well within the limits of possibility if one were willing to pay high prices. However, it involved participation in the tangled, complicated, and tortuous diplo-

[187] H. W. Steed, *Through Thirty Years, 1892-1922* (N.Y., 1924), II, 66-67. Rumania did not enter the war until August, 1916.

[188] Oxford and Asquith, *Memories and Reflections, 1852-1927* (2 Vols., Boston, 1928), II, 63; *Memoirs of Poincaré*, III, 266-267.

[189] *Livre Noire*, III, No. 497; Stieve, *Isvolsky*, pp. 141-142, 248-249; Note of the Russian Minister of Foreign Affairs to the Russian Ambassador at Paris, March 18, 1915, published by the Bolshevists and reprinted in the *Manchester Guardian*, Dec. 12, 1917.

macy of the Balkans, where intrigue and deception were usually taken for granted. Unfortunately Delcassé was no longer his old self. He was ill, nervous, and worried. Early in September 1914 Jacques Delcassé, while serving as an officer in a regiment of Chasseurs, was shot down and captured by the enemy. The name Delcassé was hated in Germany, and the French Foreign Minister naturally feared that every sort of misery awaited his unhappy son.[190] Worse still, Delcassé was hardly understood either by his associates in the Cabinet or by the other members of Parliament. Using the war as an excuse, he neglected to appear before the Chambers, which were therefore left completely in the dark as to his movements. In Cabinet meetings, he had always been very guarded in his utterances; now he was more obstinately silent than ever, and when he did speak, Poincaré noted that he seemed to be losing the thread of his thoughts. Even his best friends were afraid that he was undertaking too much in attempting to carry on his work alone, but secrecy was his passion, and all argument failed to convince him that he ought to change his methods.[191]

The idea of reconstituting the Balkan "bloc" and of winning over Bulgaria with territorial concessions seems to have originated in the fertile brain of Sazonov. Delcassé fell in with the plan rather reluctantly.[192] Similarly, British diplomacy must be held partly responsible for this ill-starred venture

[190] *Memoirs of Poincaré*, III, 145f., 153; Letter of Madame Delcassé-Noguès dated Quartier Général, Alger, Jan. 13, 1934; Interview with Camille Barrère cited above. In spite of the intercession of the American Ambassador at Paris, Charles Eugène Henri Jacques Delcassé was subjected to the rigors of a German prison camp. The German Government was anxious to exchange him for Von Schierstaedt, one of their own officers captured by the French, and demanded that the latter be freed or more severe discipline might be administered to young Delcassé. The very fact of such a threat precluded Delcassé from making any recommendation in the matter. W. Dawson, *The War Memoirs of William Graves Sharp* (London, 1931), pp. 83-86. A photograph of Lieutenant Jacques Delcassé, taken in his prison camp at Halle, was published in *L'Illustration*, June 26, 1915. He was stocky, clean shaven, and jovial, and wore a medal on his chest.

[191] *Memoirs of Poincaré*, III, 145-146, 161; Fournol, *Revue Politique et Littéraire*, July, 1921, p. 447.

[192] *Memoirs of Poincaré*, III, 258, 264, 284-285; Mévil, *Rev. Pol. et Parl.*, June, 1924, p. 400.

into the Balkan tangle.[193] However, after Delcassé had consented to engage in the enterprise, his usual enthusiasm and optimism asserted itself. Victory in the war took precedence over every other consideration in his estimation, and hence he thought it reasonable and logical that the Allies should go to any length in order to obtain Bulgaria's aid.[194]

The plan of the Allies was to offer Bulgaria certain territories in Macedonia and Thrace. The lands in question belonged to Serbia and Greece, but this fact was not regarded as an insuperable obstacle.[195] Serbia at first categorically refused to give up any part of her territory to Bulgaria but, under pressure from France, England, and Russia, agreed to sacrifice a portion of her soil in Macedonia.[196] Greece, in order to protect herself from Bulgaria, and in order to save herself from dismemberment at the hand of the Allies, thrice offered to join in the war on the side of the French and the English, provided she were given an absolute guarantee of her territorial integrity.[197] But Delcassé and the diplomats in St. Petersburg and London were determined to make Bulgaria the pivot of their Balkan policy. They reasoned that if Bulgaria joined in the war against Germany, then Turkey would be isolated, Serbia would be protected, and the Russians would be able to open communications with the Mediterranean. Consequently, in spite of the fact that Greece was a neutral State, France, Russia, and England decided in May 1915 to cede the Greek province of Cavalla to Ferdinand, and on August 4, 1915, the three Powers sent a virtual ultimatum to Athens enjoining the Greek Government to surrender both the city of Cavalla and its hinterland to Bulgaria. For the sake of appearances, Greece was offered compensation in the

[193] Cosmin, L'Entente et la Grèce pendant la Grande Guerre (2 Vols., Paris, 1926), I, 43 and note; 111; G. Deville, L'Entente, la Grèce, et la Bulgarie (Paris, 1919), pp. 205-206; 215.
[194] Deville, op. cit., p. 163.
[195] Cosmin, op. cit., I, 43 and note, 75, 90-93; 111; S. Cosmin, Diplomatie et Presse dans l'Affaire Grecque (hereafter to be abbreviated as Diplomatie et Presse), Paris, 1921, pp. 89, 93; A. Passadis, La Question D'Orient et la Grèce (Paris, 1929), pp. 238, 243f.
[196] Cosmin, L'Entente et la Grèce, pp. 92-93; Diplomatie et la Presse, p. 107.
[197] Cosmin, Diplomatie et Presse, pp. 71-80; Passadis, op. cit., pp. 238-243.

region of Smyrna, though to be sure these lands belonged to
Turkey and the Allies had not yet defeated the Turks.[198]

The Gounaris Cabinet at Athens rejected the demand to
surrender Cavalla, but fell from power almost immediately.
Venizelos then became Prime Minister. While King Constantine endeavored to maintain the neutrality of Greece,
this new Premier sought to bring his country into the war
on the Allied side.[199] Late in the afternoon of September 22,
1915, Venizelos asked the ministers of France, Russia, and
England to have 150,000 troops sent to Salonika. The Bulgarians, who were playing a double game, had by this time
mobilized their army on the Serbian frontier. The Greek
Premier alleged that he wanted 150,000 men so that he could
assist Serbia if the latter were attacked by the King of Bulgaria. Legally, Venizelos had no right to take this important
step without the previous consent of both King Constantine
and the Greek Parliament.[200] However, that fact bothered the
Allies very little. Upon receiving the request for troops, Delcassé calculated that the Allies could hardly afford to spare
150,000 men, but decided to answer Venizelos in the affirma-
tive in order "to sound King Constantine," who was suspected
of being pro-German.[201] Such is the explanation that Delcassé gave of his conduct in 1916. Doubtless he also hoped
that Italy or Russia might somehow be able to find the necessary 150,000 bayonets, if they were really needed. At any rate,
after receiving the consent of the Cabinet, Delcassé telegraphed the French representative at Athens, September 23,
1915: "You may say to M. Venizelos that the Government of
France, wishing to enable Greece to fulfill her treaty obligations to Serbia, is ready to furnish the soldiers which have been
requested."[202]

[198] Cosmin, *Diplomatie et Presse*, pp. 93-97; *L'Entente et la Grèce*, p. 111;
Deville, *L'Entente, la Grèce, et la Bulgarie*, p. 156; Passadis, *op. cit.*, pp.
243-244.
[199] Cosmin, *Diplomatie et Presse*, p. 110.
[200] *Ibid.*, pp. 121-125, citing articles 32 and 99 of the Greek Constitution.
[201] Delcassé, *J.O.*, Oct. 28, 1919 (*Comité secret* of June 16, 1916), p. 77f.
[202] *Ibid.*, p. 77f.

This telegram was communicated to Sir Edward Grey, who immediately gave his approval.[203]

Meanwhile Delcassé still thought that he might be able to secure Bulgaria for the Allied cause. He cherished this illusion in spite of repeated warnings of the danger of placing too much faith in King Ferdinand's promises.[204] On September 26, 1915, Joseph Reinach attempted to write in Le Figaro that the Bulgarian King was selling himself to Germany. Delcassé's official censor would not permit the statement to be printed. Reinach carried his grievance to the Premier. The Minister of Foreign Affairs then asked the writer to come to see him at the Quai d'Orsay. The meeting, which took place on September 27, was dramatic. The veteran diplomat, who had long ago commenced his career on the République Française, stood face to face with a journalist who attempted to show him the folly of his Balkan policy. But the man who had desired to advise Flourens refused to hearken to the dire predictions of Reinach.[205] The Minister continued his original plan. However, it is only fair to note here that Delcassé's gullibility was shared in an equal degree by Sir Edward Grey and Sazonov. All three statesmen seem to have closed their eyes and to have refused to see the situation in its true light.[206]

Toward the first of October 1915, Russia declined to coöperate in the Salonika expedition on the ground that she had reached the limit of her resources. Italy raised the same excuse. Frightened by the prospect of having to weaken the French line on the western front, Delcassé himself began to oppose the idea of sending Allied troops into Greece. He said later in his own defense:

The prospect of having to export French troops when the enemy was still on our soil filled me with anxiety. I had never wished to contemplate such a move; because it was clear to me Germany's first effort to crush us would be made in France. Hence

[203] Ibid., p. 77f.   [204] Deville, op. cit., pp. 205-206, 215.
[205] This Joseph Reinach may have been Delcassé's former collaborator on the République Française. See page 17. Le Figaro, Aug. 2, 1917, p. 3.
[206] Deville, op. cit., pp. 205-206; Mévil, Revue Hebdomadaire, June, 1923, p. 143; Cosmin, L'Entente et la Grèce, I, 43, 142.

it was necessary for our country . . . to retain all her forces in a block and to keep them on the frontier where the German attack had been made.[207]

But other men in the French Government were now determined to send soldiers to Salonika. Certain officers in the army also advocated the scheme. Delcassé therefore found himself at loggerheads both with his colleagues in the Cabinet and with powerful military officials.[208] Then, on October 12, Ferdinand of Bulgaria threw off his mask and declared war on Serbia, thereby associating himself with the Central Powers. Delcassé immediately resigned from the Ministry of Foreign Affairs, partly on account of the failure of his Balkan policy and partly as a protest against the Salonika expedition, to which he was now uncompromisingly opposed.[209]

As in June 1905, Delcassé was careful to supply himself with documentary materials before leaving the Quai d'Orsay. He told Mévil that he had all the evidence he needed to justify the policy which he had pursued in 1914 and 1915. His last speech in Parliament was made in a secret session of the Chamber of Deputies held June 16, 1916, and was designed to defend his stand with regard to Bulgaria and Greece.[210] Otherwise he took little part either in politics or in the conduct of the war. History justified his last-minute opposition to the Salonika campaign. In order to carry out the plan, it was necessary for the Allies to violate the neutrality of Greece. Then, too, they were unable to spare enough men and supplies to guarantee the success of their undertaking.[211]

At the conclusion of the World War, Delcassé refused to vote for the Treaty of Versailles on the ground that it gave France "neither reparations nor security."[212] He did not pre-

[207] Delcassé, *J.O.*, Oct. 28, 1919, pp. 76f. and 79 (*Comité secret*, June 16, 1916); Cosmin, *Diplomatie et Presse*, pp. 133 and 135.

[208] Cosmin, *Diplomatie et Presse*, pp. 135-136.

[209] *Ibid.*, p. 135; Delcassé, *J.O.*, Oct. 28, 1919 (*Comité secret*), p. 79; Mévil, *Revue Hebdomadaire*, June, 1923, p. 143.

[210] *J.O.*, Oct. 28, 1919, pp. 75ff.

[211] Cosmin, *Diplomatie et Presse*, pp. 118-136, 144-165, 220-223; Passadis, *op. cit.*, pp. 246-256.

[212] *Le Matin*, Feb. 23-24, 1923, article by Stephane Lauzanne and letter of Delcassé.

sent himself in the general elections of 1919 but went into definite retirement. For thirty years he had been a member of the Chamber of Deputies. Twelve years of that long period had been spent in some one of the various departments of government connected with the national defense—two years as head of the French colonies, two years as Minister of Marine, and eight years as Minister of Foreign Affairs. After such service to his country, he had earned the right to a good long rest. Besides, as he said to his friends, what should he do in the new Chamber which would be filled with the faces of men unknown to him? He would have felt as though he were in a strange place. To be sure, he might have become a candidate for the Senate, but the two senators from Ariège were his friends and he could not think of opposing them. It is possible that he would have accepted a senatorial post if the people of Alsace-Lorraine had offered it to him, but the name Delcassé was already being forgotten.[213]

Freed at last from the worries of public life, Delcassé divided his time between Ariège, Nice, and Paris. Summer found him at Ax-les-Thermes; winter at Mont Boron on the heights above Nice and not far from the grave of Gambetta. With the advent of spring, he made short trips to Paris to see and to talk with his friends. His last years were saddened by the death of Jacques Delcassé, who died in Switzerland shortly after being released from captivity in Germany. Moreover both Delcassé and Madame Delcassé were in poor health. But his spirits remained lively, and his judgment was as keen and as penetrating as ever.[214]

Although Delcassé seems to have had his files bulging with private papers, and perhaps with documentary evidence as well,[215] he refused to publish his memoirs. Neither would he give the newspapers any information regarding his fall from power in 1905, although this subject was raised once more after the Germans began publishing the secret documents

[213] Mévil, *Rev. Pol. et Parl.*, June, 1924, pp. 400f.
[214] *Ibid.*, pp. 401-402.
[215] See Mévil, *Echo de Paris*, Feb. 28, 1923.

of the Wilhelmstrasse. At that time (1922), he wrote letters to Jean Bernard and André Mévil, and this correspondence was published, but he had been so careful in his wording that the real secret of his resignation was not disclosed.[216]

The misunderstanding between England and France over the question of German reparations profoundly grieved Delcassé. In May 1923, when his health appeared to be a little better than usual, he for a moment dreamed of undertaking a diplomatic mission to London in the interest of more cordial relations.[217] He desired France to occupy permanently the left bank of the Rhine and was confident that England could be made to agree to this settlement if the question were presented to her with sufficient tact and skill.[218]

In February of 1923 Léon Garibaldi, editor of the *Eclaireur* of Nice, interviewed Delcassé at Mont Boron. The retired statesman declared that he had refused to vote for the Treaty of Versailles because it did not give any guarantee for the future. "The Treaty of Versailles gives us neither reparations nor security," he said. The indemnity would not be paid either in ten years, twenty years, or in forty-four years. It was necessary to seize the German banks and to force Germany to pay at once. As for the other defect in the treaty, there was no security because the endorsement of the United States was lacking and because England no longer felt obligated to France.[219] The Rhine would have to be taken from Germany and placed under French control, he argued in a letter to Stephane Lauzanne. Thus France would get her "natural frontier" and with it her safety. Moreover, the region could be made to yield four billions annually in the form of taxes, and this sum, together with the agriculture and commerce of the left bank of the Rhine, would assure France of the reparations which she claimed.[220]

[216] *Le Figaro*, March 24, 1922 (letter to Jean Bernard); *Revue Hebdomadaire*, June, 1923, p. 134 (letter to Mévil, dated March 22, 1922); Paléologue in *Le Temps*, March 16, 1922.

[217] Mévil, *Revue Hebdomadaire*, June, 1923, p. 144.

[218] *Ibid.*, p. 145.   [219] *Le Matin*, Feb. 24, 1923.

[220] *Ibid.*, Feb. 23-24, 1923. Delcassé's letter was written some weeks before his death which occurred on Feb. 22, 1923.

The climate of Nice and its environs is ordinarily mild and healthful, but the winds are variable and often change several times a day. In the spring, the sudden changes of temperature demand great care on the part of the residents. After *déjeuner* on February 22, 1923, Delcassé left his villa at Mont Boron and went to the local bishopric where Madame Yvette Guilbert and her American pupils were giving a performance for the benefit of the youth of the diocese. The wind blew very hard, and Delcassé left M. Gabriel Hanotaux and other companions in order to rest in a nearby garden. There, silently and alone, as he had fought all the great battles of his career, he fought his last fight—with death. Late that day and early the next morning, the papers of the world recalled that Delcassé had been one of the greatest of French statesmen. The Kings of England, Spain, and Italy, the President and Vice-President of the National Russian Committee all paid genuine tribute to his memory. Conscious at last of the greatness of this "noble servitor of the country" and "patient worker for the grandeur of France," the French people gave him a state funeral. The burial took place in the cemetery of Montmartre in Paris. Among those in attendance were the Premier of France, the chiefs of the army and navy, the entire Cabinet, the diplomatic corps, two regiments of infantry, and the family and friends of Delcassé. Speeches were made by Georges Leygues, Victor Bérard, and Raymond Poincaré.

It is a noteworthy fact that the public which showered all these honors upon Delcassé in death dismissed him from mind almost immediately. For a while the French journals argued about the exact time and place in which he had died, but they did not settle the questions which they had raised. There was a terrific uproar in the Chamber of Deputies on March 9, 1923, when the Government brought in a bill to defray the expenses of the state funeral. The late Minister of Foreign Affairs was then denounced as the Alcibiades of France by some and extolled as the Richelieu of the Third Republic by others.[221] At length the saner elements gained

[221] *J.O., Chambre,* March 9, 1923, pp. 1121-1126.

control of the Chamber and passed the bill by a tremendous majority, thereby ratifying the labors of Delcassé, but twelve years after his death, aside from a bronze tablet at 11 Boulevard de Clichy, there is still no suitable monument to him.[222]

Yet he had devoted nearly his whole life to the defense of France and had been a pioneer in colonial enterprise as well as the greatest Minister of Marine and greatest Foreign Minister of the Third Republic. His long period of service had been equaled only by the magnificent record of his accomplishments and by the remarkable manner in which he had achieved a set program. Before 1889 he had popularized the idea of a French alliance with Russia in order to press certain claims against Germany. Even then he had already spoken a good word for the *Entente Cordiale,* agitated for a reconciliation with Italy, proposed an entente with Spain, and advocated making Morocco into an essentially Franco-Spanish problem. He had sounded the alarm upon the accession of William II, and had demanded greater French and Russian military preparations. All this had been inspired in him by the loss of Alsace-Lorraine at the end of the Franco-Prussian War and by Bismarck's subsequent efforts to "isolate" France and keep her impotent. Wounded to the heart by the dismemberment of France, his spirit revolting against the weakness and helplessness of his country, Delcassé had dedicated himself to the rehabilitation of French power, to the restoration of the national prestige, and to the recovery of the losses of 1870. Between 1893 and 1914 he had contributed to the strengthening of France through colonial expansion. He had reconciled France and Italy, won the friendship of Spain, and perpetuated the tradition of Franco-American amity. He had begun the active penetration of Morocco, and it was he who made the *Entente Cordiale* with England, thereby gaining not only Morocco, but also the friendship of the greatest colonial and naval Power in the world. He had completely rejuvenated the decadent French marine and had

[222] This was not unveiled until Oct. 4, 1934. See *L'Echo de Paris,* Oct. 4, 1934, and *Le Temps,* Oct. 5, 1934.

further increased its fighting ability by securing invaluable naval agreements with Russia and England. The Franco-Russian Alliance—a passive union of doubtful value at the time of Fashoda—had been modified by him in 1899 into a fruitful, working diplomatic instrument capable of supporting a foreign policy; and, between 1901 and 1914, he had been chiefly responsible for transforming it into the closest and most efficient diplomatic and military alliance in all Europe. This, of course, includes the naval accord of 1912, the arrangements of 1901 and 1913 for the construction of Russian strategic railroads, and other work which tended to consolidate the alliance or increase Franco-Russian solidarity. Similarly, more than any other person, he was the man of the Triple Entente. Along with Gambetta, he had been its prophet; he had consciously laid the basis for it during his first term of office at the Quai d'Orsay and notably at the time of the Hull incident; he was the central figure in its naval and military preparations in the period 1912-1914. During the war, although his Balkan policy failed, he was, together with Grey and Sazonov, one of those who brought Italy into the war on the French side. Certainly the man who accomplished all this was not only the principal author of the Allied coalition but also the chief artisan of Allied victory. Doubtless the "war guilt" controversy has caused French writers to pass hurriedly over the deeds of this journalist and statesman who played the triple rôle of strategist, organizer, and pivot-man in the opposition to Germany between 1882 and 1915. However, perhaps it would be better to admit that even as Germany had her Bismarck, France had her Delcassé. Bismarck seized Alsace-Lorraine. Delcassé restored the lost provinces to France.

BIBLIOGRAPHY

Manuscript Sources

Archives of the Department of State, United States:
    From France, vols. 116-125 (1898-1906). Despatches of Horace
    Porter, Vignaud, and R. S. McCormick.
    From Morocco, vol. 1. Despatches of S. R. Gummeré.
    From German Embassy, vol. 34.
Library of Congress. President Roosevelt's Papers.
Archives of the Faculty of Letters of the University of Toulouse.
    Papers relating to the academic record of Théophile Del-
    cassé.

Parliamentary Debates and Parliamentary Papers

France.
    Débats parlementaires and *documents* in *Journal officiel de la
    République Française, Chambre* or *Sénat.* Imprimerie du
    Journal Officiel, Paris (annual) or *Annales de la Chambre
    des Députés* or *Sénat.* Imprimerie des Journaux Officiels,
    Paris (annual).
Great Britain.
    Parliamentary Debates, Commons, 4th and 5th Series.
        London (annual).
    Parliamentary Papers:
        Egypt and the Upper Nile, 1899.
        Madagascar, 1899.
        China, 1900.
        Agreements between the United Kingdom and Japan,
            1902.
        Declaration Respecting Egypt and Morocco, 1905.
Germany.
    *Stenographische Berichte ueber die Verhandlungen des Reich-
    stags.* Berlin (annual).

Printed Documentary Sources

France.
    Ministère des Affaires Etrangères, *Documents diplomatiques.*
    Imprimerie Nationale, Paris, 1893-   .

Afrique: arrangements, actes et conventions, 1881-1898.

Affaires du Siam, 1893-1902.

Affaires du Haut-Mékong (Paris, 1893).

Affaires du Siam et du Haut-Mékong (Paris, 1896).

Haut-Nil et du Bahr-el-Ghazal.

La convention franco-anglaise du 14 juin, 1898, et la déclaration du 21 mars, 1899.

Affaires d'Orient (May-December, 1897).

Affaires d'Orient: autonomie Crétoise (Jan.-Oct., 1898).

Négociations pour la paix entre l'Espagne et les Etats-Unis, 1898.

Affaires de Turquie, 1900-1901.

Chine (5 vols., 1898-1901).

Saint-Siège (1899-1903).

Accords entre la France et l'Angleterre. Nos. I and II.

Affaires du Maroc, 1901-1905.

Protocoles et comptes rendues de la conférence d'Algésiras.

La Guerre Européene, 1914.

L'alliance franco-russe (Paris, 1918).

Les accords franco-italiens de 1900-1902 (Paris, 1920).

Commission de Publication des Documents Relatifs aux Origines de la Guerre de 1914, *Documents diplomatiques français, 1871-1914*. 1. Série 1871-1901, 2. Série 1901-1911, 3. Série 1911-1914. Imprimerie Nationale, Paris, 1929-

Great Britain.

British and Foreign State Papers, vols. 90-107. London, 1898-

Collected Diplomatic Documents Relating to the Outbreak of the European War. London, 1915.

Gooch, G. P., and Temperley, H., editors, *British Documents on the Origin of the War, 1898-1914*. London, 1926-

United States.

Foreign Relations of the United States. Washington, 1896-1906.

Germany.

Lepsius, J., Mendelssohn-Bartholdy, A., and Thimme, F., editors, *Die Grosse Politik der Europäischen Kabinette, 1871-1914*. 40 vols. Berlin, 1922-1927.

Belgium.

Schwertfeger, Bernhard, editor, *Die Belgischen Documente*

zur Vorgeschichte des Weltkrieges, 1885-1914. 5 vols., 2 supplementary vols., and 2 vols. of commentary. Berlin, 1925. Russia.

Marchand, René, *Une livre noire: diplomatie d'avant guerre d'après les documents des archives russes (1910-1917).*

Printed Works of Théophile Delcassé

(Other than Parliamentary Reports and Diplomatic Documents)
Alerte! Où allons-nous? pp. 34. Paris, 1882. (On politics and national defense).
Signed articles in *République Française,* August 1, 1885-January 5, 1888. (On foreign affairs and national defense) .
Signed articles in *Paris,* April 3, 1887-May 16, 1889. (On foreign affairs and national defense) .

Memoirs, Biographies, Privately Printed Diplomatic Documents and Historical Literature

Anderson, Eugene N., *The First Moroccan Crisis.* Chicago, 1930.
Baratier, Colonel, *Epopées africaines.* Paris, 1912. A detailed account of the Monteil expedition.
Barclay, Sir Thomas, *Thirty Years Anglo-French Reminiscences, 1876-1906.* Boston, New York, and London, 1914.
Barnes, H. E., *In Quest of Truth and Justice.* Chicago, 1928.
Barrère, Camille, "Les responsabilités du Prince du Bülow." *Revue des Deux Mondes,* May 1, 1931.
———— "La chute de Delcassé." *Revue des Deux Mondes,* August 1, 1932.
———— "Le prélude de l'offensive Allemande de 1905." *Revue des Deux Mondes,* February 1, 1932.
———— "La chute de Delcassé: II, le duel d'Algésiras." *Revue des Deux Mondes,* January 1, 1933.
Bérard, Victor, *Questions extérieures (1901-1902).* Paris, 1902.
———— *L'affaire Marocaine.* Paris, 1906. A justification of Delcassé's policy by one of his close friends.
Billot, Albert, *La France et l'Italie: Histoire des années troublées, 1881-1899.* 2 vols. Paris, 1905.
Boden, C. F., *Zur Psychologie der französischen Diplomatie.* Brauschweig, 1912. A diatribe aimed in part at Delcassé.
Boghitschewitsch, Dr. M., *Die auswärtige Politik Serbiens, 1903-1914.* 3 vols. Berlin, 1931.

Bourgeois, E., *Manuel historique de politique étrangère*. 4 vols. Paris, 1900-1926.

Bourgeois, E., and Pagès, G., *Les origines et responsabilités de la Grande Guerre*. . . . Paris, 1921.

Brandenburg, E., *Von Bismarck zum Weltkrieges*. Berlin, 1924.

Bülow, Bernhard Fürst Von, *Denkwürdigkeiten*, 4 vols., Berlin, 1930-1931. Translated by F. A. Voigt, *Memoirs of Prince von Bülow*. 3 vols. Boston, 1931, 1932.

Burgoyne, Alan H., editor, *The Navy League Annual*. London, 1908-1913.

Caillaux, Joseph, *Agadir: ma politique extérieure*. Paris, 1919.

Cambon, Jules, *Essays and Addresses*. New York, 1903. Of interest in connection with the cultural rapprochement of France and the United States.

Cambridge History of British Foreign Policy. Sir. A. W. Ward and G. P. Gooch, editors, vol. III. Cambridge, 1923.

Carroll, E. M., *French Public Opinion and Foreign Relations, 1870-1914*. New York and London, 1931.

Castellane, Count de, *Articles et discours sur la politique extérieure, 1901-1905*. Paris, 1905. Very critical of Delcassé's policy.

Churchill, Winston, *The World Crisis, 1911-1914*. New York, 1928.

Combarieu, Abel, *Sept ans à l'Elysée avec le Président Emile Loubet: de l'affaire Dreyfus à la Conférence d'Algésiras, 1899-1906*. Paris, 1932. By the President's Secretary. Particularly useful in connection with the Donnersmarck incident.

Converset, J. (Colonel), *Les trois ans de diplomatie secrète qui nous menèrent à la guerre de 1914*. La Flèche, 1924.

Cosmin, S., *Diplomatie et presse dans l'affaire Grecque 1914-1916*. Paris, 1921.

—— *L'Entente et la Grèce pendant la Grande Guerre*, tome I, 1914-1915. Paris, 1926. A valuable study.

Coubertin, Pierre de, "M. Delcassé: a character sketch." *Fortnightly Review*, January 1, 1902.

Dawbarn, Charles, "Théophile Delcassé; the Man and His Policy." *Fortnightly Review*, September 1, 1914.

—— *Makers of New France*. London, 1915. One chapter is devoted to Delcassé.

Dawson, W., editor, *The War Memoirs of William Graves Sharp, American Ambassador to France, 1914-1919*. London, 1931.

Dennis, Alfred L. P., *Adventures in American Diplomacy, 1896-1906*. New York, 1928. Written largely from unpublished documents.

Deville, Gabriel, *L'Entente, la Grèce, et la Bulgarie; notes d'histoire et souvenirs*. Paris, 1919. By a former French Ambassador at Athens. Hostile to Delcassé.

Dickinson, G. L., *The International Anarchy, 1904-1914*. New York, 1926.

Duchêne, Albert, *La politique coloniale de la France*. Paris, 1928. By one who had served as political director for the Ministry of Colonies.

Durand-Viel, G. (Captain), "Delcassé et la Marine." Reprinted from *Revue Maritime*, May, 1923. Paris, 1923. The best single account of Delcassé's work as Minister of Marine.

Dutrèb, M., (Pseud. Marthe Du Bert), *Marchand*. Paris, 1922.

Eckardstein, H. F. von, *Die Isolierung Deutschlands*. Leipzig, 1921.

Enthoven, H. E., *De Val van Delcassé*. Utrecht, 1930. Lectures delivered at Leiden.

Ewart, J. S., *The Roots and Causes of the War, 1914-1918*. 2 vols. New York, 1925.

Fay, Sidney B., *The Origins of the World War*. 2 vols. in one. New York, 1931. Still the best work on the subject.

Feis, Herbert, *Europe the World's Banker, 1870-1914*. New Haven, 1930.

Fischer, Eugene, "Der Sinn der russich-französischen Militärkonvention." *Preussiche Jahrbücher*, April, 1923.

Fournol, E., "Le moderne Plutarque; ou, La vie des hommes illustres de la Troisième République." *Revue Politique et Littéraire* or *Revue Bleue*, July 16, 1921.

Fullerton, W. M., "Théophile Delcassé, the Man who Undid the Work of Bismarck." *World's Work*, March, 1915.

Gaffarel, P., *Notre expansion coloniale en Afrique de 1870 à nos jours*. Paris, 1918.

Gérard, Auguste, *Mémoires d'Auguste Gérard*. Paris, 1928.

Gerin, René, *Comment fut provoquée la Guerre de 1914*. Paris, 1933.

Giffen, Morrison B., *Fashoda; the Incident and Its Diplomatic Setting*. Chicago, 1930.

Gooch, G. P., *Franco-German Relations, 1871-1914*. The Creighton Lecture for 1923. London, 1923. Brief but authoritative.

———— "Delcassé." *Contemporary Review*, April, 1923. A valuable article somewhat too favorable.

Grey, Viscount, of Fallodon, *Twenty-five years, 1892-1916*. 2 vols. London, 1925.

Hale, Oron J., *Germany and the Diplomatic Revolution; A Study in Diplomacy and the Press, 1904-1906*. Philadelphia, 1931. This work brings together a great deal of valuable material relating to Delcassé and is invaluable as a guide to the newspapers of the period.

———— "Prince von Bülow: His Memoirs and His German Critics." *Journal of Modern History*, June, 1932.

Halévy, E., "Franco-German Relations Since 1870." *History*, April, 1924.

Hammann, Otto, *Der missverstandne Bismarck*. Berlin, 1921.

———— *Deutsche Weltpolitik, 1890-1912*. Berlin, 1925. Translation, *The World Policy of Germany, 1890-1912*. London, 1927.

Hanotaux, Gabriel, *Le partage de l'Afrique, Fachoda*. Paris, 1909.

———— *L'Entente cordiale*. Paris, 1912.

Hauser, Henri and Renouvin, P., *Manuel de politique européenne, histoire diplomatique de l'Europe (1871-1914)*. Paris, 1929. A valuable work written from the orthodox French point of view.

Hohenlohe-Schillingsfürst, Fürst Chlodwig zu, *Denkwürdigkeiten der Reichskanzlerzeit*. Berlin, 1931.

Hosotte, Louis, *Histoire de la Troisième République, 1870-1910*. Describes the scandals in the French marine and the fall of Clemenceau, 1909.

Jerrold, Laurence, *The Real France*. London, 1911. Contains an interesting chapter on the fall of Delcassé and describes Delcassé's share in precipitating the fall of Clemenceau.

Joffre, Maréchal Joseph (Col. T. B. Mott, translator), *Personal Memoirs of Joffre, Field Marshal of the French Army*. 2 vols. New York and London, 1932.

Jourdain, Sauvaire, "L'œuvre de M. Delcassé, Ministre de la Marine." *L'Echo de Paris*, Jan. 28, 1913. A very fine summary.

Judet, E., *Ma politique, 1905 à 1917*. Paris, 1923.

Kantorowicz, Hermann, *The Spirit of British Policy and the Myth of the Encirclement of Germany*. London, 1931.

Koepfe, Fritz, *Von Gambetta bis Clemenceau*. Stuttgart and Berlin, 1922.

Lauzanne, Stéphane, *Great Men and Great Days*. New York and London, 1921. By the patriotic editor of *Le Matin*. Chapter I is entitled, "Delcassé—the Man who Prepared Victory."

Laloy, Emile, "Les débuts de l'affaire marocaine d'après les documents allemands." *Mercure de France*, May 1, 1926.

—— "La chute de Delcassé d'après les documents allemands." *Mercure de France*, July 15, 1926.

Langer, W. L., *The Franco-Russian Alliance, 1890-1894*. Cambridge, Mass., 1929. One of the basic secondary works.

—— *The Diplomacy of Imperialism, 1890-1902*. 2 vols. New York and London, 1935. The best account in English based on a penetrating analysis of the sources.

Louis, Georges, *Les carnets de Georges Louis*. 2 vols. Paris, 1926.

Lutz, Herman, *Lord Grey and the World War*. New York, 1928.

Marchand, René, *La condemnation d'un régime*. Paris, 1922. By the author of *Un livre noire* (See above).

Marès, Roland de, "L'artisan de la Triple-Entente: M. Delcassé, ministre et diplomate." *Je Sais Tout* (Paris), Nov. 15, 1915. A popular contemporary portrait of Delcassé. Well illustrated.

Maurois, André, *Edouard VII et son temps*. Paris, 1933. The author had access to some of the personal papers of Delcassé.

Mende, Elsie Porter, *An American Soldier and Diplomat, Horace Porter*. New York, 1927. Cites the personal papers of General Porter, United States Ambassador at Paris, 1897-1905.

Mendelssohn-Bartholdy, A., "Alte Diplomatie: Der Sturz Delcassés." *Wissen und Leben*, February 1, 1925.

Mévil, André, (A confidant of Delcassé) "M. Delcassé and the Entente Cordiale." *National Review*, July, 1908.

—— *De la paix de Francfort à la conférence d'Algésiras*. Paris, 1909. An apologia inspired by Delcassé.

—— "Quelques souvenirs personnels sur M. Delcassé." *Revue hebdomadaire*, June, 1923.

—— "Delcassé et son œuvre." *Revue politik et parlementaire,* June 10, 1924.

Michon, Georges, *L'Alliance Franco-Russe, 1891-1917.* Paris, 1927.

Millet, René, *Notre politique extérieure de 1898 à 1905.* Preface by Gabriel Hanotaux. Paris, 1905. Critical of Delcassé's policies.

Mommsen, Wilhelm, "Die elsass-lothringische Frage von 1897-1904." *Archiv für Politik und Geschichte,* December, 1924.

Monteil, Lieutenant-Colonel, *Une page d'histoire militaire coloniale, la Colonne de Kong.* Paris, 1902.

Morel, E. D., *Diplomacy Revealed.* London, ——.

Morhardt, Mathias, *Les preuves.* Paris, 1922.

Newton, Lord, *Lord Lansdowne.* London, 1929. Based partly upon private papers of Lord Lansdowne.

Nicolson, Hon. Harold George, *Sir Arthur Nicolson, bart., first Lord Carnock; A Study in the Old Diplomacy.* London, 1930.

Nuova Antologia. . . . Rome, June, 1905, and Sept., 1916. Unsigned articles on Delcassé.

Ormesson, Wladimir d', *Portraits d'hier et d'aujourd'hui.* Chapter II, pp. 53-166, "Vergennes et Delcassé." Paris, 1925.

Paléologue, Maurice, *Un prélude à l'invasion de la Belgique, le plan Schlieffen 1904.* Paris, 1932. Also in *Revue des Deux Mondes,* Oct. 1, 1932.

—— *Un grand tournant de la politique mondiale, 1904-1906.* Paris, 1934.

Pinon, René, *La France et l'Allemagne, 1870-1913.* Paris, 1913.

Poincaré, Raymond, *Au service de la France.* Paris, 1926- . Translated by Sir George Arthur, *The Memoirs of Raymond Poincaré.* New York, 1926- .

Pressensé, Francis de, "The Fall of M. Delcassé and the Anglo-French Entente." *Nineteenth Century* (New York edition), July, 1905. Violently critical of Delcassé's policies.

Preussische Jahrbücher, "Delcassés Sturz." July, 1931.

Rath, Hermann vom, "Der Abgeordinete Delcassé." *Die Zukunft* (Berlin), February 8, 1908.

Recouly, Raymond, "Le septennat de M. Delcassé." *Revue politique et parlementaire,* December, 1905.

—— *De Bismarck à Poincaré; soixante ans de diplomatie républicaine.* Paris, 1932.

Reinach, Joseph, *Le ministère Gambetta, histoire et doctrine (14 novembre 1881-26 janvier 1882)*. Paris, 1882.

Renouvin, Pierre, La crise européenne et la grande guerre (1904-1918). 2 vols. Paris, 1934.

—— "L'Allemagne et la conclusion de l'alliance franco-russe." *Bulletin de la Société d'Histoire Moderne,* June, 1924.

Reventlow, Graf Ernst, *Deutschlands auswärtige Politik, 1888-1914*. Berlin, 1918.

Reynald, Georges, *La diplomatie française: l'œuvre de M. Delcassé*. Paris, 1915. From *Pages d'Histoire—1914-1915*. A short sketch written by a friend of Delcassé.

Saint-Cyr. Charles de, *Pourquoi l'Italie est notre alliée. . . .* Paris, 1915.

Sazonov, Serge, *Fateful Years, 1909-1916*. New York, 1928.

Schefer, Christian, *D'une guerre à l'autre; essai sur la politique exteriéure de la troisième république (1871-1914)*. Paris, 1920.

Schierbrand, Wolf von, "The John Hay of France. A Character Sketch of Delcassé, the French Minister of Foreign Affairs." *Public Opinion* (New York), June 10, 1905.

Schmitt, Bernadotte E., *The Coming of the War: 1914*. 2 vols. New York and London, 1930.

Schuman, Frederick L., *War and Diplomacy in the French Republic*. New York and London, 1931.

Sembat, Marcel, *Faîtes un roi, sinon faîtes la paix.* ——. 1913.

Siebert, B. De and Schreiner, G. A., *Entente Diplomacy and the World*. New York and London, 1921.

Sontag, Raymond J. *European Diplomatic History, 1871-1932*. New York, 1933.

Steed, H. W., *Through Thirty Years, 1892-1922*. New York, 1924.

Steinheil, Marguerite, *My Memoirs*. New York, 1912.

Stieve, Friedrich, *Isvolsky and the World War*. New York, 1926.

Stone, Melville E., *M.E.S. His Book*. New York and London, 1918.

Stuart, Graham, *French Foreign Policy from Fashoda to Serajevo, 1898-1914*. New York, 1921.

Taillandier, G. Saint-René, *Les origines du Maroc française, récit d'une mission (1901-1906)*. Paris, 1930. Based in part on diplomatic correspondence.

Taube, Baron M. de, *La politique russe d'avant-guerre et la fin de l'empire des Tsars, 1904-1917*. Paris, 1928.

Tardieu, André, *Questions diplomatiques de l'année, 1904*. Paris, 1905.

―――― *La conférence d'Algésiras*. Paris, 1909.

―――― *La France et les alliances*. Paris, 1909.

Terrier, Auguste et Mourey, Charles *L'œuvre de la IIIe République en Afrique occidentale. . . .* Preface by Eugène Etienne. Paris, 1910.

Toury, F. G. de, *Jaurès et le parti de la guerre*. Paris, 1922.

Tramond, J., and Reussner, *Eléments d'histoire maritime et coloniale contemporaine, 1815-1914*. Paris, 1924. Published under the direction of the Historical Service of the Chief of Staff of the marine.

Truhos, P., *M. Delcassé et son politique*. Paris, 1910. Short. Very hostile to Delcassé.

Valentin, V., *Deutschlands Aussenpolitik*. Berlin, 1921.

Wallier, René, *Le vingtième siecle politique*, années 1901-1907. Paris, 1902-1908.

Note. Almost every secondary work and practically every collection of documents dealing with European diplomacy from 1898 to 1915 has some important reference to Delcassé.

Newspapers and Periodicals

French

Annales politiques et littéraires.

Afrique française, L'.

Dépêche de Toulouse, La. Supported Delcassé.

Echo de Paris, L'. André Mévil, the foreign editor was a staunch defender of Delcassé's policies.

Figaro, Le. Opposed to Delcassé after 1905.

Gaulois, Le. Monarchical and strongly nationalistic.

Matin, Le. The editor, Stéphane Lauzanne, was an admirer of Delcassé and the paper is generally credited with close relations to the latter.

Paris. Delcassé was the foreign editor of this paper, 1887-1889.

Questions diplomatiques et coloniales: revue de politique extérieure.

République Française, La. Delcassé wrote for this paper, 1879-1889. In 1887, 1888, and 1889, he was secretary of the editorial staff.

Revue des deux mondes. Enjoyed close relations with the Quai
d'Orsay. Cambon, Barrère, and Paléologue have made valu-
able contributions to it.
Revue d'histoire de la guerre mondiale.
Revue historique.
Revue d'histoire diplomatique.
Revue maritime.
Revue de Paris.
Revue politique et parlementaire.
Revue politique et littéraire or *Revue Bleue.*
Temps, Le. Generally regarded as the semi-official organ of the
Ministry of Foreign Affairs.

English

Fortnightly Review.
Manchester Guardian.
National Review.
Nineteenth Century.
Saturday Review.
Spectator.
The Times.
Westminster Gazette.

German

*Berliner Monatshefte: Zeitschrift zur Vorgeschichte und Ge-
schichte des Weltkrieges.*
Berliner Tageblatt.
Berliner Lokal Anzeiger.
Deutsche Rundschau.
Die Post.
Hamburger Nachrichten.
Kölnische Zeitung.
Preussische Jahrbücher.
Vossiche Zeitung.

American

American Monthly Review of Reviews.
Baltimore Sun.
Boston Transcript.
Christian Science Monitor.
Philadelphia Public Ledger.
The New York Times.

INDEX